Changing Boundaries

CHANGING BOUNDARIES

Gender Roles and Sexual Behavior

Edited by
ELIZABETH RICE ALLGEIER
Bowling Green State University
and
NAOMI B. McCORMICK
State University of New York, Plattsburgh

 MAYFIELD PUBLISHING COMPANY

Library of Congress Catalog Card Number: 82-60885
International Standard Book Number: 0-87484-536-X

Manufactured in the United States of America
Mayfield Publishing Company
285 Hamilton Avenue, Palo Alto, California 94301

Special projects editor: Liz J. Currie
Managing editor: Pat Herbst
Manuscript editor: Linda Purrington
Art director: Nancy Sears
Production manager: Cathy Willkie
Compositor: Viking Typography
Printer and binder: George Banta Company

The editors acknowledge permission to reprint the following copyrighted material:

Quotation on p. 26 from Horney, K. Flight from womanhood. *International Journal of Psycho-Analysis*, 1926, 7, 327–328.

Illustrations on pp. 46 & 47 from Koch, P. B. A comparison of the sex education of primary aged children in the United States and Sweden as expressed through their art. Proceedings of the International Symposium, Children and Sexuality, Montreal, Éditions, Études Vivantes, 1980. Used by permission of P. B. Koch.

Quotation on p. 76 from Perper, T., & Fox, V. S. Flirtation and pickup patterns in bars. Paper presented at the meeting of the Eastern Conference on Reproductive Behavior, New York, June 1980. Used by permission of Timothy Perper.

Quotation on p. 76 from Perper T., & Fox, V. S. Special focus: Flirtation behavior in special settings. Paper presented at the meeting of the Eastern Region of the Society for the Scientific Study of Sex, Philadelphia, April 1980. Used by permission of Timothy Perper.

Quotation on p. 115 from Extent of love reactions questionnaire from Kanin, E. J., Davidson, K. D., & Scheck, S. R. A research note on male/female differentials in the experience of heterosexual love. *Journal of Sex Research*, 1970, 6, 64–72. Reproduced by permission of *Journal of Sex Research* and the authors.

IN a society that provides many alternatives, an individual contemplating the apparent benefits of a particular lifestyle may embark on a path with little awareness of its implications. We dedicate this book to our students and children in the hope that they will be able to achieve greater satisfaction with their choices, having made them with prior knowledge of both the costs and the benefits of each lifestyle. We also dedicate this book to our friends and families, whose love and support enabled us to write it.

C O N T E N T S

PART TWO

Contemporary Perspective   159

P R E F A C E

The past few decades have produced a great deal of rhetoric about two important aspects of human experience: appropriate roles for women and men and the purpose and meaning of sexual intimacy. Public enthusiasm for these issues has captured the attention of the scientific community. Increasing numbers of researchers have become specialists in the study of either gender roles or human sexuality. An influx of new investigations and major books reviewing existing knowledge about men, women, and sexuality has caused a minor revolution in higher education. Existing courses have changed, and new ones have been created to meet the demand for information about intimate human relationships.

Today, a popular and scientific interest in relationships and intimacy has taken an exciting turn. For the first time, social scientists have begun to focus on the *interaction* between gender roles and sexual behavior. Armed with the question "How do real and assumed differences between men and women affect sexual expression?" the scholarly community has been drawing some thought-provoking conclusions. Very much a part of this Zeitgeist, the contributors to *Changing Boundaries* challenge our often complacent assumptions about how men and women are supposed to behave, view themselves, and experience sexuality and love.

The purpose of this book is to synthesize what is known about the relationship of gender roles, differences, and similarities with information about sexual attitudes and experiences. This text, then, may supplement courses in sociology, psychology, women's studies, health and human development, and home economics. More specifically, it will be useful in courses on human sexuality, developmental and social psychology, marriage and the family, and in courses focusing on gender similarities and differences. The book may be used in introductory courses in these areas, for the contributors have not assumed that students have prior knowledge or statistical background. At the same time, the material will intrigue advanced students because the chapters have been written by experts.

The chapters in the first part of *Changing Boundaries* focus on life span development from sexual and gender-role socialization in childhood and adolescence through courtship strategies and the beginnings of sexual intimacy. Differences and similarities in men's and women's expectations of love, sex, and relationships are described. Part One concludes with a consideration of the relationship of gender roles to sexual expression during the second half of life.

Relying on the framework presented in Part One, the second part focuses on some of the contemporary issues involved in sexuality and gender roles. It begins with a consideration of how beliefs and behaviors regarding sex and gender relate to reproductive roles. Next, attitudes toward sex in the workplace and perceptions of the increasing number of people selecting single lifestyles are examined. The following chapter is an analysis of the extent to which the relationships of gay males and of lesbians are circumscribed by, or freed from, sexual and gender-role prescriptions. Rape is considered in the subsequent chapter, which asks how societal responses to sexual assault are influenced by differing beliefs about men's and women's sexuality. Finally, in the last chapter of Part Two, sex is analyzed as a commodity; similarities and differences between men's and women's reactions to erotic materials are described. In the "Afterword," we make some predictions regarding changes in male and female roles and how these may affect sexual interactions.

In developing the book, we sought contributors who were actively conducting research and had the additional skill to describe the findings in specific areas clearly, with little reliance on specialized jargon. Thus, the original material presented here will be of interest to undergraduates, scholars, and the general public.

For us and for many of the other contributors, *Changing Boundaries* has a great deal of personal meaning. Although academicians are often accused of being out of touch with "reality," nearly all the contributors to this book, while doing research on the impact of changes in gender-role norms, are also dealing with these changes in their own lives. We and our colleagues are simultaneously attempting to observe the consequences of these changes and make personal decisions about many of these issues. We are products of our culture, ranging in age from our twenties through our fifties. Thus, most of us were socialized to behave in accordance with traditional gender-role norms and have, at some point, shifted in our intentions regarding how we will live our lives.

In our own struggles with these issues, we have developed personal values, which of course are bound to influence the questions we ask as we conduct our research. For each of us, however, professional training and ethics have also had their influence. Scientific training stresses the importance of examining as much evidence as possible in order to reach objective conclusions. In other words, even when the evidence contradicts some cherished beliefs, we are obligated to take these findings seriously and report them to our colleagues and to the public in general. Therefore, it is our intent to share with you the results of the research that has been conducted to date relevant to how changing gender roles have influenced the satisfaction men and women feel with their relationships and with themselves. We hope you will share our enthusiasm for the study of how the "fallout" from several important social movements has produced changes in men's and women's sexual lives even as many traditional values about masculinity and femininity survive and continue to have their influence.

In developing this book, we have been pleased not only with the individual chapters, but with the authors' willingness to read one another's manuscripts, providing valuable suggestions and criticisms with the aim of strengthening the book as a whole. Elizabeth Allgeier gratefully acknowledges the comments and suggestions of Rick Allgeier, Anne Peplau, and Diane Phillis in response to an early draft of her chapter. Letitia Anne Peplau and Steven L. Gordon wish to acknowledge the helpful comments of Elizabeth Allgeier, Charles T. Hill, Randall Jones, and Naomi McCormick, and are grateful for the assistance of Patricia Linton in preparing their manuscript.

In addition, the text as a whole benefited from reviews by Georgia Babladelis, California State University at Hayward; Carol Copp, California State University at Fullerton; Beverly Fagot, University of Oregon; Shirley Feldman-Summers, University of Washington; Jeanne Gullahorn, Michigan State University; Carol Lindquist, California State at Fullerton; Hilary Lips, University of Winnipeg; Judy Stevens-Long, California State University at Los Angeles; Susana Urbina, University of North Florida; and Barbara Yanico, Southern Illinois University.

About the Contributors

Elizabeth Rice Allgeier is in the psychology department at Bowling Green State University. She received her Ph.D. from Purdue University in 1976. In addition to co-authoring *Sexual Interactions* and conducting numerous studies on public policies toward abortion with Rick Allgeier, she has studied sexual and contraceptive attitudes and behaviors. She is a consulting editor for the *Journal of Sex Research* and a member of the board of directors of the Society for the Scientific Study of Sex.

Naomi B. McCormick is in the psychology department at the State University of New York at Plattsburgh and is currently director of the Psychological Services Clinic. She received her Ph.D. at UCLA in 1976. Her research interests include adolescent contraception and courtship. Applying her research to her clinical practice, she specializes in psychotherapy with adolescents and their families.

A. R. (Rick) Allgeier is a staff psychologist at Northwest Community Mental Health Center in Lima, Ohio. He received his M.A. from the American University of Beirut in Lebanon and his Ph.D. from Purdue University in 1974. His research interests include sexual dysfunction and sexuality and aging. He and Elizabeth Allgeier are co-authors of a human sexuality text, *Sexual Interactions* (1983).

Frances Cherry is a social psychologist interested in social power and the historical and philosophical bases of social psychology. She earned her B.A. and M.A. degrees at York University in Toronto and her Ph.D. from Purdue University. Presently she is associate professor at Carleton University in Ottawa, Canada, teaching courses in social and community psychology.

William A. Fisher is assistant professor of social and personality psychology at the University of Western Ontario in London, Canada. Dr. Fisher received his B.A. from Tel Aviv University and his M.S. and Ph.D. from Purdue. His research focuses on reactions to erotic stimuli and on the psychology of adolescent contraceptive behavior. With Don Byrne, he coedited *Adolescents, Sex, and Contraception*, which deals with reasons—and possible remedies—for teenagers' failure to use contraception.

Jacqueline D. Goodchilds is a social psychologist. A Cornell Ph.D., she is a member of the psychology department at the University of California at Los Angeles and a research scientist at the Rand Corporation. A past editor of the *Journal of Social Issues*, she is concerned that her research enterprises be informative in socially responsible ways.

Steven L. Gordon is associate professor of sociology at California State University at Los Angeles. He received his Ph.D. from UCLA. Dr. Gordon was awarded an NIMH Postdoctoral Fellowship in Personality and Social Structure at the University of California at Berkeley. His sociological interests include role theory, socialization, intimate relationships, and cultural influences on emotions. His publications include "The Sociology of Sentiments and Emotion," appearing in *Social Psychology: Sociological Perspectives* (1981), edited by Rosenberg and Turner, and "Boundaries of the Self," co-authored with Ralph H. Turner and appearing in *The Self Concept* (1981), edited by Lynch et al. With Letitia Anne Peplau, he co-authored "Women and Men in Love: Sex Differences in Close Relationships," an article in *Women, Gender, and Social Psychology* (1982), edited by O'Leary, Unger, and Wallston.

Barbara A. Gutek is associate professor of psychology at the Claremont Graduate School. She received her Ph.D. in organizational psychology from the University of Michigan in 1975. She was assistant professor at UCLA before joining Claremont. Her research topics include women and work, sexual harassment and sexuality in the workplace, job satisfaction, and the effects of office automation. She has edited a monograph, "Facilitating Women's Career Development" (1979), for the Jossey-Bass series on Education, Work, and Careers and has co-authored, with Veronica F. Nieva, a book that is a literature review and synthesis, *Women and Work: A Psychological Perspective* (1981).

Elaine Hatfield is chair of the psychology department at the University of Hawaii. She received her B.A. from the University of Michigan in 1959 and her Ph.D. from Stanford in 1963. She has taught at the University of Minnesota, the University of Rochester, and the University of Wisconsin, and she has been a guest research professor in Mannheim, West Germany. She has published in a variety of areas. Her work on love is available in Hatfield and Walster's *A New Look at Love* (1981), a book that won the American Psychological Foundation's National Media Award. Her work on marriage, equity, and marriage contracts is available in Hatfield, Walster, and Berscheid's *Equity: Theory and Research* (1978). She has also conducted research on physical attractiveness, human sexuality, and the life span.

Clinton J. Jesser is in the sociology department at Northern Illinois University. He received his Ph.D. in 1962 from Michigan State University. He is coeditor of *The Family in Latin America* (1980) and the author of *Social Theory Revisited* (1975). His current research interests include male gender roles and a comparison of women's and men's crying behavior.

Charles Y. Nakamura is director of the training program in clinical psychology at the University of California at Los Angeles. His research interests include relations among children, parents, and families, with a recent focus on characteristics of capable children. A long-standing interest is in issues related to the progress of women in society such as education, work, child care, and social policies. His Ph.D. is from Stanford University.

Jacquelynne Eccles Parsons is in the psychology department at the University of Michigan. She received her Ph.D. from UCLA in 1974. She has edited *The Psychobiology of Sex Differences and Sex Roles* (1980) and co-authored *Women and Sex Roles: A Social Psychological Perspective* (1978). Her research interests include social attribution and the development of sex-role awareness.

Letitia Anne Peplau is an associate professor of social psychology at the University of California at Los Angeles. She received her doctorate from Harvard. Her research focuses on close relationships and has included studies of heterosexual, lesbian, and gay male relationships. She coedited (with Daniel Perlman) *Loneliness: A Sourcebook of Current Theory, Research and Therapy* (1982).

Diane E. Phillis is a Ph.D. candidate in the psychology department of Bowling Green State University. After receiving her M.A. there in 1977, she taught for three years in the psychology department at the University of

Wisconsin at Plattesville. Her research interests include the lifestyles of singles, adolescent contraceptive behavior, and communication between parents and their children about sex and contraception.

Shirley Radlove is in the psychology department at the University of Cincinnati and is an Educational Seminars Consultant in Cincinnati. She received her Ph.D. from Miami University in 1976 and has done postdoctoral work in human sexuality at the Masters and Johnson Institute in St. Louis. Her research interests include female sexuality, alcohol-related sexual dysfunctions, and stress factors in intimate relationships.

Peter J. Stein is associate professor of sociology at William Paterson College. He received his B.A. from the City College of New York and his Ph.D. from Princeton University. He has recently completed (with Beth Hess and Liz Markson) *Sociology*, an introductory text, and has edited *Single Life: Unmarried Adults in Social Context*, an anthology covering many aspects of single life. He is the chair of the Family Division of the Society for the Study of Social Problems. He is continuing his research on singles, adulthood, and friendships.

Gail L. Zellman is a research scientist at the Rand Corporation. She received her Ph.D. in 1973 from UCLA in social/clinical psychology. Her research interests include social cognition and social aspects of information processing. Her most recent work focuses on problems of adolescence, including pregnancy and delinquency.

Changing Boundaries

INTRODUCTION

The Intimate Relationship Between Gender Roles and Sexuality

During the dinner celebrating their second anniversary, Sally and Bob decided that it was time to have a baby. Later that night, and over the course of the next month, they made love very tenderly, enjoying the idea that—with the absence of the birth control they had always used in the past—Sally might conceive.

When Sally's period failed to appear several weeks later, she called her doctor but was told to wait another month until her next period was due before getting a pregnancy test. After missing a second period, she went to her doctor for examination and a pregnancy test and was delighted when the results indicated that she and Bob were going to become parents. The doctor said that she was six weeks pregnant, and she and Bob talked about whether they were going to have a girl or a boy.

Had they been able to see into her uterus at that point, they would not have been able to tell whether she was carrying a boy or a girl, because the sexual and reproductive structures of a male and female fetus are identical at six weeks. Between the eighth and twelfth weeks of gestation, however, the fetus develops in a male or female direction. It develops either the structures of a male (testes, penis, and genital ducts and organs that later convey sperm or secrete seminal fluid) or the structures of a female (ovaries, fallopian tubes, uterus, clitoris, vagina, and labia—vaginal lips).

Just before she was due to give birth, Sally learned that she was carrying twins. As each baby was born, the doctor glanced quickly at its genitals and proclaimed, first, "It's a boy!" and then, "It's a girl!" They were the parents of fraternal twins! Both babies, healthy and strong, began receiving attention and presents from all their delighted relatives and grandparents. John was given little blue overalls, blocks, balls, and stuffed animals. Jennifer received pink and white frilly dresses and baby dolls.

1

During childhood, John and his father wrestled and played ball in the back yard, and sometimes John would help his father fix the car or mow the grass. Jennifer was encouraged to help her mother in the kitchen, setting the table and cooking. Although John and Jennifer played with each other, each had his or her own circle of friends. John spent a lot of time with other boys in the neighborhood playing whatever sport was in season. Jennifer and her girlfriends played with dolls and later began getting together for slumber parties, at which they would talk about clothes, makeup, and boys.

Aside from their haircuts and clothing styles, John and Jennifer looked a great deal like each other through childhood. With puberty, however, Jennifer began to develop rounded curves, and, somewhat later, John's shoulders began to broaden, and he became several inches taller than Jennifer.

Jennifer began dating before John did, and her parents insisted on meeting her dates. They were quite strict about where she went, when she would be home, and so forth. When she began going out exclusively with one particular boy, her mother warned her not to "let him go too far" or he would "lose respect" for her. When John began dating, they didn't require him to bring his girlfriends home before permitting him to go out, and he was allowed to stay out later, even though he'd been dating for a shorter period of time than had Jennifer. When John became increasingly involved with one girl, his father, feeling he was being quite enlightened, told John to make sure he didn't get her pregnant and explained the use of condoms (although John already knew about them from his friends).

One night while Jennifer and her boyfriend were at the drive-in movies, they went beyond their usual kissing and necking and began playing with each other's genitals. Within a few minutes after she began touching his penis, he ejaculated. He continued to play with her, and although it felt very good, she asked him to stop because she didn't want to seem too interested in sex. She arrived home, almost an hour late, feeling guilty. She and her parents had quite an argument over what she perceived as their greater restrictiveness with her than with her brother. The argument was punctuated by the arrival of John an hour after she'd gotten home. He was not scolded or punished, and Jennifer stomped off to bed, exclaiming, "It's not fair!"

Why are Sally and Bob treating Jennifer and John differently? Do they favor one of their children over the other? Are they being unfair to Jennifer, as she claims? Do they care less about what John is doing with his dates? Depending on your point of view, you may answer each of these questions yes or no. Actually, Sally and Bob care a great deal about both of their children, and they are trying to raise them to be healthy adults. However, in North America, our cultural definition of a healthy adult woman is different from our beliefs about the personality and behavior of a healthy adult man. Most people in our culture believe that men are, and should be, different from women, beyond their obvious genital differences. That is, a person's *gender* defines our expectations of his or her personality, attitudes, and the behaviors we think are appropriate for men and women. These expectations that men will be different from women are particularly strong in the area of sexual experience and expression. Before discussing cultural beliefs about the nature of male versus female sexuality, however, we will discuss the development of gender.

THE VARIABLES OF GENDER

Most of us think of *gender* in simple either/or terms: either you are a male, or you are a female. However, gender is more complex than this. To understand the variables influencing gender, we have to go back to the day that Sally and Bob conceived the twins.

At conception, the fertilization of an egg by a sperm determines *genetic gender*. That is, an egg, carrying an X chromosome, can be penetrated by either an X-bearing sperm, in which case the fertilized egg is XX—a genetic female. Alternatively, the egg may be penetrated by a Y-bearing sperm, resulting in a genetic (XY) male. In Sally and Bob's case, two of Sally's X-bearing eggs were released in a single month and were penetrated by two sperm. One of them was X-bearing (producing Jennifer); the other was Y-bearing (producing John).

During the next six weeks, John's and Jennifer's sexual and reproductive structures were identical. That is, they had not yet begun to differentiate in a male or female direction. About eight weeks after conception, *gonadal gender* began to develop. That is, the internal part of the gonads (heretofore, identical in John and Jennifer) of the male (XY) fetus began to differentiate—to develop into testes. In John's case, the testes began to secrete the masculinizing hormone testosterone, which further influenced the development of the internal and external sexual and reproductive structures in a male direction. If the fetus is XX—female—the gonads remain undifferentiated for another six weeks, at which point they begin to develop into ovaries, as in Jennifer's case.

Our knowledge of the gender differentiation process and of the influence of *hormonal gender* is very dependent on research with people who have experienced atypical gender differentiation (Money, 1980). That is, if the gonads of an XY (male) fetus fail to differentiate, or if they fail to secrete enough testosterone, or if the fetal cells are unable to respond to the testosterone, the genetic male may take on a female appearance. Similarly, if a genetic female is exposed to testosterone during the period of prenatal gender differentiation, she will develop internal and/or external structures (testes, penis, etc.) characteristic of males. Normally, however, *genital gender* is consistent with genetic gender. Generally, babies with inward folding genitals are genetic females; babies with outwardly folding genitals are genetic males.

To summarize, then, *genetic gender* (XX or XY) is determined at conception. *Gonadal gender* (testes or ovaries) unfolds between the eighth and twelfth weeks following conception. *Hormonal gender*—principally the presence or absence of testosterone, the masculinizing hormone, also exerts its influence during the latter part of the first trimester of pregnancy. The presence or absence of testosterone, in turn, influences the differentiation of the genitals to produce *genital gender.* If testosterone is absent, regardless of *genetic*—XX or XY—*gender*, the external genitals of a baby will include two labia, a clitoris, the entrance to the vagina, and so on. If testosterone is present, the tissues making up the labia fuse together to make a scrotum, and a penis rather than a clitoris develops from the earlier genital structures.

By the beginning of the second trimester—that is, the second three months of pregnancy—the process of prenatal biological gender differentiation is complete. No further physical development in a male or female direction occurs until 10 or 15 years later, with the onset of puberty. Our description of prenatal gender differentiation is brief and somewhat simplified. For those wishing a more complete description, we recommend Money and Ehrhardt's (1972) book, *Man and Woman, Boy and Girl.*

Nine months after conception, the social and psychological variables of gender begin to exert their influence. The proclamation, "It's a _____ (boy or girl)!" is called *gender assignment.* That is, the genitals of a baby are examined at birth, and it is assigned the gender label "boy" or "girl." You might ask how a gender could be *assigned,* when it is biologically determined during the prenatal differentiation process. That being the case, the birth announcement of a baby's gender ought to be a simple process of recognizing whether it is a boy or a girl. Most of the time that is true, but the variable gender assignment becomes important when you realize that people are sometimes assigned the *wrong* gender. That is, had Jennifer received testosterone during the prenatal differentiation period, Sally and Bob might have been told that their twins were boys when in fact Jennifer was a genetic female, perhaps even possessing the internal structures of a female but having the external genitals of a male. Alternatively, Sally and Bob might have been informed that both their twins were girls if John's gonads failed to differentiate in a male (testes) direction or if he did not secrete, or was unaffected by the secretion of, testosterone. In either case, when errors occur, assigned gender is a more influential determinant of gender identity than is genetic gender (Money & Ehrhardt, 1972).

With gender assignment, John and Jennifer received markedly different treatment by their parents and relatives. They received different kinds of toys, with expectations and encouragement for "boyish" behavior in John and "girlish" behavior in Jennifer. By the time they are from 18 months to three years of age, children develop *gender identity* — that is, a definite sense that they are boys or girls. At the same time, they are learning about *gender roles*, the traits and behaviors stereotypically expected of males versus females in their culture. People vary in the extent to which they incorporate those expected roles into their own personalities. Varying in *gender-role identification*, individuals internalize to a greater or lesser extent the expected behaviors and traits for their gender into their personalities. If John's personality characteristics and behaviors conform to those expected of males in his culture, his gender-role identification is masculine. Similarly, if Jennifer internalizes many expected female traits, her gender-role identity will be feminine. Alternatively, each of them may develop *androgynous* role identities.

The term *androgynous* refers to the possession of both "masculine" and "feminine" characteristics. A person with a masculine gender-role identity might assertively confront an employer about an unfair demand, whereas a person holding a feminine gender-role identity might be more likely to yield to the employer's demands. Conversely, the individual with a feminine gender-role identity might gently soothe a hurt friend, whereas the person holding a masculine gender-role identification might back away from such tender expressions. An androgynous person engages in both kinds of behaviors (confronting unfair demands, providing comfort and support to others) depending on the situation.

Before further defining terms (also, see the Glossary) to be used in this book, we want to point out that the terms *masculine* and *feminine* as applied to gender-role identification, involve some rather unfortunate assumptions, although they are widely used by researchers in the area. Specifically, rather than assuming that attributes such as assertiveness, nurturance, tenderness, and athletic ability can be possessed by *both* men *and* women, these traits have been assumed to be characteristic of men *or* women. Hence, a whole constellation of traits and behaviors is currently described as "masculine," when in fact both males and females may possess these capacities. There are similar problems with the description of particular traits (such as gentleness and passivity) as "feminine" traits. Some scholars have attempted to get around this problem by using the terms "agentic" versus "communal," or "instrumental" versus "expressive," to characterize behaviors others have stereotyped respectively as "masculine" and "feminine."

Clearly, there are advantages to using these more neutral terms to describe the vast range of human behavior. Nevertheless, most researchers have relied on the terms *masculine* and *feminine*. Consistent with the scholarly literature, these terms are used throughout this book to describe the extent to which people conform to expected gender roles. However, we hope that readers will avoid gender-role stereotypes—the trap of expecting men and women to be polar opposites. Research has demonstrated that, with the exception of specific traits related to reproduction, such as menstruation, impregnation (donation of sperm), gestation (capacity for pregnancy), and lactation (milk production), all other skills, traits, and behaviors may be possessed by *both* men *and* women. Although only a minority of people have developed masculine and feminine qualities equally, each person has the potential to be androgynous. For this reason, *gender-role stereotypes*—a simplified or standardized image of males and females that fails to discriminate between observable and illusory differences—should be called into question.

GENDER AND SEXUAL BEHAVIOR

By the time they reach the age where they engage in sexual interaction with one another, most men and women in our culture have gone through a long process of *gender-role socialization*—training to conform to the attitudes and behavior stereotypic for their gender. As will be seen in subsequent chapters, *gender-role norms*—expectations about appropriate sexual behavior of women versus men—emphasize noninitiatory, passive sexual behavior for women. Men, in contrast, are expected to push for sexual contact and to determine the kind of sexual stimulation, the length of sexual contact, and the coital positions used during sexual interaction.

The purpose of this book is to examine the impact of contemporary changes in gender-role norms for women versus men on various aspects of their sexual interaction. Traditionally, gender-role norms have defined people's experience of their sexuality. The stereotype of men as more interested in sex, more goal-oriented, more aggressive, and more powerful than women (Gross, 1978) has done much to shape both heterosexual and homosexual courtship. The stereotype of women as passive-receptive, interpersonally oriented, and incompetent in the world outside of the home (Broverman et al., 1972) has led many women to experience themselves as alienated from their sexuality. Although they may perceive themselves as sex *objects*, they do not perceive themselves as sexual *actors* in their own right (Phelps, 1979).

The major premise of this book is that gender roles provide us with information about how to be sexual. Gender roles—the socially prescribed rules for being masculine or feminine—have established and continue to reinforce *boundaries* or limits for expected sexual conduct. These boundaries are not invulnerable, however. Boundaries for sexual behavior considered appropriate for each gender are changing as society itself is changing. All of us have been touched by a number of movements for civil rights and human liberation. In particular, the women's movement, the sexual freedom movement, and gay liberation have had an impact on our notions about appropriate gender-role behavior. The title of this book, *Changing Boundaries*, reflects our belief that the increasing demands for equality for men and women in politics, the workplace, and the home may also be changing our experiences with and expectations of sexuality.

This book is also relevant to changing boundaries because of changes in the contexts regarded as appropriate for expressing sexual feelings. Increasing numbers of people agree that women, as well as men, are entitled to have sexual intercourse before marriage (Bauman & Wilson, 1976; Glenn & Weaver, 1979). With this shift in attitudes, both women and men may begin to approach other sexual freedoms. Instead of being sexual martyrs who permit intercourse in exchange for nonerotic rewards such as economic support, protection, and marriage, women may be increasingly able to enjoy sexual intimacy for its own sake. And men, at least those who favor the liberation of women, may feel less oppressed by what Gross (1978) has described as the need to prove manhood through sexual conquests or "successes" in achieving and bringing partners to orgasm.

Finally, we have entitled our book *Changing Boundaries* because of issues raised by gay-rights advocates (Berzon et al., 1979; Weinberg, 1973). In particular, lesbian separatists, disillusioned by heterosexual women who rejected them from women's right's groups (Bunch, 1980; Simpson, 1976) have pointed out that people may need to accept the legitimacy of homosexual lifestyles before they can truly change maladaptive sexual and gender constraints.

Could it be that our appreciation of sexuality will be enhanced as gender-role limits are challenged in a variety of ways? Perhaps we should not be overly optimistic, at least in the short run. As Tavris and Offir (1977, p. 20) note, "Stereotypes, like laws, usually persist even after the realities have changed."

CONFLICTING ROLES: WOMEN

Regardless of whether people argue for traditional or "liberated" gender roles, decision making at this point is likely to be self-conscious and burdened with concerns about the possible prices to be paid for choices. For instance, the young "liberated" career woman may agonize over what she perceives to be the cost of her liberation when a divorce results over the difficulties that she and her husband have in finding jobs in the same location. She may wonder in the dead of the night whether she might not have been wiser to follow a more traditional pattern. Should she have concentrated on a housewife role or at least selected an occupation, such as elementary school teaching or nursing, that would have allowed her greater flexibility to fit in with her husband's career needs? In her pain, she may cast an envious glance at some of her more traditional sisters.

Sexual liberation can cause the same conflicts for women as does economic and political liberation. A teenage girl who directly initiates sex with her date by attempting to arouse him physically before he makes the first move may threaten her partner's budding but vulnerable sense of masculinity. Such activity on her part could lead to rejection, name calling, and cruel gossip. One liberal male college student described himself as a man who would enjoy sleeping with a sexually liberated woman but then told how repulsed he was when a beautiful 21-year-old female student suggested they "ball." He said he "didn't feel too good" and decided not to see her again because he was "taken aback by her forwardness" (Gross, 1978, p. 97; Komarovsky, 1976, p. 91).

Traditional women are no more free from conflict about their lives than are women who are "liberated." Consider the example of a woman who, after she had her first child, quit her job to fulfill the homemaker-mother role in the most time-honored fashion. Fifteen years later, the woman learns of her husband's enchantment with a better educated woman who offers intellectual companionship of the sort that she herself has not provided because of her emphasis on her husband's or children's development. Bitterness and confusion would be an understandable reaction to such a situation.

Traditional women are also vulnerable to sexual conflict in our changing times. Often reared to save themselves for marriage, many women continue to feel alienated from their sexuality and to feel put upon by their male partners' sexual demands. The following segments from interviews with two working-class, married women in their 30s illustrate this dilemma:

> We had sex four or five times a week like clockwork all those years and I just laid there like a lump. I couldn't figure out what all the noise was about. [Rubin, 1976, p. 149]

> It feels like somebody's always wanting something from me. Either one of the kids is hanging on to me or pulling at me, or my father needs something. And if it's not them, then Tom's always coming after me with that gleam in his eye. Then, it's not enough if I just let him have it, because if I don't have a climax, he's not happy. I get so tired of everybody wanting something from me all the time. I sometimes think I hate sex. [Rubin, 1976, p. 151]

Unfortunately, the sexual freedom movement has placed additional demands on some already heavily burdened women in traditional relationships.

CONFLICTING ROLES: MEN

Lest it appear that we have placed too much emphasis on the plight of women in changing times, let's talk about the conflicts faced by men. The husband in the traditional relationship has often found himself blamed for his wife's lack of development. His confusion and resentment at being faulted for behaving in a manner consistent with the way in which he was raised are understandable. His resentment may be compounded by the realization that, in this period of inflation and recession, he is bearing an increasingly heavy economic burden for the support of the entire family.

Some men may also face conflicts in the bedroom. If they live with traditional women who are uncomfortable with sexual intimacy and fearful of trying new things, these men may feel that their lives lack the sexual pleasure they desire. One man married 12 years describes this conflict:

> I've always been of the opinion that what two people do in the bedroom is fine; whatever they want to do is okay. But Jane, she doesn't agree. I personally like a lot of foreplay, caressing each other and whatever. For her, no. I think oral sex is the ultimate in making love; but she says it's revolting. (With a deep sigh of yearning:) I wish I could make her understand. [Rubin, 1976, p. 138]

Such men are unlikely to feel comforted by the blitz of magazine and newspaper articles and television talk show appearances by sex experts who praise the glories of the sexual revolution.

Nontraditional men are also paying a price for changes. The husband who agrees to participate in a less traditional division of house maintenance and child care may wonder, as he slips on the spilled milk in the middle of a cluttered kitchen while getting the baby's cereal, whatever possessed him to choose a liberated woman for a marital partner. A few men are quite comfortable with the realities of a marital relationship that incorporates the notion of role equality. Occasionally, however, they may become understandably defensive in response to negative reactions from relatives, friends, and outsiders. For example, the husband of a working mother frequently took his son to the community playground during the afternoons. He was taken aback when he overheard one neighborhood woman whisper to another, "That poor little boy. His mother must be dead—it's always his father who brings him here" (Lein, 1979, p. 491).

Women in egalitarian marriages may occasionally express their discomfort with their nontraditional partner, thereby hurting their spouses in subtle but hard-to-pin-down ways. A friend of ours reported being teased by a colleague's wife who had seen her unemployed husband at the supermarket during the work day. Our friend confessed conveying her embarrassment to her husband with an insensitive remark, although part of the reason for his unemployment was to give his wife an opportunity to pursue her career.

Furthermore, nontraditional men are confronted by conflicts in their sex lives. For example, it is not considered very "macho" for a teenager to admit that he isn't particularly attracted to the images of women presented in popular soft-pornography magazines such as *Penthouse* and *Playboy*. And many people have negative stereotypes about the manhood of gay men, men who choose other men as lovers. Ironically, heterosexuals themselves are not immune from such prejudices. The man with nontraditional attitudes toward sex even risks being denigrated by his own spouse. Men who express a willingness to use a male contraceptive pill, if one becomes available, have been characterized by their wives as less admirable and self-assured than those who refuse to take such contraceptive responsibility (Gough, 1979). Although lauded by advocates of responsible family planning, men who are willing to try a male pill have been described by wives as "restless and changeable; think(ing) and behav(ing) differently from others; submissive; giv(ing) in easily; lacking in self-confidence; awkward and ill-at-ease socially; easily embarrassed; feel(ing) inferior and inadequate; (or taken in total—not very manly)" (Gough, 1979, p. 34).

THE CONSEQUENCES OF LIFESTYLE CHOICES

No lifestyle is painless. Those of us who subscribe to traditional gender roles, as well as those of us who are less traditional, are vulnerable to "the inevitable anxiety that occurs during any period of major transition, when old and new values exist at the same time" (Bardwick, 1979, p. 7). Bardwick's conclusion is a good starting place to tell you more about this book. Many of the chapters deal with powerful emotional and political issues, but we are not trying to sell a particular point of view. The writers neither advocate liberation for everybody nor encourage North Americans to return to traditional values, to the so-called good old days when strict gender norms prevailed. Rather, we explore what is currently known about the costs and benefits of individual choices relevant to the maintenance of traditional norms versus an emphasis on individual development and freedom from the constraints of gender roles.

The contributors to *Changing Boundaries* are social scientists who are actively involved with the growing body of research on gender roles and human sexuality. This research indicates that gender-role norms, or rules for being males and females, can and do program overt sexual behavior, interpretations of sexual feelings, and even individuals' public accounts of their sexual lives. Further, there is convincing evidence that gender-role considerations may be central to the sexual feelings and experiences of people regardless of their age, marital status, or sexual preference. Our interest in gender roles extends beyond their relevance to purely erotic behavior. Gender-role norms may define our behaviors in clearly nonerotic, but socially critical, sex-related areas such as contraception, interaction between employees and supervisors, and rape.

HOW THIS BOOK IS ORGANIZED

In order to review what is known about the impact of changes in traditional gender-role norms on the quality of people's relationships with themselves and each other, we have organized this book into two parts.

Relying on a developmental perspective, Part One describes gender roles and sexual expression from childhood to old age. Both unmarried people and those involved in long-term relationships are considered in chapters that examine gender-role socialization processes throughout the life span.

Part Two examines some of the contemporary sexual issues revolving around changes in gender-role norms. Gender-role-bound versus gender-role-free relationships between men and women are included in Part Two, which ends with a consideration of the responses of men and women to erotic material.

FEMINISM AND CHANGING BOUNDARIES

Before concluding this introductory chapter, we want to acknowledge that the push for changes in the roles and relationships between men and women is still primarily limited to the middle and upper classes. As with other political and social movements, it is rarely the most down-trodden victims of particular social processes who press for change. The poorest members of society rarely have the resources or the leisure to consider methods for altering their environment; they are too busy trying to survive within it.

For instance, the man and woman who have a number of children but little in the way of education or marketable skills may perceive the women's movement as nonsense. At the lower end of the economic ladder, the husband may find himself working at two jobs, both of which pay the minimum wage, in the effort to support his family. After from 12 to 16 hours of work, he is exhausted and is not likely to be receptive to pressures to participate in home maintenance, dishwashing, and so on. The wife may feel quite trapped if she remains in the house all day, especially if she has many small children. But it is likely that she will see poverty, rather than gender-role restrictions, as being the cause of her unhappiness. If the wife is employed, as many such women are, she works for sheer survival. Like their husbands, such women tend to have "jobs" rather than "careers." Moreover, they are at a greater economic disadvantage than are working men because women are paid substantially less than men for performing similar work (Blau, 1979) and are especially susceptible to hardship when they are unemployed "breadwinners" (Schlozman, 1979).

Despite the fact that poor women are more oppressed than well-to-do women, they are unlikely to identify with feminist rhetoric. From the perspective of an economically insecure, hand-to-mouth existence, they may perceive their social class or minority group as their special-interest group and may not feel any particular identification with the women's movement. Poor women may be too occupied with raising their children and vainly trying to make ends meet to be concerned with confronting themselves or their men or with raising their "consciousness."

For these and other reasons, this book may have a middle-class bias in its consideration of relevant research. Most researchers in the field, ourselves included, have greater access to college students and families from the typically white, middle-class communities near colleges and universities where we work. Consequently, a large proportion of the studies that are reported in this book may not be generalizable to people from different socioeconomic groups and those from ethnic minorities. Admittedly, then, this book may be more relevant to white, middle-class North Americans than to others. As stated previously, the push for women's rights seems to have had a more positive impact on the affluent than on those in the lower socioeconomic classes.

It is appropriate to end this chapter by looking at the complexity of changing gender-role boundaries in greater detail. We will do this by returning to the lives of the twins, John and Jennifer. As the parent-child battles of their adolescence subside, John and Jennifer enter young adulthood. Continuing to be close, they decide to enroll in the same college. Although they take many of the same courses and move into the same dormitory, their ideas about ideal gender roles become quite dissimilar, largely as the result of associating with a very different group of friends.

Within his first year at college, John is accepted into a fraternity and makes the college's basketball team. His new friends are a self-confident and traditional group of men who feel there are two kinds of women — those they sleep with and those they might marry. Influenced by his friends, John maintains *traditional gender-role attitudes*. He believes women should center their lives on men. As dates, he selects attractive women who encourage him to talk about himself. He expects his future wife to be a full-time homemaker and mother, as his mother was.

Naturally, John expects his dates and future wife to let him take primary responsibility for decision making and economic support. When he takes someone out, he decides where to go and pays for the date. John enjoys sex and often makes the first move in a sexual encounter. Nevertheless, his traditional gender-role attitudes are not consistent with all his hopes and desires. Sometimes he gets tired of having to be the sexual expert. Less interested in marrying a virgin than are some of his buddies, he secretly hopes to meet a woman who will occasionally take the sexual initiative and let him be on the receiving end of lovemaking. In John's case, changing gender-role boundaries have not influenced his general behavior with women. However, they have influenced his expectations about sex.

Jennifer's development during college presents an interesting contrast with that of her twin, John. Unlike her traditional brother, Jennifer becomes involved with the campus feminists. She and her friends advocate *profeminist* values including support for the Equal Rights Amendment (ERA), advocacy of reproductive freedom, and opposition to any policies that discriminate against women. As part of her extracurricular activities, Jennifer has worked to establish a day-care center for working mothers and has passed around a petition that protests the fact that few women professors are hired at her college.

Not surprisingly, the men that Jennifer goes out with share her pro-feminist or *egalitarian* values. She prefers to spend her time with men who are comfortable letting her share the expenses for dates and who support her political views. Jennifer looks forward to living with or marrying someone who is quite unlike her twin brother. She expects to fall in love with an egalitarian man who thinks her career is just as important as his own, especially one who would assume half of the child-care and housework responsibilities.

Feminism aside, Jennifer has a difficult time taking on a liberated role during sex. Sometimes she wonders if her dates say they are profeminist just to influence her to go to bed with them. She is confused as to whether she or her partner should take the major responsibility for using contraception. Despite her feminist beliefs, she is rather traditional during lovemaking. She prefers that the male make the first move during a sexual encounter. Instead of being willing to tell a man what makes her feel good, she hopes her partner will have enough expertise in lovemaking to anticipate her sexual needs.

Changing boundaries for gender roles and sexuality have influenced Jennifer very differently from the way they have influenced John. Jennifer's advocacy of women's liberation is limited to the home and workplace; she expects traditional male dominance during sex. John's traditional values, in contrast, do not extend to sex. He wishes women would take a more dominant role during lovemaking.

John's and Jennifer's attempts to grapple with changing gender-role norms during their years at college have heuristic value. As the following chapters point out, social change does not touch everyone in the same way. Changing gender-role boundaries have contributed to a variety of adaptations. One group remains traditional in both their beliefs about men and women and their approach to sexuality. A second group holds on to traditional gender-role norms and attitudes while expecting men and women to be equally enthusiastic and active during sex. A third group advocates liberation from male political and economic domination but continues to expect men to take the dominant role during sex. Only a few people have been able to pursue liberation in both sexual and nonsexual male-female relationships. Still, if social change continues in the same direction, people who are doubly liberated may prevail in the future. Unlike John and Jennifer, tomorrow's children may grow up in a world that offers expanding social and sexual options for both men and women.

PART ONE

Developmental Perspective

Change is our one certainty. From birth through old age, our lives are characterized by a variety of changes. As our bodies mature and then age, we also grow psychologically and socially. It is no wonder, then, that each age group develops different understandings of what it means to be masculine or feminine. Also, every generation must adjust to changing sexual standards. It goes without saying that 5-year-olds, 15-year-olds, and 50-year-olds have widely varying ideas about what is sexually normal. With the acceleration of changing values in the latter part of this century, the generation gap between younger and older peoples' beliefs about sexuality may be widening.

Throughout human development, identification with and attitudes toward gender roles are core parts of one's personality. In this part of the book, the relationships between these core parts of personality and sexuality are considered in detail. A key assumption characterizes each chapter in Part One: regardless of age, the understanding of women's and men's "proper" places in the world is intimately bound up with human sexual expression. Chapters 1 through 6 consider the way in which gender-role norms influence sexuality across the life span.

Chapter 1 describes the acquisition of a gender role and its relatively weak association with childhood sexuality. Beginning in their first years of life, most children are taught to live within strict gender-role boundaries. Adults pay close attention to whether or not boys are "masculine" and girls are "feminine." At the same time, children receive little sex education from parents and other adults. Given the common belief that childhood sexuality is unnatural, it is not surprising that well-meaning adults overlook the fact that children, boys in particular, masturbate, engage in sexual play, and tell bathroom jokes. In our culture, both boys and girls are expected to be

15

ignorant, until puberty, about sex. For this reason, childhood may be the period of life when the relationship between gender-role identity and sexual behavior is least prominent.

Chapter 2 describes how the process of identifying with a gender role that was initiated in childhood becomes integrated with sexual behavior during adolescence. Peers assume a larger role than elders in socializing the adolescent. Encouraged by their peers, adolescents come to accept a rigid code for appropriate masculine and feminine sexual behavior. Traditional and nonegalitarian expectations prevail. Boys are seen as obsessed with and driven by sexual urges. They are expected to initiate and control sexual interactions, sometimes forcibly. In contrast, girls are seen as sexy looking but as less sexually interested than boys. They are expected to be the passive but responsible partners within sexual relationships.

Chapter 3 describes how gender-role norms influence courtship, the institutionalized way in which men and women become acquainted before marriage. Most young adults seem to adhere to the gender-role stereotypes for heterosexual behavior that were established during adolescence. Men are more likely than women to initiate dates and sexual intercourse. Women more frequently take a limit-setting role. Nevertheless, maturity begets flexibility. Unlike adolescents, some young adults do challenge strict gender-role norms. For example, women are just as likely as men to initiate a flirtation in a bar. And a number of men welcome woman partners who take the sexual initiative.

With adulthood, people are expected to be capable of enjoying their sexuality. As indicated in Chapter 4, this ideal is not always achieved. Despite a great similarity between men's and women's physiological responsiveness to effective sexual stimulation, women are more susceptible to sexual dysfunctions than are men. Gender-role identification seems to be implicated in these difficulties. The major reason for many women's sexual problems is that they are too "feminine" to seek the sexual stimulation they need. Like the majority of men, however, androgynous women are comfortable taking an active role with a lover. For this reason, the androgynous woman receives more pleasure from sexual relations than does the feminine or gender-typed woman.

Chapter 5 describes gender differences in love relationships from young adulthood to old age. Whereas women are more likely to suffer from sexual dysfunctions, men are more likely to become "love-sick" in new relationships. Men fall in love and become deeply committed before women do. Once the couple develops a long-term relationship, however, gender-role norms favor the man. From the time dating begins, to very late in marriage, women provide men with more emotional support than they receive in return.

Finally, aging brings about gender-role equality. During old age, men return love with intensity equal to or greater than their spouses.

For those fortunate enough to hold on to good health and a partner, old age can bring about liberation from traditional gender roles. Chapter 6 describes how middle-aged and elderly couples may experiment with converging gender roles. In such relationships, the man may contribute to housework and accept his nurturant side, and the woman may become more comfortable with her competent, dominant side. Although young people associate sex with reproduction and expect their elders to be sexless, those who were sexually active in the past are likely to continue to enjoy sex during their final years. Because little research has been done in this area, we have little information on how the assumption of less stereotyped gender roles in old age influences sexual expression. One gender difference that characterizes the entire life span remains, however: women have sex less frequently than men. Although women outlive men, the few men of their own age who survive are able to attract younger partners, because there is a double standard of aging. Hence, women have increasingly fewer opportunities for sexual intercourse as they grow older.

Now that each of the developmental chapters has been summarized, a comparison between the issues raised in the chapters concerned with early development and those dealt with in the chapters on adulthood is timely. Chapters 1 through 3 indicate that growth and change follow a fairly predictable course in youth. Childhood, adolescence, and young adulthood, each seem to be characterized by particular developmental changes in gender-role socialization and sexuality. All three chapters point out that the young live in accord with strict gender-role norms and even stricter notions about appropriate sexual behavior. In contrast, Chapters 4 through 6 describe the variety of sexual and affectional options available to older adults. Because there is so much individual variation in adult development, the physiological, psychological, and social changes discussed in these chapters cannot be pinpointed to particular chronological age groups. Nonetheless, one generalization is possible: older people seem to adhere to more flexible guidelines for gender-role and sexual behavior than do the young.

1 Sexual Socialization and Gender Roles in Childhood

JACQUELYNNE ECCLES PARSONS

The next six chapters examine the influence of gender-role norms throughout different stages in the life cycle. In this chapter, Jacquelynne Parsons focuses on the socialization of gender roles and of sexual attitudes and information. She begins by describing several components of gender roles and sexual behavior. Specifically, children learn which gender they are and the role behaviors associated with being male or female in their culture. While they are learning these roles, children also learn about sexuality. First, they acquire beliefs and attitudes about sexual interactions. Second, they learn facts about sex, to a greater or lesser extent. Third, children learn specific sexual behaviors. The extent to which explicit training is given in these last two areas varies from one culture to the next. North American culture tends to provide little information, resulting in many inaccuracies in sex knowledge.

Parsons then describes three influential theories of childhood gender-role and psychosexual development. These include Freudian or psychoanalytic theory, social learning theory, and social cognitive theory. She compares these models and notes the contributions of each to our understanding of the child's development. Relatively little research has been conducted on sexuality in childhood, perhaps due to cultural beliefs that there is no such thing. However, Parsons reviews what is known about sexual development from birth to puberty. She provides a table describing the acquisition of sexual behavior and sexual knowledge from birth to puberty that may be very useful for adults in their roles as parents and/or researchers. Among the issues discussed in this section are the development of childhood modesty at about age 6 or 7, the use of sexual humor and jokes by children, and the exploration of sexuality with same and other gender friends.

Parsons notes the paucity of children's sexual knowledge in North American culture and compares their understanding of reproduction, for instance, with that of Swedish children. She discusses the hotly debated issue of sex education in this country and describes the three basic positions: ignore, minimize, or cultivate children's interest in learning about sex. She points out that although most parents support formal sex education in the schools, a vocal minority believe education should be provided by parents, *not* by public schools. Unfortunately, research indicates that most parents provide only very rudimentary information, if that. The result is that most children rely on friends who may be equally ignorant. Parents may avoid providing information for fear that this will encourage sexual activity, but as we will see in later chapters, research does not support that hypothesis.

A little girl asked her mother the age-old question, "Where did I come from?"

"The stork brought you," her mother nervously replied.

But the little girl persisted. "Where did Daddy come from?" she queried.

"I think the doctor brought him in his little black bag," Mom anxiously retorted.

Undaunted, the little girl asked again, "Well, where did Grandma and Grandpa come from?"

"They were found in a cabbage patch. Now, that's enough questions," Mom scolded.

The next day, the little girl went to school and reported to her second-grade class, "For over three generations, there has not been a normal birth in my family!" [Koch, 1980, p. 1]

As we were walking casually down the street one afternoon, my daughter asked, "How long does it take to make a baby?" Automatically, I replied, "Nine months." Amy looked at me tolerantly and then pointed to her crotch and said, "I mean, how LONG does it take to make a baby." Realizing that she was referring to how long intercourse takes rather than how long pregnancy takes, I answered, "That depends, it can take different amounts of time." Undaunted, she asked, "Well, if you take longer, do you get a bigger baby?"

These anecdotes clearly depict children's interest in sexuality. Unfortunately, few children in North American culture are as lucky as either of these children. Usually they do not have enough accurate information to be able to judge the misinformation provided by their parents and their culture. Furthermore, their parents are rarely receptive to their questions. Despite the fact that Freud brought the reality of childhood sexuality to the attention of

Western civilization as early as 1933, most parents in this culture still prefer to either ignore or punish their children's interest in sex. Similarly, few social scientists have deemed it an appropriate topic for study. This chapter summarizes the major theories of gender-role acquisition and psychosexual development and reviews the little existing empirical research on childhood sexuality and the development of sexual behavior patterns.

BASIC COMPONENTS IN THE DEVELOPMENT OF SEXUAL MATURITY

The construct of sexuality is broad and varied in its scope. Freud stressed throughout his writings that sexuality encompasses the full range of sensual pleasures. Poets and philosophers have long nested the concept of sexuality within the full range of human emotions. Social scientists and experts in sex education include most aspects of intimate, interpersonal activity as well as our knowledge and understanding of them as part of the domain of sexuality. Given this broad range, it is difficult to select just what should be included in a discussion of childhood sexuality. But at the very least there is agreement that the development of sexual maturity consists of five basic components, which emerge and take shape with age.

1. *Gender identity:* Sometime around 18 months of age, children learn whether they are a boy or a girl. Not long after they learn their gender, it becomes a critical component of their self-concept. Gender identity, then, grows out of the awareness of one's gender and the incorporation of gender as an important part of one's basic identity. Psychologists now believe that gender identity develops very early. Children begin organizing their understanding of their social world and their conception of themselves around gender by 2-1/2 years of age (see Frieze et al., 1978). In fact, recent work by Money and his associates on the effects of changing a child's gender label suggests that a rudimentary form of gender identity may be firmly in place by 24 months of age (see Money & Ehrhardt, 1972). Once formed, it is now clear that gender identity has a major impact on all subsequent development, especially on all aspects of gender-role acquisition and psychosexual development.

2. *Gender role:* During the process of socialization, we learn many behaviors and attitudes. Some of these are specifically linked to gender and to the prescribed roles expected of men and women and boys and girls in each culture. As children begin to monitor their own behavior and to identify themselves as either males or females, they develop a sense of what it means to be a boy or girl in their culture. Gender-role identity motivates many behaviors including the clothes we select to wear, our

---

Gender Reassignment

Each year, Money and his colleagues see children who need to have their gender reassigned. Some of these children, because of prenatal hormonal imbalances, were born with ambiguous genitalia; for example, an enlarged clitoris, or a fused labia majora, or a rudimentary penis. Consequently, the attending doctor mislabeled the gender of the child at birth; that is, he or she may have called a female with an enlarged clitoris a "boy," or a boy with a rudimentary penis a "girl." When this mistake is discovered, the doctor and parents usually decide to have the child's gender reassigned. Other children, primarily boys, have sustained severe injury to their genitals, and the doctor and parents decide it is better to have the child's gender reassigned. In both of these cases, surgery is often necessary to make the child's anatomy coincide more accurately with his or her gender label. However, even if surgery is not necessary, the child must undergo a psychological change that can have severe debilitating effects. Money and his colleagues have found that gender reassignment after the age of 2-1/2 is psychologically dangerous. Gender reassignment, with or without surgical corrections, carried out before the child is 2, is usually successful provided that people in the child's environment accept the reassignment.

---

career choice, and whether or not we call up a member of the other gender to ask for a date.

3. *Sexual scripts and attitudes:* As we grow up, we acquire a wide range of attitudes toward sexuality. These attitudes include the value we attach to sexuality, our comfort with our own sexuality, and a set of norms and expectations regarding the manner in which intimate relationships are to be acted out. These norms and expectations are called sexual scripts (see Gagnon & Simon, 1973; Gagnon, 1977). These scripts dictate many aspects of sexual interactions, including the appropriate sequence of events, the pool of acceptable partners, and the range of acceptable behaviors at various points in our lifetime.

4. *Specific knowledge of sexual and reproductive facts and skills:* In addition to gender-role identity, sexual scripts, and sexual attitudes, as we grow up we learn some of the facts of sexuality. Unfortunately, children in this culture do not learn very many of these facts. As a consequence, we spend most of our lives rather "illiterate," sexually speaking. This failure to educate children sexually is discussed in more detail later.

5. *Sexual behaviors:* In addition to all the attitudinal components of psychosexual development already listed, actual sexual behavior is a critical component of sexuality. In fact, most of us assume that sexual behavior is *the* essence of sexuality. But there are several important points to bear in mind in thinking about sexual behavior. First, sexual behavior is generally dictated by sexual knowledge, sexual attitudes, and sexual scripts; it is the tip of the iceberg resting on a vast network of conscious and unconscious beliefs and physiological processes that scientists do not yet understand. Second, sexual behaviors are perhaps the most difficult aspect of sexuality to study. People are not as willing to discuss their sexual behaviors as they are to discuss their attitudes toward sexuality. Third, the sexual meaning of any particular behavior is very personal. People vary a great deal in the behaviors they consider to be sexual and the behaviors that "turn them on" sexually. Finally, although children are sexual, the nature of their sexuality, as well as their understanding of sexuality, varies from age to age. For example, the interest of a 4-year-old in observing and touching other people's bodies may reflect curiosity about anatomical differences rather than sexual interest. In contrast, similar interests in a 16-year-old are more likely the result of erotic desires. Similarly, homosexual play during the early years may be quite distinct in meaning and motivation from homosexual play among 16- or 18-year-olds. Parents, grandparents, and teachers are likely to apply adult connotations to the actions of children. In doing this, adults may react in inappropriate, and often harmful, ways to children's behavior. Research in this area underlines the need for caution in inferring the motives or goals behind the seemingly "sexual" behaviors of children.

The interaction of these five basic components provides a broad and complex part of our adult identity. Therefore, it is important to realize that in North America sexuality is always learned but seldom taught. Cross-cultural studies have uncovered wide variations in both childhood and adult sexuality that coincide with variations across societies in the prevalent attitudes toward teaching sexuality. In a few cultures, many aspects of erotic sexuality are taught explicitly. In many other cultures, however, sexuality is learned in back alleys and locker rooms. Our society fits into the latter category. Because societies with more liberal teaching philosophies also have freer expression of childhood sexuality, the relatively repressed state of childhood sexuality in this culture is to be expected.

There is a growing concern in America with the failure of our culture to "teach" sexuality. Rising rates of unwanted pregnancy, rape, incest, and venereal disease are coupled with the exploitation of erotic sex for a multitude of purposes. These problems have created alarm among social scientists, public policy makers, educators, moralists, and parents. Various remedies have been proposed, ranging from increased sexual repression to mandatory sex education of all children. People are increasingly aware of the importance of prevention (see Yates, 1978, 1980) through educating our young people. Such programs would be designed to teach healthy sexual attitudes to children and adolescents in order to prevent problems from developing later in adulthood. There is growing consensus that such programs are badly needed, but the exact nature of these programs is still the subject of much heated debate.

THEORIES OF GENDER-ROLE ACQUISITION AND PSYCHOSEXUAL DEVELOPMENT

One of the first steps in sexual socialization is the acquisition of a well-defined gender role. Many theorists argue, in fact, that sexuality is the essence of one's gender role. They assert that the behaviors and characteristics differentiating females from males are primarily designed to facilitate sexuality and intimacy between men and women. Other theorists stress the impact of gender role on sexuality, arguing that the entire character of our sexuality is shaped by the same processes that shape gender roles. But whichever perspective one takes, it is clear that gender roles and sexuality are linked to each other in many ways. From a developmental perspective, gender-role socialization is one of the major forces shaping adult sexuality.

Three major theoretical frameworks have emerged to explain the acquisition of gender role and of psychosexual development. These are psychodynamic theories based on Freud's work; social learning theories; and social cognitive theories. Advocates of each approach have analyzed the acquisition of gender roles, but only Freud and his followers explicitly and directly linked it to psychosexual development. Nevertheless, the concepts that have emerged in both social learning theories and social cognitive theories can be used to explain psychosexual development.

Freudian Theory

In his efforts to understand the development of the human personality, Freud (1933/1965, 1938) proposed what was, for that time, a rather revolutionary argument. He suggested that the child's relationship with his or her same-gender parent had a tremendous impact on the child's developing personality. "Identification" was Freud's term for the unique learning process through which the child molds his or her own ego (identity) after that of the parent model. Through identification, the child quite literally incorporates or takes the personality of the model into him- or herself. Thus, in the

Freudian view, identification is the means by which children acquire the behaviors expected of them as adults—including gender-role and sexual behaviors.

Over the past 40 years, Freud's ideas have been reworked into a number of modified theories of the identification process. These interpretations all share the acceptance of identification as the critical building block of psychosexual development. Identification is thought of as the means by which a child acquires total, complex patterns of behavior, attitudes, feelings, wishes, and standards of conduct, such as would constitute gender-role and sexual orientation. But what is meant by a "complex pattern" of behavior and attitudes? Consider the following example.

Mary and Billy watch their mother balancing her checkbook. Their mother sighs and complains repeatedly. Now and then, she stops and starts over again. Finally, she gives up, voicing her disgust for mathematics to Mary and Billy. Later, when Mary and Billy begin to learn mathematics in school, Mary, ordinarily a good student, exhibits her mother's pattern of responses to mathematics. She too struggles and complains. She too gives up easily. Moreover, she expresses a similar set of attitudes about math: "I hate math." "I'm no good at math." "Math is for boys." In contrast to his sister, Billy exhibits none of his mother's responses to math.

Identification theorists would argue that regular learning theories are not capable of explaining the acquisition of the entire set of mother's attitudes toward mathematics by Mary but not by Billy. Instead, they maintain that Mary has come to model her mother so closely because of her identification with her mother—an identification that Billy cannot share.

What is critical in this notion of identification is the assumption that girls identify with their mothers and boys identify with their fathers. Freud's theory of psychosexual development dealt specifically with the forces that would motivate this gender-differentiated identification pattern. This is the aspect of Freud's theory that I elaborate on here; but some basic comments are in order before beginning that summary.

First, Freud was a stage theorist: he believed that psychosexual development usually proceeds in an orderly fashion, culminating with *the* mature stage. This perspective led Freud to conclude (1) that heterosexuality is the mature state and that homosexuality is an immature state; (2) that mature female sexuality focuses on the vagina, not the clitoris; and (3) that mature male sexuality requires an aggressive, intrusive personality. These aspects of Freudian theory have been widely criticized by contemporary scientists. Nonetheless, they still influence many therapists and psychiatrists.

Second, Freud adopted the male as the standard for his theory; he considered the female to be the deviant. Karen Horney (1926, pp. 327–328) was the first to point out this bias. She concluded,

The present analytical picture of feminine development (whether that picture be correct or not) differs in no case by a hair's breadth from the typical ideas that the boy has of the girl.

We are familiar with the ideas that the boy entertains. I will therefore only sketch them in a few succinct phrases, and for the sake of comparison will place in a parallel column our ideas of the development of women.

The Boy's Ideas	Psychoanalytic Ideas of Feminine Development
Naive assumption that girls as well as boys possess a penis.	For both sexes it is only the male genital which plays any part.
Realization of the absence of the penis.	Sad discovery of the absence of the penis.
Idea that the girl is a castrated, mutilated boy.	Belief of the girl that she once possessed a penis and lost it by castration.
Belief that the girl has suffered punishment that also threatens him.	Castration is conceived of as the infliction of punishment.
The girl is regarded as inferior.	The girl regards herself as inferior.
	Penis envy.
The boy is unable to imagine how the girl can ever get over this loss or envy.	The girl never gets over the sense of deficiency and inferiority and has constantly to master afresh her desire to be a man.
The boy dreads her envy.	The girl desires throughout life to avenge herself on the man for possessing something which she lacks.

Recent critics of Freud have agreed with Horney's analysis and have discredited Freud's male bias.

Third, Freud believed that much of psychosexual development is driven by unconscious processes. As a result, the psychological consequences of "faulty" socialization are very difficult to correct, creating a need for years of intensive psychoanalysis.

Finally, Freud believed that sexuality in its broadest sense (including all bodily pleasures) is one of the basic motivational forces behind all behavior. Freud also believed that the sources of bodily pleasure change as one develops. Consequently, the conflicts between one's id (the internal force seek-

ing pleasure) and the social demands for conformity change as one grows older. As these conflicts shift, the developmental tasks facing the child also shift, and new components of personality take shape. In the first stage, the oral stage, the child confronts the world with his or her need for sucking. At the same time, the world confronts the child with feeding schedules. In the second stage, the anal stage, the world confronts the child with toilet training. At the same time, the child is learning to enjoy power over excretory functions. Freud assumed that development during these two early stages (which comprise the first three years of life) was comparable for boys and girls. At the next stage, the phallic stage, boys and girls diverge in their development.

Freud suggested that once children learn to discriminate between the genitals of males and females and to experience sexual pleasure (at approximately age 4), the identification experiences of boys and girls diverge. For the boy, budding sexual awareness initiates the oedipal complex. He begins to desire his mother sexually and to resent and fear his father as a rival. However, the event that forces the boy to resolve his feelings is the sight of the female's genitals—or, rather, her embarrassing lack of genitals. With childish reasoning, the boy concludes that girls have lost their penises and that a similar fate threatens him. There are two reasons why this discovery is a threatening one. First, because identification with his mother makes him want to be like her, the boy now sees that he must give up his penis to identify successfully. Second, the boy fears that his father will castrate him as punishment for his harboring of lusting thoughts about his mother.

In either case, fear of castration now motivates the boy to shift his identification to his father. The boy assumes that by identifying with the father he can incorporate the father into himself. Then he will no longer be competing with father. He can instead enjoy the father's status vicariously. Thus, in choosing to be like his father, he can both keep his penis and possess his mother. As a result of this shift in identification to the father, the boy begins to take on his father's characteristics and behaviors.

For the girl, resolution of the phallic stage begins when, in comparing herself to boys, she discovers that she lacks a penis. Freud believed that girls, on discovering this difference, feel

> seriously wronged, often declare that they have "something like it too," and fall victims to "envy for the penis," which will leave ineradicable traces on their development and the formation of their character and which will not be surmounted in even the most favorable cases without a severe expenditure of psychical energy. [Freud, 1933/1965, p. 589]

The girl's first reaction to this "traumatic discovery," according to Freud, is to deny that she does not have a penis. Eventually, however, she must face

Fear of Castration

When my son, Chris, was about 3 years old, he commented on the anatomical differences between boys and girls. Specifically he noted, "Girls don't
have any penises." Being curious about his reaction to this discovery, I asked
him, "Why don't girls have penises?" He thought about the question for
approximately 30 seconds and replied, rather matter of factly, "Someone
must have cut them off." Needless to say, I almost fell off my chair. After
years of explaining in my classes that there is little evidence to support
Freud's idea of fear of castration, my son, in one casual comment, had
shaken my conviction to the soul. But when I quizzed him some more to
find out his feeling about castration, my conviction was restored. It was
apparent, from his subsequent comments, that he did not fear castration for
himself. He had simply reached the conclusion that all children must start
with penises like his, and then it seemed logical to him that girls must have
lost theirs somewhere along the way. With the delightful innocence of
childhood, he had accepted this conclusion as logical without attaching any
fear or anxiety to it.

the fact that not only does she lack a penis, but that she shares this fate with
her mother and all other females. She may believe that she once had a penis,
but that she somehow lost it. In any case, she blames her mother for her lack
of a penis. Because she holds her mother responsible for her "loss" and
because the mother also lacks the "highly valued" penis, Freud believed that
the mother, and all females, are devalued by the girl. Thus, the girl begins to
regard men with profound envy, and joins all males in disdaining women.

The girl's "penis envy" motivates her to renounce her love for her mother
and turn to her father. At the same time, she renounces her clitoris and shifts
her erotic focus to the vagina—the mature female sex organ, according to
Freud (1938). Her shift of love to her father derives from her desire to possess
his penis. She believes that she can take in the father's penis, thereby uncon-
sciously perceiving her vagina in a new positive light. She also comes to
equate penis and child. She takes her father as a love object in order to have a
child by him, which symbolically represents attaining a penis. This process
places the girl in a position of unconscious competition with her mother.
Thus, according to Freudian theory, the girl playing with dolls is really expressing her wish for a penis. The original penis wish is transformed into a
wish for a baby, which leads to love and desire for the man as bearer of the
penis and provider of the baby.

Penis Envy

Here we have a classic example of the bias discussed earlier. Freud assumed that all children would accept the male body type as the norm and that consequently females would feel inferior because they lacked the male organ. Many of Freud's own students (namely, Adler, Horney, Thompson, and Erikson) later rejected this notion. Evidence supporting the concept of penis envy is sparse. Drawing on a variety of different types of studies, Sherman (1971) reported on nine that could be interpreted as being related directly or indirectly to penis envy. Of these nine studies, three found no evidence of penis envy or castration anxiety in either males or females. Three found some evidence of penis envy and castration anxiety in a very small percentage of both the males and females in their samples. Two reported finding a higher incidence of penis envy in females than males, and one reported the reverse. Thus there is little agreement among these studies on which to base a conclusion. Furthermore, of these nine studies, five used questionable measures (dream analyses and various projective techniques). For example, Landy (1967, p. 576) assessed penis envy by observing the way a person opened a pack of cigarettes:

> for women, having penis envy and the desire to possess a penis would constitute reaction formation; they would reject phallic images in everyday life and recreate . . . the cavity. . . . Thus, female smokers should tend to open an unopened pack of cigarettes and obtain a cigarette by lifting open the folded part of the cigarette pack, lifting the flap up to make a form similar to a cavity, and pushing the bottom of the pack to expel the cigarette from the top. In this manner the female creates a cavity in the bottom of the pack and expels the cigarette.

Landy assumed that the cigarette is a phallic symbol and that by pushing the cigarette out of the pack, the woman is symbolically rejecting the penis. He took this as evidence of penis envy because he assumed that rejection was compensation by women for the recognition that they cannot have the highly desired penis. Such studies clearly have major methodological problems, making interpretation of the results impossible. Thus, at present there is little evidence to support Freud's suggestion that female psychosexual development is motivated by penis envy. A little girl may occasionally pretend that she has a penis, just as a little boy may pretend that he is pregnant. But it seems likely that this play behavior reflects curiosity about the anatomical differences between the genders rather than deep-seated envy of what one does not have.

The shift from clitoral to vaginal sexuality is basic to Freud's developmental theory, because to him the clitoris is "masculine." Clitoral sexuality must be eliminated if mature femininity is to develop. To Freud, one of the immediate consequences of penis envy is that the girl struggles to renounce clitoral masturbation, which may remain a conflict for her throughout childhood. It is, after all, difficult for the girl to give up this activity, which has provided her with such pleasure. She does so, according to Freud, because of the terrible narcissistic wound of not possessing a penis.

For a girl, the "discovery of castration" initiates the female counterpart to the Oedipus complex, known as the Electra complex. However, Freud believed that girls remain in the grips of Electra conflicts for an indeterminate length of time, and never fully escape them. Partial resolution does occur through the girl's identification with her mother as a symbolic means of possessing her father. She then acquires her superego (a set of moral values) and her feminine identity from her mother. However, Freud concluded that women cannot have as strong a superego as men, because the motive for its formation (in men, fear of castration by their fathers) is lacking. Thus, women are doomed to remain morally and ethically less mature than men.

A woman, according to Freud, usually responds to the Electra complex with one of the following patterns: (1) She may renounce sexuality in general. (2) She may develop the "mature" feminine attitude, with all eroticism concentrated in the vagina. (3) She may cling to the clitoral "masculine" sexuality in obstinate self-assertion. Abnormal resolution of these phallic stage conflicts can lead to masculine identification and homosexuality, or to overly strong "penis envy" and masculine behavior.

Although only one of these three paths involves the renunciation of sexuality, Freud did believe that the libido, or human sexual force, functions less effectively in women than in men. He stated that the libido is essentially active or "masculine." According to Freud, the libido is more constrained "when pressed into the service of the feminine function" (1933/1965, p. 595). In short, he believed that the normal process of female development demands more sexual repression than does the normal process of male development.

After passing through the phallic stage and oedipal conflict, both genders enter the latency stage, which lasts from approximately age 7 until the time of puberty. During this time, about which Freud wrote comparatively little, the child is assumed to have no central erogenous focus and sexuality is largely repressed. Finally, in the genital stage, both girls and boys are oriented toward heterosexual intercourse. This means that the girl's erotic focus is the vagina and the boy's is the penis. For both genders, though, the interest is in intercourse rather than in masturbation.

The Freudian theory of psychosexual development has come under extensive criticism and in some instances has been proven incorrect. (For example, we now know that children are sexually active and very interested in sex during the latency period.) However, it has had a tremendous impact on our thinking about psychosexual development. Most importantly, Freud made us aware that children are sexual and that sexuality is a very powerful motivating force even during childhood. He also introduced the idea of unconscious processes. Finally, he pointed out the formative importance of the relationship between parents and their children during the first five years of life.

Social Learning Theories

Psychodynamic theorists have argued that identification with one's same-gender parent is the force behind the acquisition of a gender-role identity and of the associated sexual scripts. In contrast, social learning theorists (Bandura & Walters, 1963; Mischel, 1970; Skinner, 1953; Watson, 1925) argue that the concept of identification is not necessary. Imitation of same-gender individuals and reinforcement (rewards or punishments) for gender-appropriate behaviors are sufficient to explain the acquisition of gender-role identity and sexual behaviors. Identification, it is argued, is an oversimplification that hides a wide range of learning mechanisms responsible for gender-role acquisition. Furthermore, social learning theorists argue that it is not necessary to hypothesize a separate "identification" process to explain gender-role learning. Instead they argue that gender-role learning can be adequately explained by the basic principles of learning theory. They suggest that there are laws governing imitation and that these laws can account for identification. Consequently, there is no need to distinguish between imitation and identification. The rules explaining imitation in the laboratory should be equally useful in explaining imitation in the home. Finally, the most ardent social learning theorists have denied the need to include internal motivational variables such as the Oedipus conflict in the theoretical explanation of gender-role acquisition. Indeed, they suggest that we learn gender-role behaviors just as we learn a variety of other behaviors—by reinforcements (rewards and punishments) from our environment.

Learning theory posits that children are differentially rewarded by their parents and their society for exhibiting behaviors appropriate to their gender roles. As a result, gender-appropriate behaviors take on greater value for the child and are exhibited with greater frequency (Mischel, 1970). Little girls are rewarded with big hugs for dressing femininely. Little boys who run away from fights are punished by the disappointed looks on their fathers' faces. Similarly little girls who are sexually "forward" are punished by the stern looks of disapproval from their parents, relatives, and friends. These differential patterns of rewards and punishments shape the behaviors of boys and girls into the gender-typed behavior patterns we find among adult men and women.

Rewards and punishments also shape the patterns of sexual behaviors and attitudes we find among adults. Girls, it is argued, learn not to be assertive, especially in sexual encounters and in interactions with boys. Boys learn that they should be the initiators of intimate relations. A girl learns that success in life is a rich, handsome husband who can take care of her. A boy learns that success in life is a good job and a pretty wife who stays at home.

Much of this, it is argued is learned by direct reinforcement. Some of it, however, is learned by a second set of mechanisms: imitation and role modeling. Impressed by the fact that children can learn without direct rewards, several social learning theorists (for example, Bandura & Walter, 1963) have suggested that children learn from the behavior of those around them (models), especially if the models are reinforced for their behavior.

One characteristic of a model that influences whether children imitate that model or not is gender. Children have little difficulty distinguishing between males and females. Thus, they have ample opportunity to learn about behaviors appropriate to gender roles and sexual scripts from the myriad of people they can observe both in real life and on the television and motion picture screens. Gender-role stereotypes are the common denominator of most mass media presentations. Furthermore, in most cases actors and actresses are rewarded for adhering to the gender-role stereotypes and are punished for violations. This is especially true for behaviors associated with sexual scripts.

Social learning theorists argue (see Bandura & Walters, 1963; Mischel, 1970) that exposure to both a gender-stereotyped society and the different patterns of rewards and punishments administered to boys and girls is sufficient to explain gender-role development.

Unlike Freud, social learning theorists do not expect gender-role behaviors and sexual behaviors to emerge in tandem, nor do they expect that negative experiences in childhood will require extensive psychotherapy. Furthermore, social learning theorists do not define an optimal course of psychosexual development. People's sexual scripts and gender-role identity are assumed to be shaped by their experiences; variations do not reflect developmental immaturity. Instead, variations reflect either the models one has been exposed to or the experiences one has had. Heterosexuality is the most common pattern, primarily because it is the pattern we are most likely to be exposed to and because early signs of homosexuality are very likely to be punished, especially if one is a boy. Homosexuality is not considered immature or deviant. It is merely a variation. If, for example, a girl is exposed to homosexual models and has rewarding sexual experiences with other girls, social learning theorists would predict that she will continue to engage in homosexual behaviors. If, on the other hand, she is never exposed to homosexual models or if her parents have repeatedly criticized homosexuality, then it is much less likely that she will engage in homosexual behavior even if she has very positive experiences with other girls. Thus, both the gender of one's sexual partner and the range of sexual behaviors one exhibits is assumed to be a function of one's past and present experiences. Changes in one's role models or in the pattern of rewards and punishments for various behaviors and attitudes related to gender role are expected to produce changes in sexual behavior.

Social Cognitive Theories

In recent years, several psychologists whom I will loosely group into the social cognitive camp (Kohlberg, 1966; J. Parsons, 1978; T. Parsons & Bales, 1955; Piaget, 1932/1948), have criticized the social learning approach for its overemphasis on rewards and punishments. These psychologists have argued quite vehemently that children play an active role in their own socialization. They believe that children are motivated to learn gender roles because they want to master the demands of their culture; that is, children want to become "good" members of their society. The critical difference between the social cognitive perspective and the social learning perspective is the importance placed on the child as an *active* participant in his or her own development. Social learning theorists have, in the past, assumed that the child is rather passive in the process of gender-role socialization; gender-appropriate behaviors are produced by the rewards and punishments administered to the child by members of his or her society. In contrast, social cognitive theorists view the child as very active; the child seeks out information about gender roles and then monitors his or her own behavior so that it is consistent with the gender-role norms. Rewards, punishments, and role models are assumed to be important precisely because they help the child distinguish between appropriate or "good" behavior and inappropriate or "bad" behavior.

Social cognitive theorists differ from social learning theorists on one other dimension: the role of the child's maturity in gender-role acquisition. Social cognitive theorists (for example, Piaget, 1932/1948; Kohlberg, 1966; and Parsons, 1978) believe that children's understanding of gender roles and sexual scripts is tempered, in part at least, by their level of cognitive development. For example, because 3-year-olds are very concrete in their thinking and because they tend to overgeneralize newly discovered facts, they are expected to hold very rigid beliefs regarding gender roles: doctors simply cannot be women, and nurses simply cannot be men.

Advocates of the social cognitive perspective believe that, once gender identity emerges, children use gender as a social category. That is, they organize much of the social information available to them according to gender. In keeping with their active view of the child, these theorists assume that the children create these categories and seek out the information needed to fill out the content of each category (that is, male and female). In forming these categories, children use any available information. For example, when my son Chris was 3 years old, I was a graduate student and my husband worked for the Veterans Administration Hospital. Consequently Chris was accustomed to having his mother go to school while his father went to work. One day, I told Chris that I was going to work. He looked at me in total disbelief and informed me that "Mommies do not work, they go to school—Daddies work." Apparently, he had assimilated our behavior into his categories of male (Daddy) and female (Mommy). His conception of male and female had come to include the distinction between school and work. Interestingly, my daughter Amy reached the same conclusion at 2-1/2. At that time I was teaching at Smith College. Consequently, she saw a lot of female students attending school and knew that I went to "school" each day also. At the same time her father worked at the Veterans Administration Hospital. As we were driving to the Smith College Child Care Center one day, she informed me that ladies go to school while men go to work. She refused to believe me when I told her that I worked at Smith College and that some ladies work other places. Apparently both of my children at age 3 were trying to formulate for themselves what it means to be a male or a female. They were developing a concept of what gender means in terms of the behaviors and sexual object preferences of those they observed.

Social cognitive theorists suggest that all children form these gender-role concepts. Furthermore, once formed these concepts are assumed to provide children with a framework for interpreting what they see and for predicting future behavior. New information will be incorporated into these concepts, and children will develop expectancies regarding human behavior based on these concepts. It is this process—the formation of male and female concepts through categorization and assimilation—that is the basis for the creation of gender-role stereotypes. In addition, it is assumed that this process is a direct consequence of children's desires to understand their social world.

Having formed these gender-role categories, children are then assumed to strive to become like the categories they have created. They will imitate behaviors they assume to be important and will adopt attitudes congruent with their image of a "good" boy or girl. For social cognitive theorists, this process of monitoring one's own behavior is the crux of gender-role acquisition.

In sum, according to social cognitive theories, gender-role acquisition depends on two basic processes. First, it depends on the child's capacity and desire to form social concepts, in particular gender-role concepts. The information necessary to fill out these concepts is provided by each culture. It includes the behaviors of the child's parents and relatives, the gender roles portrayed in mass media, and the behaviors of all the individuals that the child encounters. From this mass of information, the child abstracts a system of social concepts that includes the appropriate behaviors and attitudes of each gender, sexual scripts, values and attitudes associated with sexuality, and the gender of potential sexual partners. The quality and rigidity of these concepts are assumed to change with the child's age and with the range of behaviors to which the child is exposed. If the child lives in a culture that has well-defined gender roles and rigid rules governing sexual behavior and sexual partners, then the child will develop rigid gender-role concepts. In contrast, if the child lives in a society with more egalitarian gender-role prescriptions, then the child's gender-role concepts will be less rigid and more tolerant of variation.

Gender-role acquisition depends on a second process as well. In particular, it depends on the children's desire to model themselves after their gender-role concepts. For example, boys typically do not wear dresses and rarely express the desire to do so. But dress wearing is so rare that it is unlikely to ever have been punished. Why, then, do boys avoid it? Social cognitive theorists argue that the boys' avoidant behavior pattern is a consequence of their need to be "boyish." This need to be "boyish" if one is a boy or "girlish" if one is a girl is the force that motivates the acquisition of gender-role behaviors and attitudes.

Conclusions

In this section, the three major theoretical explanations for gender-role acquisition and psychosexual behavior have been reviewed. Each theory stresses the importance of a different influence. Freudian theory focuses on the process of identification and on parents as the critical socializers. Social learning theory focuses on the processes of reinforcement and modelling and on parents, mass media, teachers, and peers as the critical socializers. Social cognitive theory focuses on cognitive processes and on the child as the critical actor in his or her own socialization. The three approaches make similar predictions for some aspects of gender-role acquisition. For example, all three stress the importance of parents and of early childhood. Scientific studies have supported these predictions. On other issues, the three approaches yield quite different predictions. For example, Freudian theory predicts that heterosexuality is the natural result of mature psychosexual development, while social learning theory makes no such prediction. Similarly, social cognitive theory predicts that gender stereotypes are created by the child, while social learning theory predicts that gender stereotypes have to be taught to the child. Scientific studies have found support for some aspects of each theory and have failed to find support for other aspects of each theory. A full account of this work, however, is beyond the scope of this chapter. (Interested students should read Brooks-Gunn & Mathews, 1979; Frieze et al., 1978; Maccoby & Jacklin, 1974; and Huston, in press.)

What, then, can be concluded about the processes underlying gender-role acquisition and psychosexual development? Like all human behavior, the acquisition of a gender role reflects the complex interaction of many processes. The determinants of a person's behavior at any given point in time are many. The processes responsible for the acquisition and change of responses over time are even more numerous and complex. It is clear that no one theory tells the complete story. Each of the three major theoretical approaches provides insight into various aspects of gender-role acquisition. As suggested by psychodynamic theorists, close personal relations between parents and children are undoubtedly conducive to the adoption of the parents' standards. Consequently, to the extent that a child's parents exhibit clearly defined gender roles, the child's acquisition of a gender role will be enhanced by identification. Similarly, reinforcement for behaviors appropriate to a gender role speed up gender-role acquisition and punishments for behaviors inappropriate to a gender role reduce the incidence of these behaviors. Finally, because the child must interpret all information in the environment before it can alter her or his behavior, the child's gender-role concepts must play a critical role in the process of gender-role acquisition.

Four factors are clearly of prime importance in the acquisition of gender-role and sexual behavior: (1) the behaviors of the individuals around the child, (2) the child's interpretation of the behaviors of these individuals, (3) the reactions of these individuals to the child's behavior, and (4) biological changes within the child. Biological changes may be especially critical for sexual behavior patterns at puberty.

Typically, the first three factors operate in conjunction with each other producing a strong push toward the acquisition of a role identity appropriate to gender. But as children grow older, experiences increasingly arise that make gender roles seem more arbitrary. Moreover, children learn that they can select the individuals who make up their social world. As these two processes occur and as biological forces make the need for sexuality greater, some children move beyond rigid gender roles and adopt more androgynous or egalitarian views of appropriate behaviors and sexual scripts.

Finally, the implications of gender-role acquisition for our understanding of sexuality are often indirect. Nonetheless, there are some clear and important links. In acquiring a gender role, we learn a set of behavioral dispositions (for example, passivity, dependence, aggressiveness, and nurturance), a notion of our own sexuality, stereotypes of the characteristics and preferences of the other gender, and a set of social scripts for how romantic and intimate encounters should be acted out. These behaviors and belief structures lay the foundation for double standards regarding the monitoring of premarital sexual encounters, the initiation of sexual and/or intimate heterosexual contacts, and the character of the continuing interaction between men and women. Gender roles also affect the very nature of intimate interactions by structuring the roles men and women play. In Ghana, for example, gender roles dictate that adult men and women spend most of their time in homosocial groups (groups comprised of only one gender); adults interact with members of the other gender primarily for sexual contact. In contrast, in middle-class American society, husbands and wives are assumed to be companions, interacting with each other for social as well as sexual reasons. The nature of heterosexual intimacy in each culture is quite different largely as a result of these differences in the gender-role prescriptions for adult social interactions.

Storms (1981) has recently advanced a theory of erotic orientation (that is, the gender of the individuals whom a person finds sexually appealing). His theory captures the complexity of the interaction of gender role and sexuality in shaping our behavior. He stresses the importance of three aspects of psychosexual development: (1) the shift in the gender of children's play groups as they pass into puberty, (2) the increase in sex drive associated with puberty, and (3) the frequency of engaging in sexual behaviors during the latter part of latency (that period of development from age 6 to the onset of puberty). Latency is a period of homosocial play (play that takes place primarily in groups of the same gender). Storms argues that homosexual erotic orientation is more likely to develop if a child's sex drive increases early (relative to other children), while he or she is still interacting mostly with other children of the same gender. If this child's sex drive increases while he or she is still a member of homosocial groups, then the likelihood that the child's erotic fantasies will include same-gender partners is increased, especially if the child also acts out those fantasies with one of his or her same-gender friends. In contrast, if a child's sex drive does not increase markedly prior to the shift from homosocial to heterosocial groupings that occurs in high school, then the likelihood is reduced that his or her erotic fantasies will include members of the same gender. In essence, Storms is suggesting that the erotic fantasies of children whose sexual impulses increase prior to age 12 or 13 are more likely to include members of the same gender than are the erotic fantasies of children whose sexual impulses increase after 12 or 13. This difference is the result, Storm argues, of the differences in whom one is likely to be thinking about or spending time with when one experiences the upsurge in sexual impulses associated with puberty. Whether his theory will be supported by research remains to be seen; I have included it in this discussion primarily as an example of how complex the interactions between gender roles and sexuality can be in the course of growing up.

CHILDHOOD SEXUALITY: CHANGES WITH AGE

The very definition of sexuality in childhood is problematic. In agreement with the broad conceptualization of Freud and the advocates of a broadly defined sex education curriculum, both overt behaviors (such as masturbation, homosexual and heterosexual play, bathroom humor, and other displays of affection and intimacy) and sexual knowledge (regarding such varied aspects as body parts and functions, reproduction and contraceptive procedures, and sexual scripts, rules, and norms) have been included in this review. Unfortunately, we know very little about any of these aspects of childhood sexuality. Most of what we do know has been gained through self-report questionnaires and interviews with children and parents reporting on current behaviors and knowledge and recalling past behaviors and knowledge (for example, see Broderick, 1966; Elias & Gebhard, 1969; Hunt, 1974; and Kinsey et al., 1948, 1953). These reports undoubtedly underestimate both the incidence and the range of childhood sexual behavior and knowledge. It is not surprising that a colleague of mine was totally unprepared for the quantity of sexual activity she saw in a recent observational study of nursery school behavior (Crandall, personal communication, June 1980). Interested in assessing gender-typed behavior in natural settings, Crandall and her colleagues at Wright State Medical College designed an observational scheme for a preschool setting. They did not include any codes for sexual play. To their amazement, however, both girls and boys engaged in a lot of discreet "sexual" play, such as rocking back and forth on the monkey bars and rubbing up against objects. Because they were unexpected and because there were no codes for these behaviors, the sexual behaviors were not recorded. Studies that do record the frequencies of such behaviors are badly needed. Until we have such information based on real observations, we will have to rely on what children and parents tell us about childhood sexuality. A basic summary of what we now know is provided in Table 1-1.

The expression of sexuality in children varies as a function of culture, gender and the individual. Ford and Beach (1951) found little overt sexual behavior and sexual knowledge in some cultures; in other cultures, children masturbated openly and frequently, and engaged in both oral-genital sexual play and intercourse. Reporting on the interviews done by Kinsey et al. during the late 1940s, Elias and Gebhard (1969) found that 52 percent of males and 35 percent of females in America had engaged in prepubertal homosexual

TABLE 1-1

Development of Sexuality from Birth to Puberty

AGE	SEXUAL BEHAVIORS	SEXUAL KNOWLEDGE
0–12 months	1. Penile erection/vaginal lubrication 2. Sensual pleasure from body contact, sucking, bathing 3. Genital stimulation from diapering and bathing 4. Masturbation	
12–18 months	1. Masturbation 2. Play with feces 3. Mutual seeking and giving of affection	1. Boys become aware that they can cause erections
18 months–3 years	1. Continued masturbation 2. Retention of feces as means to exercise control over one's body 3. Continued interest in contact and affection 4. Low modesty 5. Interest in genitals of others, especially members of other gender	1. Gender identity emerges 2. Discovery of gender differences but may classify gender on hair length and clothing rather than genitals 3. Beginning of language opens possibility that child can learn correct labels for body parts if provided with them. Most children are not. 4. Genital area may become negatively associated with excretory processes if toilet training is not handled carefully 5. Common belief in "agricultural fallacy": Babies come from seeds planted in Mommy's tummy

TABLE 1-1 (continued)

AGE	SEXUAL BEHAVIORS	SEXUAL KNOWLEDGE
3–6 years	1. Masturbation increases 2. Expressions of affection begin to take on erotic quality 3. Desire to look at or touch adult bodies and the genitals of other children 4. High incidence of playing "doctor" with children of both genders 5. Dirty words and bathroom talk become a major component of the child's conversation 6. Desire for privacy begins to emerge toward the end of this period 7. Imitation of "Mommy" and "Daddy" roles	1. Gender identity becomes stabilized 2. Gender-stereotypes emerge and rigid beliefs regarding appropriate and inappropriate behaviors develop 3. Concepts of marriage and intimate relationships begin to emerge 4. Boys switch their identification to their fathers 5. Increased interest in babies, pregnancy, and birth 6. "Agricultural fallacy" still widely believed (that babies are created when Daddy "plants a seed" inside Mommy)
7–10 years	1. Public masturbation decreases and frequency of sex play in private with peers increases 2. Modesty emerges 3. Imitation of gender roles expands to include more extended aspects of masculinity and femininity 4. Children tease each other for violations of gender-role norms 5. Homosocial play groups become the norm 6. Homosexual play is common	1. Identification with same-gender parent and peers increases. Girls are more ambivalent about their gender-role status than boys 2. Increase in interest in sex accompanied by an increase in question asking and information seeking. If parents are not receptive, children will turn to peers for information 3. Gender-stereotypes become less rigid and prescriptive

AGE	SEXUAL BEHAVIORS	SEXUAL KNOWLEDGE
	7. Heterosocial and heterosexual play is unusual 8. By 9 or 10, testosterone and estrogen begin to be produced	4. Interest in "dirty" jokes increases dramatically 5. Most American children still do not associate intercourse with reproduction
10–12 years	1. Dramatic increase in hormone production 2. Secondary sex characteristics begin to emerge especially for girls 3. Menstruation may begin. Nocturnal emissions may occur in a small portion of the boys 4. Frequency of spontaneous erections increases 5. Erotic impulses increase 6. First major crush or love 7. Beginning of transition from homosocial to heterosocial interests 8. Masturbation increases for boys and emerges for the first time for many of those girls who had not masturbated before	1. Intense preoccupation with body 2. Reawakening of concern over gender roles and anxiety over proper way to behave in heterosocial activities 3. Increased interest in learning sexual scripts from books, movies, and magazines. Since these sources are very stereotyped and romantic, preteens develop very stereotyped and romantic sexual scripts 4. Lack of understanding of reproduction, contraception, and sexuality still common. Children usually turn to peers or books for information at this point. Misinformation is very common

SOURCE: Adapted from a table developed by Cathy MacDonald, University of Michigan, 1979.
Major references: Bernstein, 1978; Bernstein & Cowen, 1975; Broderick, 1966; Gagnon, 1965;
Gadpaille, 1975; Hyde, 1979; Martinson, 1976; Moore & Kendall, 1971; Thornburg, 1974;
Uslander, Weiss, Telman, & Wenick, 1973.

play, and 34 percent of the males and 37 percent of the females had engaged in a variety of heterosexual play by puberty—including, primarily, genital exhibition and touching, but also oral-genital play and intercourse. By 1967, Reevy found that 33 percent of females and 60 percent of males had engaged in homosexual play by age 13; and in 1974, Hunt found that 63 percent of males and 33 percent of females had masturbated by age 13. Thus, although Ford and Beach (1951) judged our society to be sexually repressed, there is quite a bit of self-reported sexual play among American children. But boys, for the most part, are more likely to engage in these sexual behaviors than are girls (and men are more likely to do so than women).

Again, like adults, children vary widely in their interest in sexuality. In an informal interview with friends and colleagues, the parents reported that their children vary markedly in their level of interest in both sexual activity and information. In one family, one daughter (8 years of age) openly admits to masturbating daily, while the other children (5 to 10 years of age) rarely masturbate, or at least do not admit to masturbating. In fact, in this family, everyone has adopted a label for what the more "sexual" daughter does. They refer to her sexual activity as her "daily exercises." Because this family is so open sexually, I am willing to accept their reports of the differences in levels of interest in sexual activity among the children. Comparable variations have also been reported by Kinsey and his associates (Kinsey et al., 1948; Elias & Gebhard, 1969). Although masturbation to orgasm was found to be common in infancy, both the frequency and the probability of engaging in this activity varied across the children in their studies. For example, while one male infant had about eighteen orgasms in 38 minutes, several other infants did not appear to masturbate at all.

The character of sexual expression also varies with the children's age. In general, as one might expect, there is a gradual increase in sexual knowledge. The character of sexual behaviors over the childhood years, however, is more erratic. For example, while the incidence of masturbation increases steadily until age 6 or 7, it appears to drop in frequency after age 7. This drop may reflect an increase in modesty or in fear of punishment rather than an actual decrease in the incidence rates. Parents do increase their censure of public masturbation just before their children enter school. As a consequence, 8- and 9-year-olds may simply be restricting their behaviors to private places more than they did earlier. By puberty, the reported rates of masturbation have gone back up.

There are other rather dramatic shifts in sexual behavior. For example, both modesty and embarrassability increase abruptly at about age 6 or 7; children who only a year earlier were quite content to run around nude suddenly insist on closing bathroom doors and react with horror to the mere suggestion that they go skinny-dipping. This shift seems to occur even in families that are quite open sexually and do not have rules prohibiting nudity. I was absolutely amazed when this intense modesty emerged in my son at age 7 and again, right on schedule, in my daughter at age 7. Occasionally we went skinny-dipping in a wonderful pond in Vermont. The first summer we all went swimming in the nude. The next summer, Chris was 7-1/2; Amy was 4. Chris refused to take off his clothes; so he put on his swimsuit while the rest of us swam nude. By the time Amy reached 7, we had moved away; but her modesty emerged nonetheless: she refused to let anyone in the bathroom while she was taking a bath.

Children's interest in sexual humor also emerges quite dramatically at about age 6 (see Hyde, 1979). Analysis of children's jokes indicates a strong interest in sex even though overt displays of genital play may decrease during the years between 6 and 9. Children's jokes during this period also reflect a subtle awareness of the difficulty parents have in communicating about sexuality (Zumwalt, 1976): many of the children's jokes rely on the humor inherent in the mislabeling of body parts and sexual activities that is common among adults. For example, they tell stories about finding their parents nude in the shower and being told by their parents that "Mommy's breasts are her headlights, Mommy's vagina is her garage, and Daddy's penis is his car." The punchline relies on the use of these mislabels to describe intercourse in an innocuous fashion: "Mommy, please turn off your headlights so Daddy can put his car in your garage." Zumwalt (1976) concluded that children find these jokes to be humorous precisely because they acknowledge parents' embarrassment over sex and at the same time acknowledge the children's sophisticated understanding of intercourse. Alternatively, these kinds of jokes may reflect the mutual game playing of children and adults around sex education. Both are aware of sex; both know the other is aware of sex; but nobody wants to acknowledge the existence of either sex itself or of sexual knowledge publicly. Adult sexuality is a shared "secret."

Another important shift occurs in the gender of one's most likely sexual partners. Homosocial and homosexual play is very characteristic of the latency period. At puberty, sexual interest in the other gender increases dramatically. A similar shift has been noted for gay men and women (Green, 1980; Marmor, 1980). High levels of heterosocial play are common in the backgrounds of many gay individuals. At puberty, they also appear to shift in their sexual interest. In these cases, however, the shift is to a same-gender rather than other-gender partner.

The most disturbing aspect of childhood sexuality is the low level of sexual knowledge children have acquired by the time they reach puberty. This aspect of development is discussed in the next section.

SEX EDUCATION: SOCIALIZATION OF SEXUAL KNOWLEDGE AND BELIEF SYSTEMS

There are three basic philosophies regarding sexuality: (1) Sexuality is bad and should be eliminated. (2) Sexuality is inevitable and should be co-existed with, as well and as minimally as possible. (3) Sexuality is good and should be cultivated. The majority of Americans fall into Category 2; a very vocal minority fall into Category 1 (Swan, 1980). Thus it should come as no surprise that American children have so little sexual knowledge. By the second grade, Swedish children (who get carefully programmed sex education in their schools) know the connection between intercourse and pregnancy and have a good understanding of the birth process (Koch, 1980). In contrast, many second-grade American children have no idea how pregnancy comes about, and many still do not have a clear understanding of the connection between intercourse and pregnancy by the time they are 10 or 11 years old. Their lack of knowledge is even more astounding when it comes to the more difficult topics such as menstruation, contraception, sexual techniques, and rape (Gagnon & Roberts, 1980).

Why aren't we educating our children, given the fact that most parents would like to have sex education in the schools? The answer is that a very vocal group opposes it. This group presents basically two arguments against sex education in the schools. First, sex education ought to take place in the family, and schools should not usurp any more of the family's socialization responsibilities. Second, sex education in the schools will put ideas into young children's heads and will increase the promiscuity of the youth.

With regard to the first argument, the fact is that parents just aren't providing adequate sex education. American youth acquire most of their knowledge about appropriate sexual scripts and practices, contraception, and so forth from their friends (Gagnon, 1965; Gagnon & Roberts, 1980; Rothenberg, 1980; and Spanier, 1977) or from books and the mass media (Hunt, 1974). For example, of 21 possible topics related to sexuality, Gagnon and Roberts (1980) found that mothers had discussed an average of 7 with their preadolescent children, while fathers had discussed only 4. The most commonly discussed topics included pregnancy and birth, love, physical differences between the males and females, marriage and divorce, nudity, being a tomboy or a sissy, and rape or kidnapping. Very few had discussed sex play, masturbation, intercourse, venereal disease, or contraception (topics likely to be of impending concern to their children). In a related study, Rothenberg (1980) found that only 26 percent of mothers had talked to their children about birth control by the time the children were 10 to 14 years of age. Only 34 percent had explained intercourse, and most of the children reported that they had learned about birth control from a teacher at school.

The problem is compounded further by the fact that much information provided by parents is either incorrect or prohibitive in nature (Gagnon & Roberts, 1980; Libby & Nass, 1971; and Yates, 1978, 1980). Parents are much more likely to tell children what not to do than what to do. Many parents and grandparents still react with concern when their children masturbate or exhibit cross-gender behaviors. They mislabel parts of the body or fail to label them at all. Few parents provide children with a full picture of the functions of their genitals. Consequently, boys tend to think about their penises as sexual rather than reproductive organs. In contrast, girls tend to think about their genitals as reproductive rather than sexual organs, especially because few girls even know they have a clitoris or that it is a separate organ from their vagina.

Perhaps most importantly, Gagnon and Roberts (1980) found that sexual discussions between parents and children typically result from the child's initiative. Very few parents take it on themselves to provide any systematic program of education. Guiding one's own sexual education is a very tenuous proposition when you know very little to begin with and live in a society that actively distorts the truth.

In response to the second argument, little evidence exists that supports the conclusion that sex education increases sexual activity. Spanier (1977) found no relation between college students' current sexual practices and their participation in sex education courses in high school. Furthermore, Levine (1970) found that adequate sex education programs can produce a significant drop in the rate of venereal disease among high school students.

But not all sex education in schools is good. It takes a very special kind of teacher to provide a good program (Chesler, personal communication, March 1979). Most teachers represent the same population as the parents described in the previous paragraphs. I can still remember my high school biology teacher. He had the responsibility of teaching us the reproductive facts, which were covered in the last two chapters of our textbook. His pace slowed as we approached those chapters, culminating in a three-week session on tuberculosis (the chapter immediately preceding reproduction). Then we spent two days on reproduction; films were shown on both of those days. With adequate training and appropriate curricular materials, however, good teachers can be produced.

CONCLUSION

Surveying the literature on childhood sexuality in America, one is struck with one obvious contradiction: children are sexual, yet adults do not want to admit it or deal with it. As Abramson (1980) has suggested, Americans do not include childhood sexuality as part of their "sexual system" (a cognitive

Children's Views of Reproduction

In a recent cross-cultural study, Patricia Barthalow Koch (1980) compared the reproductive knowledge of first-graders in Sweden and America. Swedish children are typically introduced to sex education in the first grade. The impact of that exposure on their knowledge and understanding of reproduction is clear in Koch's study. She asked children to explain reproduction and to draw a picture illustrating "where babies come from and how babies are born." American children provide explanations like these:

> God makes babies and puts them in your stomach. I don't know how the baby gets into the stomach, but the doctor cuts her out. [p. 5]

> I don't know how the baby gets in but the doctor will have to put holes in the stomach to get it out. [p. 5]

> Babies grow when you dream about them and they squeeze out. [p. 5]

> Babies are formed of the stomach and come out the rear end. Ouch! [p. 5]

> Mom has a baby when she eats a certain kind of food, then the doctor has to cut her open. It hurts a lot. [p. 6]

American Children's Drawings

Only one child in the class had any concept of birthing taking place through the mother's vagina. Their pictures reflect this low level of understanding.

In contrast, Swedish children provide quite accurate descriptions of reproduction and draw rather straightforward and accurate representations of the entire process.

Swedish Children's Drawings

© 1974 by P. B. Koch

system that contains and organizes our knowledge and attitudes about sexuality). Consequently, we do not see the need to educate our children, and we are taken by surprise when they exhibit signs of sexuality. This failure to incorporate the notion of childhood sexuality into our sexual system creates problems for children (see Yates, 1978, 1980), for adolescents (see Abramson, 1980), and probably for adults as well (see Yates, 1978, 1980).

Let me end with an anecdote that typifies what might be a healthier state. In one of our many "Where do babies come from?" discussions, I felt the need to provide my daughter Amy (8 years old) with some contraceptive information. I introduced the idea of the pill as I was explaining that one might want to have intercourse for fun rather than for procreation. She looked up at me and asked, "Are you giving me those pills now?" I said no. To which she replied, without missing a beat, "But you will when I'm 13, right?"

2 Becoming Sexual in Adolescence

GAIL L. ZELLMAN
and
JACQUELINE D. GOODCHILDS

By the time they enter their second decade, as Parsons documented in the last chapter, children in North American culture have vague, and in many cases, highly inaccurate notions about sexuality. In this chapter, Gail Zellman and Jacqueline Goodchilds examine sex education and sexual relationships in adolescence.

The contemporary neglect of sex education in childhood continues into adolescence. Most teenagers rely on each other for information or, more frequently, for misinformation. Although many schools do provide coverage of menstruation, such topics as sexual arousal, the use of contraception, and the avoidance of sexually transmitted diseases are either omitted or dealt with very superficially. The failure of parents and schools to provide systematic education about sexuality results in large numbers of teenagers who are ignorant about basic reproductive physiology. Their knowledge of the social and emotional aspects of sexuality is even more skimpy.

However, adolescents have learned the behaviors and attitudes stereotypically associated with their gender extremely well. At no other time in the life cycle is conformity to these norms quite so rigid or exaggerated. Perhaps because of their eagerness for adult status, adolescents sometimes appear to be portraying caricatures of stereotypic adult gender roles. The competent assertiveness expected of men may be expressed as cocksure aggressiveness, while the gentle, other-centered nurturance associated with the traditional woman may appear as approval seeking and cultivated incompetence. Such exaggerated role playing may help to fill the vacuum created by the lack of information young people receive regarding how to be sexual.

Zellman and Goodchilds's review of their own work indicates that adolescents' attitudes and behaviors regarding their emerging sexuality are heavily laden with exaggerated gender-role stereotypes. Males are expected to initiate and control sexual interaction to the point where they sometimes use force to have sex with women. Men are also believed to have driving sexual urges, whereas women are inherently free of sexual desires. Therefore, women must bear the responsibility for sexual outcomes, because men cannot physically control themselves. Many teenagers simply do not believe the notion that men might at times not want to have sex. Describing a pattern that is discussed more fully in Cherry's chapter on sexual assault (Chapter 11) Zellman and Goodchilds note that the great majority of teens in their sample could imagine conditions under which the use of force might be acceptable in the context of a sexual relationship.

The authors conclude that the costs of conforming to extreme gender-role norms in adolescence are enormous. Beyond the problem of over a million unwanted adolescent pregnancies each year, such conformity limits the extent to which adolescents may learn how to form consensual, mutually satisfying sexual and emotional bonds.

 One event—both at the time and forever—looms large in the history of maturing men and women: the first full sexual experience with a partner. The initiation of adult sexuality—traditionally called "losing one's virginity"—is often anticipated with impatience, fear, and uncertainty.

For most young people today, this event takes place during their teenage years. Taking biological age as a rough proxy for social, developmental, and physiological age, we obviously must acknowledge that sexual maturation takes place over time for the individual, and at different times for different individuals. It is variously pegged as occurring between the boundary ages of 10 and 25 years. In the interests of simplicity and brevity, we have not divided this broad period into stages ("early" versus "late," for example). We also wish to include major subgroups whose stages most probably would be different and differently ordered.

However important and central to human development sexual initiation may be, establishing the sexual self is but one among several crucial tasks of growing up. Achieving adult status, both self-defined and socially defined, simultaneously requires three major developmental tasks in today's society. First, the adolescent must adopt a long-term perspective on the likely implications and future consequences of his or her present behavior. Second, the adolescent must come to terms in a realistic way with career, social, financial, and personal goals and take appropriate steps to achieve these goals. Third, the adolescent must disentangle him- or herself from the parental nest (or web), literally and emotionally. This list, of course, could be extended Each of these three tasks presents the adolescent with hard choices whose resolutions require a quantum leap in social and psychological development. In short, the years of adolescence are characterized by irreversible decisions and actions.

In the midst of all this turmoil, adolescents also become aware of their own and others' sensuality, and they explore partnered sexual behaviors. They come to "understand" sex (with varying degrees of accuracy), and more or less settle on the place and form that sexuality will play in their adult lives. In making this last choice, they must deal with major questions about partnering such as these: (1) "Can one adjust to the special sort of closeness of a sexually intimate relationship?" (2) "Can one sustain such a relationship over a long time, maybe a lifetime?" and (3) "Is the partner to be of the other or of the same gender?" Cross-gender partnering entails the possibility of pregnancy and, subsequently, parenting. These two aspects of adulthood pose major, although often unacknowledged, challenges to maturing young people as well as to the whole society.

In this chapter, we examine ideas and discuss evidence that touch on the socially prescribed gender-linked behaviors in the sexual realm; that is, we consider the sexual scripts that adolescents adopt and attempt to adapt to their own experience.

Our reference group comprises the here and now; that is, U.S. teenagers today. Within this group are subgroups with serious social, physical, and/or emotional difficulties (for example, the severely retarded and the physically handicapped) whose special circumstances so set apart their adolescent experiences as to make this chapter largely inapplicable to them. Most of the research cited here encompasses the full range of social class categories and minority-majority statuses that characterize this young mainstream population. This chapter considers socially imposed restrictions on sexual interactions and, specifically, the learning and initial practice of these interactions.

Following the theme of this book, this chapter considers how current gender roles shape adolescent sexual expression. We examine the extent to which today's teenagers adhere to or break out of traditional gender-role boundaries. First we consider how adolescents learn to be sexual. This section builds on the previous chapter's discussion of contemporary sex education. Second, we examine the expectations adolescents have for male-female sexual encounters. We explore the extent to which youthful sexual interactions are intimate partnerships versus power struggles between female and male combatants. Third, we look at the consequences of the high incidence of adolescent coital activity. We provide material on teenage fertility and contraceptive behavior (also considered in Chapter 7). Finally, we summarize what is known about teenage sexuality and speculate on its future directions.

LEARNING FROM ADULTS

A number of factors often diminish opportunities for formal instruction or even informal discussion between teenagers and adults about issues relating to sex and intimacy. Sexual behavior among teenagers is a source of great concern to most parents and educators. Reports in the public media citing the "epidemic" of teenage pregnancy or an increase in the incidence of sexual intercourse among young people fuel these concerns. For many adults, premarital intercourse violates deeply held religious tenets or moral beliefs. Moreover, teenage sexuality subjects young people to the risks of venereal disease and pregnancy, as well as to the less concrete risks often associated with physical intimacy that occurs prior to emotional readiness.

A small but vocal group of these concerned adults believes that talking to teenagers about sex will "put ideas into their heads"; that is, motivate them to engage in sexual behaviors. This is most likely to occur, the argument goes, when the information is presented in a group context (particularly school) where the discussion cannot be tailored to each individual's level of knowledge, psychological readiness, or personal value system. Accordingly, this group opposes school discussions about sex. They are convinced that withholding sex information will be effective in inhibiting sexual behavior (Kasun, 1979).

Another group of concerned adults believes that discussion of sexuality is important but is too personal a matter to be presented in any but a family setting. These people feel that other societal institutions, particularly schools, have no business in this area because discussion in an institutional context cannot address the many and diverse religious and moral viewpoints held by individual families. Such people object to attempts to provide so-called value-free curricula as (1) misguided and (2) doomed to failure.

Still others feel that sex should not be discussed in school because the schools have other work to do. The schools are seen as having increasing difficulty in teaching basic skills—expecting them also to take on sex education and teach it effectively seems an unfair burden. Many school personnel agree. In a recent survey of school staff in 11 school districts across the country, Zellman (1981) found that many school staff resent the new problems they are supposed to solve. High on their resentment lists are premarital sex, pregnancy, and drug use. Many note that they were trained to teach a particular subject or to do academic advising and do not have the skills, motivation, or time to take on these enormous social problems.

In spite of these objections, some schools are attempting to teach sex education. But in designing curricula in this area, educators have often bowed to vocal minorities by targeting sex education courses only to high school juniors and seniors and by excluding the most "objectionable" topics—intercourse, contraception, and abortion (Alan Guttmacher Institute, 1981). Such courses are most often limited to what one educator has called "an organ recital"—what is connected to what in the body, with no discussion of how or why two bodies might connect with each other.

In recent years, growing numbers of parents and educators have begun to press for the inclusion of nonbiological aspects of sexuality in sex education courses. They note that issues surrounding the formation of sexual relationships, deciding whether or when to have sex, and expectations for one's own as well as peers' behavior, are rarely discussed. Yet this kind of discussion is important as a means of questioning norms, establishing new behaviors, and clarifying the teenager's developing sexual self-concept.

Discussions of this type have been ignored for two contradictory reasons. One is *misplaced romanticism,* which leads some to believe that sex should be totally natural and thus cannot be taught. The second is *misplaced rationalism.* In this view, teenagers who are taught the basic facts about contraception and pregnancy risks can then make the appropriate inferences and applications. Accordingly, they have no need for special training in building relationships and communication skills. As a result, when sex education is taught at all, it is usually offered in the last years of high school. By this time, however, one-third to one-half of the students have already begun having sex (Chilman, 1979; Hass, 1979; Zelnick & Kantner, 1979, 1980), and most have already formed stereotyped attitudes about appropriate ways of relating to people of the other gender. Coupled with the narrow focus of the curriculum on biological aspects of reproduction, the whole social psychological side of sexuality generally is ignored.

Given these implications, it is not surprising that sex education has so little impact on teenagers. Even when asked directly about topics covered in their sex education classes, many teenagers do not know the correct answer. For instance, they don't know the time in the menstrual cycle when women are most fertile (Zelnik, 1979).

Under these circumstances, responsibility for transmitting sex information from adults to adolescents largely rests with the family. However, it is evident that usually the family is not performing this socially assigned function. A recent review of the available research literature concluded gloomily, "The role of the parents as sex educators of their children is minor at best" (Fox, 1979, p. 22). A consistent finding is that only a small minority of teenagers report their parents as a primary or even important source of education about sexuality. Daughters are somewhat more likely to look to parents, especially mothers, as a source of such information than are sons (Fox, 1979; Spanier, 1977).

Rare and discounted though it may be, parent-child communication about sex does appear to have an impact on sexual behavior. Adolescents who received most of their sex education from a parent (usually the mother) were less likely to have had sexual intercourse, to be generally less experienced sexually, and to be better contraceptors if they were sexually active (Fox, 1979; Spanier, 1977). However, as Fox notes, the cause-and-effect relationship between parental communication and sexual behavior is not at all clear. Family discussions may inhibit sexual behavior, or inexperienced teenagers may be embarrassed to admit their inexperience to friends and therefore seek out their parents for advice or information.

In any case, the link between parental discussion and sexual constraints suggests that parents might be a good source of sex education. Yet most don't take on this role. Therefore, teenagers get this information from their peers.

LEARNING FROM EACH OTHER

When teenagers are asked where they learned about sex, they mention peers as the major source of information (see Chapter 1). In a recent study of 432 Los Angeles young people aged 14 to 18, we asked, "How or where did you learn what you know about sex?" The most common response was same-gender peers. Parents, a class in school, and personal experience all played lesser roles (in order of mention) in providing information.

Teenage peers also teach each other how to be sexual. However, adolescents recognize peers to be poor sex education teachers. In our research, only a third of those who reported learning about sex from same-gender peers thought this source "most useful"; personal experience and discussion with parents were seen as more valuable. These findings suggest that, although there may be a lot of talk about sex among same-gender peers, the talk is often not informative. Hass (1979, p. 81) quotes a 16-year-old boy whose view of the usefulness of peers may be typical: "My older brother talked to me about it, but it was pretty general and I don't think I had a very clear idea of what it was all about."

Indeed, teenagers *don't* know what it is all about. Many studies indicate that large numbers of teenagers are ignorant about basic reproductive physiology (for example, see Zelnik, 1979). Knowledge of the more emotional aspects of sexuality is even less prevalent. Scales (1977) differentiates "factual" knowledge (types of contraceptives and methods of use) from "relationship knowledge." Knowledge about relationships, he says, doesn't get communicated from any source. Teenagers seem to agree. In surveying adolescents' interests and concerns, Smith (1980) found that dating and dating relations were rated as being of concern by the largest number of adolescents in his sample. In a peer culture that stresses independence from elders, teenagers learn about dating and courtship primarily on their own and from one another (see Chapter 3).

GENDER-ROLE STEREOTYPES

As researchers, we have been concerned with the ways in which gender-role prescriptions affect adolescents' sexual beliefs and experiences with sexuality. We recently studied the attitudes and expectations teenagers bring into dating relationships. These attitudes and expectations—which for our sample seemed fully formed by age 14—tend to be traditional and nonegalitarian.

Both young men and young women reflected back to us with startling clarity the view that heterosexual relationships necessitate an unequal power structure. This group of 14- to 18-year-olds generally expected that the male partner will initiate and control a sexual interaction, that there are occasions where he may use force to have sex, and that the female may be held responsible for outcomes. The teenagers we interviewed strongly endorsed the traditional view of heterosexual relationships. According to them, the male is naturally the active, aggressive pursuer who sees sex and love as quite separate. The female is generally the passive, disinterested resistor who sees physical sex as an expression of romantic love (Schwartz & Merten, 1967). Similar findings (see also Chapters 3 and 11) have been reported by others, notably Hass (1979) and a group of researchers studying Israeli adolescents (Antonovsky et al., 1980).

Many expectations about gender-linked differences in sexual behavior stem from very different stereotypes about "what boys are like" and "what girls are like." The key to these stereotypes is the notion that men have enormous physical drives that can be contained only with the greatest difficulty and sometimes not at all. Women are portrayed as lacking such drives; therefore, in romantic encounters the male cannot be responsible for controlling sexual behavior. Responsibility must fall on the "less easily aroused" female.

A generation ago, these prejudicial views (for which there is no basis in fact—see Peplau & Hammen, 1977) led to a number of standard dating precautions. For example, "mad money" was money a parent gave a daughter before her date arrived, "just in case you need to get home by yourself." The possible reasons for such an eventuality were never discussed, but the girl *knew* she might have to use the money if her date got drunk, tried sexual blackmail, or did some other irresponsible thing. A quaint and outmoded tradition? Our data and those of other researchers (also see Chapter 11) show that the stereotypes that spawned "mad money" are still very much with us.

In our study, teenage men and women were asked if they agreed with the following statement: "Guys have a greater physical need for sex than girls do." Nearly half of our respondents agreed with this statement, one that provides a rationale for male sexual aggressiveness. Additional confirmation of the persistence of the "physical need" stereotype came in response to the question "What would a boy do to let a girl know he didn't want to have sex without saying so directly?" Respondents couldn't imagine this scenario and had great difficulty formulating an answer to the question. Typical responses were "That's not possible; guys always want sex" and "He must be gay, that's the only explanation."

Both male and female adolescents expect the girl to set the limits in sexual behavior. Toward the end of each interview in our study, the teenage respondents were read a series of little stories, each involving a brief encounter between a boy and a girl that ended in (1) consensual sex, (2) agreement not to have sex, or (3) forced sex. After each vignette, respondents were asked, "How much was the boy responsible for what happened?" and "How much was the girl responsible for what happened?" We were most interested in how young people reacted to the vignettes describing situations in which the boy wants to have sex, but the girl does not, and despite her reluctance they do have sex. For example,

> A guy and a girl who are dating are at a friend's party one evening, and decide to sit out in the yard. It is very dark and, after a while, they start to kiss and hug. The guy slips his hand under his girlfriend's blouse, but she pulls away and tells him to cut it out. Her boyfriend says that he wants to have sex with her, and when she refuses he threatens to hurt her. Although the girl does not want to, they have sexual intercourse.

Overall, in assigning responsibility in the forced-sex stories, our teenagers surprised us by assigning 84 percent of the responsibility "for what happened" to the boy and 27 percent to the girl. These young people confirm the old notion that the female shares responsibility for dating outcomes no matter what the circumstances.

Other studies indicate that additional aspects of the stereotypes continue to exist. For example, Hass (1979) found that female teenagers in his sample were more likely to have been the recipients rather than the initiators of sexual behavior. More girls reported having had their genitals touched than reported having touched boys' genitals. They also reported more pleasure from being touched than from touching. Said Hass, "Girls were more comfortable letting things happen to them rather than having to take responsibility for assuming a more active sexual posture" (p. 49). Girls also differ from boys in their evaluation of sexual relationships. Girls are much less likely to approve of "noninvolved" or casual sex than their male peers (Antonovsky et al., 1980).

Views about adult gender roles were also far from "liberated." More than half of our sample agreed with the statement "Although many women work outside the home, their most important job is still in the home." And only a bare majority (52 percent) agreed "with the goals of the women's rights movement." Consistent with their traditional beliefs, 82 percent of our teenage participants said that they expected to marry some day, and 85 percent indicated the desire to have children.

These stereotypes concerning gender roles and sexual behavior are saddening, because, more than anything else, they make it difficult for the individual to *be* an individual. Although boys in our sample often hooted at the idea that a boy might not want sex at a particular time, in fact sometimes boys would rather not have sex. And, although girls are aware that sex can be a bargaining tool to gain other ends, such as love, they also have strong sexual feelings and know that such feelings must be controlled in order to regulate sexual behavior for which they are considered and feel themselves to be responsible. (See Peplau & Hammen, 1977, and Pleck & Brannon, 1978, for reviews of the evidence on these topics.)

SEXUAL BEHAVIORS

Widespread support for stereotyped views of gender roles and sexual behavior suggests that the so-called sexual revolution may be only an illusion. Or have some things changed? In the remaining sections of this chapter, we look at some factors that influence dating behavior.

Researchers who study sexual behavior generally agree that the sexual revolution is at most a sexual evolution (Berg, 1975; Diepold & Young, 1979). Although some things have changed substantially, the changes continue to be rooted in a traditional network of stereotyped norms and attitudes. The most obvious change is that increasing numbers of women have experienced sexual intercourse, especially at younger ages (Chilman, 1979; Zelnik, Kim, & Kantner, 1979; Zelnik & Kantner, 1980). In recent studies, nearly equal numbers of women and men over 15 years old report having had sex (Diepold & Young, 1979). However, several studies of teenagers have revealed that this increased sexual behavior is not accompanied by changes in attitudes about sex. For girls, sex continues to occur most often in the context of close, romantic relationships (Antonovsky et al., 1980). And for many girls, being sexually active is seen as a means to such close relationships, rather than an end in itself. For example, Hass (1979) has found that many more girls than boys in his sample reported that sex was not important at all. Says Hass, "Many girls only feel comfortable experiencing their sexuality within a love relationship. . . . For many of those not romantically involved, sexual expression is almost irrelevant" (p. 14).

Consistent with these attitudes, girls report having fewer sexual partners. They also report less interest in sex, per se. Compared to boys, girls are more apt to see sex as a means of deepening communication or expressing affection in a committed relationship. They understand, however, that boys are more likely to see sex as a valued end in itself. In a number of studies, young women reported that they first agreed to have sex to satisfy the demands of the partners to whom they were emotionally committed. Some have had sex simply to keep boyfriends.

As more girls have intercourse (and at a younger age), having sex becomes increasingly expected by both boys and girls. Girls who might have refused in an earlier generation know that boys who threaten desertion if they don't have sex *can* go elsewhere for sex, probably to another member of their friendship group. Besides, not having had sex has become a sign of personal failure to many young people of both genders. Two-thirds (68 percent) of the teenagers in our study reported that their friends "think it is OK" to have sex. In contrast, less than half (42 percent) thought that their friends would approve of abstinence.

Approval of sexual activity is widespread among American adolescents of both genders. Nor does giving in to pressure to have sex indicate a person is deviant or insecure. Research on the relationship between self-esteem and sexual behavior suggests that individuals high in self-esteem are the most likely to accept and act on normative attitudes. For example, in their study of women aged 13 to 20, Herold and Goodwin (1979) found that self-esteem was significantly correlated with endorsement of sexual intercourse when the partners felt strong affection toward each other. No significant relationship was found between self-esteem and acceptance of "intercourse without affection." Herold and Goodwin concluded that permissiveness with affection is the prevailing norm. Conformity to social norms is associated with positive self-evaluation (high self-esteem) during adolescence.

Although intercourse is more likely to occur on a date than was true in the past, dating behavior seems otherwise to have stayed very much the same. We asked our teenage respondents a large number of questions about various aspects of dating situations. Among these aspects were desired characteristics of a date, the implications of various date behaviors, and the significance of where the dating couple go on a date in terms of their having or not having sex.

Asked to describe attributes of a desirable date, girls were more likely to mention personality and sensitivity whereas boys emphasized physical appearance. Another set of questions dealt with the meanings attached to the wearing of certain articles of clothing. Respondents were asked whether a girl's low-cut top, shorts, tight jeans, or see-through clothes meant she wanted to have sex, and whether similar meaning was implied if a guy wore an open shirt, tight pants, jewelry, or tight swim trunks. Female respondents were less likely to report that clothing of *any* type worn by either gender would be a signal for sexual interest or availability than were male respondents. Gender differences were larger for judgments of female clothes, however, because boys tended to agree with girls that male apparel does not signal sexual interest.

Another set of questions concerned a date's prior reputation. We asked, "Suppose a girl dates a guy that she's heard has had sex with a lot of girls. Do you think she would expect him to come on to her?" When the respondent had indicated a response, the interviewer asked, "Would she feel that she had agreed to have sex because she has accepted a date with a guy with that kind of reputation?" Teenagers of both genders generally agreed that a girl who had accepted a date from a guy with a reputation would expect a "come-on." But girls were significantly less likely than boys to feel that in accepting such a date a girl had agreed to have sex.

Views changed markedly when the person with the reputation was a girl. Both genders agreed that a boy was likely to "come on" to such a girl on a date. However, girls were more likely than boys to feel that a man had a right to expect sex on a date from such a woman. These reactions fit the old stereotypes perfectly. Women are to be protected unless they act unworthy. One way to be not worthy of protection is to express one's sexuality, particularly if its expression involves "a lot of guys" (Schwartz & Merten, 1967).

Interest in or willingness to go certain places with a date may be a way to signal that a person wants to have sex. We asked teenagers to tell us the sexual implication of "meeting for the first time in a public place and going somewhere together," "going to the guy's house alone when there was nobody home," "going to a park or beach alone together at night," and "going to a party where there will be grass, drugs, or drinking." Both genders rated these places in the same order: meeting in a public place and going somewhere together was the least likely signal for sex, and going to the male's house alone when there is nobody home was the strongest signal. All agreed that in each situation the girl was less likely than the boy to want sex, although the differences were small. However, female respondents were less likely than male respondents to view any location or activity as a signal for sex, regardless of which partner was the initiator. These results indicate that a boy may attach an unwarranted sexual meaning to a girl's being in a given place. These data underscore the stereotype, warning women not to act in a way that gives even the appearance of immodesty lest they encourage male advances.

SEXUAL COMBATANTS

Highly consistent with the preceding research were our findings concerning the use of force in sexual activity. Each respondent was asked, "Under what circumstances is it OK for a guy to hold a girl down and force her to have sexual intercourse?" In response to this question, 72 percent of our respondents said there were *no* circumstances that justified force. We then asked a series of "what if" questions, providing nine specific circumstances under which force might be considered. For each circumstance, we asked if it was "OK then for a guy to hold down and force her to have sexual intercourse?"

For specific instances, many males and females reported acceptance of the idea of force. The percentage replying "Definitely not" to all nine specific force items dropped to 21 percent from the 72 percent opposed to force in the abstract. A significantly larger percentage of women (27 percent) than men (15 percent) rejected the use of force across all nine circumstances, but the two genders agreed completely on the relative "appropriateness" for the use of force in the separate circumstances. Force was seen as most acceptable in such cases as when "she gets him sexually excited," "she has led him on," or "they have dated a long time."

Further insight into the acceptability of the idea of force among this sample of Los Angeles teenagers is contained in their responses to the final question asked about each of the small stories of nonconsenting sex, described earlier. In each forced-sex story, the boy was described as employing one of the following three levels of force: (1) threatening to "tell lies or spread rumors" about the girl; (2) threatening to "hurt her"; or (3) actually using physical force—specifically, pushing her down or slapping and hitting her. In addition, we also varied the degree of prior acquaintance between the two individuals. The boy and girl were described as a couple who (1) had just met, (2) were known to each other and friendly but had never dated, or (3) were in a dating relationship. All these stories ended with the identical line: "Although the girl does not want to, they have sexual intercourse."

As noted earlier, the average perceived percentage of relative responsibility for the outcome was 84 percent to the boy and 27 percent to the girl in all the forced-sex stories (there was no requirement or suggestion that the two percentages should total 100). However, as we expected, the reported level of force did affect the perceived responsibility for outcome. When the threat was to do verbal harm, responsibility was assigned 79 percent to him, 34 percent to her; when physical harm was threatened, it was 84 to 27 percent; and when the description involved actual physical force, it became 89 to 20 percent. Responsibility assigned to the young woman in the forced-sex stories fell below 20 percent only in the case of nondating couples where the male actually slugged his partner.

In an attempt to pin down adolescent perceptions of forced sex, we asked our teenagers after each story, "Do you think this was rape?" They were asked to respond on a scale from 1 ("definitely yes") through 5 ("definitely no"). The average response across stories was 2.5, halfway between "Probably yes" and "Unsure." When the couple was presented as dating, reluctance to label the activity as rape was the most pronounced.

Overall, our data show that teenagers of both genders are quite accepting of forced sex between acquaintances and often don't view it as rape. There was general agreement that girls share at least some of the blame when forced sex occurs. Adolescents evidently share highly stereotyped attitudes concerning appropriate sexual behavior. They agree to a remarkable extent on which places and behaviors have a "sexy" meaning, although male teenagers see each cue as more sexual than do females. They also agree that females are responsible for controlling sexual behavior, even when the male uses physical force to have sex. Violence, although rejected in the abstract, is reported as "OK" by the great majority in at least some circumstances. The acceptable circumstance involves relationships or events (for example, "leading him on") that are seen as under the control of girls. The stereotypes persist.

SEX AND PREGNANCY

The pressures teenagers feel to engage in sex have unintended and serious consequences. It is projected that one out of every ten U.S. women will have had at least one pregnancy by age 18 (Tietze, 1978; Zelnik, Kim, & Kantner, 1979). Births to teenage mothers are accounting for a growing proportion of all births as the birthrate to adult mothers declines (Baldwin, 1978a, 1978b; National Center for Health Statistics, 1979).

More teenagers are keeping their babies and raising them alone, although research indicates that the children of teenage mothers may suffer learning and emotional deficits. And the teenage mothers themselves may drop out of school, thereby limiting their prospects (Baldwin & Cain, 1980; Dryfoos & Belmont, 1979; Marecek, 1979; Moore et al., 1979). Some births are at least partly planned as a means of keeping boyfriends, having an excuse to leave school or home, or getting "something of my own." Most are not. These unplanned pregnancies are a result of the many difficulties teenagers have in using effective contraception. Risk taking is likely among younger teenagers, especially those newly initiated to sexual intercourse (Zabin, Kantner, & Zelnik, 1979) and those in more casual as opposed to steady heterosexual relationships (Fisher et al., 1979).

A major cause of teenage pregnancies is that contraceptive responsibility is rarely discussed or shared among teenagers. Unfortunately, adolescent thinking, stereotyped gender roles, and contraceptive technology all inhibit effective contraceptive use among the young.

Surveys repeatedly find that many young women do not use contraception because they just can't believe that their sexual activity might result in pregnancy. Their stated reasons for failing to use birth control were disconcerting; for example, "I didn't expect to have sex," "I forgot," "I can't swallow pills," "I was too young," or "We only did it two times" (Rogel et al., 1979; Zellman, 1981; Zelnik & Kantner, 1979). This reasoning mimics the feelings of children, who also believe that nothing can happen to them. Such denial of reality is believed by many researchers to reflect cognitive immaturity, which makes it difficult for adolescents to think rationally about themselves (see Elkind, 1967; Cvetkovich & Grote, 1977). Others suggest that teenagers may, for all their sophistication, simply fail to understand elementary probability theory. Instead of realizing that each month an individual has the same probability of conceiving as in the previous month, teenagers may develop false notions about the probability of becoming pregnant.

Gender-role stereotypes that make the girl ultimately responsible for whether or not pregnancy occurs don't help matters. Many teenage boys don't worry about impregnating a partner and don't feel the need to discuss contraception (Scales, 1977, 1978; Sorensen, 1973). It is no surprise, then, that girls rarely trust boys with any contraceptive responsibility. However, girls may also be reluctant or unable to take on contraceptive responsibility because doing so would mean that they accept themselves as assertive, sexually active individuals.

The cost to the female partner of this continuing pattern of response to the consequences of unprotected intercourse is enormous, emotionally, financially, and in terms of self-image and future life course. Equally damaging, if more subtle, is the effect on a male-female relationship (and the male partner himself) of the asymmetry in their partnering, which attributes full responsibility for consequences to her and assigns and/or allows him no share whatsoever.

BARRIERS TO TOGETHERNESS

The fact that each generation learns as part of the growing-up process certain gender-linked behaviors, especially in respect to sexuality, is not surprising. Stereotypes, roles, and "scripts" do have their function. Simplifying assumptions about people and shared symbolizations about actions can make prediction of interpersonal behaviors quick and easy. It is the content of the gender boundaries and the rigidity of the roles that are of concern. Informal observation and more formal investigations make it painfully and poignantly evident that traditional nonegalitarian "he-she" behaviors continue to be impressed on each new generation of teenagers.

These maturing women and men embark on sexual activity with a detailed scenario spelling out the actions, attitudes, and even the feelings considered appropriate and acceptable for each gender. They accept the scenario and for the most part attempt to adhere to it. It is distressing to contemplate the fact that the range of interactions in this sphere is strictly narrowed so early. The option of deviating from the traditional is closed off to a new generation, and formula sex is prescribed for them, too.

Three major negative aspects of this present formula need particularly to be noted. First, the gender roles assigned for sexual activity accord exceedingly well with the traditional gender-role differentiations for behaviors in general: the woman is the passive recipient, and the man is the active, aggressive initiator. Changes in the social norms vis-à-vis the two groups thus are negated by the retention of this boundary setting.

Second, recent examinations of the sexual interaction itself emphasize the crucial importance for satisfactory adult sex of mutual pleasuring and consensual sex. The existing formula, however, suggests to both partners that the degree of consent and active involvement the woman contributes is of trivial concern.

Finally, and following directly on the fact that the pattern has a built-in disregard for consent, there is a larger need expressed by many in our society today for meaningful intimacy. The sexual script, featuring an adversarial encounter—a "battle of the sexes," if you will—effectively keeps our maturing young people from forming the close relationships they so desire and require if they are to live full happy lives.

This is not to say that more satisfying, egalitarian male-female relationships are impossible. But change of this type is difficult. Adolescents are actively involved in developing adult identities for themselves. Rigid adherence to traditional roles may be perceived by some as necessary for this achievement. Furthermore, these issues often are not discussed either with adults or among teenagers themselves. Recent trends toward openness about these matters in some segments of our society—as exemplified in a recently published self-help manual for teenagers, *Changing Bodies, Changing Lives* (Bell, 1980)—point the way to more discussion and concern about the quality of relationships. These trends are an encouraging sign of movement toward sexual relationships that are more individualized, equal, and satisfying.

3   The Courtship Game: Power in the Sexual Encounter

NAOMI B. McCORMICK
and
CLINTON J. JESSER

As they move into the latter part of adolescence, young people begin developing more serious relationships with one another. In their overview of courtship in late adolescence, Naomi McCormick and Clint Jesser see more room for optimism than do the authors of the last chapter.

After a brief discussion of courting across different cultures, McCormick and Jesser focus on courtship norms in North America. Ample evidence indicates that the gender roles that were learned in childhood and adolescence have enormous impact on the dynamics of the courtship process. Contemporary dating norms illustrate the different ways in which power is used by men and by women. The authors describe the strategies that young men and women use in flirting, initiating new relationships, asking for dates, and moving toward greater (or lesser) physical intimacy. Fascinating quotes are included from young men and women who describe how they try to seduce a partner, as well as how they attempt to sabotage the seductive efforts of partners they don't desire. Young men are still more apt to involve themselves with the former strategy: attempts at seduction. Young women continue to put more energy into the sabotage of seduction than into trying to initiate sexual intimacy. When the persuasive efforts of young men (or, more rarely, young women) to engage in sexual intercourse are successful, the impact of gender-role norms still persists in the sexual behaviors and coital positions practiced by adolescents and young adults.

Despite the continued existence of stereotypic roles in the courtship of most adolescents, some young men and women are beginning to relate in more egalitarian ways. McCormick and Jesser conclude that the double standard implicit in many of our traditional courtship patterns is beginning to fade. They applaud these shifts toward a single standard for their potential to provide men and women alike with greater flexibility and more rewarding relationships.

64

The boundaries of heterosexual courtship—the institutional way that men and women become acquainted before marriage—have changed dramatically since a physician (Robinson, 1929, p. 262) offered the following advice:

> Fortunate are you, my young girl friend, if you come from a well-sheltered home. . . . But if you have lost your mother at an early age, or if your mother is not the right sort . . . if you have to shift for yourself, if you have to work in a shop, in an office, and particularly if you live alone and not with your parents, then temptations in the shape of men, young and old, will encounter you at every step; they will swarm about you like flies about a lump of sugar; they will stick to you like bees to a bunch of honeysuckle.

In the 1800s and the beginning of this century, courtship among middle-class North Americans was a sober process that strongly emphasized the end goal of marriage. Almost everyone, including feminists, valued sexual self-control (Hersh, 1980). Unmarried people were severely restricted as to *whom* they might court and *what* went on during courtship (Gordon, 1980). Because the respectable unmarried woman was constantly supervised by older adults, sexual experience with her courtship partner was unlikely (Kinsey et al., 1953).

Power—the ability to influence another person's attitudes or behavior—is an essential component of courtship. As societies become increasingly industrialized and urbanized, family and kin exercise less power over the young. "The world, as a whole, seems to be moving toward the idea of free choice in marriage" (Murstein, 1980, p. 778). The absence of parental power does not imply that courtship has become a free-for-all. Now, unmarried people have most of the power in determining the course of their own courtship.

To some extent, the sexual revolution is the result of this shift in power. As premarital sex has gained peer acceptance (see Chapter 2), increasing numbers of youthful North Americans, especially women, have sexual intercourse before marriage (Zelnik & Kantner, 1977, 1979, 1980). Sex and intimacy, not always leading to marriage, may be the new end goals of courtship.

In this chapter, we look at the ways people use power in courtship. Given the limited research in the area, some of our discussion is more relevant to never-married, heterosexual, middle-class youth than to other groups. Fortunately, two other chapters in this book help make up for our limited focus: Chapter 9 provides useful information about the ways in which older singles, including the divorced and separated, negotiate courtship relationships. Chapter 10 includes some information about power within gay and lesbian relationships.

We examine gender differences in using and responding to power, and explore all levels of courtship, from meeting someone to having sex. (Because of space limitations here, readers may want to refer to Chapter 5 for additional information on power within long-term relationships.) In this chapter, we focus predominantly on new dating relationships (such as how people flirt and ask dates out). We ask who holds most of the power in a dating relationship, the man or the woman. After this inquiry, we subject the sexual encounter itself to rigorous power analysis. We view sexual expression in political terms. And we inquire how and why people use particular strategies for having and avoiding sex and prefer some coital positions over others.

POWER AND COURTSHIP

Power is one person's ability to impose wishes on another more than that other can impose his or her wishes (Weber, 1964, p. 152). The exercise of power is effective when one person succeeds in changing another person's thoughts, attitudes, or behavior (Raven, 1965, 1971). People acquire power and dominance in many ways. Sometimes they acquire and use power in a heavy-handed way. They use physical strength, social position in organizations and politics, and control over land and money, and often take unfair advantage of an influencee, or target (Collins & Raven, 1968; French & Raven, 1959).

Rape occurs when an influencing agent uses physical strength or the threat of violence to influence a victim (influencee) to have sex. Using superior wealth or the authority one has acquired as the boss or leader to convince a less-than-willing influencee to have sex is also heavy-handed. In the very least, such a use of power is sexual harassment. At its most extreme, it is rape. Because these more coercive uses of power are discussed in Chapters 8 and 11, we are free in this chapter to focus entirely on more subtle uses of power in courtship.

Students sometimes balk when we suggest that nice people, not just sadists, use power during courtship. "If both the man and the woman like each other or want sex," they argue, "then power is irrelevant." According to these romantic students, lovers just happen to meet, just happen to get carried away and have sex. Characteristic of this attitude, some California college students are unable to relate to the question "Assuming you are very desirous of sexual intercourse . . . describe how you would try to influence your date to have sex" (McCormick, author's files):

- I don't think I would try to influence my date to have sex. If it's time and everything is right, sex will follow its own pattern.
- I would not try. In time we would make it.

■ It must come about naturally. No persuasion should be necessary. Otherwise, lovemaking is not a sign of affection but rather a disgusting sexual act.

Not everyone sees dating and mating in the same romantic light as these three students. Many, ourselves included, speculate that people are able to plan strategies carefully for attracting and seducing sexual partners. Power, the potential to influence another person's attitudes or behavior, may be an essential component of any romantic attraction or sexual relationship.

As we said before, there is more than one way to acquire and use power. The development of skills and knowledge, being perceived as attractive and likeable, and even acting helpless or "needy" can all be used to influence someone else (Collins & Raven, 1968; French & Raven, 1959). Often, these less obvious kinds of power are more effective because they avoid hitting the influencee over the head.

People often assume that their behavior is self-motivated when they receive relatively little feedback indicating that they are being influenced by someone else (Bem, D. J., 1972). For this reason, the effective strategies for influencing courtship tend to be subtle enough to convince a partner that he or she wanted what happened as much as the influencing agent wanted it. Flirtation in bars is an excellent example:

> We begin with a woman entering the bar. She is nicely dressed, and perhaps she expects to meet someone. As she enters, she characteristically stops, and nearly always adjusts some item of clothing, an accessory, or her hair. Then she looks around the bar, a deliberate scan, not a casual glance. . . . Then, she goes to the bar itself, walking directly to it and ends up standing next to some man. . . . If he fails to look at her, or if he turns away, the interaction is likely to cease immediately. But we assume that he moves slightly, perhaps looking at her briefly, perhaps just shifting his weight. His seeming trivial action is essential, since it has communicated to her that she has been noticed. . . . If things go further, he may well believe that *he* picked up *her*. [Perper & Fox, 1980a, p. 12]

MEN AS PURSUERS, WOMEN AS PURSUED

Sex and the broader conditions of life cannot be separated. This fact is especially important today with the changing circumstances and opportunities in men's and women's lives. Because societies vary greatly, it is difficult to generalize about the relationship between sex and power.

Where or under what conditions do women have the most control over their sexual lives? Generally speaking, in five specific situations women have greater say over who they have sex with and how they have sex (see Hacker,

1975, pp. 212–214). First, women enjoy more sexual freedom where there is little or no emphasis on warfare and militarism. Second, women control their own sexuality more where men participate in child rearing or where child-care services are available. Third, women have greater power in their sexual relationships when they have political representation. Fourth, women enjoy greater sexual freedom where they have helped mold the mythology, religious beliefs, and world view of their groups. Finally, women are more sexually emancipated where they have economically productive roles such as control over tools, land, produce, and products.

In most societies, women's sexuality is more restricted than that of men (Safilios-Rothschild, 1977). A *double standard*—the expectation that premarital and extramarital sex is more permissible for men—has been employed. The cultural conditions just cited modify the extent to which the double standard is enforced. On the other hand, cultures that emphasize male dominance in society as a whole severely penalize premarital sex by women (Safilios-Rothschild, 1977). For example, in some Arab socieities, women who break sexual conventions may be executed, sometimes by their brothers or fathers (Critchfield, 1980, p. 67).

Fortunately, not all societies oppress the sexual choices of women. The more power women have in society as a whole, the weaker the double standard is. The double standard is weak or absent in matrilineal societies, where descent and inheritance occur through the mother and land is owned or controlled by women (see Jesser, 1972, pp. 248–249). The double standard is also on the wane in societies that reward women for bearing children by encouraging them to be sexually permissive, as in Polynesia. Finally, the double standard dies in societies that have an overabundance of men. For example, in the Marquesa Islands, where men greatly outnumbered women at one time, men did all the work, including housework and child care. In contrast, Marquesan women spent their time attracting and pleasing sexual partners. In glaring contrast to North American culture, Marquesan men catered to women's whims, women were viewed as hypersexual, and sex started only after the woman gave the signal (Leibowitz, 1978).

Intriguing as they were, the Marquesans were unusual. Most societies are politically controlled by men. Consequently, sexual access to women is part of the property system (see Stephens, 1963, pp. 240–259). In societies in which women are regarded as property, men try to "enrich" themselves by having sex as frequently and with as many women as possible. Correspondingly, women try to keep themselves "precious" by staying beautiful or desirable while they refuse to give themselves to any but the "right" men—their present or future husbands (Safilios-Rothschild, 1977).

Male-dominated societies seem to permit men to use power to have sex with women while women are allowed to exercise power only to avoid sex with unsuitable partners. In such a society, a woman who uses power to seduce a man openly is regarded as "bad" and possibly dangerous. A man who uses power to avoid sex with a "turned-on" woman is regarded as "religious" at best, and inept, stupid, and unmanly at worst. This chapter explores the extent to which this value system about power in sexual encounters survives in North American society.

POLITICS OF COURTSHIP IN NORTH AMERICA

It would be difficult to describe adequately the conditions of North American society that have affected the status of women and, consequently, their sexual relations with men. Essentially, what happened is that the industrial system has become so successful during the last 70 years that men's and women's spheres of work have separated. Except for lower-class women and during times of war, many women were eliminated from the expanding workforce. Place of work and place of residence separated under industrialization, and for the "secure and successful" workforce, a man's paycheck became adequate for the support of the family (see Deckard, 1975, pp. 199–375). A "cult of domesticity" emerged (Degler, 1980), supposedly reigned over by women. This involved the attempt on the part of the middle class to upgrade (professionalize) full-time housework.

Such developments were not without strains, which have become especially noticeable within the last 25 years. Middle-class women became dissatisfied with the "gilded cage"—the house—in the midst of their declining and unrewarded domestic functions. More educated than ever before and trying their best to manage while the family's income was eaten away by inflation, housewives did not find their lot easy. As a more companionate marriage of equality became the ideal, middle-class homemakers became even more sharply aware of their unhappiness.

Divorce, when it did break the trap, sometimes resulted in more difficulties than it solved (see Chapter 9). Outside employment or going back to college also posed dilemmas for women. Domestic duties could be reduced but not completely eliminated (Davidson & Kramer-Gordon, 1979); instead of having one job, working and student mothers now had two. Eager to pacify insecure husbands, employed women retained major responsibility for child care and housework (Berkove, 1979; Hooper, 1979; Pleck, 1979).

Just as the balance of power between the genders influences sexual relations in other cultures, North American women's subordinate economic and political status severely limits their sexual freedom. It should come as no surprise that the "battle of the sexes" in the living room spills over into the bedroom.

Although it is less severe in North America than in the Third World, a double standard—unfavorable to women's premarital and extramarital sexual expression, while favorable to such expression by men—has prevailed. Admittedly, this standard is looser than in the past (Hopkins, 1977; Komarovsky, 1976; Peplau, Rubin, & Hill, 1977). Also, it is important to remember that the double standard is stronger among white, lower-middle-class people. It is rare among certain ethnic or racial groups, including working-class U.S. blacks, who do not stigmatize children who are born out of wedlock (Broderick, 1979; Scanzoni & Scanzoni, 1976). Here, too, women's relative power outside of sexual relationships is important. Although economically oppressed in their own right, lower-class black women are less dependent on men for their livelihood than are white women. Consequently, they may enjoy sex for its own sake rather than expecting it to be an economic bargaining tool (Coleman, 1966).

Unlike their lower-class black counterparts, middle-class white women use sex as a bargaining tool with some hazard to themselves because of the lingering double standard. Specifically, they are tacitly expected to exchange sexual and emotional companionship for economic support from men (Scanzoni, 1970, pp. 4–25). The sexual revolution hasn't changed matters much. Instead of waiting until she marries the "right man" before having sex, today's middle-class woman waits until she *finds* the "right man" to have *premarital* sex (Hunt, 1974).

For some, the goal of courtship continues to be finding the right man to marry. Such arrangements give women veto power over sex and thus a bargaining lever for other things for which sex might be exchanged. The extent to which this veto power operates successfully, or even the desirability of that kind of power in the first place (as compared to true independence and initiative power), can be questioned (Gillespie, 1971, p. 448). Nevertheless, current researchers continue to find that women are less interested in having sex than men (Mancini & Orthner, 1978; Mercer & Kohn, 1979) and have greater power than men when a couple makes the decision to abstain from sexual intercourse (Peplau et al., 1977). If men are really more enthusiastic about sex, it is likely that the traditional pattern of bargaining continues.

CHANGING BOUNDARIES OF COURTSHIP

Not all North American women view sex as a bargaining tool for finding men who will take care of them. Courtship patterns are changing and these changes could alter the balance of power between the genders. As described in Chapter 9, the decrease in the number of people marrying early and staying married weakens the once close connection between successful courtship and marriage. Courtship now occurs for a variety of other purposes, such as for having "a good time," for sexual release only, and for proving one's competence and status. Nevertheless, these changes in themselves may not lead to substantial social change.

The sexual politics of courtship may be especially resistant to change because couples beginning to court often engage in posing—the tendency to fall back on those gender roles that are stereotypically appropriate or safe (Heiss, 1968, p. 82). For example, even if such stereotyped behavior is uncharacteristic, a woman might be careful to appear as sweet and unassertive as possible on the first date so as to make a good impression.

In the next two major sections of this chapter, we question the extent to which "posing" continues in sexual encounters (in bars, bedrooms, or the back seats of cars). The following types of questions arise:

1. Do men and women desire (seek) different types of benefits, satisfactions and goals in the courtship process, and if so, what are they, and who actually achieves them?
2. Who may touch whom, and how or where?
3. When sex and sexual signaling occur, to what extent do the values of the society and the gender roles disadvantage one or the other party in the form, content, timing of the acts or in the benefits to be derived?

DYNAMICS OF DATING

Despite some speculation that the traditional date is disappearing (Murstein, 1980, p. 780), dating remains a crucial part of courtship for many young people (Bell, 1979, p. 49), although now, with more mixed gender places available and more casualness as the norm; people don't date as much, or they just call it "going out." Dating enables courting partners to get away from their parents and have the opportunity to know each other better. However, there is more to dating than just being alone together. Dating is also a bargaining process in which the man provides certain goods and services in exchange for others provided by the woman. In other words, dating is similar to marriage because it requires negotiations to take place. Perhaps this point would be much clearer if we analyze how the genders use power on the typical date. The best and most enjoyable way to do this is to imagine a traditional date.

When we imagine the classic North American date, the following narration comes to mind. On Tuesday, Herbert Dumple makes the first move. He calls Mildred Smedly, doing his best to sound sophisticated and desirable over the telephone. Herbert asks Mildred out for the following Saturday. Mildred accepts, especially impressed that he phoned a few days in advance.

She assesses that this means that Herbert *values* her. She might have refused, even if she had nothing to do but wash her hair, if he phoned only one day before.

On Saturday, Herbert arrives at Mildred's home promptly at 7 P.M. He is neatly attired in a sports jacket and dress slacks. His neat appearance brings home the fact that he values Mildred (jogging shoes and old jeans would be a "putdown") and that he himself is valuable. Herbert's middle-class status or aspirations are clear from his respectable appearance. In other words, he looks like "a good catch."

Mildred isn't ready yet, accidentally on purpose. Consequently, Herbert has about ten minutes to chat with her family. He sits on the loveseat, somewhat anxious about making a good impression, and tries to sound intelligent and responsible. Meanwhile, Mildred's Mom and Dad look him over. The assessment process is so critical that the family has turned off the television set and are even checking out Herbert's manners, asking, "Would you like a snack while you wait?"

Mildred finally comes down to the living room at 7:10 P.M. However, perhaps we are jumping the gun. Before we describe her entrance, it might be useful to speculate about her reasons for being late. Actually, Mildred has two reasons for taking her time, both of which are relevant to our previous discussion of courtship as a bargaining process. First, by being late, she has more time to make herself attractive (put on make up, fix her hair, make sure she has chosen the right outfit). Second, by being late, she is telling Herbert that she is a valuable person, a woman *worth* waiting for.

At last, Mildred comes down the stairs from her room. She looks "beautiful," at least according to Herbert and her father. Some parent-child negotiations take place concerning where the couple is going and when Mildred can be expected home. "Oh, Mom!" she says, "Can't you trust me?" Finally, the awkward process is over, and Herbert escorts Mildred to his car. He opens the door for her, an excellent example of the posing we described earlier.

Mildred is relieved that Herbert has a car. This increases his marketability. Apparently, he might have some money. She dislikes dating men who expect her to travel on the bus. After all, dates are potential husbands, and it is important to find a good provider.

Mildred and Herbert go to dinner. Again, Herbert provides evidence of his potential as a good provider by taking her somewhere expensive and paying for their meals. Furthermore, he shows that he is appropriately masculine (posing again) by ordering their meals and taking responsibility for assessing the quality of the wine.

During dinner, Mildred tries her best to be a good conversationalist. This means that she asks Herbert about school or his job, focusing on *his* interests and trying her best to sound enthusiastic. Mildred's selfless concern for Herbert's interests is not accidental. After all, she wants to present herself as a valuable person, a potential spouse. She has already established that she is attractive ("beautiful"); her market value could only increase if she also seems empathic and emotionally supportive.

After dinner, the couple goes to Herbert's apartment. He has carefully made sure that his roommates are out so that the two of them can be alone. Mildred and Herbert smoke a couple of joints and share a small bottle of imported wine. Then Herbert begins to make some sexual moves. Now Mildred must make a choice. It is up to Mildred (the woman) to decide "how far to go" (Peplau, Rubin, & Hill, 1977).

Back in the 1950s, Mildred would probably have gone along with Herbert until they engaged in heavy petting. She would have been unlikely to have had sexual intercourse. In those days, many women remained "technical virgins" until marriage because coital experience would have "cheapened them" or decreased their market value for marriage.

As beautifully documented in Chapter 2, the values of the 1950s are over. These are the 1980s. More and more women, including young adolescents, are having sex before marriage. Today, a woman's market value might be increased by being a good lover (providing, of course, that she has sex with only one man at a time in a relationship). There are still strong prejudices against women who have many partners.

If Mildred really likes Herbert (she may convince herself she loves him), she will probably have sex. However, she will let Herbert make most of the moves. Although it is acceptable for today's woman to have sex, it is still risqué for her to ask for it.

Mildred and Herbert do have sex. Before they straighten out their hair and clothing, trying to look innocent for the benefit of parents, it is appropriate to analyze the power implications behind Mildred's decision to have sex. Mildred's potential power during her sexual encounter depends heavily on her age. If she is a young adolescent, she is probably trading off sex for Herbert's esteem. Indeed, if this is the case, Mildred may have traditional gender-role attitudes and be looking toward Herbert to fulfill multiple dependency and status needs (Scanzoni & Fox, 1980). Young adolescent women who wait until they are older before having sex often have higher self-esteem and more profeminist attitudes than their more coitally experienced peers (Cvetkovich et al., 1978; Larkin, 1979; Scanzoni & Fox, 1980).

Putting on your Sherlock Holmes hats, you may be confused at this point. How could Mildred be a young teenager? Wasn't she able to order wine at the restaurant? Well, if Mildred wasn't "passing" as an older woman, you have a good point. More importantly, the power implications of having sex are completely different for older, college-age women. If Mildred is a college student, having sex suggests that she feels good about herself. In contrast with younger women, sexually active college women are more independent, autonomous, assertive, and profeminist than their less sexually active peers (Scanzoni & Fox, 1980).

DATING, POWER, AND EQUITY

Our description of Herbert and Mildred's date provides some insight into how men's and women's different interests are reflected in their experience of power during courtship. Equity theory, which predicts that people prefer relationships in which each party receives equal relative gains (Hatfield & Traupmann, 1980), is useful at this point. Will Mildred and Herbert become a couple? Will they feel secure enough about each other to have sex again? Will Herbert and Mildred eventually have one of those long-term relationships described in Chapter 5?

According to equity theory, people in inequitable (or "unfair") relationships (both those receiving too little and those receiving too much) become distressed enough to either balance or end the relationship. According to equity theory, then, Herbert and Mildred will be likely to seek a balanced or fair relationship, especially if they have already made a heavy investment in one another (Walster, Walster, & Berscheid, 1978, p. 6).

As their dating relationship develops, if either Herbert or Mildred feels that he or she is getting a "raw" deal, the injured party will use power ploys to achieve a better position. For example, if Herbert "cheats" on Mildred by sleeping with another woman, she will let him have it during an argument. Mildred will continue to feel distressed until Herbert makes it up to her for cheating, perhaps by being especially considerate or even by purchasing an engagement ring. Such actions would help balance the relationship and would lead to greater happiness for both members of the couple (Hatfield & Traupmann, 1980).

Suppose, however, that Mildred's power ploys have failed. Despite her entreaties, Herbert goes out with even more women. Her friends tell her that he is sleeping around with everyone. Moreover, Herbert is into drugs quite heavily and appears to have become an insensitive lout. Unless she can convince herself that she deserves such treatment (alas, some women do this and stay around), Mildred may end or withdraw from what has become an unsatisfactory relationship. Inequitable relationships are unstable. Both the overbenefited, cheating Herbert and the underbenefited, jealous Mildred are not satisfied with the way things are going (Hatfield & Traupmann, 1980). Motivated by anger and guilt, such people would be more likely than equitable couples to use power ploys or attempt to end their relationships (see Walster, Walster, & Traupmann, 1978).

Another important issue for Herbert and Mildred is their evaluation of each other's value or marketability with different dating partners. As described earlier, Herbert and Mildred are constantly assessing each other and themselves. Early on, even Mildred's parents get into the act. This evaluation process continues throughout their relationship. Herbert and Mildred are more likely to stay together if they are well-matched in age, intelligence, educational plans, and good looks (Hill, Rubin, & Peplau, 1976).

Finally, equity theory is relevant to the quality of Herbert and Mildred's sex life together. They are more likely to continue having sex if neither partner feels "ripped off" or overbenefited. Actually, having sex in the first place suggests that this couple feels they are a good match. Couples in inequitable relationships are more likely to stop before "going all the way" (Walster, Walster, & Traupmann, 1978, p. 89). Even more relevant to power during sexual encounters, Mildred and Herbert will have very different feelings about *why* they had sex, depending on whether their relationship is equitable or unfair. If Herbert and Mildred truly make up after their argument about Herbert's affair, they will say that they had sex because *both* wanted to, citing reasons such as "mutual physical desire" and "enjoyment" (Walster, Walster, & Traupmann, 1978, p. 89). On the other hand, if their sexual relationship continues, despite the fact that Mildred still feels she is getting the short end of the stick, sex too would be seen as unfair. Herbert, for example, might feel that Mildred obliged him to make love to her to apologize for his indiscretion. In contrast, if Herbert wanted sex more than Mildred, she might blame him for taking advantage of her here, too.

STRATEGIES FOR INITIATING NEW RELATIONSHIPS

The discussion of equity theory helps explain the balance of power in long-term relationships. However, it provides very little information about how people actually use power, especially in beginning new relationships. Focusing first on flirtation and then on the process during which one person asks another for a date, we will discuss *how* men and women actually use power with new dating partners.

Flirtation

A flirtation "is a sequence of behavior, mostly nonverbal, which brings two people into increasing sociosexual intimacy" (Perper & Fox, 1980a, p. 23). To date, the best research on what actually happens during flirtation (as opposed to what people think happens) is by Timothy Perper and Susan Fox.

Clocking over 300 hours of observations of working-class and middle-class single people of varying ages in New Jersey and New York City bars, Perper and Fox have overturned two of our most beloved cultural myths. The first overturned cultural myth is that the man is always the sexual aggressor, eagerly pressing himself on the coy but reluctant woman. At least in the beginning of the flirtation process, men do not "swarm around a woman like bees about a lump of sugar." Instead, the woman often makes the first move. Because her move is subtle — usually nothing more than standing close to her target — it is understandable that the man might erroneously come to believe that *he* started the interaction.

According to the second overturned myth, men know more about flirtations and sex than women. In glaring contrast with this expectation, women are the experts:

> Typically, women are exquisitely familiar with what occurs during flirtations while men are generally quite ignorant. Women can describe in great detail how they and other women flirt and pick up men, and what men do (and just as frequently, what men do *not* do). In contrast, . . . [most] men were unfamiliar with all or most of the events of flirtations. Even quite successful men had no idea how they attracted women and what happened during a flirtation. Often men create vast and complex theories . . . but they seem to possess little or no information. [Perper & Fox, 1980b, p. 4]

Now that we have established that women know more about flirting, at least in bars, it is still appropriate to ask, "Which gender has the most power?" Egalitarians should be delighted to know that flirtations are not under the control of one person. Instead, both genders have equal power.

A successful flirtation is one that will probably result in a new dating or sexual relationship. Such a flirtation depends on the influencee or target signaling that the flirt's influence attempts are welcome at *each* stage of the flirtation. To clarify this, we have described the stages of a flirtation in Figure 3.1.

As you can see, neither gender dominates a successful flirtation. Indeed, it is hard to separate the influencing agent from the influencee. Each person takes a turn at influencing the partner and at signaling that the other's influence attempts are welcome. As the couple's relationship becomes more secure, flirtation strategies become more obvious:

> [A woman] commonly touches the man before he touches her. Her touch is made, typically with the palm of the hand flat, and not with the fingertips, in a light, fleeting and pressing gesture. . . . She might brush against him with her hip or back, she may lean on him briefly, or she might brush against him while she turns to look at something. An alternative is for the woman to remove an otherwise nonexistent piece of lint from the man's jacket (men's jackets in bars collect such lint very readily). [Perper & Fox, 1980a, p. 18]

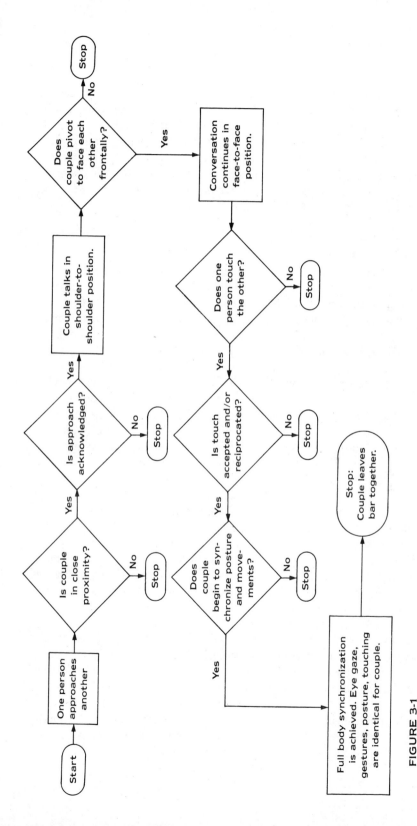

FIGURE 3-1

Flirtation in Bars (Note that either gender may initiate a flirtation. Power is shared; neither partner dominates the outcome.)

SOURCE: Based on a model proposed by Perper & Fox, 1980a and 1980b. Used by permission of Timothy Perper.

An important aspect of touching is that it is safe, in that it can be interpreted as accidental. This saves face for the influencing agent should the flirtation prove unsuccessful. Touching during flirtation is similar to body language, a popular strategy for both men and women when they approach a date to have sexual intercourse (McCormick, 1979). This strategy relates to a point made earlier: less obvious kinds of sexual power may be preferred because they are subtle enough to convince a partner that he or she wanted what happened just as much as the influencing agent did.

Asking for a Date

As you recall, Herbert Dumple asked Mildred Smedly out. North American gender-role norms are rather strict about who initiates a date. The traditional woman can, at most, make herself attractive. She is not allowed to call the man or start a new relationship. In contrast, the traditional man (shy or not) is responsible for initiating any and all relationships with women. Does the man still have all the power when it comes to initiating a new dating relationship? Perhaps not. Current research sheds light on this issue.

Research fails to clarify whether or not women take more assertive roles in dating than in the past. Nevertheless, there are strong indications that traditional gender-role norms prevail. Men are more likely to say that they would initiate new heterosexual relationships than women are (Green & Sandos, 1980). Moreover, both gender-typed and androgynous college students report that men typically initiate dates and pay for expenses incurred on dates (Allgeier, 1981).

Men still have most of the power when it comes to initiating new dating relationships. However, not everyone is happy with this situation. Already, some college students are pushing for change (see Allgeier, 1981). Liberals are experimenting with innovative dating patterns. Androgynous people, especially men, tend to have more experiences with female-initiated dates than do gender-typed individuals. Also, some men express dissatisfaction with the traditional date. Men are more positive about women initiating and paying for dates than women are.

In any event, the times may be ripe for change. A recent study at a southern university suggests that college men welcome female sexual initiation. In this study, women students approached strangers with this line: "I have been noticing you around campus. I find you very attractive." After saying this, most of the women are extremely successful in gaining men's verbal compliance with requests to go out on dates, to go to the women's apartments, and especially to go to bed with the women (Clark & Hatfield, 1981). Apparently, more than a few college men enjoy being propositioned. However, as we shall see, wishes aren't always realities.

Women are well advised to be cautious when contemplating whether or not to ask men out. The gender-role norms for male initiative in courtship are far from dead. When college students are asked how they feel about someone who either starts a friendly conversation or invites a co-worker to dinner at a restaurant, responses are stereotyped (Green & Sandos, 1980). Both men and women feel that it is more appropriate for the man than for the woman to take the initiative in either situation. Perhaps this helps explain why women are so conservative. Not surprisingly, women are more positive about men initiating dates than men are (Allgeier, 1981).

There is more to power in courtship than asking someone out. People also have the power to refuse. Women are more pragmatic than men about courtship (see Chapter 5). They want to size men up before committing themselves to relationships. Moreover, the double standard may still be operating. Women may be especially reluctant to go along with a man's sexual advances when he comes on "too strong." Clark & Hatfield's (1981) study supports this idea. When men ask strangers on a college campus for dates, they are successful. However, when they ask the new acquaintances to go to their apartments or go to bed with them, they are not greeted with the warm enthusiasm that men give women for these same requests. Instead, most are flatly refused, with such responses as "You've got to be kidding" or "What is wrong with you? Leave me alone" (p. 17).

Changing Boundaries of Dating

We may conclude at this point that North American courtship is not as rigidly bound to the double standard as many of us suspected. Traditional gender-role norms are being challenged in three ways. First, with the exception of young adolescents, sexually active women are not exploited by men. Instead, the coitally experienced woman is likely to be independent and profeminist. Also, she is unlikely to have sex outside of an equitable or balanced relationship. Second, men are not the experts when it comes to picking up dates. If knowledge is power, then women are more powerful than men when it comes to signaling men with whom they would like to become better acquainted. Finally, although it is not known if women are asking men out more than in the past, the times are ripe for change. Some men are highly receptive to women's invitations for dates and sex (Hite, 1981). Probably, the main thing that holds women back is the continued stereotype that such behavior is unfeminine or inappropriate.

Courtship has changed, at least in its preliminary stages. However, what happens once a couple does have sex? In the remainder of this chapter, we focus more specifically on the relationship between men and women during sexual intercourse. We also further identify and document the sexual value system—society's evolving rules for playing the courtship game.

ROLES AND POWER DURING SEXUAL INTIMACY

In general, dominant and extroverted people report engaging in more varied sexual behavior and with more frequency than submissive, introverted people (De Martino, 1963; Eysenck, 1971, 1972; Maslow, 1963). Extroverts of both genders are more likely than passive individuals to be sexual nonconformists, willing to deviate from expected gender roles in their sexual encounters. For example, unlike her passive counterpart, the dominant and extroverted woman may be more likely to take the active sexual role. She is also more willing to experiment with nontraditional coital positions, such as being on top of her partner during sex.

Traditionally, women have been expected to play a relatively passive role in sexual encounters in our own and in some other societies (Ford & Beach, 1951; Rainwater, 1971; Rubin, 1976, pp. 134–154). It is no accident that the stereotype of the sexually passive woman is consistent with both the sexual double standard we have alluded to previously and our culture's idealization of the "passive-receptive" woman (Broverman et al., 1972; McKee & Sherriffs, 1957; Rosenkrantz et al., 1968).

Consistent with the double standard and idealization of the passive-receptive woman, most dating and married couples report that a woman seldom actively initiates a couple's first intercourse (Peplau, Rubin, & Hill, 1977). Generally, the woman is less likely to initiate sex than the man (Bell, 1976; Carlson, 1976; Crain & Roth, 1977). These findings still leave many questions unanswered, however. For example, the need to look feminine might lead a woman to overlook or forget some subtle strategies she uses to give her partner the idea that *he* wants sex. What are the politics of deciding whether and how to have sexual intercourse?

Seduction and Rejection

Historically, the whole scenario of the sexual encounter, from initiation and timing to positioning of the bodies, was expected to be initiated by men (Long-Laws, 1979). In contrast, the woman has been expected either to passively go along with men's sexual advances or to refuse to have sex (Ehrman, 1959; Gagnon & Simon, 1973; Komarovsky, 1976; Peplau, Rubin & Hill, 1976, 1977).

Young people's sexual vocabularies characterize men as sexual actors and women as sexual objects. According to Sanders and Robinson (1979, p. 28), women describe the penis with "cute little euphemisms" such as "Oscar," "penie," "ding-a-ling," and "babymaker." In contrast, young men are more likely to use power slang such as "womp," "rod," "pistol," and "stick." Similarly, men use slang for sexual intercourse, such as "poking," "stroking a hole," and "hosing," suggesting that men perceive sex as demonstrations of power. Their language contrasts strongly with women's vague, passive, and romantic images of sex: "doing it," "being inside," "going all the way," and "loving."

Women's typical words for describing sexuality (that is, "penis," "vagina," and "make love") reveal attitudinal constraints that contrast strongly with men's verbal flexibility. Unlike women, men are able to communicate about sex with a variety of audiences (Sanders & Robinson, 1979). Less free to talk about sex, women may also feel less free to be sexual actors than are men.

On the other hand, women may feel more comfortable about being sexual actors than they did in the past. A large proportion of both men and women in ongoing relationships report persuading their partners to have sex using such straight-forward approaches as touching, snuggling, kissing, allowing their hands to wander, and asking directly (Jesser, 1978). When asked how men respond to their sexual advances, women who ask directly to have sex are *not* more likely to report being rebuffed than those who fail to report asking directly. Predictably, women who are opposed to female sexual modesty and the need for women to pursue their interests inconspicuously are especially likely to consider directly asking their dates to have sex. Equally predictable, men whose partners had directly asked them to have sexual relations are also those who disagreed with the view that women must regard their bodies more modestly than men. These same men are especially likely to disagree with the position that men's dominant interest in women is sexual (Jesser, 1978).

Could sexual role playing be on the wane among today's courting couples? Another study finds strong similarities between men's and women's use of influence in sexual encounters. When asked how they would influence a date to have sex in a hypothetical sexual encounter, both male and female college students prefer indirect strategies. For instance, one student said, "I would test my limits by holding hands, sitting closer to this person, etc." (McCormick, 1979, p. 199). As you recall, using touch as an approach is also popular in flirtations.

Indirect strategies are preferred for good reasons. In their very subtlety, these strategies provide the influencing agent with a haven from possible rejection. For example, imagine that Mildred Smedly uses another indirect approach—environmental manipulation—to influence Herbert Dumple to have sex. After doing her best to set the stage for sex by dimming the lights, providing some liquor, and playing sensual music on the stereo, she is shocked when Herbert makes fun of her. Fortunately, her strategy permits her to avoid the hot seat when Herbert ridicules her.

HERBERT (in challenging voice): Mildred, are you coming on to me?
MILDRED (firmly): No, Herbert. I just like that record a lot. Also, candlelight is good for my eyes after a long day of typing my term paper.

Clearly, indirect strategies are useful for having sex. However, seduction, a highly direct and arousal-oriented strategy, is also popular with both men and women for influencing a hypothetical partner to have sex. Here are two quotes from students' essays describing how they would seduce their dates (McCormick, author's file):

[Female college student:] I would start caressing his body and start kissing his chest, maybe stomach. I would try to be very sexy, doing this especially with lots of eye contact. Probably a few sighs here and there to let him know I feel sexually stimulated. This would probably be all I would do aside from wearing something slinky and bare. I could not get myself to perhaps start unbuckling his pants.

[Male college student:] I would proceed to use my charm and bodily contact to get what I want. (1) If she shys away in a huff, I would stop and try to talk it out. If we got nowhere from there, I would take my ass home. (2) If she gives me the come on, then I would proceed very vigorously. (3) If she pushed away gently, I would tell her what a good time we had, that we are not children, and since we relate so well, we should "Get it on."

Consistent with the stereotype that men are sexual actors and women are sex objects, men say they would use seduction significantly more than women say they would. However, both genders prefer seduction over all other strategies for influencing a potential partner to have sex. Women are clearly capable of experiencing men as sex objects.

Gender differences also disappear when college students are asked how they would avoid sexual intercourse with a turned-on partner. Both men and women prefer direct, obvious strategies. Moralizing—using religious convictions or moral opposition to argue against having sex—is one such strategy. As one volunteer put it, "I would state directly that that type of relationship is reserved for marriage" (McCormick, 1979, p. 199).

Clearly, some of today's young singles are breaking out of sexual role playing. At any rate, the previously discussed findings suggest that male and female college students have the *potential* to enjoy courtship interactions that are free of gender-role stereotypes. Nevertheless, egalitarian readers should be advised to hold their applause. It is important to note that regardless of their gender-role attitudes, the overwhelming majority of college students stereotype men as using all possible strategies to have sex and women as using every strategy in the book to avoid having sex (LaPlante, McCormick, & Brannigan, 1980; McCormick, 1976, 1979). If such stereotyping persists, it is likely that students believe that others want them to engage in sexual role playing and that such behavior will be common with future dating partners.

In contrast with their lack of sexual role playing when asked what they would do within hypothetical sexual encounters with imaginary or future partners, students report strict adherence to gender-role stereotypes during their *actual* courtship experiences. When describing their personal use of power via various strategies, men use strategies significantly more than women do to influence dates to have sex, and women use strategies significantly more than men do when the goal is avoiding sexual intercourse. Complementing this finding, when asked to describe their experiences as influencees within sexual encounters, men are more likely than women to report being influenced by all strategies for avoiding sex. Also, women report being more likely than men to be influenced by the majority of strategies for having sex (LaPlante, McCormick, & Brannigan, 1980; McCormick, 1977).

The continued importance of gender roles in sexual encounters is supported by the fact that a higher proportion of women than men say that they use extraordinarily subtle or indirect signals to indicate their sexual interest. For instance, they report using eye contact, changes of appearance or clothing, and changes in tone of voice. Could it be that these women are fearful of "turning off" their partners if they are more sexually assertive? Consistent with such an opinion, many women are hesitant about being assertive with dates with whom they want to have sex, perceiving this as unacceptable to men. Ironically, women may be holding themselves back sexually more than men would desire. Relatively unoffended by sexually assertive women (Jesser, 1978), college men are more positive about women initiating sex than are women (Allgeier, 1981). Just as they would welcome greater female initiative in dating, men also desire more assertive sexual partners. For instance, many older men agree that "it's exciting when a woman takes the sexual initiative" (Tavris, 1978, p. 113).

Overall, the research on strategies for having and avoiding sex has disappointing implications for those who prefer sexual behavior liberated from gender roles. It may be that courtship is a bastion for the strict performance of stereotyped gender-role behavior. However, before we accept this conclusion, let us look at the research on coital positions.

Coital Positions: Who's on Top

The "missionary position," in which the woman lies on her back while the man is on top of her, seems to be the most common coital position in North

American society (Allgeier, 1981; Ford & Beach, 1951, p. 23). A few decades ago, many people never attempted to use any but the man-on-top position for sexual intercourse (Kinsey, Pomeroy, & Martin, 1948). Although contemporary couples are more likely to experiment with other positions (Hunt, 1974), the man-on-top coital position may have some symbolic value. This position closely fits the stereotype in our society that the male should be active while the female remains passive during sexual intercourse.

Little is known about the relationship between gender-role identity and coital position. Recent research sheds some light on this issue. Unmarried college students were asked to give their opinions of couples who are having sexual intercourse in various positions including the ever-popular man-above and the nontraditional woman-above coital positions. Interestingly enough, women are more conservative than men in their evaluation of the woman who is on top of her partner during sexual intercourse. Women, but not men, have a real distaste for the couple in the woman-above position. They rate the woman as "dirtier, less respectable, less moral, less good, less desirable as a wife, and less desirable as a mother when she is on top than when she is beneath the man during intercourse" (Allgeier & Fogel, 1978a, p. 589). Given these feelings, it is not surprising that women report having sex with the man on top more frequently than do men. Possibly, gender-role stereotypes color their reasons for preferring this position. Women claim that the man-above position offers greater "emotional satisfaction" than the woman-above position (Allgeier, 1981, p. 326).

Advocates of social change may be even more disappointed with some additional findings. Allgeier (1981) found no relationship between gender-role identification and feelings about various coital positions. Moreover, both androgynous and gender-typed college students are likely to have greater experience with the man-above coital position than with the woman-above position. As Allgeier and Fogel suggest,

> Aside from giving birth, there is probably no other arena in which gender differences have more importance to us than in our sexual interaction. "Vive la difference" expresses our pleasure with the ways in which males and females *do* differ; and perhaps this attitude is so strong that it overwhelms the potential influence of [androgyny]. [Allgeier & Fogel, 1978b, p. 13]

Allgeier and Fogel's findings parallel McCormick's (1979) failure to find a relationship between being profeminist and rejecting the stereotype that men always initiate sex and women do everything they can to avoid sex. In addition, their findings bear some strong similarities to Jesser's research. Both Jesser and Allgeier find that women are more attached to the gender-role norms that prescribe female sexual submissiveness. Women's attitudes may present greater barriers to egalitarian sexual behavior than do men's attitudes.

ARE THE RULES FOR COURTSHIP CHANGING?

The courtship game has changed in three ways. First, thanks to the weakening of the double standard and encouragement from feminists, women are freer to make the first move in a flirtation and to have premarital sex than in the past. Second, men seem to be encouraging women to be more assertive in initiating sexual relationships. Third, given the opportunity, men would reject sex and women would try to have sex with the same strategies that are characteristically used by the other gender.

Despite these changes, the courtship game continues to follow gender-role stereotypes. Men ask women out more than vice versa. Men are more likely to influence a date to have sex; women are more likely to refuse sex. The persistence of gender-role playing is associated with a number of factors, such as women's more conservative attitudes toward sexuality. Another factor that contributes to the courtship game is that North American society views people who behave "out of role" (that is, passive men and assertive women) as less well adjusted and popular (Costrich et al., 1975).

As the women's liberation movement gains increasing acceptance, the courtship game will probably become less rigid. For instance, although women prefer masculine over feminine men, male college students are *not* more attracted to feminine women than they are to masculine women (Seyfried & Hendrick, 1973). Even more indicative of social change, recent research contradicts earlier reports (Goldberg, Gottesdiener, & Abramson, 1975; Johnson et al., 1978) that men are turned off by profeminist women. Johnson, Holborn, and Turcotte (1979) found that men were more attracted to women who support the feminist movement than they were to those who are described as nonsupporters. As attitudes toward feminist women become more liberal, people may try out more egalitarian ways of dealing with courtship. However, such experimentation is likely to be minimal at first because out-of-role behavior is especially risky within sexual encounters where people already feel emotionally vulnerable.

Some insight into future directions for male-female courtship is provided by a vocal and liberal group of physicians and sex therapists. In the past decade, a number of therapists have contributed their ideas in opinion articles with titles such as "Do men like women to be sexually assertive?," "Who should initiate sexual relations, husband or wife?," and "Who should take the sexual lead—the man or the woman?" In many of these articles, medical personnel and sex therapists indicate that they favor sexual equality in the bedroom for all but those few patients who would experience emotional turmoil as a result of such equality. The following statement is characteristic:

> The assumption that the male must be the aggressor in sexual intercourse and the female passive is simply not valid. Each partner must be both passive and aggressive and must participate mutually and cooperatively in the interaction. The unfortunate persistence of labels attributable to one sex as opposed to another has led to untold misery, creating feelings of guilt, inferiority, inadequacy, or even suspicions of homosexuality when one's inclinations are somewhat different from prevailing notions concerning sex roles. [Salzman, 1976, p. 23]

If the public continues to be exposed to these liberal ideas, values of future generations will slowly but surely change. It may not be overly optimistic to predict that college students in the year 2000 will be less likely to stereotype strategies for having sex as something only men would do and strategies for avoiding sex as something only women use. Furthermore, women in the year 2000 may be less likely to put down those who experiment with nontraditional coital positions. Before we get carried away with optimism, however, it is important to note that not all opinion leaders reject the sexist courtship game. Indeed, a powerful backlash by psychiatrists and other sex therapists has indicated that they are highly alarmed by the supposedly explosive impact of the women's liberation movement on power in the sexual encounter. According to this backlash, women who are assertive about sex endanger the security of otherwise solid relationships and make men neurotic, anxious, or insecure. Ruminating about the new impotence allegedly caused by sexually aggressive women, these conservative sex experts advise women to remain sexually passive in the bedroom or, at the very least, to be cautious when taking the sexual initiative with men (Ginsberg, Frosch, & Shapiro, 1972; also see F. Lemere's and G. Ginsberg's commentary in Kroop, 1978). Clearly, if the stereotyped courtship game does die, it will have an agonizing and elongated death rattle.

Hopefully, this chapter has shed a little light on the complexities of power in courtship. If you are still perplexed, consider this popular dirty joke: " 'I nearly fainted last night when my date asked me to kiss him,' exclaimed the sweet young thing to her escort. 'Really?' laughed the boy. 'Then you're gonna die when you hear what I have in mind' " (Fry, 1977, p. 64). Are you laughing? If you are, what tickled you? Would this joke be just as amusing if the sweet young thing was an adolescent boy and the escort was an adolescent girl?

4   Sexual Response and Gender Roles

SHIRLEY RADLOVE

The broad overview of gender roles, courtship, and sexual strategies provided in Chapter 3 is brought into finer focus by Shirley Radlove. She describes the consequences of variations in gender role identification on sexually satisfying, or in some cases, unsatisfying relationships.

Radlove begins with a brief history of our knowledge of the physical aspects of human sexual response prior to the work of Masters and Johnson. She gives a short, clear description of Masters and Johnson's major findings and incorporates newly emerging research demonstrating that both men and women are capable of multiple orgasm and ejaculation. Some of the many similarities between the sexual response of men and women at the physiological level may have been affected by differences in the training men and women receive regarding both sexual values and expected masculine versus feminine behavior.

From the standpoint of sexual pleasure, traditional gender-role socialization may be more broadly maladaptive for women than it is for men. Qualities important for the flowering of sexual arousal and orgasm run counter to the training women receive to concern themselves with the needs of others. Such qualities include the ability to give pleasure to oneself and to communicate what feels good to one's partner. Paradoxically, in the inability of some women to communicate their own sexual feelings and desires, they deny their partners the pleasure of contributing to their sensual enjoyment.

After reviewing early evidence suggesting that traditional feminine identification might interfere with healthy sexual responses, Radlove presents the highly supportive results of her own research. Specifically, she found that androgynous married women reported more active and varied sexual interactions with their husbands than was true of more traditionally feminine women. Furthermore, androgynous wives' sexual intimacy with their husbands culminated in orgasm more frequently than did the marital encounters of traditional women.

Regardless of whether they are egalitarian or traditional, the sexual responses of men appear to be less broadly affected by gender-role identification. Radlove concludes that when men have difficulty with their sexual responses, negative sexual attitudes and misinformation seem to be at the root of the problem, rather than gender-role identity per se. The one exception involves erectile dysfunction. The traditional man who is occasionally unresponsive in a sexual situation or who wilts in the middle of sexual intercourse may panic in his failure to match his ideal of male sexuality. This creates a vicious cycle and, potentially, a sexual problem that might not have persisted in the absence of anxiety over masculinity.

In the movie *Sleeper*, Miles Monroe (Woody Allen), part-owner of the Happy Carrot Health Food Restaurant in Greenwich Village, has a major problem. In 1973 he went to the hospital for a minor ulcer operation, but something went wrong. So he was wrapped in aluminum foil and frozen (as hard as a South African lobster tail), only to wake up 200 years later, defrosted, in a new world.

Miles is the first to admit to the inhabitants of this advanced new world that he is an uncurable coward. As he himself points out, "I was once beaten up by Quakers." The world in which Miles finds himself is thus rather alarming to him—a "worst dream come true," you might say. He comes across chickens that are 12 feet tall and bananas as big and as long as canoes. There are robot servants and robot dogs, and at the end of a dinner party, a hostess comments, "I think we should have had group sex but there weren't enough people." Miles is shocked to learn that group sex consists of nothing more than passing around a small crystal ball from guest to guest.

It seems apparent that in this new society all the men are impotent and all the women are frigid. What has evolved is a very simple and efficient "orgasm machine" (a tall contraption called an Orgasmitron) used for automatic (and solo) sexual release. The Orgasmitrons look like white metal shower stalls big enough for one person to enter, climax, and exit—all in the space of about 30 seconds. There is an Orgasmitron available in the home of almost every well-to-do person in this new world. When Luna (Diane Keaton), a beautiful but slightly flaky right-wing poet, tells Miles that she earned her Ph.D. in oral sex, it is clear to the film audience that she studied something as potentially unnecessary and as dead as ancient Greek.*

In Woody Allen's futuristic fantasy of a society where sexual release is fully automated and conveniently relegated to a mechanical contrivance called an "Orgasmitron," and group sex is literally a ball but orgasm is always achieved solo, something seems definitely awry. In this new world rather helpless females are still the standard model of womanliness, and sexual behavior between consenting adults has apparently become obsolete.

Why might the inhabitants of such a new world opt to reject traditional concepts of sexual behavior? Perhaps they felt there were simply too many complex and puzzling problems associated with traditional sex.

For example, why do men in our society, of whom the traditional gender role requires continuous demonstrations of strength, power, and control, often find themselves totally unable to fend off an oncoming orgasm? Why are women, who are supposed to have the biological potential to be multiorgasmic, often not orgasmic at all? Why do men and women seem to have so many problems, concerns, and difficulties in the area of sexual behavior?

Sexual response is supposed to be a healthy, pleasurable, natural phenomenon. Quite often, however, something intervenes, creating barriers and obstacles to this natural act. In this chapter, I focus on some of these intervening variables, including gender-role norms, stereotypes, attitudes, and self-concepts. The emphasis will be on how these gender-role issues can interfere with sexual behavior and cause problems in sexual response.

First, I describe the physiological components of sexual response and use this material to show that men and women are quite similar in their physiological response to sexual stimulation. This provides a foundation for understanding the differences in male and female sexual response in terms of gender-related issues and attitudes.

Second, I consider three overlapping systems involved in effective and healthy sexual functioning. Disruptive influences in any or all of these systems can result in a wide array of sexual difficulties. I define some of these difficulties in relation to sexual attitudes and gender-role norms covered in the third section of the chapter.

Third, in the last section I offer alternatives and suggestions for change. I look at some behaviors related to androgyny, describe some ways to effect personal change, and consider how to approach the resolution of sexual problems.

Of course, all this material will immediately become obsolete with the invention of an Orgasmitron. Should this come to pass, I suggest that you

---

*Adapted from Vincent Canby's review of Woody Allen's film *Sleeper*, *New York Times*, December 18, 1973.

remember to check your circuits periodically, replace worn fuses, thank Woody Allen, and make sure your voltage is always properly regulated.

THE PHYSIOLOGICAL COMPONENTS OF SEXUAL RESPONSE: MASTERS AND JOHNSON'S FINDINGS

Prior to the publication of *Human Sexual Response* by Masters and Johnson (1966), our knowledge of the physiological components of human sexual response and potential was sketchy, at best. Many small studies and a few major studies (for example, Kinsey et al., 1948, 1953; Terman, 1951), had been conducted. However, these were mainly survey studies of sexual attitudes and reported behaviors. That is, they described what people said they did, not what they were observed to do. Research in the area was not only costly but was typically hampered by narrow attitudes, embarrassment, and heated controversy. Sexual behavior was not considered a respectable topic for study, and those who did try to study it met with strong resistance.

As a result, few scientists had the definitive information badly needed and repeatedly sought by direct-service health professionals (physicians, psychologists, and social workers) who were typically called on for advice and treatment of sexual concerns.

According to gynecologist William H. Masters (Tom Snyder television interview, 1975), physicians were being asked the same unanswerable questions over and over again by their female patients:

"Am I *supposed* to have orgasms?"

"I've never had an orgasm; is there something wrong with me?"

"Will I be more sexually satisfied after my child is born?"

"How can my husband control himself longer when we're having sex?"

Responsible physicians could not answer. Science had not supplied the answers. Physicians fielded these and many other questions as best they could, but their bottom-line responses had to be "I just don't know. No one knows—the research is just not in yet."

In 1954, Dr. Masters began an intensive 10-year investigation of the anatomy and physiology of human sexual response. His results were published in 1966, a definitive and rather astonishing contribution to our knowledge of human sexual response. From a physiological standpoint, the research was apparently in.

The Sexual Response Cycle

In their report of the results, Masters and his co-researcher Virginia Johnson (1966) described four phases of human physiological response to effective sexual stimuli. These phases were (1) excitement, (2) plateau, (3) orgasm, and (4) resolution.

Excitement phase   In the male, the first physiological responses to sexual stimulation are the swelling and erection of the penis and partial elevation of the testes. Female excitement results in the production of vaginal lubrication, accompanied by clitoral swelling. The clitoris gets longer, and the vagina increases in width and length.

Plateau phase   With continued sexual stimulation, the circumference of the head (coronal ridge) of the penis increases. The testes become 50 percent larger than they are in their unstimulated state. In the female, the clitoris begins to withdraw into its hood, and there is a further increase in the width and depth of the vagina. Extreme swelling can be seen in the lips of the vulva.

Orgasmic phase   In the male, this phase is characterized by three or four contractions of the entire length of the urethra, at 0.8-second intervals. This is followed by several seconds of minor contractions, which are lower in frequency and expulsive force. The female experiences three to six intense contractions of the outer third of the vagina, at 0.8-second intervals, followed by several seconds of minor contractions, also reduced in frequency and intensity.

Resolution phase   After orgasm, the male's penis begins a rapid loss of swelling and erection. This is followed by a slower shrinking of the penis until it returns to its normal state. In the female, the clitoris returns to its normal position, followed by a slower reduction in size and level of swelling.

Similarities in The Sexual Responses of Men and Women

Throughout their lengthy report of the results just reviewed, Masters and Johnson emphasized the similarities rather than the differences in male and female sexual response. They did report one striking difference between men and women: women seemed to have a unique biological capability for multiple orgasm.

After her initial orgasm, a woman can immediately experience additional orgasms as long as effective stimulation continues and until the woman chooses to stop or becomes exhausted. Men, on the other hand, were said to experience a refractory period: an interval of time (approximately 30 minutes), after ejaculation, during which a man could not return to orgasmic levels of response. Thus, researchers thought men were not multiorgasmic.

More recent research, however, has shown that males too, may have a biological capability for multiple orgasms. Robbins and Jensen (1978) found that men who had taught themselves to be orgasmic without ejaculating could return to repeated orgasms with the same speed and facility observed in women. It was only after these men chose to have an orgasm accompanied by ejaculation that they experienced the refractory period noted by Masters and Johnson (1966).

Apparently, even where the issue of multiple orgasm is concerned, men and women are similar in their sexual response. If there is any remaining difference between the sexes, is it perhaps that only men can ejaculate and women cannot? There is new evidence indicating that such an assumption is unwarranted.

In a series of studies concerning ejaculation in women, researchers noted that women have a biological capability for ejaculation (Addiego et al., 1981; Belzer, 1981; Perry & Whipple, 1981). In women, orgasm may be accompanied by an expulsion of liquid from the urethra. Chemical analysis indicates that it is not urine. Interestingly, Belzer (1981) hypothesized that orgasm accompanied by ejaculation in women may also be followed by a temporary inability to be multiorgasmic—a refractory period, as in men.

Multiple orgasm in males and ejaculation in females are behaviors that are not currently found with great frequency in the population (Robbins & Jensen, 1978; Perry & Whipple, 1981). They do exist, however, as sexual behaviors that can be developed through learning. Although Masters and Johnson (1966) did not observe male multiple orgasm and female ejaculation in their research subjects, it is doubtful these behaviors would have been researched without their initial impetus. In short, the concept of similarity between the sexes had valuable impact on the scientific community.

The Impact of Masters and Johnson's Research

Human Sexual Response was written for physicians and scientists, in terms that few laypeople would ordinarily find captivating. It was not long, however, before journalists began translating the material into popular language, and it began to appear in a number of popular magazines and newspaper articles, and as a topic on television interviews. For instance, Tom Snyder interviewed Masters and Johnson and featured their findings on one of his television programs in 1975.

In a questionnaire designed for a couples sexual communication workshop (Radlove, 1979), men and women were asked if they had read the results of Masters and Johnson's research or other articles describing their work, and if so, whether it had any impact on their attitudes, behavior, or significant relationships. Many of the individuals who shared their insights and experiences indicated that the Masters and Johnson data did indeed have an impact on them.

Women, it seemed, were accorded a new physiological status (sexually speaking). Those who had never been orgasmic, or had never given much thought to their sexual selves, now sought sexual fulfillment from their partners. Others, who worried whether or not their technique for achieving orgasm was legitimate, took comfort in Masters and Johnson's conclusion that orgasms were the same, no matter how achieved. Specifically, there was a serious challenge to the Freudian assumption that women had two kinds of orgasms (see Deutsch, 1944, 1945). The new research seemed to refute the existence of two separate types of female orgasms, a vaginal orgasm reached without clitoral stimulation by sexual intercourse alone and a clitoral orgasm reached when a partner or the woman herself stimulated the clitoris directly. Women's feelings about their sexual functioning improved when they were no longer told that needing clitoral stimulation for orgasmic release was somehow less mature and feminine than achieving orgasm through sexual intercourse (Hite, 1976; Kaplan, 1974).

The new doctrines about sexuality liberated many women, but it was not all "roses." Many men, feeling threatened by the new message, found their own sexual problems exacerbated. Some who had earlier functioned effectively now seemed to falter under the pressure to provide their partner with multiple orgasms. Old "shoulds" were replaced by new ones; people continued to be anxious about their sexual adequacy.

The major question raised by Masters and Johnson was "Why do so many more women than men suffer from sexual dysfunction? If there is no longer a physiological and/or anatomical rationale for this, what is the problem?"

In 1970, Masters and Johnson published another book describing their work with sexually dysfunctional men and women. Their book was not written for the layperson, and, although it did seem to create some stir among the general population, it offered no easy solutions. It did, however, provide repeated and compelling indications that sexual problems in both men and women could best be understood in terms of disruptive influences on one or more of three overlapping systems involved in sexual response.

THREE SEXUAL RESPONSE SYSTEMS

Each person has three sexual response systems. The *biophysical system,* based on our biological capacity to respond to sexual stimulation, determines the physiological limits of sexual response. The *psychosocial system,* based on the culture's sexual scripts for appropriate male and female sexual behavior, and the *sexual value system,* an individual's unique set of beliefs about sexuality, are equally important. People are not naturally sexual. They must learn

Couples Sexual Communication Questionnaire: Excerpts Concerning the Masters and Johnson Data

This excerpt is from a woman who had been nonorgasmic for 14 years prior to reading about Masters and Johnson's results:

I remember after my second child was born in 1959, how disappointed I was that I still could not reach a climax with my husband. I asked my doctor about it, told him about some marriage manuals I was reading and he just grinned at me and said to put the books away and just relax. Then he said, "some women do experience orgasms and some never do, and they should just forget about it." I took this to mean that some women were just physically incapable of climaxing under any and all circumstances, and that I was just one of those unfortunate women. I left his office thinking, "Well, kid, that's that. You might as well go and try to change the color of your eyes." I stopped reading the books, and I stopped masturbating too (mostly). All it ever did was make me nervous anyway. Then (approximately 10 years later) I read a magazine article that seemed to tell me that my doctor had been wrong because some new research had shown that all women could have orgasms. I got the book they were talking about (Masters & Johnson, 1966) and sat there with the dictionary, trying to read it and understand it. I really didn't understand most of it, but the main thing I did understand was that it was definitely possible for all women, and for me, to have orgasms, just the same as it's always been possible for men. Knowing that was like the key for me, and it wasn't long after that, a few days, that I was able to masturbate to my first orgasm. I was 32 years old and married 14 years at the time, but I finally made it!

Another woman wrote that the material had helped her to feel less guilty and far more spontaneous and sexually open in her marriage:

I was always able to have clitoral orgasms, but never vaginal orgasms,* and it really bugged me and made me feel sort of ashamed of myself because I felt that my husband's manual stimulation of my clitoris during intercourse should not be necessary, and that it made me

scripts that tell them how to have sex, who to have it with, and even the extent to which they are allowed to take advantage of their biophysical capacity for responsiveness (Gagnon & Simon, 1973; Gagnon, 1977).

The Biophysical System

The biophysical system involves the body's natural capacity to respond to sexual stimulation. It includes the genitals, the internal sex organs, the ner-

somehow "weird" or "perverted" to him, even though he never said so. When I found out that vaginal orgasms were mainly a Freudian myth, my feelings about myself and my sexual behavior really improved. The little guilts and undercurrents of embarrassment were gone, and I could ask for what I wanted and needed sexually.

Freud got an additional slap on the hand from the husband of the woman who had waited 14 years for her first orgasm:

> I think Freud was very wrong when he said that women have penis-envy. If a woman isn't being satisfied in the bedroom, or if she isn't having orgasms and the man is, it stands to reason that she's going to be jealous of him or his standard equipment. I don't think it's really penis-envy at all. I think it's orgasm-envy. Now that women are supposed to be having multiple orgasms, maybe the shoe will be on the other foot.

Another man offered that his new understanding of the similarities between the sexes made him feel closer to his wife:

> I wouldn't exactly say that I used to be a sexist type, but I will admit that I always believed that men and women (my wife included) were very different and women were tough to figure out. It blew my mind to read that women and men were so much alike sexually, and I figured that if it was true, then I ought to be able to be a much better sex partner. I mean, I ought to know what might please my wife sexually, and where and how to touch her, because I know what pleases me and where and how I like to be touched. Anyway, even though I can't claim any sexual miracles, that understanding did improve our sex life. I think it brought us closer in other ways too.

*A "clitoral" orgasm results from direct stimulation of the clitoris. A "vaginal" orgasm supposedly results from stimulation of the vagina during coitus with no separate massaging of the clitoris.

vous system, the circulatory system, and every physiological structure and process involved in sexual response. This system tends to be dominant. That is, it is not easily disrupted or wiped out by negative influences such as anger or resentment toward one's partner or the attitude that sexual response or excitement is bad or dirty. However, negative attitudes and beliefs can partially diminish the body's natural tendency to respond to sexual stimulation. For example, a woman may experience high levels of physiological tension and excitement during masturbation or intercourse. But she may not be orgasmic if she is frightened or ashamed by the intensity of her sexual response.

The Psychosocial System

The psychosocial system involves the learned and internalized messages and myths transmitted to men and women by the culture. For example, men receive permission to value and explore their sexual feelings by our society, while women are taught to conceal their sexual feelings and remain naive. Men are directed to increase their sexual knowledge and sexual performance skills via masturbation and/or multiple-partner experience, while women are advised to avoid sexual self-exploration and multiple-partner experience lest they be labeled oversexed or promiscuous. In addition, although the culture dimly approves when men's sexual tensions find outlet in casual sex, the resolution of women's sexual tensions are permitted only in the context of love, affection, commitment, and/or movieland romanticism.

The psychosocial system—all the culturally imposed limitations to free-flowing biophysical response—does not automatically create sexual problems for men and women. Problems occur, however, when the realities of individual experience fall short of cultural ideals. For example, if a man has not fully developed his sexual skill and sexual technique, it is unlikely that he will be able to satisfy appropriately and effectively a naive and inexperienced woman who is completely dependent on him for sexual direction. Similarly, if a woman ignores the cultural directive to remain sexually unsophisticated until romantically committed and/or married, she may find that her partner responds to her sexual expertise with erectile difficulties grounded in his perception of her as loose or immoral.

The Sexual Value System

The sexual value system involves the individual's sexual attitudes and beliefs. It consists of family attitudes and personal learning beyond that which is generally transmitted by the culture at large. For example, although the culture may approve and promote sexual skill building via exploration of the male's sexuality, an individual man's religious beliefs may be such that he prefers to remain sexually inexperienced prior to marriage.

North American culture imposes many restrictions as to what sexual behaviors are more appropriate for women or for men. It does not, however, advance the notion that sex is dirty, sinful, or painful for either gender. These negative perceptions are learned in a more personal context. A woman who is raped, for example, may come to devalue sex as a painful and frightening experience. Similarly, men and women whose religion has taught them that masturbation and any other nonreproductive sexual activity is dirty or sinful may bury their natural potential for sexual response and may associate sex with guilt and shame. Such individuals would be said to have a negative sexual value system.

In sum, although men and women are quite similar in their biophysical potential for sexual response, they tend to be dissimilar with regard to their cultural learning of sexual behavior norms. They may also differ greatly (from each other as well as the culture at large) in their sexual value system—the degree to which they value or devalue sexuality. For women, the available research seems to show that cultural learning of feminine role behaviors may be implicated in female sexual problems. In men, sexual problems seem to be more often related to negative sexual values than to a stereotypic masculine role.

GENDER-ROLE AND SEXUAL PROBLEMS IN WOMEN

Statistics compiled by Kinsey and his colleagues (1953) and by Fisher (1973) suggested that approximately 60 percent of North American women have orgasms very rarely or not at all, during sexual intercourse. The currently held belief (for example, see Masters & Johnson, 1970; Kaplan, 1974) is that women seldom get or seek the sexual stimulation they need in order to reach orgasm. Orgasmic dysfunction in females is seldom associated with emotional disturbance, negative sexual attitudes, physiological problems, and/or anatomical abnormalities (Cooper, 1969; Fisher, 1973; Masters & Johnson, 1966; Pomeroy, 1965; Raboch & Bartak, 1968; Radlove, 1977; Winokur, Guze, & Pfeiffer, 1959).

However, many research clues suggest that identification with the traditional feminine role may be related to women's reluctance to ask for or go after the sexual stimulation they need. For example, Masters & Johnson (1970) and Kaplan (1974) report that, in part, the achievement of orgasm requires some behavioral independence or sexual autonomy in a person—the ability and desire to take active responsibility for one's own pleasure. They indicate that a woman (or a man) must be capable of behaving in what they called a "sexually selfish" manner. That is, the individual must be able to focus at times only on his or her own sexual sensations and pleasure. Such focus may be particularly difficult for women, for several reasons.

First, the culture has not traditionally given women the same tacit permission to be fully sexual, with honor and/or praise, that it has given men. That is, during her formative years, a woman learns to repress her sexual needs and feelings in order to abide by cultural norms calling for her to remain a "good girl" (see Chapters 1 and 2). If women are taught to avoid sexual exploration and sexual experience in order to remain "good girls," how are they supposed to learn and understand what their sexual needs are, much less focus on them?

Second, if indeed orgasm requires independence, autonomy, and active responsibility for the self, it is no wonder that so many women are nonorgasmic. How can a woman take active and independent responsibility for her sexual self, when the culture does not promote or support these behaviors in her nonsexual self?

Early research suggesting a link between gender-role norms and orgasmic dysfunction was done by Terman (1951). He noted that nonorgasmic women were less likely to "rebel inwardly at orders" and were also less persistent and more emotionally sensitive than were orgasmic women. No attempt was made by Terman to interpret these findings in terms of traditional or socially approved expressions of femininity. Nevertheless, they do seem to describe traditionally feminine role characteristics, including passivity, dependency, altruism, sensitivity, and harmony. Similarly, Fisher (1973) found a relationship between consistent achievement of orgasm and a typically masculine characteristic (endurance) often associated with traits such as persistence, task orientation, and other instrumental approaches to life.

More recent research indicates that women who take an active, autonomous, and responsible role in their own sexuality not only tend to be orgasmic and/or multiorgasmic but also have a greater likelihood of experiencing ejaculation than women who do not. For example, Kegel (1949, 1952) reported that sexual feeling in the vagina is closely related to muscle tone and that women can increase the probability of coital orgasm by engaging in voluntary contractions of the pubococcygeus muscle ("Kegel exercises"). Perry and Whipple (1981) noted that women who revealed an active and independent effort to condition their sexual muscle tone, doing Kegel exercises for many months, often had orgasms accompanied by ejaculation.

It seems clear that gender-role norms directing women to be passive and dependent, rather than active and autonomous, can prevent many women from becoming orgasmic. How is it, then, that some women are able to overcome such normative influences and/or behave actively and independently in spite of these influences? Quite simply, the behavior of individuals is not entirely or exclusively controlled by gender-role norms. Many individuals achieve a sense of self or unique identity that can supersede psychological allegiance to a set of stereotyped role behaviors.

By actively interacting with the environment and testing our limits, we eventually establish ourselves as adult human beings with unique traits, talents, and abilities. When this is accomplished, we can begin to define ourselves in terms of our special traits as a person rather than in terms of a collection of gender-role traits. That is, we may know that in addition to having traits typically associated with being male or female, we also have traits that are neither masculine nor feminine (for example, we may be skillful, musically talented, successful). Unfortunately, the early learning and acceptance of gender roles may delimit the development of a personalized self-definition or unique identity in many women.

Wynne (1958), for example, conceived of the achievement of unique identity as requiring an environment in which the individual is motivated to test a large variety of behaviors during the course of development. When the environment does not encourage active self-testing, the probability of achieving an identity outside of one's gender role is substantially diminished. In such a case, the culturally prescribed role may become a substitute for a unique self. Wynne further noted that the individual may then invest a great deal of psychological energy in maintaining the stereotypical role, because underneath this pseudo-identity there is no other person: there is a void.

Bardwick and Douvan (1971) noted that establishing a unique identity may be particularly difficult for the majority of presumably healthy women, given socialization practices that reward conformity, dependence, and passivity in women, rather than independence, self-sufficiency, and objective achievement. In other words, many women may be highly dependent on gender-role norms for self-definition. This situation seems additionally serious in that women may have to step out of their stereotypic feminine role in order to function well sexually.

Masters and Johnson (1970) and Kaplan (1974) noted that the likelihood of orgasm is increased when a woman takes the woman-above position during intercourse. This position creates an increase in clitoral pressure and sexual stimulation. Similarly, it is believed to be helpful for a woman to engage periodically in active coital thrusting. But many women reportedly perceive such behaviors as "masculine," and thus inappropriate for them. Perhaps this is why women gave more negative evaluations of a couple depicted in photographic slides of intercourse in the woman-above position in Allgeier and Fogel's (1978) research (see Chapter 3). Consistent with this, Kaplan (1974) reported that the woman-above position seems to give rise to anxieties in nonorgasmic women. These women fear that they will be sexually unattractive in the woman-above position. Moreover, Kaplan noted, these fears may have some basis, for husbands may in fact become resentful or rejecting if they feel their role is being preempted.

The possibility that women may monitor themselves in line with what they believe to be role-appropriate behavior is also implied in clinical reports of progress in sex therapy. Masters and Johnson (1970) and Kaplan (1974) have noted that the nonorgasmic woman seems to have difficulty abandoning herself to the sexual situation, behaving more like a passive spectator than an active participant in sexual intercourse.

Although researchers have long sensed there might be a relationship between gender-role identity and sexual dysfunction, the relationship could not be strongly substantiated (Terman, 1951; Fisher, 1973). This was probably because early tests of gender-role identification could only reveal whether a woman was masculine *or* feminine; these tests could not tell the *extent* to which a woman was masculine or feminine. With the advent of Bem's (1974) measure of gender role identification described in Chapter 2, however, it became possible to ask whether a feminine woman might be more likely to have sexual problems than a woman who is more androgynous (both masculine and feminine) in her gender-role identification.

In a study designed to explore the relationship between female orgasm and gender-role identification, I found that androgynous women tended to achieve orgasm more often than feminine women (Radlove, 1977). Androgynous women were also more likely than feminine women to take active responsibility for their own clitoral stimulation. Compared to feminine women, androgynous women were more likely to perceive active sexual behaviors such as coital thrusting or being on top of one's partner as equally appropriate for men and women. Thus, it appears that feminine role norms can be a disruptive influence in women's sexual behavior. Women who do not define themselves solely in terms of the female stereotype are more apt to be orgasmic than women whose gender-role identification is strictly feminine.

GENDER-ROLE AND SEXUAL PROBLEMS IN MEN

Although men are not free of sexual difficulties, far fewer men than women have sexual problems that seem directly related to gender-role stereotypes. Men, for example, do get the stimulation they need in order to reach orgasm. The behaviors that lead to the stimulation necessary for orgasm in both the male and female are apparently already a part of the masculine gender-role repertoire. That is, the masculine role involves behaving in an active, instrumental manner. When men are sexually dysfunctional, the source of the problem is more often traced to sexual values and attitudes than to adherence to gender-role norms.

For example, in discussing the inability to achieve erection under any circumstances, Masters and Johnson (1970) reported that long-term negative sexual attitudes seem to be at the core of the problem. In the majority of cases they treated, sexual histories revealed restrictive sexual attitudes—a perception of sex as "dirty" or only for purposes of procreation—originating with intense religious training. For these men, the overwhelming psychological barrier against sexual pleasure tended to wipe out completely the body's natural ability to respond to physical stimulation.

Similarly, in the majority of males treated for the inability to have orgasm during coitus,* Masters and Johnson noted that the problem appeared to stem from severe religious training, dislike or open disgust for the marital partner, and/or sexual trauma, more often than to gender-role norms. In some cases, a man's earlier excessively intimate relationship with his mother resulted in overwhelming sexual guilt and a maze of unconscious defenses against "letting go" with any woman. Other men revealed that the problem began after they had been ridiculed by impatient prostitutes for "not coming fast enough."

In the case of premature ejaculation—the inability to exert control over speed of ejaculation—it appears that attitudes are again a major factor. In this case, however, it is less often a result of negative sexual attitudes per se, and more often a result of naivetè and/or lack of concern for the sexual needs of women. For example, Masters and Johnson (1970) reported that grade school or early high school dropouts rarely request treatment for premature ejaculation. When treatment is sought, it is usually the wife, not the husband, who seeks it. The husbands of these women seem to be quite unaware and/or unconcerned that their speedy ejaculation is leaving their partners sexually frustrated. Masters and Johnson further noted that men's level of concern for controlling ejaculation and sexually satisfying their partners seems to increase in direct parallel to their level of formal education.

Interestingly, it might be hypothesized that males who are sexually aware and well educated, and who tend to be more profeminist in their attitudes, might also have problems. Overly invested with a sense of responsibility for satisfying the potentially multiorgasmic female, these men may exercise high levels of control—possibly diminishing their own sexual pleasure.

The foregoing overview of the association of various attitudes to the development of a number of male sexual dysfunctions is not meant to imply that identification with the stereotypic masculine role is never a factor in male sexual dysfunction. In the case of the inability to maintain an erection, Masters and Johnson (1970) clearly seem to suggest that identification with the stereotypic masculine role can be a major factor in the onset of the problem. Such men usually have a history of success in having erections. For a variety of reasons, including exhaustion, alcohol excess, and marital tension, they may have an initial experience with erectile dysfunction. Such a man may look on this as a sign that his manhood is in danger. To overcome

*Penis-in-vagina intercourse.

the difficulty, he may become quite tense, hoping erection can be achieved if he works at it. It is as if he is convinced that by the sheer force of his masculine strength and will, he can forcibly produce an erection. However, forcing, exerting, and demanding are masculine gender-role characteristics that tend to work against the man with erection problems. Healthy responses generally come only when he allows himself the luxury of not trying at all. In other words, he should give in to the moment, become somewhat more passive sexually, so as to let the erection occur naturally, of its own accord. Like the woman, he may be better off sexually if he is less psychologically bound to traditional gender-role behaviors and is able to behave in either an active or passive manner depending on the situation.

It is surprising that the incidence of sexual dysfunction among men tends to be less than among women. The sexual myths that men learn in North American culture seem to be enough to give any man an overdose of performance anxiety. Zilbergeld (1978) devoted two chapters in his book on male sexuality to a discussion of these myths. Although Zilbergeld, tongue-in-cheek, refers to these myths as the "Fantasy Model of Sex," he clearly believes the effects of the fantasy model to be psychologically and behaviorally disturbing to most men. The model is summarized in the accompanying box. Zilbergeld closes his discussion of the cultural myths with the saddest myth of all: "In this enlightened age, the preceding myths no longer have any influence on us" (p. 53).

ALTERNATIVES AND SUGGESTIONS FOR CHANGE

We have seen that from a physiological perspective, males and females are quite similar in their sexual response. We have seen too, that from a psychosocial perspective, gender-role behaviors can diminish sexual pleasure and create problems for otherwise healthy men and women. The remaining issue is what to do about it. And here, unfortunately, the scientific literature does not provide much help.

Are there alternatives to the traditional masculine and feminine gender roles that tend to reduce our options and cause difficulties in the sphere of sexual behavior? Can we give up a one-dimensional set of role behaviors and still maintain our unique sense of pride and value as male and female partners in sexual activity?

Androgyny as an Alternative

One possible answer may be found in S. L. Bem's (1972, 1974, 1975) concept of the androgynous person. A number of studies seem to indicate a positive relationship between an androgynous role orientation and effective function-

---

The Fantasy Model of Sex

The Equipment: All you need is a penis. In Fantasyland, penises come in only three sizes—large, gigantic, and so big you can barely get it through the door.

The Partner: The women in Fantasyland are all gorgeous and perfectly formed. They want sex all the time, and want to be handled roughly, no matter how much they request gentleness.

The Feelings: Men should not have, or at least not express certain feelings. Aggressiveness, competitiveness, anger, and the other feelings associated with being in control are OK, but weakness, confusion, fear, vulnerability, tenderness, compassion, and sensuality are allowed only to girls and women.

The Performance: In sex, as elsewhere, it's performance that counts. The three A's of manhood are "Achieve, Achieve, Achieve."

The Responsibility: The man must always be the one to take charge of and orchestrate sex.

The Desire: A man constantly wants and is always ready to have sex. Men are like machines, and can perform any time the button is pushed.

The Goal: All physical contact must lead to sex. Cuddling, hugging, kissing, holding, and caressing are neither valuable nor pleasurable in their own right; they are useful only in paving the way for sex.

The Main Thing: There is only one main thing—intercourse. All other forms of sex are only preliminaries. Oral sex is not sex. Only intercourse is sex.

The Main Thing (Part II): An erection is everything.

The Vigor: Sex must be hard-driving and drive women into paroxysms of pleasure. Sex should not be slow or leisurely, with time for resting, talking, laughing.

The Natural Expertise: There is no necessity for learning any new skills, talking about sex, or taking any corrective measures, for there is nothing to learn and nothing to correct.

SOURCE: Adapted from Zilbergeld, B. *Male sexuality; A guide for sexual fulfillment.* Boston: Little, Brown, 1978. Copyright © 1978 by B. Zilbergeld. Reprinted with permission of Little, Brown and Co.

---

ing in general, as well as effective sexual functioning. Allgeier (1975), for example, reported that androgynous individuals felt less guilt over masturbation and tended to begin their contraceptive education at a younger age than nonandrogynous individuals. Spence, Helmreich, and Stapp (1975) examined the relationship between androgyny and self-esteem in men and women, and found that androgynous subjects tended to be higher in self-esteem than were traditionally gender-typed individuals.

However, recent evidence (Jones, Chernovetz, & Hansson, 1978) indicates that self-esteem, flexibility, and overall emotional adjustment tend to be associated with masculinity more often than with androgyny for both males and females. Furthermore, research by Allgeier (1981) shows that where heterosexual interaction is concerned, the strength of the androgyny variable seems to diminish. Apparently, engaging in behaviors defined by the culture as "role inappropriate" can be very difficult in a heterosexual context, even for androgynous individuals. Perhaps, in a heterosexual context, the possibility of rejection by a person of the other gender can make the translation of androgynous attitudes into androgynous behavior much more risky.

At the present time, very little in the literature on androgyny indicates clearly how one can become more androgynous. It appears that a great deal more work must be accomplished in this area before androgyny can be seen as a truly viable alternative to the restrictive gender roles implicated in sexual dysfunction.

Personal Change

Regardless of whether or not it is possible simply to choose to become more androgynous, a number of options are open to an individual who wants to effect personal behavior change in the context of a sexual relationship. One such option may be to engage in the desired behaviors despite the psychological discomforts that may initially be associated with these behaviors.

D. J. Bem (1972) has shown that the observation of oneself actually engaging in a particular behavior tends to shape our perceptions of our internal attitudes and emotions. In other words, actually doing so-called role-inappropriate sexual behaviors can positively change our own perception of "appropriateness."

Because any sexual partnership obviously involves more than one person, however, the suggestion that one person might independently engage in new behavior without the understanding and cooperation of the other seems, at best, to greatly undermine the probability of a successful result.

Although it is often suggested that partners in sexual interaction need to communicate more, it seems more important to suggest that they need to communicate more effectively. Appropriate ways to communicate feelings, needs, desires, hurts, and/or fears, in a nonthreatening and nondemanding way, may be found in classes, workshops, and reading material on effective couple communication or training in assertiveness (Bloom, Coburn, & Pearlman, 1975; Alberti & Emmons, 1978; Bower & Bower, 1976).

Another way to effect personal change may be found in books specifically designed for self-help. Barbach's (1975) book on female sexuality and Zilbergeld's (1978) book on male sexuality give exercises for improving sexual response.

Where sexual problems already exist or are suspected to exist, however, professional help may be useful. Some of the issues an individual may want to consider are (1) the need for gynecological and/or urological examination (to rule out physical or anatomical pathology), (2) the need to choose wisely from available sex therapists by asking questions regarding the therapist's professional background and training in the treatment of sexual concerns, and (3) the desirability of placing sexual concerns in the context of a relationship. Masters and Johnson (1970, p. 2) note, "There is no such thing as an uninvolved partner in any marriage (or relationship) in which there is some form of sexual dysfunction. *Sexual response represents ... interaction between people*" (our emphasis). Where there is a breakdown in the nonsexual aspects of a relationship—a long-term buildup of resentment, a loss of trust, or a lessening of mutual concern and respect—it is typically reflected in the sexual aspect of the relationship. Thus, the initial focus in sex therapy is often the relationship itself (Kaplan, 1974; Masters & Johnson, 1970).

Whatever an individual chooses to do to resolve or prevent sexual difficulties, the effort can be greatly enhanced by a more open and accepting view of one's own behavior and that of others. With such a view, the restrictive roles we fill as men and women may eventually give way to a healthier, more spontaneous, and more productive reality for all.

5 What Do Women and Men Want from Love and Sex?

ELAINE HATFIELD

The benefits of egalitarian over traditional gender-role identification for women's and men's sexual pleasure were well documented in the last chapter. But what are the wishes and expectations of men and women for their love relationships in the long run? In this chapter, Elaine Hatfield reviews research on the similarities and differences in the goals of adult men and women regarding love, sex, intimacy, and sexual performance.

Love means different things to different people, and Hatfield begins reviewing possible gender differences in six variations of love, including romantic, self-centered, sensible, and altruistic (selfless) love. Her research review indicates that men view love more romantically. They also tend, however, to be more cynical about love. Women tend to be willing to sacrifice more for love than is characteristic of men.

Hatfield goes on to examine gender differences in the meaning of sexuality. After reviewing sociobiological versus social learning speculations regarding the sexual interests and responses of men and women, she reviews research on gender similarities and differences in adults' responses to erotic materials, tendencies to initiate sexual activity, enjoyment of sexual stimulation, desire for intimacy, and sexual performance expectations.

Some theorists speculate that the expectations and desires of the two genders are so different that men and women are essentially incompatible with one another. But Hatfield's review of research in the area leads her to an entirely different perspective: "Nature has arranged things more sensibly." She concludes that, although the goals of men and women do differ in a few superficial ways that are largely shaped by differential gender-role socialization, both men and women share the same goals for intimacy, sex, and love.

106

Love has not been protected from ravages of the battle between the sexes. From time immemorial, men and women have been accusing one another of being incapable of feeling or returning love; for example, "Men can't love" (Firestone, 1971, p. 152) and "Men love women; women merely love love" (Anonymous).

The controversy is far from over. Recently, a woman posed an intriguing question in my human sexuality class: "Why are love affairs generally such disasters?" She had decided it was hopeless—"Men and women just want different things." Her bitter feelings sparked an intense debate.

Most of the students said they believed that men and women were really very much alike. They might talk about things differently, but in truth they both cared about the same kinds of things.

"Not so," said an indignant minority. Students then suggested a bewildering list of ways in which they thought men and women differed:

"Women care about love. They have to trust their partners if they're to have good sex."

"What men care about is sex; they want to have a lot of sex, with a lot of partners, in a lot of ways." ("Yeah! Yeah!" came a rowdy chorus.)

"Men claim to be egalitarian, but they all want to marry virgins; women want someone who is sexually experienced."

"Women are capable of intimacy. Men aren't. They won't talk about their feelings."

"Women want commitment; men don't want to be pinned down."

"Women say they want intimacy, but just let a man express a little weakness, and they really give it to him."

What an array of sexual stereotypes! Is there any truth in them?

REVIEW OF THE RESEARCH LITERATURE

I reviewed the research literature in order to find the answer to two questions: (1) What do men and women want out of their intimate relationships—the same things or markedly different things? and (2) What, specifically, is the nature of these differences?

Most theorists seemed to agree that—in the main—men and women hope for very similar things from their intimate relationships. There are, however, probably *some* significant differences in the things they desire.

Sociobiologists contend that men and women are *genetically* programmed to desire different things from their intimate relations (see Hagen, 1979; Symons, 1979; and Wilson, 1975). Symons (1979) argues that gender differences are probably the most powerful determinant of how people behave sexually. Symons's sociobiological argument proceeds as follows: According to evolutionary biology, animals inherit those characteristics that ensure that they will transmit as many of their genes to the next generation as possible. It is to men and women's advantage to produce as many surviving children as possible. But men and women differ in one critical respect—in order to produce a child, men need only to invest a trivial amount of energy; a single man can conceivably father an almost unlimited number of children. On the other hand, a woman can conceive only a limited number of children. It is to a woman's advantage to ensure the survival of the children she does conceive. Symons observes, "The enormous sex differences in minimum parental investment and in reproductive opportunities and constraints explain why *Homo sapiens,* a species with only moderate sex differences in structure, exhibits profound sex differences in psyche" (p. 27).

What are the gender differences Symons insists are "wired in"? According to Symons,

1. Men desire a variety of sex partners; women do not.
2. Men are inclined to be polygamous (possessing many wives); women are more malleable in this respect; they are equally satisfied in polygamous, monogamous, or polyandrous marriages (possessing many husbands).
3. Men are sexually jealous. Women are more malleable in this respect; they are concerned with security—not fidelity.
4. Men are sexually aroused by the sight of women and women's genitals; women are not aroused by men's appearance.
5. For men, "sexual attractiveness" equals "youth." For women, "sexual attractiveness" equals "political and economic power."
6. Men have every reason to pursue women actively. They are programmed to impregnate as many women as possible. Women have every reason to be "coy." It takes time to decide if a man is a good genetic risk—is likely to be nurturant and protective.
7. Men are intensely competitive with one another. Competition over women is the most frequent cause of violence. Women are far less competitive.

In contrast, social learning theorists insist that gender differences are learned. Men and women are very adaptable. A half century ago, Margaret Mead in *Sex and Temperament in Three Primitive Societies* (1969) discussed three cultures of New Guinea (now Papua New Guinea) and their gender-role standards. She described the Arapesh, a culture in which both genders had "feminine" traits; the Mundugamur, among whom both genders were "masculine"; and the Tchambuli, among whom the men were "feminine" and women were "masculine."

Thus, learning theorists argue, if men and women desire different things from intimate relationships, it's because they've been *taught* to desire different things (see Bernard, 1972; Byrne & Byrne, 1977; Firestone, 1971; Griffitt & Hatfield, in press; Hatfield & Walster, 1981; Safilios-Rothschild, 1977; and Tavris & Offir, 1977).

Learning theorists do not always agree about what men and women have been trained to want from intimate relationships. For example, some argue that men are quicker to love, and love more deeply, than do women (Hobart, 1958; Kanin, Davidson, & Scheck, 1970; Hill, Rubin, & Peplau, 1976). Others argue that women love more deeply (Firestone, 1971; Kanin, Davidson, & Sheck, 1970). Some think it is men who are most possessive and jealous; others think that women are (see Clanton & Smith, 1977).

What does research indicate? Are there gender differences in what men and women want out of their intimate love relationships? Theorists have speculated that male-female differences are probably most striking in four areas: (1) concern with love, (2) concern with sex, (3) desire for intimacy, and (4) desire for control.

CONCERN WITH LOVE

According to folklore, it is women who are most concerned with love. Theorists of every political persuasion have assumed that the cultural stereotype—women love; men work—has a ring of truth.

Aristotle argued that it could hardly be otherwise. He theorized that, by nature, men are superior in every respect to women; not only are they superior in body and mind, but even in the ability to live on via the next generation. Aristotle erroneously believed that semen transmitted the soul to the embryo. "Feminine secretions" transmitted only a temporary earthly body to the next generation. Thus, Aristotle argued that "because the wife is inferior to her husband, she ought to love him more than herself; algebraically, this would compensate for their inequality and result in a well-balanced relationship." For Aristotle, the "fact" that women are concerned with loving and being loved, while men care far less, is written in their genes (or rather, in their "semen" and "secretions").

Interestingly enough, modern feminists have tended to agree with Aristotle—they too assume that women are the more romantic of the two genders. For example, Dorothy Dinnerstein (1977, p. 70) writes,

> It has often been pointed out that women depend lopsidedly on love for emotional fulfillment because they are barred from absorbing activity in the public domain. This is true. But it is also true that men can depend lopsidedly on participation in the public domain because they are stymied by love.

Shulamith Firestone (1971) agrees. In *The Dialectic of Sex*, she observes, "Men can't love." She comments, "That women live for love and men live for work is a truism. . . . Men were thinking, writing, and creating, because women were pouring their energies into those men; women . . . are preoccupied with love" (pp. 126–127). Firestone does not argue that women should cease being lovers. She argues, instead, that men and women must become equals, so they *both* can love.

This commonsense view—that women are intensely concerned with love while men's feelings are more muted—has been echoed by a wide array of psychologists and sociologists (see, for example, Parsons, 1959; Langhorn & Secord, 1955; and Parsons & Bales, 1955). The theorists agree—but do the facts support the theorists?

Research suggests that the facts are more complicated than one might expect: Men and women seem to differ in what they mean by love. But who is defined as the "romantic" depends on your definition of love.

The Meaning of Love

What do we mean by "love"? Lee (1977) and Hatkoff and Lasswell (1979) argue that "love" means very different things to different people. Hatkoff and Lasswell (1979) have concluded that men and women differ in the way they conceptualize love. They interviewed 554 blacks, whites, and Asians as well as members of several other ethnic groups. The lovers' ages ranged from under 18 to 60. They concluded that men are more romantic and self-centered lovers. Women are more dependent, companionate, and practical. No one is very altruistic.

Research by other investigators suggests that their conclusions might have some validity. Let us consider the evidence regarding gender differences in the different kinds of love.

Romantic love   Several theorists agree with Hatkoff and Lasswell's (1979) finding that men are more romantic than are women. In 1958, sociologist Charles Hobart asked 923 men and women to respond to a series of statements related to romanticism. Why not try seeing how you feel about Hobart's 12 statements? You might also want to ask your current dating partner how he or she feels (see Table 5-1).

Hobart (1958) found that men had a somewhat more romantic view of male-female relationships than did women. On the average, women agreed with about four of the romanticism items. Men agreed with about five of them.

Recently, social psychologists tried to replicate Hobart's work in an effort to determine if it is still men who are the real romantics. They found evidence to indicate that men may still be the more romantic sex (see Dion & Dion, 1973, 1979; and Knox & Sporakowski, 1968).

TABLE 5-1
Romanticism Scale

	AGREE	DISAGREE
*1. Lovers ought to expect a certain amount of disillusionment after marriage.	____	____
*2. True love should be suppressed in cases where its existence conflicts with the prevailing standards of morality.	____	____
3. To be truly in love is to be in love forever.	____	____
*4. The sweetly feminine "clinging vine" girl cannot compare with the capable and sympathetic girl as a sweetheart.	____	____
5. As long as they at least love each other, two people should have no trouble getting along together in marriage.	____	____
6. A girl should expect her sweetheart to be chivalrous on all occasions.	____	____
7. A person should marry whomever he loves regardless of social position.	____	____
8. Lovers should freely confess everything of personal significance to each other.	____	____
*9. Economic security should be carefully considered before selecting a marriage partner.	____	____
*10. Most of us could sincerely love any one of several people equally well.	____	____
11. A lover without jealousy is hardly to be desired.	____	____
*12. One should not marry against the serious advice of one's parents.	____	____

NOTE: What's your romanticism score? If you agreed with Items 3, 5, 6, 7, 8, or 11 (the items without an asterisk), give yourself one point per item. If you disagreed with Items 1, 2, 4, 9, 10, or 12 (the items with an asterisk), give yourself one point per item. Record your total score here _____ .

SOURCE: Hobart, C. W. The incidence of romanticism during courtship. *Social Forces*, 1958, *36*, p. 364. Copyright © 1958 by The University of North Carolina Press. Used by permission.

Other researchers support Hatkoff and Lasswell's findings that men—as the romantics—are more likely to fall in love at first sight, become deeply committed to a romantic dream, and suffer bitterly when their romantic fantasies fall apart. For example, Kanin, Davidson, & Scheck (1970) interviewed 700 young lovers. "How early," they asked, "did you become

---

Six Definitions of Love

ROMANTIC LOVE

Romantic lovers believe in love at first sight. They're in love with love. They can remember when they met, how they met, and what their partners were wearing when they first touched. They expect their partners to remember, too. Romantic lovers want to know everything about their beloved; to share their joys and sorrows and their experiences. They identify totally with one another. They are thoroughly committed to their lovers. Theirs is a sexual kind of love. Romantic lovers try hard to please their loved ones. They give generous presents.

SELF-CENTERED LOVE

Self-centered lovers play at love affairs as they would play at games. They try to demonstrate their skill or superiority; they try to win. Such lovers may keep two or three lovers on the string at one time. For them, sex is self-centered and exploitative. As a rule, such lovers have only one sexual routine. If that doesn't work, they move on to new sexual partners. Self-centered lovers care about having fun. They get frightened off if someone becomes dependent on them or wants commitment. If a partner ends the relationship, they take loss gracefully: "You win a few, you lose a few—there'll be another one along in a minute."

DEPENDENT LOVE

Dependent lovers are obsessed. They are unable to sleep, eat, or even think. The dependent lover has peaks of excitement, but also depths of depression.

---

aware that you loved the other?" Of the men, 20 percent fell in love before the fourth date; only 15 percent of the women fell in love that early. At the other extreme, 30 percent of the men, compared to 43 percent of the women, were not sure if they were in love by the twentieth date. Men seemed willing to fall headlong into love; women were far more cautious about getting involved.

There is also some evidence that it is men who cling most tenaciously to an obviously stricken affair and who suffer most when it finally dies. A group of Harvard scientists (Hill, Rubin, & Peplau, 1976) charted the course of 231 Boston couples' affairs for two years. They found that usually it was the women who decided whether and when an affair should end; men seemed to

They are irrationally jealous, and become extremely anxious when their loved ones threaten to leave, even for a short time.

COMPANIONATE LOVE

Companionate lovers are basically good friends. They take it for granted that their relationships will be permanent. The companionate relationship is *not* an intensely sexual one. Sex is satisfying, but not compelling. Temporary separations are not a great problem. If their relationship breaks up, such lovers remain close and caring friends for the rest of their lives.

PRACTICAL LOVE

Practical lovers are intensely pragmatic. They look realistically at their own assets, assess their market value, and set off to get the best possible deal in their partners. They are faithful in love so long as the loved one is a good bargain. Practical lovers think carefully about education, make sensible decisions about family size, and so on. They carefully check out their future in-laws and relatives.

ALTRUISTIC LOVE

Altruistic lovers are forgiving. They assume the best. If their lovers cause them pain, they assume the lovers didn't mean to do so. Altruistic lovers are always supportive, self-sacrificing. They care enough about their lovers' happiness to give them up, if their lovers have a chance for greater happiness elsewhere.

stick it out to the bitter end. When an affair finally did flicker out, the men suffered most. The men felt most depressed, most lonely, least happy, and least free after a breakup. They found it extremely hard to accept the fact that they were no longer loved, that the affair was over and there was nothing they could do about it. They were plagued with the hope that if only they said the right thing or did the right thing everything would be as it was. Women were far more resigned, and thus were better able to pick up the pieces of their lives and move on. And the contention that it is men who suffer most when an affair flickers out, is consistent with the fact that three times as many men as women commit suicide after a disastrous love affair (Bernard, 1972).

Self-centered love   Self-centered lovers see love as a pleasant pastime. Following the Roman poet Ovid's advice, they play the game of love for their own purposes. The rules of the game are to exploit a relationship to its fullest without getting deeply involved.

Few social psychologists have explored self-centered love, probably because most people don't consider it to be love at all. Hatkoff and Laswell (1979) do, and they found that men are far more likely to be self-centered lovers than women. Replicating their findings, Dion and Dion (1973) also found that men can be more exploitative in love relationships than women.

Dependent love   A number of scientists have studied dependent love, although they have chosen to label this intense state as "passionate love" (the term we prefer), "puppy love," "infatuation," or "falling in love" (as opposed to "being in love").

Hatfield and Walster (1981, p. 9) defined passionate love as "A state of intense absorption in another. Sometimes lovers are those who long for their partners and for complete fulfillment. Sometimes lovers are those who are ecstatic at finally having attained their partners' love, and, momentarily, complete fulfillment. A state of intense psychological arousal." Tennov (1979) argues that passionate love has the following basic components:

1. Lovers find it impossible to work, to study, to do anything but think about the beloved.
2. They long to be loved in return.
3. Their mood fluctuates wildly; they are ecstatic when they hope they might be loved, despairing when they feel they're not.
4. They find it impossible to believe that they could ever love again.
5. They fantasize about how it would go if their partner declared his or her love for them.
6. They're shy in the other's presence.
7. When everything seems lost, their feelings are even more intense than usual.
8. They search for signs (a squeeze of the hand, a knee that doesn't move away, a gaze that lingers) that signify that the other desires them.
9. Their heart aches when they imagine they might lose the other.
10. They feel like walking on air when the other seems to care.
11. They care so desperately about the other that nothing else matters; they are willing to sacrifice anything for love.
12. Love *is* blind; lovers idealize one another.

Contrary to the evidence presented earlier that men tend to be more romantic, researchers have found that, while a relationship is at its highest pitch, women experience the euphoria and agony of romance more intensely than do men. Kanin, Davidson, and Scheck (1970) asked men and women to rate (on the following scale: 1 = none; 2 = slight; 3 = moderate; 4 = strong; 5 = very strong) how they felt when they were in love; that is, to what extent did they experience the following love reactions:

( ) Felt like I was floating on a cloud
( ) Felt like I wanted to run, jump, and scream
( ) Had trouble concentrating
( ) Felt giddy and carefree
( ) Had a general feeling of well-being
( ) Was nervous before dates
( ) Had physical sensations: cold hands, butterflies in the stomach, tingling spine, and so on
( ) Had insomnia

In this study, the women appeared to be the most passionate. They generally experienced the symptoms of passionate love with some intensity. Men did not, with one exception: men and women were both nervous before dates. The recent work of Tennov (1979) provides additional support for the contention that women feel more "symptoms" of love than do men.

Researchers have found only one exception to this conclusion. Traup-mann and Hatfield (1981) interviewed men and women at all stages of life about their feelings for their partners. They interviewed 191 dating couples and 53 newlywed couples right after their marriages and then again a year later. They also interviewed 106 older women, but (unfortunately, for our purposes) they did not interview women's husbands. These people were asked how much passionate love they felt for their partners and how much love they thought their partners felt for them. Possible answers were (1) "None at all," (2) "Very little," (3) "Some," (4) "A great deal," and (5) "A tremendous amount." Unlike previous researchers, they found that during courtship and the early years of marriage, men and women felt equally passionate about one another. Both steady daters and newlywed men and women felt "a great deal" of passionate love for their partners. It was only in old age that men *may* begin to love their partners with slightly more passion than they are loved in return. Older women reported that their husbands loved them with "some" passion. They reported feeling slightly less passionate about their husbands. Whether or not their husbands agree with this assessment is unknown (see Figure 5-1). In summary, women appear to love the most passionately, at least until old age.

Companionate and practical love   Women appear to *like* their partners more than their partners like them in return. Researchers have talked about this friendly kind of love as companionate love, practical love, or just plain love. For most people, this is the essence of love.

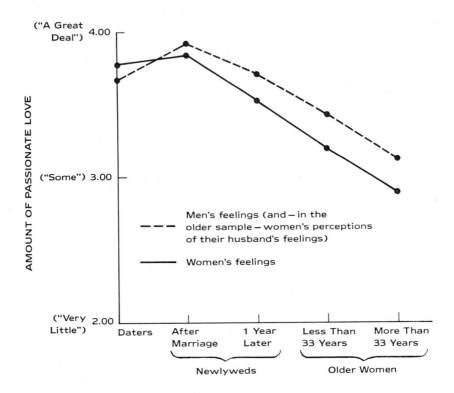

FIGURE 5-1

Dating Couples', Newlywed Couples', and Older Women's Passionate
Love for Their Partners

SOURCE: Traupmann, J., & Hatfield, E. Love: Its effect on mental and physical health. In J. March, S. Kiesler, R. Fogel, E. Hatfield, & E. Shanas (Eds.), *Aging: Stability and change in the family.* New York: Academic Press, 1981, p. 261. Used by permission of Academic Press and the authors.

Hatfield and Walster (1981) agree that liking and companionate love have much in common. They define companionate love as "The affection we feel for those with whom our lives are deeply entwined" (p. 9). Rubin (1970) explored some of the components of love. He argued that love includes such elements as idealization of the other, tenderness, responsibility, the longing to aid and be aided by the loved one, intimacy, the desire to share emotions and experiences, sexual attraction, the exclusive and absorptive nature of the relationship, and finally, a relative lack of concern with social norms and constraints.

Again, researchers find that, from the first, women are the friendly lovers. Traupmann and Hatfield (1981), also asked dating, newlywed, and older people how *companionately* they loved their partners and how much they thought they were loved in return. They found that from the dating

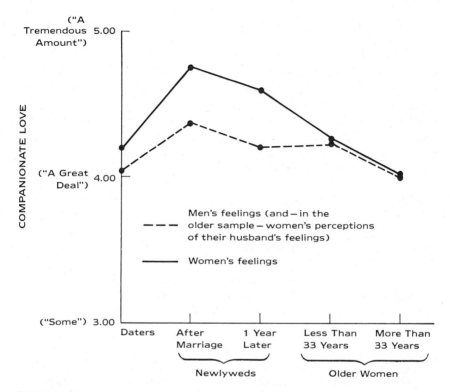

FIGURE 5-2

*Dating Couples', Newlywed Couples', and Older Women's Companionate
Love for Their Partners*

SOURCE: Traupmann, J., & Hatfield, E. Love: Its effect on mental and physical health. In J. March,
S. Kiesler, R. Fogel, E. Hatfield, & E. Shanas (Eds.), *Aging: Stability and change in the family.* New
York: Academic Press, 1981, p. 262. Used by permission of Academic Press and the authors.

period until very late in life, women admitted they loved their partners more
companionately than they were loved in return. Both steady daters and
newlyweds expressed a "great deal" to "tremendous amount" of companionate love for their partners. By age 50, most people still expressed "a great
deal" of companionate love for their mates—even after many years of marriage. As one can see from Figure 5-2, at each point in time women feel more
companionate love than do men. It is only in the final years of life that men
and women come to love one another companionately with equal intensity.
With long experience, equal respect and love evidently comes.

For many women, the fact that they love more passionately and companionately than they are loved in return is deeply unsettling. They continue
to long for love throughout their marriages.

My colleagues and I (Hatfield et al., 1981) interviewed casually dating and newlywed couples in an attempt to determine what they wished from their sexual relations. Men and women's concern with love was assessed via such questions as "During sex, I wish my partner was . . . " (possible answers ranged from "Much more caring and considerate" to "Much less caring and considerate") and "I wish my partner would . . . " ("Talk lovingly much more during sex" to "Talk lovingly much less during sex"). Both dating and newlywed women said they wished their partners would be more affectionate during sexual intercourse; men thought the amount of affection they received was "just about right."

Altruistic love   Altruism is a classical form of love—love that is patient, kind, that never demands reciprocity. All the great religions share this concept of love. For example, St. Paul, in his letters to the Corinthians, wrote that Christians have a duty to care about others, whether the others are deserving of their love or not.

The data on who is most altruistic—men or women—are confusing. Sociologist John Lee asked Americans, Canadians, and Britons about their love experiences. He didn't find anyone, man or woman, who was very altruistic. Lee (1974, p. 50) admits,

> I found no saints in my sample. I have yet to interview an unqualified example of [altruism], although a few respondents had brief [altruistic] episodes in relationships that were otherwise tinged with selfishness. For instance, one of my subjects, seeing that his lover was torn between him or another man, resolved to save her the pain of deciding; he bowed out gracefully. His action fell short of pure [altruism], however, because he continued to be interested in how well his beloved was doing, and was purely and selfishly delighted when she dropped the other man and returned to him.

Hatkoff and Lasswell (1979) interviewed blacks, whites, and Asians, ranging in age from 18 to 60, about their perceptions, memories, and experiences of love. In Hawaii, it was women (especially Asian women) who were most altruistic. In the mainland United States, men had higher altruism scores than women. Thus, cultural factors probably have an enormous influence on altruism.

Recently, however, other research suggests women may be willing to sacrifice more for love than are men. Psychologists have begun to study couples' implicit "marriage contracts"—men and women's unconscious understandings as to what sort of give-and-take is fair. In his book on marriage contracts, for example, Sager (1976, pp. 4–5) observes,

The concept of . . . marriage contracts has proven extremely useful. . . . But what must be emphasized above all is the reciprocal aspect of the contract: What each partner expects to give and receive in exchange are crucial. Contracts deal with every conceivable aspect of family life: relationships with friends, achievements, power, sex, leisure time, money, children, etc.

And researchers have attempted to determine how fair men and women perceive their respective "contracts" to be (Hatfield, Walster, & Traupmann, 1979; Utne et al., in press; Traupmann & Hatfield, in press; Traupmann, Hatfield, & Sprecher, 1982). The researchers contacted dating couples, newlyweds, and elderly couples who had been married for up to 60 years, and asked them how fair they thought their relationships were.

Couples in this series of studies were asked to focus on four possible areas of concern:

1. *Personal concerns:* How attractive were they and their partners? How sociable? Intelligent?
2. *Emotional concerns:* How much love did they express for one another? How much liking, understanding, and acceptance? How much sexual pleasure did they give and get? Were they faithful? How committed to one another? Did they respect their partners' needs for freedom?
3. *Day-to-day concerns:* How much of the day-to-day maintenance of the house did they and their partners do? How about finances? Companionability? Conversation? Decision making? Remembering special occasions? Did they fit in with one another's friends and relatives?
4. *Opportunities gained and lost:* How much did they gain simply from going together or being married? (For example, how much did they appreciate the chance to be married? To be a parent or a grandparent? Having someone to grow old with?) How about opportunities forgone?

After considering all these things, men and women were asked how fair they thought their relationships were. Were they getting more than they felt they deserved? Just what they deserved? Or less than they thought they had coming from their relationships?

Researchers found that regardless of whether couples were dating, newlyweds, or long marrieds, both men and women agreed that the men were getting the best deal. Both men and women agreed that, in general, men contribute less to a marriage than women do and get more out of marriage than do women.

Bernard (1972) provides additional support for the notion that women sacrifice more for love than men do. In her review of the voluminous litera-

· ture contrasting "his marriage" versus "her marriage," she observes a strange paradox. Women are generally thought to be more eager to marry (and marry anyone) than are men. Yet women are the "losers" in marriage. She notes that "being married is about twice as advantageous to men as to women in terms of continued survival" (p. 27). As compared to single men, married men's mental health is far better, their happiness is greater, their earning power is greater, after middle age their health is better, and they live longer. The *opposite* is true for married as compared to single women. For example, all symptoms of psychological distress show up more frequently than expected among married women: nervous breakdowns, nervousness, inertia, insomnia, trembling hands, nightmares, perspiring hands, fainting, headaches, dizziness, and heart palpitations. They show up much less frequently than expected among unmarried women.

These data, then, suggest that, like it or not, women sacrifice the most for love. Perhaps for women, marriage should carry a warning label: "This relationship may be hazardous to your health."

Summary

The evidence, then, makes clear that there is no simple answer to the question "Who is most loving—men or women?" Men tend to have a more romantic view—and a more exploitative view—of love than do women.

When we turn to passionate love, it is women who are the great lovers. Women experience the euphoria and the agony of love more intensely than do men. Yet, for most people, it is probably companionate love that represents "true love" at its best. Here, the evidence is clear. Women love more than they are loved in return. It is unclear who loves most unselfishly, men or women. Most evidence suggests, once again, that it is women who are willing to sacrifice the most for love.

CONCERN WITH SEX

The second type of gender difference that scientists have investigated is in concern with sex. Traditionally, theorists have assumed that sex is far more important for men than for women. According to cultural stereotypes, men are eager for sexual activity; women set limits on such activity (see Chapter 3). Theorists from the sociobiological and cultural-contingency perspectives can agree with this observation. What they disagree about, is *why* such a gender difference exists.

A number of biological determinists, most notably Freud, have argued that biology is destiny, and that interest in sexual activities is determined primarily by genes, hormones, and anatomy. Sociobiologists contend that men and women are genetically programmed to be differentially interested in sexual experience and restraint (see Hagen, 1979; Symons, 1979; Wilson, 1975). They argue that men are genetically programmed to seek out sexual activity; women, to set limits on it.

At the other end of the spectrum are social learning theorists, who argue that sexual behavior is learned (see Bernard, 1972; Byrne & Byrne, 1977; Firestone, 1971; Foucault, 1973; Griffitt & Hatfield, in press; Hatfield & Walster, 1981; Rubin, 1973; Safilios-Rothschild, 1977; Tavris & Offir, 1977). These authors argue that the sociopolitical context determines who is allowed to be sexual and who is forbidden to be, who is punished for violating sexual rules and who is not, and even what kinds of foreplay and sexual positions are considered to be normal. Because this is a male-dominated society, they argue, existing sexual norms meet the needs of men. Men are encouraged to express themselves sexually; women are punished for doing so. The style of intercourse men prefer (for example, the "missionary" position) is considered normal; the activities that women prefer (such as cuddling and cunnilingus) are neglected. No wonder, then, that men find sex in its common forms more appealing than do women.

Regardless of theorists' debates as to *why* men and women may differ in their enthusiasm for sex, they generally agree that men and women *do* differ. But, as we have seen earlier, cultural stereotypes are not always correct. What does research indicate?

In the earliest sex research, scientists found fairly sizable gender differences. In more recent research, researchers find that although gender differences still exist, they are not always so strong as theorists have assumed. Gender differences have begun to narrow, or disappear.

Gender Differences in Liking for Erotica

Early research supported the traditional assumption that men, not women, are interested in erotica (Kinsey, et al., 1948, 1953). Recently, however, researchers have found that there are few, if any, gender differences in response to literary erotica (Veitch & Griffitt, 1980) or to audiotapes of sexual encounters (Heiman, 1977). For Fisher's comprehensive review of research in this area, see Chapter 12.

Willingness to Initiate Sexual Activity

In Kinsey's day, a double standard existed. Men were allowed, if not encouraged, to get sex whenever and wherever they could. Women were supposed to save themselves for marriage. In light of the double standard, it was not surprising that both men and women agreed that men were more likely to initiate sex and that women were more likely to resist sexual advances (see Baker, 1974; Ehrmann, 1959; Kaats & Davis, 1970; Reiss, 1967; Schofield, 1965; Sorensen, 1973).

Recent evidence suggests that traditional standards, although changing, are not yet dead. Contemporary college students reject a sexual double standard (Hopkins, 1977; Komarovsky, 1976; Peplau, Rubin, & Hill, 1976). Yet, this new single standard does not seem to have changed the cultural stereotype of male as sexual initiator and female as limit setter. Even today, it is almost always the man who initiates sexual activity (see Chapter 3). In a recent study of unmarried students, the man was found to have more say than the woman about the type and frequency of sexual activity (Peplau, Rubin, & Hill, 1976) except when a dating couple had decided to abstain from coitus in which case the woman's veto was the major restraining influence (Peplau, Rubin, & Hill, 1977).

Gender Differences in Sexual Experience

There is compelling evidence that men and women are becoming very similar with regard to sexual experience, however.

In the classic studies of sexuality, researchers found that society's double standard influenced sexual experience. For example, Kinsey and his colleagues (1948, 1953) tried to assess how sexually active men were throughout their lives, compared to women. They found that (1) indeed, men did seem to engage in more sexual activity than did women, and (2) men and women had strikingly different sexual histories.

At 18, it was usually the man who pushed to have sex. Kinsey and his associates reported that most men were as sexually expressive at age 15 as they would ever be. In fact, according to Masters and Johnson (1966, 1970) 25 percent of men are impotent by age 65; 50 percent are impotent by age 75.

Women's experience was markedly different. Most women were slow to begin sexual activity. At 15, most women are quite inactive. Sometime between the ages of 16 and 20, they slowly shed their inhibitions and begin to feel more enthusiastic about sexual exploration. They continue their high rates of sexual activity for fully two decades. Not until their late 40s does their sexual behavior begin to ebb.

In commenting on women's sexual histories, Kinsey and his colleagues (1953, pp. 353–354) observed,

> One of the tragedies which appears in a number of the marriages originates in the fact that the male may be most desirous of sexual contact in his early years, while the responses of the females are still underdeveloped and while she is still struggling to free herself from the acquired inhibitions which prevent her from participating freely in the marital

activity. But over the years most females become less inhibited and develop an interest in sexual relations, which they may then maintain until they are in their fifties or even sixties. But by then the responses of the average male may have dropped so considerably that his interest in coitus, and especially in coitus with a wife who has previously objected to the frequencies of his requests, may have sharply declined.

Moreover, the age differential that is common in marriages (the men being older) may contribute to this problem.

Since Kinsey's day, researchers (DeLamater & MacCorquodale, 1979; Ehrmann, 1959; Schofield, 1965; Reiss, 1967; Sorensen, 1973); continued to interview samples of young people about their sexual behavior: Had they ever necked? At what age did they begin? French kissed? Fondled their lover's breasts or genitals? Had their own genitals fondled? Had intercourse? Oral-genital sex? When responses from these studies are compared, we find that indeed, a sexual revolution *is* occurring. In the early studies, in general, men were far more experienced than were women. By the end of the 1970s, these differences had virtually disappeared. As DeLamater and MacCorquodale (1979) observe,

> There are virtually no differences in the incidence of each of the behaviors. Unlike most earlier studies which generally reported lower frequencies of more intimate activities among females, we find that women are as likely as men to have ever engaged in these behaviors. The only exception occurs with coitus, which women . . . are less likely to have experienced. (*Among students*, 75 percent of men and 60 percent of women had had intercourse. *Among nonstudents*, 79 percent of men and 72 percent of women had had intercourse.) [p. 58]

DeLamater and MacCorquodale continue:

> Thus, the gender differences in lifetime behavior which were consistently found in studies conducted in the 1950s and 1960s have narrowed considerably. This is also an important finding; it suggests that those models which have emphasized gender as an explanatory variable are no longer valid. [p. 58]

When men and women are together in a close, loving relationship, they seem equally likely to desire to engage in sexual activity. There is only one type of situation in which scientists find women are still more reserved than men: if men and women are offered a chance to participate in uncertain, unconventional, or downright bizarre sexual activities, men are more willing to take the risk than are women.

For example, in the Clark and Hatfield (1981) study described in Chapter 3, college men and women were hired to approach Florida State University students of the other gender. If a woman requested a date, suggested that the man visit her apartment, or even go to bed with her, she was generally very successful in getting the stranger to agree. Men were generally at ease with such requests. They said such things as "Why do we have to wait until tonight?" or "I can't tonight, but tomorrow would be fine." When a man made such a request, however, he was much less successful. Although the majority of women would date a man who approached her, few would go to his apartment, and none would agree to go to bed with him. Typical responses to males were "You've got to be kidding" or "What's wrong with you? Leave me alone."

Sociobiologists such as Symons (1979) argue that the gender differences Clark and Hatfield describe are genetically "wired in"; that women are genetically programmed to desire one, deeply intimate, secure relationship, while men are programmed to desire anonymous, impersonal, casual sex. Other scientists have documented that, even today, men are more eager to have sex with a variety of partners, in a variety of ways, and so on. (Sociobiologists such as Symons, 1979, would argue that these gender differences too, are "wired in.") For example, Hatfield and her colleagues (in press) interviewed casually dating and newlywed couples about their sexual preferences. They assessed desire for variety via such questions as

1. "I wish my partner were . . . " (Answers range from "Much more unpredictable about *when* he or she wants to have sex," to "Much more predictable about *when* he or she wants to have sex.")
2. "I wish my partner would be . . . " (Answers range from "Much more experimental sexually" to "Much more conventional sexually.")
3. "I wish my partner were . . . " (Answers range from "Much more variable about *where* we have sex" to "Much more conventional about *where* we have sex.")
4. "I wish my partner were . . ." (Answers range from "Much more wild and sexy" to "Much less wild and sexy.")

The authors predicted that men would be more interested in exciting, diverse experiences than women would be. That is exactly what they found. The men wished their sex lives were a little more exciting. Women tended to be slightly more satisfied with the status quo.

In summary, then, recent evidence suggests that, although some gender differences remain in men and women's concern with sex, a sexual revolution *is* occurring. The gender differences we have described—in responsiveness to pornography, willingness to initiate sex, and sexual experience—are rapidly disappearing. Recent studies indicate that women and men are becoming increasingly similar in their sexual preferences and experiences.

DESIRE FOR INTIMACY

The third way in which theorists agree men and women differ is in desire for intimacy. What is intimacy? Intimacy is not a static state, but a *process*. Intimacy may be defined as a process by which a couple—in the expression of thought, emotion, and behavior—attempts to move toward more complete communication on all levels. According to many clinicians, one of the major tasks people face is the achievement of a separate identity while, at the same time, achieving a deeply intimate relationship with others (Erikson, 1968; Kantor & Lehr, 1975; Kaplan, 1978). Both separateness and intimacy are generally considered to be basic human needs (see Freud, 1922; Maslow, 1954). Kaplan suggests that adults spend much of their lives resolving the dilemma between achieving a sense of self while at the same time establishing close nurturant relations with others.

According to family therapists, men have the easiest time achieving an independent identity; women have the easiest time achieving closeness with others. Napier (1977) describes two types of people who seem, with uncanny accuracy, to attract one another. Type I (Usually a woman) is only minimally concerned with maintaining her independence. What she cares about is achieving emotional closeness. She seeks "fusion with the partner," "oneness" or "we-ness" in the marriage. She puts much energy into planning "togetherness" activities. Type I fears rejection and abandonment. She feels rejected when her partner chooses to spend an evening alone, or with other friends. Her feeling of rejection may even extend to times when her partner is engaged in necessarily exclusive activities—such as earning an income, studying for exams, or writing a manuscript.

Type I's partner, Type II (usually a man), is most concerned with maintaining his sense of self and personal freedom and autonomy. He feels a strong need to establish his territory within the common household: to have "my study," "my workshop," "my car." Similarly, he feels compelled to draw sharp lines around psychological space: "my night out," "my career," "my way of handling problems." What he fears is being "suffocated," "stifled," or "engulfed..." or in some manner intruded on by his spouse.

Napier observes that men and women's efforts to reduce their anxieties make matters worse. Women (seeking more closeness) clasp their mates tightly, thereby contributing to the men's anxiety. The men (seeking more distance) retreat further, which increases their wives' panic, inducing further "clasping." Sociobiologists such as Symons (1979) argue that the gender difference Napier describes is genetically "wired in"; that women are genetically programmed to desire one, deeply intimate, secure relationship; men, to desire anonymous, impersonal, casual sex.

Theorists can agree, then, that women are far better at intimacy than are men. Family therapists take it for granted that the fact that women are very comfortable with intimate relationships and men are not is a common cause of marital friction. And there are literally dozens of books exhorting men to share their feelings. Therefore, it is startling that there has been so little research devoted to gender differences in intimacy. Worse yet, it is difficult to draw any conclusions from the research that does exist. If I were forced to guess what future research will reveal, I would guess as follows: Women's complaints that men just won't share their deepest feelings is a legitimate one. In general, women *are* more comfortable with intimacy than are men. But paradoxically, even though women complain about men's lack of intimacy in love relationships, male-female differences are *smallest* in a love affair. Women find it fairly easy to be intimate with their lovers, with men friends, with other women, and with children. Many men can be intimate only with their lovers. It is here that they reveal most of themselves— not as much as their lovers might like, but far more than they share with anyone else. It is most difficult for men to be close to other men.

These are broad conclusions—too broad, perhaps. What are the sparse data on which these overgeneralizations are based? A few social psychologists have explored gender differences in people's willingness to get close to others. Generally, they have defined intimacy as a willingness to disclose one's ideas, feelings, and day-to-day activities to lovers, friends, or strangers, and to listen to their disclosures in return.

Psychologist Sidney Jourard (1964) developed one of the most commonly used measures of intimacy, the Jourard Self-Disclosure Questionnaire (JSDQ). The JSDQ consists of 60 questions in all. It asks people to think about how much they typically disclose to others in six difference areas of life. A few of these items are shown here. Take a look at these items and think about how much you have disclosed to the person you love most. How much has he or she disclosed to you?

Jourard calculates respondents' self-disclosure scores by adding up their scores in each of the six areas. What was your score? What was your partner's score? Were the differences between the two of you typical of those social psychologists find between men and women in general?

In self-disclosure research, four findings have consistently emerged. First, both men and women disclose far more about themselves in intimate than in casual relationships. In casual encounters, most people are willing to reveal only the sketchiest, most stereotyped information about themselves. The Renaissance French essayist Montaigne (quoted in Thomas, 1979) observed that everyone is complex, multifaceted:

> All contradictions may be found in me . . . bashful, insolent; chaste, lascivious; talkative, taciturn; tough, delicate; clever, stupid; surly, affable; lying, truthful; learned, ignorant; liberal, miserly and prodigal: all this I see in myself to some extent according to how I turn. . . . I have nothing to say about myself absolutely, simply and solidly, without confusion and without mixture, or in one word.

In intimate relationships, more of the complexities and contradictions are revealed. In deeply intimate relationships, friends and lovers feel free to reveal far more facets of themselves. As a consequence, intimates share profound information about one another's histories, values, strengths and weaknesses, idiosyncracies, hopes, and fears (Altman & Taylor, 1973; Huesmann & Levinger, 1976; Jourard, 1964; Worthy, Gary, & Kahn, 1969).

Second, in their deeply intimate relationships, men and women often differ little, if at all, in how much they are willing to reveal to one another. For example, Rubin and his colleagues (1980) asked dating couples via the Jourard Self-Disclosure Questionnaire how much they had revealed themselves to their partners. Did they talk about their current relationships? Previous opposite-sex affairs? Their feelings about their parents and friends? Their self-concepts and life views? Their attitudes and interests? Their day-to-day activities? The authors found that, overall, men and women did *not* differ in how much they were willing to confide in their partners.

There was a difference, however, in the *kind* of things men and women were willing to share with those they love. Men were more willing to share their views on politics and their pride in their strengths. Women were more likely to disclose their feelings about other people and their fears. Interestingly enough, Rubin and his colleagues found that the stereotyped form of communication is most common in traditional men and women.

Some authors have observed that neither men or women may be getting exactly the amount of intimacy they would like. Women may want more intimacy than they are getting; men may want far less. There is evidence that couples tend to negotiate a level of self-disclosure that is bearable to both. In the words of the movie *My Fair Lady*, this ensures that "*neither* really gets what either really wants at all" (Chaikin & Derlega, 1975).

Third, in less intimate relationships, women disclose far more to others than do men (Jourard, 1971; Cozby, 1973). Rubin and his colleagues (1980, p. 306) point out that "The basis for such differences appears to be in socialization practices. Whereas women in our culture have traditionally been encouraged to show their feelings, men have been taught to hide their feel-

---

The Jourard Self-Disclosure Questionnaire

0 = Have told my friend nothing about this aspect of me.

1 = Have talked in general terms about this item. My friend has only a general idea about this aspect of me.

2 = Have talked in full and complete detail about this aspect; my friend could describe me accurately.

Attitudes and Opinions

1. What I think and feel about religion; my personal religious views _____

2. My views on the present government—the president, government, policies, etc. _____

3. My personal views on sexual morality—how I feel and how others ought to behave in sexual matters _____

Tastes and Interests

1. My favorite food, the ways I like food prepared, and my food dislikes _____

2. The kind of party, or social gathering I like best, and the kind that would bore me, or that I wouldn't enjoy _____

Work (or studies)

1. What I find to be the worst pressures and the strains in my work _____

2. What I feel are my special strong points and qualifications for my work _____

3. What I feel are my shortcomings and handicaps that prevent me from working as I'd like to, or that prevent me from getting further ahead in my work _____

---

ings and to avoid displays of weakness (Pleck & Sawyer, 1974). As Kate Millett (1975) has put it: "Women express, men repress." The authors argue that it is traditional men and women who differ most on emotional sharing. They discovered that more egalitarian couples were more likely to disclose themselves fully to one another.

Fourth, and last, women receive more disclosures than do men. This is not surprising in view of the fact that the amount of information people

Money

1. How much money I make at my work, or get as an allowance _____

2. My most pressing need for money right now; e.g., outstanding bills, some major purchase that is desired or needed _____

3. My total financial worth, including property, savings, bonds, insurance, etc. _____

Personality

1. What feelings, if any, that I have trouble expressing or controlling _____

2. The aspects of my personality that I dislike, worry about, that I regard as a handicap to me _____

3. Things in the past or present that I feel ashamed and guilty about _____

4. The kinds of things that make me just furious _____

5. The kinds of things that make me especially proud of myself, elated, full of self-esteem or self-respect _____

Body

1. How I wish I looked: my ideas for overall appearance _____

2. Any problems or worries that I had with my appearance in the past _____

3. My feelings about different parts of my body—legs, hips, waist, weight, chest or bust, etc. _____

SOURCE: Jourard, S. M. *The transparent self* rev. ed. Copyright © 1971 by Litton Educational Publishing, Inc. Reprinted by permission of Wadsworth Publishing Company, Belmont, Calif. 94002.

reveal to others has an enormous impact on the amount of information they receive in return (see Altman, 1973; Davis & Skinner, 1974; Jourard, 1964; Jourard & Friedman, 1970; Marlatt, 1971; Rubin, 1975; Worthy, Gary, & Kahn, 1969).

There does seem to be some evidence, then, that women feel slightly more comfortable with intense intimacy in their love relationships than do men, and are far more comfortable revealing themselves in more casual relationships than are men. Tradition dictates that women should be the "intimacy experts." And today, women *are* more comfortable sharing their ideas, feelings, and behavior than are men. But what happens if this situation changes? Rubin and his colleagues (1980) suggest that such changes have already begun.

The prognosis is mixed. Young women usually say they would be delighted if the men they love could be intimate. I'm a bit skeptical that it will be this easy. Change is always difficult. More than one man has complained that when he finally dared to reveal his weaker aspects to a woman, he soon discovered that she was shocked by his lack of "manliness." Family therapists such as Napier (1977) have warned us that the struggle to find individuality *and* closeness is a problem for everyone. As long as men were fleeing from intimacy, women could safely pursue them. Now that men are turning around to face them, women may well find themselves taking flight. In any case, the confrontation is likely to be exciting.

And the change should have real benefit. As Rubin and his colleagues (1980, p. 316) observe,

> Men and women should have the freedom to decide for themselves when they will reveal themselves—and when they will listen to another's revelations. "Full disclosure" need not be so full that it eliminates all areas of privacy, even within the most intimate relationships . . . [given that] we believe the ethic of openness is a desirable one. Especially when contemplating marriage, it is valuable for women and men to be able to share rather fully—and equally—their thoughts and feelings about themselves, each other, and their relationship. . . . It is encouraging to discover that a large majority of the college students we studied seem to have moved, even if incompletely, and sometimes uneasily, toward the ethic of openness.

There is one final way in which theorists have speculated that men and women may differ—in their desire to flow with the moment versus to dominate, to achieve.

DESIRE FOR CONTROL

Traditionally, men are supposed to control themselves, other people, and the environment. The ideal man carefully controls his thoughts. He is objective, logical, and unemotional. He hides his feelings, or if he does express any feelings, he carefully telescopes the complex array of human feelings into a single emotion: anger. Men are supposed to be dominant; women, to be submissive. A "real man" is even supposed to control the environment by taming nature.

In contrast with the ideal man, the ideal woman is supposed to be emotional and responsive to other people and the environment. The ideal woman is expressive and warm. She shares herself openly with others but is, at the same time, highly vulnerable to their disapproval. Comfortable expressing a rainbow of feminine feelings—love, anxiety, joy, and depression—she is less in touch with anger. Tears and smiles come easily; anger is an alien emotion. A "real woman" is regarded as somewhat like a child; she is attractive and caring but not independent or competent.

There is considerable evidence that, even today, most men and women hold these stereotypes. Inge Broverman and her colleagues (1972) asked people what men and women *should be* like and what they really *are* like. The answer was clear: "women are expressive and nurturant; men are in control and instrumental."

What is the purpose of all this male control? Achievement. Some people, usually men, view intimate relations—the one place where people can be themselves, totally relaxed, confident that they will be accepted no matter what, a place for exploring the possibilities of life—as yet another arena for achievement. In reviewing male sexual myths, Zilbergeld (1978) observed that, even in their most intimate relationships, men are more goal oriented than women (see Radlove's description of Zilbergeld's work in Chapter 4). In summary, he concludes that "In sex, as elsewhere, it's performance that counts" (p. 35).

According to theorists, then, there are marked gender differences in three areas: (1) desire to be "in control"; (2) desire to dominate their partners or submit to them, and (3) desire to "achieve" in their love and sexual relations.

Unfortunately, although a great deal has been written about these topics, there is almost no research documenting that these differences do in fact exist. Let us review what scientists do know.

Desire to Be in Control

As I said in the previous section, it appears that even in love relationships, men are more concerned than women about possessing and expressing appropriate thoughts, feelings, and behaviors. It is especially difficult for men to acknowledge their weaknesses.

Desire to Dominate or Submit to Others

Sociobiologists have argued that gender differences in dominance-submission are genetically "wired in." Males can ensure the survival of their genes by dominating women; women, by submitting to one man.

There is little evidence, however, to support such a contention. The only study relevant to this issue examined gender differences in the desire for dominance-submission on couple's intimate sexual encounters (Hatfield et al., 1981). The study reviewed a number of reasons why men's and women's desires might differ.

Most men and women accept traditional roles. They believe that men and women ought to be very different: men "should" be dominant; women "should" be submissive (Broverman et al., 1972). In fact, however, men and women are surprisingly similar in dominance-submission (Maccoby & Jacklin, 1974). Thus, perhaps both men and women secretly fear they do not "measure up." Men may worry that they're not sufficiently "masculine"—they may feel compelled to exaggerate their "macho" image, to deny any hint of weakness. They want their partners to be as submissive as possible. Women, worried about their "femininity," may wish to deny any hint of strength; they may want their partners to be "real men," dominant and strong. If such a dynamic is operating, men might be expected to wish secretly that their partners would be more feminine, women, to wish their mates would be more dominant.

That's one possibility, but there is another. Gender roles are limiting. Modern men and women may secretly wish that they could express themselves more honestly, but they may be afraid to do so. Some men may want to express their submissive side, and some women may want to express their dominant side in sexual relations. Some theorists have argued that men, forced to be more dominant than they wish to be in their daily activities, are especially attracted to masochistic sexual experiences (Gibson, 1978; Green & Green, 1973; Kamiat, 1936; Krafft-Ebing, 1903/1939). According to this same logic, we might expect women to find sadism equally appealing. Few theorists, however, have ever suggested that they do (Robertiello, 1970; for an exception to this statement, see Stoller, 1978). According to this reasoning, then, we might expect to find that *both* men and women wish their sexual repertoires could be expanded—men wishing their partners would some-times take the lead, women wishing their partners would sometimes behave more submissively.

To determine which, if either, of these possibilities is true, I and my colleagues (Hatfield et al., 1981) asked dating and newlywed couples how they *wished* things were in their sexual relationships. We measured men and women's desire for dominance submission via such questions as

1. "During sex, I wish my partner would . . . " (Answers range from "Give many more instructions and requests" to "Give many less instructions and requests.")
2. "I wish my partner was . . . " (Answers range from "Much more willing to do what I want sexually" to "Much less willing to do what I want sexually.")

3. "I wish my partner would play . . . " (Answers range from "The dominant role in sex much more" to "The dominant role in sex much less.")
4. "I wish my partner would play . . . " (Answers range from "The submissive role in sex much more" to "The submissive role in sex much less.")

When we examined men and women's reactions to these items, a surprising result emerged: there is no evidence that couples wish men could be more dominant and women could be more submissive—nor any evidence that they wish they could be more androgynous in their sexual lives. What *do* the data show? Interviews suggested two surprising conclusions. First, as family therapists have noted, couples seem to have a communication problem. Both men and women wish *their partners* would be a little clearer about what they want sexually, but these same men and women are evidently reluctant to say what *they* want. Second, in general, if anything, *both* men and women wish their partners would be more assertive about what they want sexually. Of the two, men are the more eager for their partners to take an active role. Evidently, in spite of some therapists' concerns (see Chapter 3), women have not yet become so dominant and demanding that they frighten men away.

Desire to Achieve in Love and Sex

It is fascinating to speculate about the effects that such gender differences, if they exist, would have on love and sexual relations. Are most men so concerned about acquiring an impressive reputation that, if they had a choice between having a warm, wonderful, sexual encounter and having a reputation of being the world's greatest lover, they would choose the latter? Is women's definition of a "good lover" someone who is loving, tender, and intimate? Do the very men who are most eager to succeed at being "a great lover" focus on "achievements" that women care little about—the objective facts of a sexual encounter such as the size of their partners' breasts, length of their own penises, the number of their conquests, how long they last sexually, and the number of their orgasms? These are interesting speculations, but no one has conducted research on these questions.

In summary, men are more concerned than women about being in control, dominating others, and achieving at love according to the theorists. However, empirical research is needed to determine whether these theoretical speculations are accurate.

CONCLUSIONS

In this chapter, I have explored what is known about gender differences in four areas: love, sex, intimacy, and control. Many theorists have seen men and women as very different—to the point of almost being incompatible. A consideration of the evidence, however, indicates that nature has arranged things more sensibly. Men and women are surprisingly similar in what they want out of their most intimate relations. Everyone, male *and* female, wants love *and* sex, intimacy *and* control. Yet, if one is determined, one can detect some slight differences between the genders. Women may be slightly more concerned with love; men, with sex. Women may be somewhat more eager for a deeply intimate relationship than are men. Men may be a little more eager to be in control of things, perhaps to dominate their partners, to "achieve" at love than are women. This last contention is badly in need of research: the available research clearly indicates far greater similarities than differences in the feelings of men and women about sex and love.

6 Sexuality and Gender Roles in the Second Half of Life

A. R. ALLGEIER

Our life span perspective of the interaction of the changing boundaries of gender roles and sexual behavior culminates with Rick Allgeier's examination of sexual expression between older people who are generally beyond the responsibilities involved in reproduction. A consideration of the sexual expression of the aging could have been the opening chapter of this book. As Allgeier points out, North Americans are exploring sexuality beyond its reproductive function for its recreational value and for enhancing egalitarian intimacy. In that exploration, knowledge of the sexual lives of the elderly may provide younger people with very helpful information.

Allgeier begins his consideration of the impact of aging on sexual expression by noting that an increasingly large proportion of the population consists of people in their fifth decade and beyond. There has been a corresponding increase in concern for the quality of aged people's lives. Examining the quality of their sexual lives is a very recent phenomenon, however.

Aging does carry with it some inevitable physical changes, and the effects of these changes on sexual response are described in this chapter. Allgeier devotes most of his attention to the effect of beliefs about aging on the way in which we view ourselves once we've aged beyond the first few decades of life. One factor that interacts heavily with gender-role stereotypes is the double standard of aging. Men are seen as retaining their attractiveness or even increasing it if they have managed to accumulate a certain amount of power. In contrast, women beyond their reproductive years just get old—or, at least, that is the stereotype. Allgeier suggests that the extreme youth orientation that characterizes our culture may be particularly damaging for women's self-esteem and sexual enjoyment. He also describes the phenomenon of midlife transition and its relationship to gender-role expectations, and

135

reviews research on the impact on men versus women of various life span events, including retirement and the death of a spouse.

In the final section of the chapter, Allgeier provides a very positive picture of the possible models that aging people can offer. After retirement, they are freed of the constraints of occupational, reproductive, and parental pressures. Thus, aging people may finally be able to escape from the constricted kinds of interactions that engulf adolescents and young adults who are bound by strong expectations of what it means to be a man or a woman in North American culture, as was described in Chapters 2 and 3. As Allgeier points out, we are badly in need of more research on the sexual patterns that characterize the lives of the elderly. The currently available research demonstrates two things, however. First, couples beyond the middle of life remain physically capable of all of the aspects of sexual expression that were theirs in their youth. And some of the elderly are enjoying mutually satisfying sexual intimacy to a greater extent than they did when younger.

 People in the United States have had a strong investment in the perception of themselves and their country as youthful—and for most of their history this perception has been accurate. When the first U.S. census was taken in 1790, half the people in the country were 16 years old or younger. As recently as 1970, the median age was under 28. By the year 2000, it is expected that the median age will reach 35 and, within about 30 years from that date, will approach 40. Over the same time span, the number of people over 65 will more than double to about 52 million beings—close to one out of every five U.S. citizens.

This "graying of America" will dramatically affect the social and psychological climate of the United States. For better or worse, the changes created by this gradual shift in the age of our citizens are unavoidable. Indeed, some changes are already apparent, such as increased pressure on Florida politicians from their elderly constituents and increased funding for research on aging. Advertisers, in their continual vigilant survey of the consumer population, have already started to gear up for America's aging. The models representing the Pepsi generation have broken out in wrinkles, sagging tummies, and eyeglasses.

A prime force behind this shift is the postwar baby boom. In the decade after World War II, 43 million babies were born—about one-fifth of the present population. This was followed by a dramatic drop in the total fertility rate, from a postwar high of 3.8 children per woman in 1957 to 1.8 in 1976. The children of the baby boom crowded the schools in the 1950s and 1960s and flooded the job market in the 1970s. In the next two decades, they will constitute a middle-aged bulge in the population, swelling the 35- to 44-year-old group from 23 million in 1977 to about 41 million by the year 2000.

It is somewhat ironic that the young of the 1960s thought they could change the institutional basis of society and create a different set of values. They still may very well change our society in a fundamental way—but from their leverage as the aged rather than from the zeal of their youth.

AGING AND SEXUALITY

This chapter is concerned with the meaning of sexuality and gender roles in the second half of life. It is based primarily on those individuals who are heterosexual whites and who have been married one or more times. The major reason for this limitation is that most research in this area has used this population.

Biological Changes

As we shall see, sexual activity among people during middle and old age varies greatly. However, the organs associated with sexuality unavoidably age, regardless of how often we use those organs. The onset of the noticeable effects of changes in our bodies may vary, but sooner or later they must be dealt with and incorporated into our sexual self-image. A good deal of our knowledge about aging and sexuality comes from the work of Masters and Johnson (1966). They studied 61 women whose ages ranged from 41 to 78, and 39 men between the ages of 51 and 87. These volunteers were observed in an effort to understand the physical changes in sexuality during the aging process.

Male aging   As men age, the size and firmness of their testicles diminish. During sexual excitement, the testicles do not lift upward toward the body as markedly. The threadlike structures within the testes (seminiferous tubules) that produce sperm thicken and sperm production is gradually reduced. Normal sperm, however, may be produced even after potency is lost (Stokes, 1951). The semen becomes thinner and is not expelled as forcefully. The prostate gland, whose secretions account for much of the seminal fluid, often enlarges, and its contractions during orgasm are weaker. The secretion of male sex hormones dwindles steadily from 30 to the age of 60 and then remains fairly constant.

Also, the phases of the sexual response cycle appear to lengthen, particularly after age 60. According to Masters and Johnson (1966), it takes longer periods of stimulation to produce erection. Pelvic thrusting and ejaculation diminish in intensity, and there is an increase in the time after orgasm during which the male is unable to respond to sexual stimulation. "The psychosexual pleasure of the ejaculatory process may be impaired . . . the young male . . . is aware not only of the force of the explosive contractions but also of the localized sensation of fluid emission . . . the aging male, particularly if his erection has been long maintained, may have the experience of seepage rather than of seminal fluid expulsion" (Masters & Johnson, 1966, p. 259).

Female aging The most obvious and dramatic sign of aging in females is menopause. The reduction in hormone secretion that occurs at "change of life" can produce a number of physical symptoms. Headaches, dizziness, heart palpitations, and pains in the joints are often related to hormone imbalances during this period.

Perhaps the best known symptom of menopause is the "hot flash", caused by an irregular fluctuation in the blood vessels. This fluctuation permits more blood to flow at one time, resulting in the feeling of waves of heat spreading over the face and upper half of the body. The hot flash usually lasts for a few seconds or longer and may be followed by chills or perspiration. Some of these symptoms affect about three out of every four women to some degree. However, only about 10 percent of those affected are inconvenienced by these problems (Katchadourian & Lunde, 1980).

The postmenopausal woman experiences marked changes in her genitals. The vaginal walls lose their thick, corrugated texture and elasticity and become very thin, with a pale complexion. In this state, they do not give adequate protection to the bladder during sexual intercourse. This lack can result in discomfort following sexual intercourse, which is often experienced as a burning sensation during urination. The uterus or womb experiences a gradual shrinking and becomes less involved in sexual response. The breasts also experience some shrinking of tissue.

The rate and production of vaginal lubrication generally diminishes in most women. Some women, however, are lucky exceptions (Masters & Johnson, 1966). Specifically, women who are consistently sexually active, having coitus once or twice weekly, show no reduction in lubrication. In any event, older women may continue to experience sexual pleasure, as the clitoris seems relatively unaffected by age. Its response to sexual stimulation remains relatively unchanged even in very old age.

Physical Problems Associated with Aging

As our bodies age, we become more susceptible to a variety of ailments that can affect sexual behavior. It is important for individuals who wish to engage in erotic activity to be aware of the effects of physical impairments on their sexuality so that they can modify their lovemaking techniques when necessary. Because so much of the writing on sexuality has stressed the psychological aspects of sexual behavior, some individuals may feel that a change in their sexual feelings is somehow due to a "mental" problem rather than to a physical condition. It is particularly important for elderly people to rule out physical problems before examining psychological reasons for abrupt changes in their erotic feelings and behavior. In the following section, some of the more common problems encountered in middle and old age are reviewed.

Prostate Problems   An increase in the number of cells of the prostate gland (prostatic hyperplasia) resulting in the enlargement of that organ occurs in many men over 60 years of age. This benign form of the disease is usually treated by chemotherapy or minor surgery. Potency is often maintained after treatment. Prostatic surgery may affect potency, however, if major surgery is involved, which is usually the case with a malignancy of the prostate gland.

Diabetes   Diabetes, a hormone disorder, can impair sexual functioning in men. Over half of 200 diabetic men were unable to become erect in one study (Weiss, 1973). The difficulty with erection is thought to be the result of a disorder involving the nerve fibers that supply the penis and bladder. The problem usually disappears when control of the diabetes is established. The effects of diabetes on the sexuality of women is not known.

Vascular illness   Vascular disease is another problem for the sexuality of the aging male. A high volume of blood flow is necessary for erection. Blocking of the arteries or their tributaries to the external genitals may result in problems in producing erection. Individuals who have suffered heart attacks or strokes may fear sexual activity because it produces increases in blood pressure, heart rate, and stress on the cardiovascular system. The severity of the damage to the cardiovascular system will determine the limits of exertion during sexual activity. In most cases, though, vascular illnesses do not impose a permanent ban on sexual expression.

In the case of hypertension and recovery from a heart attack, the individual is usually encouraged to practice minimal exertion during sexual activity and to rest after coitus. One study (Weinstein & Como, 1980) found that higher levels of information about the heart and sexual functioning were associated with lower anxiety about sexual activity following a coronary. The ways in which these problems affect females have not been reported in any detail. This lack of information concerning the relationships of women's sexual response to diseases that occur primarily in the second half of life probably reflects a general social bias. That is, scientists may not have considered the sexual response of women who have lost their reproductive capacity to be of much importance.

Many other diseases and disabilities can affect sexual expression. It is important to stress, in relation to all of these problems, that if sexual intercourse is impaired by infirmity, other sex-related needs continue to persist. Closeness, sensuality, and being valued as a man or woman do not depend on an erect penis or a lubricating vagina.

Hysterectomy   Many early attempts to account for sexual behavior used biological explanations and were often used to justify the status quo. It was argued that biological factors could not be changed. Therefore, there was little to do but accept one's fate. Today the predominant view is that sexual behavior is relatively plastic; that is, it can be molded in many directions, depending on the particular social environment.

This view has helped to overturn outmoded theories that sexuality is the mere summation of biological drives. However, it tends to oversimplify the complex interaction between biological, psychological, and social systems in producing sexual behavior. This overreliance on psychological and social variables to explain sexual behavior has some potentially damaging implications.

An interesting example of this point is our current view of the relationship between sexuality and hysterectomy. It is estimated that half of all women in the United States will have a hysterectomy by the age of 65 if this type of surgery continues at its present rate (Morgan, 1978). A hysterectomy involves removal of the uterus and usually the cervix. Women frequently make the decision to have a hysterectomy and often an ovariectomy (removal of the ovaries) after being told that such surgery will not change their sexual responses. Morgan (1978) has outlined the potentially harmful effects of this assertion for women who *do* experience problems. In a hysterectomy, hormonal levels are not altered, because the ovaries remain intact. But sexuality *can* be affected, because the uterus is involved during sexual arousal (see Chapter 4). During the excitement phase, blood flow increases to the entire pelvic area; this vasocongestion is felt as arousal. Removal of the uterus leaves less tissue to be aroused. Obviously, there can be no elevation of the uterus. During this phase, the vagina can increase in diameter by as much as three inches and in length by as much as an inch. The scar tissue replacing the cervix is inelastic, however, preventing full ballooning of the vagina.

The plateau phase involves further elevation and ballooning, with the uterus increasing to as much as twice its normal size. This additional sexual tension will not be felt by a woman after hysterectomy. During orgasm, the uterus contracts. The more intense the orgasm, the stronger are the contractions. After hysterectomy, orgasms may not reach their previous intensity.

Finally, in the resolution phase, some females can attain additional orgasms if they maintain sexual tension. There is less vasocongestion after hysterectomy, though, which makes multiple orgasms less probable.

Thus, a number of physical and emotional changes can affect sexuality after hysterectomy. Perhaps the most reasonable summary comes from The Boston Women's Health Book Collective, in *Our Bodies, Ourselves* (1976): "For women whose uteruses have an active role in their sexual response, a hysterectomy may affect sexual sensations" (p. 149). It is important to understand the possible effects of hysterectomy on sexuality so as to be prepared to deal with any changes in sexual response. Even more importantly, this knowledge can keep people from blaming changes in sexuality following hysterectomy on psychological problems or conflicts. The problem may not be just in the head.

Sexuality and Health

A number of writers have commented on the contribution of an active sexual life to general health. Sexual activity may have beneficial effects in relieving the pain of arthritis by boosting cortisone levels in the blood (Butler & Lewis, 1973). Sexual dysfunction or decreased sexuality is linked with an increase in suicide among the aged (Leviton, 1973). Depression—a not unusual affective state in the aged—is manifested by reduced sexual interest and activity (Beck, 1968). Generalizing from animal research, Verwoerdt (1976) suggests that continued sexual activity is associated with or may contribute to increased longevity and that maintained sexual activity is positively related to continued vigor. Sexuality can be a drug-free treatment for insomnia (Butler & Lewis, 1973). And sexual activity may also be useful in relieving anxiety states.

Of the various systems within the body, sexual function has a relatively low status, because it does not appear essential for the individual's life or health. When the body is under attack from physical and/or psychological stress, sexual functioning may be sacrificed to foster the systems that are more important for survival or health (Schumacher & Lloyd, 1981). An abrupt change or diminishing of sexual functioning may be an early warning that the body is being threatened by illness or psychological threat. For instance, one study of 131 male patients (Wabrek & Burchell, 1980) who had suffered heart attacks found that two-thirds of them reported significant sexual problems *before* they suffered the heart attack. Of these men, 64 percent had difficulties achieving or maintaining an erection, 28 percent reported a more than 50 percent decrease in frequency of sexual activity, and 8 percent had ejaculation problems. Thus, sexual functioning may be a rough indicator of the general state of bodily health.

Beyond the physiological effects, sexual activity during the second half of life would appear, intuitively, to be related to a sense of well-being. That is, to the extent that sexuality can fulfill the needs for human contact, caring, and love, it should contribute to a state of general health. We now need to move beyond such intuitive and logical speculations toward research.

Aging and Sexual Behavior

In this section, the relationship between aging and sexual activity is examined. Then I review some of the major social events and challenges faced by people in the second half of life.

Male sexual behavior   The average human man's sexual responsiveness diminishes as he ages. Kinsey, Pomeroy, & Martin (1948) found no factor that affected the frequency of sexual outlet as much as age did. They defined "total sexual outlet" in terms of six sources of orgasm: masturbation, nocturnal emissions, heterosexual petting, heterosexual intercourse, homosexual relations, and intercourse with animals. They reported that the median frequency of orgasm per week from all of these sources reaches a peak in the late teens and then drops regularly until age 60. Kinsey felt that he did not have enough data on men over 60 to permit generalizations. Perhaps the most noticeable characteristic of the waning of sexuality in males is its gradualness. That is, the decrease in sexual expression from one age to another (as measured in five-year intervals) is steady—there is no specific age at which there is a dramatic reduction (Botwinick, 1978).

Kinsey and his colleagues (1948) found that frequencies of sexual expression were 3.3 per week at age 20, with relatively little change to age 30. By age 40, the average was two per week. The frequency of sexual expression declined even further to 0.8 per week by age 60 and 0.2 per week by age 75. Married men reported more frequent sexual activity in their teens than did single men (4.8 versus 3.2 per week), but this difference leveled out; both groups were comparable by age 50.

Female sexual behavior   Because of the greater cultural restrictions on female sexuality, it is more difficult to assess women's sexual functioning over the life cycle. In addition, much sexual activity of women does not result in orgasm, while men rarely fail to reach orgasm in their sexual activities. This difference is probably related to societal prohibitions.

Kinsey's data (Kinsey et al., 1953) indicated that the frequency of total sexual outlet for single women, as measured by median frequency of orgasm per week, was about 0.3 at 20. At ages 40 and 50, the frequencies were around 0.5, and at age 55 it was 0.35. For married females, the median frequency at age 20 was 2 per week. The frequency of orgasm declined to 1.5 per week at 35 and to 0.8 per week at age 50. At age 55, it was 0.6 per week.

Kinsey and his colleagues felt that the best index of female sexuality was frequency of masturbation. Because of the social restrictions on nonmarried women and the decline over time in marital intercourse (which Kinsey thought was largely due to husbands), he felt that autoeroticism was a more accurate longitudinal measure. Using this standard, he and his colleagues found little evidence for diminishing sexuality in women at least until late in life. Rates of masturbation for women declined only slightly with age.

Some evidence, however, shows that there is a reduction in the sexual activity of women as well as in men, but that it appears later in life (Christenson & Gagnon, 1965). Among women aged 50 to 70, masturbation showed a gradual decline over this 20-year period. Of some interest is the comparison of masturbation frequencies between (1) married and (2) divorced or widowed women. The latter masturbated at nearly twice the frequency of the former. This suggests that women who are deprived of coitus because they lack partners rely more heavily on masturbation as a sexual outlet.

Variation in behavior   On most social, psychological, and biological measures, significantly greater variations exist among the scores of older groups of individuals than among those who are younger. Increased variation rather than increased similarity seems to occur with advanced age (Maddox & Douglas, 1974). For instance, there is greater variation in intelligence test scores among older groups than among younger groups of people. Sexuality is no exception to this general rule. Although sexual activity progressively declines with advanced age, large differences in sexual capacity and performance exist among older people. The capacity for sexual intercourse is found among 70-, 80-, and 90-year-old individuals (Kinsey, Pomeroy, & Martin, 1948; Pfeiffer, Verwoerdt, & Wang, 1968; Verwoerdt, Pfeiffer, & Wang, 1969). In general, the frequency of women's sexual activity is much more variable than is the frequency of men's sexual activity. The Kinsey data revealed that the average man is sexually active more frequently than is the average woman. However, 1 percent of single females aged 16 to 30 reported having 7 to 29 orgasms per week. A little less than 1 percent of single females from age 46 to 50 reported having 7 to 18 orgasms per week. A slightly higher percentage of married women reported these frequencies in their respective age groups than did their unmarried counterparts.

More recently, investigators at Duke University studied 260 older female and male volunteers over a nine-year period. The volunteers ranged in age from 60 to 94. Intercourse declined more than 50 percent during the early 60s and an additional 10 to 20 percent after age 80 (Pfeiffer, Verwoerdt, & Wang, 1968; Verwoerdt, Pfeiffer, & Wang, 1969). When married and unmarried women were compared, there was little difference in reports of sexual interest. However, married women engaged in more sexual activity. Obviously, lack of partners is a major reason for diminished sexual activity among aging women. This issue, discussed in detail later in this chapter, is particularly problematic, because women now outlive men by an average of eight years.

One factor that does seem to be related to continued sexual activity in old age is previous behavior. High rates of sexual activity in old age have usually been preceded by high rates of sexual activity in early adulthood and middle age (Newman & Nichols, 1960). The North American stereotype of the sexless older person is inaccurate. Sexy young people mature into sexy middle-aged and elderly people. The sexually disinterested elderly person was probably not very enthusiastic about sex in youth.

Although the decline in sexuality is more apparent in men than in women, the sexual activities of men, for various reasons, are more frequent than those of women throughout the life span. Given the double standard of sexuality, which was much more evident when Kinsey's data were collected, it is not surprising to find this difference. As noted, the other imposing obstacle to sexual expression for heterosexual women in late middle age and old age is the scarcity of men. This obstacle is dramatically reflected if you look at people 65 or older. In this group, there are about 75 men to 100 women. In 1970, older bridegrooms outnumbered older brides two to one. Among unmarried older people, there are about 50 men to every 100 women. Of the 31,000 older men who married in 1970, 59 percent married women under the age of 65. The imbalance is dramatically reflected in the marriage rates: 15.6 marriages per 1,000 men per year for men over 65, and 2.4 per 1,000 per year for women over 65 (Troll et al., 1979).

Habituation, novelty, and midlife transition   The term *midlife crisis* has become increasingly popular in our culture. Basically, it refers to dissatisfaction with one's current and/or past life style. It can occur anywhere between age 30 and age 60. In terms of sexuality, people experiencing midlife crisis may seek new partners in the attempt to resolve their dissatisfaction.

The middle-aged man who searches for comfort in the companionship of a young woman has been a standard image in our culture. What has become more visible recently is the increased sexual activity of middle-aged women. The frequency of extramarital sex for women is now approaching that for men (Hunt, 1974). Like men, women often begin affairs when they enter their mid-30s, seeking passion, reaffirmation of their sexual attractiveness, and the rollercoaster of courtship and love (Wolfe, 1975). New relationships provide a novelty and risk that make life and our feelings more vivid. Excitement, joy, and fear color the canvas of courtship. Relationships that are not yet stable are attractive because their very precariousness produces romance and obsession, which push to the background the more mundane demands of a long-term relationship. Issues such as who pays the bills, feeds the dog, or takes responsibility for the dozen of other minor but necessary chores that encumber our lives become unimportant within the risk and unpredictability of a beginning relationship.

Tripp (1971) asserts that compatibility and commitment in a monogamous* relationship dull eroticism because heightened sexual feelings require tension and resistance between the partners. Monogamous relationships are perhaps the most difficult of all human contracts, because they are expected to satisfy so many of the varied needs of the individuals involved. The needs for passion, security, and play, to name a few, are channeled into this relationship. Most marriages overloaded by these needs are also buffeted by the problems of children, jobs, and paying bills. Slowly and often imperceptibly, these relationships drift toward "friendly, unpassionate companionable security" (Bardwick, 1979, pg. 93). As the relationship habituates over time, the partners are limited to a constricted range of experience. It is difficult to maintain the excitement of a relationship when enmeshed in the rituals of security.

Troll and Smith (1976) have postulated that there is a fundamental relationship between attraction and attachment. Attraction is high in the beginning of a new relationship, but attachment is low. Over the years, attraction wanes as novelty wanes, but attachment may increase (see Chapter 5). If marital satisfaction or happiness is measured in terms of attraction, a steady decrease over time would be inevitable. There may be a temporary rise when the children leave, creating a new situation for husband and wife.

Perhaps the most dramatic change that has occurred in the pattern of the typical family life cycle is the increase in the length of the "empty nest" period in this century. This term refers to the period of time after children are raised and have left their parents' home. The increase from 2 years to 30 years (Glick, 1977) is largely a consequence of rising survival rates. Among the many implications of this increase is that there is a longer period in which husbands and wives live together in the absence of children. This situation has the potential for developing either a more harmonious or a more discordant relationship between the two.

Retirement and death of a spouse   Research on the effects of retirement on marriage has centered primarily on the division of household tasks (Kerckhoff, 1972) and concomitant changes in gender-role differentiation (Lipman, 1961). Generally, there is a shift away from expressive behavior by the wife to mutually expressive behavior. That is, the husband shifts from the instrumental role of provider to the more expressive role of helping in the house. His wife moves from a relatively less expressive homemaker to a more expressive, loving, and understanding role. Whether the retired husband who shares in household tasks is comfortable about these activities probably de-

---

*Restricting sexual expression to one's marital partner.

pends on his value system. If he considers "woman's work" demeaning, then he will probably feel devalued if he engages in it (see Chapter 7).

Fengler (1975) classified women into three categories based on their attitudes toward their husbands' retirement: optimists (39 percent), neutralists (29 percent), and pessimists (32 percent). The optimists saw retirement as the opportunity for a different life together based on more companionship and shared activities. The neutralists felt that retirement would have little effect on their marriage. The pessimists feared intrusion into their domestic domain by husbands who would have too much time on their hands.

There is little information on how retirement affects sexuality. It certainly creates the possibility for more erotic spontaneity, because leisure time increases. Patterns of sexuality, however, probably remain relatively unchanged after retirement. As noted earlier, the frequency of sexual activity in old age is related to previous levels of sexual expression during early adulthood and middle age. This area is certainly open to investigation and is one in which the retirement of women and men should be examined. It would seem that the more one's gender-role identity and sexuality are tied into notions of reproduction, the more difficult it would be to continue or maintain eroticism.

The death of a spouse is often more traumatic for men than for women, according to assessments of morale and psychological symptoms (Lowenthal et al., 1967). Men also seem to have more difficulty adjusting to divorce than women do (Chiriboga & Cutler, 1977). This finding may be related to the reports that men name their wives as confidantes far more often than women name their husbands as intimates. Beyond underscoring differences in the concept of a close relationship between men and women (see Chapter 5), Lowenthal and her colleagues (1967, 1975) found that men are less likely to have people other than their wives to whom they feel close or intimate. This situation may create greater trauma for men than women when marriage ends due to death or divorce.

Because of the gender differences in mortality rates, heterosexual widows have a hard time finding partners. As pointed out earlier, among unmarried older people there were 50 men to every 100 women in 1970. In lieu of trying to establish a polygynous* relationship or altering one's sexual preference, half of these unmarried women are left with the alternative of entering into affairs with married men, masturbation, or asexuality. One other alternative that may become more popular is a relationship with a younger male.

---

*In which one man is sexually intimate with more than one woman.

Self-image and social stereotypes   Many abilities that are more important to daily functioning than is sexuality—such as vision, hearing, and psychomotor skills—also decline in later life. However, these declines do not seem to cause the consternation and threat that waning sexuality does. Sexual decline in later life is intimately tied to our feelings of self-worth, which are built up over decades of exaggerated emphasis on sexual performance in North American culture.

Our ideas of what sexual men and women are like are intimately bound up with our anatomy. Parts of our bodies, particularly those associated with sex, become symbolic of who we are. As parts of the body change with age, fail to function properly, are damaged, or are removed, some individuals feel that their masculinity or femininity has been partially diminished or lost. Surgical removal of the breasts (mastectomy) or uterus (hysterectomy) results in the loss of a significant symbol of femininity, and a woman may react to such loss as though a critical aspect of her identity has been obliterated. A man who is not able to control or effectively use his penis, the major symbol of his masculinity, may develop identity problems and experience feelings of incompetence and inadequacy in his day-to-day activities.

Sexuality is one of the cornerstones of identity and self-esteem. The erotic impulse is more than some nebulous summation of biological drives; it is an expression of basic needs for human contact, love, and life itself. Indeed, the erotic impulse may be the fundamental expression of an appetite for life.

It is perplexing for aging individuals to experience intense desires that are at odds with the feelings society has shaped them to expect of themselves. That noted author of the erotic, Henry Miller, described his own feelings during a love affair when he was 75: "The old man! How vulnerable he is! How pathetic! How he needs love—and how easily he accepts the counterfeit of it" (1974, p. 9). Yet Miller also wrote, "Mark my words, that where love is concerned, nothing, nobody, no situation can be utterly ridiculous" (p. 3).

In North America, our aversion to serious discussion about sex in older people may also stem from our tendency to identify older people with our parents and from the discomfort most of us experience when we think of our parents as sexual beings. Pocs and Godow (1976) asked 646 students at a midwestern university to estimate the extent and kinds of sexual activity engaged in by their parents. The researchers did not have data on the parents' actual sex lives. Therefore, they used figures from the Kinsey studies (collected more than 30 years before) for comparison purposes, although Kinsey's data probably underestimated the parents' real sexual activity. The college students' estimates were markedly lower than the Kinsey figures for all sexual activities measured. For instance, more than half the students thought their parents engaged in sexual intercourse once a month or less. Kinsey reported that parents in this age range (41–45 for married women,

46–50 for married men) had intercourse about seven times a month. There were even wider discrepancies for other activities such as oral-genital sex and extramarital sexual activity. Of these students, 90 percent felt their parents were happily married and still in love although the students apparently believed that their parents' happiness was achieved without the help of sex, or at least without much sex.

If we are treated as though we are sexless, our attitudes about ourselves may gradually change. If previously rewarded expressions of our sexuality are now ignored or punished, we begin to feel and behave differently. Different self-perceptions may arise when sexual behaviors once considered appropriate are now viewed as no longer acceptable. One of the most persistent factors affecting assumptions about sexuality in the second half of life is our implicit and explicit equation of sexuality with reproduction. Defining sex as reproduction leads to the view that only the young (i.e., fertile) are sexual beings. This view also makes penis-in-vagina intercourse the goal of all erotic interaction. Primary emphasis is placed on the physical attributes needed to attract sperm carriers and on the physique and attributes needed to ensure that one is able to deposit sperm in the proper receptacle. I am only slightly exaggerating here to underline the difficulty the older North American encounters in the sexual sphere. Just how pervasive the sexuality-reproduction association can be is illustrated by a report by Mazor (1980) on her research with over a hundred infertile couples. Most of her sample consisted of middle-class business and professional people. They were between the ages of 28 and 40 and were involved in long-term, stable relationships with their partners. The recognition that they were unable to conceive affected many of these individuals' sense of masculinity and femininity. Some of the women reported feeling like "neuters," not belonging to a male or female category. Male patients sometimes referred to intercourse as "shooting blanks." Both men and women felt decreased sexual desire, and half of the men suffered ejaculatory disturbances of a temporary nature.

The stages of a woman's life, viewed by herself and others, are often defined by events related to her reproductive function (Notman, 1978). The awareness of her own mortality, her sense of differentiation from older and younger generations, and her self-esteem are all closely interwoven with the experiences of childbearing, parenting, and easing her children into the adult world. Perhaps, given the current threat of overpopulation and the increasing number of middle-aged and old people, such perceptions of sexuality and reproduction will begin to change.

The double standard of aging Aging is much more of a crisis for women in North American culture. A man's graying hair is often described as distinguished. The lines on his face, increasing with age and becoming more deeply etched, are thought to bestow character. His sexual value is defined more by power and status than by physical characteristics.

A woman's physical appearance, however, has traditionally defined her "attractiveness." The physical characteristics regarded as attractive in women—smooth skin, slim physique, firm breasts—tend to wane earlier than the physical qualities considered "sexy" in men. Thus, those women who can afford it may enlist cosmetic devices and plastic surgery as aids to counter the effects of aging.

This double standard of aging is aptly illustrated by a 1979 survey of employment of actors and actresses undertaken by the Screen Actors Guild. Actresses aged 20 to 29 slightly outnumbered actors, in both days worked and average income. From age 30 to 39, the situation is reversed. At 40 years of age and older, the differences between men and women become dramatic. For instance, in 1979 there were 500 more women than men aged 20 to 29 in the Screen Actors Guild. There were, however, 3,000 fewer women than men aged 40 to 49. Female members of the Guild over 40 work approximately one day for each three days worked by male members over 40. In addition, 40-year-old actors earn 59 percent more money than actresses each day they work, and 50-year-old actors earn more than double the daily money paid to 50-year-old actresses (Harmetz, 1980).

These figures reflect dramatically the double standard of aging found in North American culture. Not only do the media perpetuate these stereotypes, but the media also help to create unrealistic fantasies. Women are not considered as viable sexual beings over 40, whereas men are often just beginning to play romantic leads at this age. The contemporary stereotypes regarding the double standard of aging was stated concisely by actress Joanne Woodward during a recent television interview. She compared her own public image to that of her husband, actor Paul Newman: "He gets prettier; I get older."

To evade the negative stereotypes associated with aging in women, many women use cosmetic devices to disguise the physical characteristics that accompany the aging process. Some of these women feel sensuous and vigorous in middle and old age but feel they must camouflage their true age in order to be accepted by others. In sad irony, they therefore perpetuate the stereotype that aging, or at least its physical manifestation, brings about the end of sexuality. Graying hair, for example, is disguised and is not perceived as part of the aging, attractive, sensuous woman. We need gray-haired women as models of vitality and energy who can challenge the association of gray hair with asexuality in women. We need to overcome our fears about aging and attractiveness. If we can allow ourselves to age gracefully and sensuously, we can begin to alter the way aging and sexuality is viewed.

I hope that the double standard of aging will begin to wilt under pressure from the women's movement in the presence of more accurate information to replace stereotypes regarding the effect of aging on sexuality.

GENDER AND AGING

What is the relationship between sexuality and gender roles during the second half of life? Do our identities, roles, and values that revolve around being masculine or feminine remain stable or change over time? The answers to these questions are quite complex.

The noted personality theorist Carl Jung suggested that characteristics in the first half of life are developed at the expense of others that are suppressed. These suppressed characteristics begin to push for expression in middle age. He theorized that values, and even bodies, tend to change into their opposites. Physiologically, the male becomes more feminine and the female more masculine. Psychologically, there is a counterbalancing of personality traits between men and women. There is some evidence that gender roles become less distinctive from middle age onward. That is, both men and women shift toward personality attributes traditionally defined as characteristic of the other gender (Gough, 1964; Kahana & Kahana, 1970; Livson, 1976, 1978; Neugarten & Gutman, 1968; Strong, 1943; Terman & Miles, 1936).

As women age, they tend to become more tolerant of their aggressive and self-centered impulses. In contrast, men appear to become more tolerant of their nurturant and affilitative impulses. Older women are seen as more dominant than older men by 55- to 70-year-olds of both genders (Neugarten & Gutman, 1968). Older men rate older women as more active, involved, handy, and stable than they rate themselves (Kahana & Kahana, 1970).

Such research suggests that more androgynous individuals may be found among older people than among their younger counterparts. Perhaps, as we grow older we are able to express masculine and feminine psychological traits to a more equal degree.

Androgyny

Most authors writing on androgyny (Bazin & Freeman, 1974; Bem, 1974; Bernard, 1975; Block, 1973; Hefner, Rebecca, & Oleshans, 1975; Johnson, 1977; Kaplan & Bean, 1976) implicitly or explicitly view an androgynous person as one who is better able to adjust to the environment than a more traditional individual. Certainly the challenges of gender roles pose different tasks across the life span. Humans are androgynous at birth, with gender-role differentiation beginning shortly thereafter in all cultures.

In North American culture, gender roles diverge sharply in middle childhood (see Chapter 1). For most people, roles converge during the early work years, only to diverge again during childrearing. Gender roles become less distinct when the children have grown. This progression suggests that individuals deal with their gender roles, and the behaviors that stem from them, in different ways depending on the stage in their life. Sinnot (1977) has proposed that a person's ability to show life span variations in gender roles indicates a general flexibility that is associated with more successful aging and a longer life span. Sinnot reviewed a number of studies that supported her position, at least indirectly. However, many of these investigations leave much to be desired from a scientific point of view. Defining gender-role flexibility or androgyny in older people is difficult because of measurement problems.

Measuring androgyny   The tests designed to measure androgyny have been constructed using mainly adolescents and young adults. Therefore, it may be inappropriate to use these tests to measure the gender-role identities of older men and women. This problem is illustrated in a study by Hyde and Phillis (1979), who administered the Bem Sex-Role Inventory (BSRI) to 289 people 13 to 85 years of age. The number of androgynous males increased with age. In contrast, the number of androgynous females decreased with age. In attempting to explain their results, Hyde and Phillis pointed out that females would have to add masculine traits to their personality as they age. On the BSRI (Bem, 1974) many of the masculine traits, such as "athletic" and "ambitious," are youth oriented and are difficult to achieve as one gets older. On the other hand, many of the feminine traits, such as "gentle" and "loves children," are relatively easy characteristics for aging men to attain. Bem's scale may have tapped a domain of "youthful" masculine traits and may have left out traits that describe masculinity in middle and old age. The other possibility is that the traits we associate with masculinity are inherently youthful.

Even when considering the results of gender-role research on younger people, the results sometimes conflict with the concept of androgyny as being a more mentally healthy stance than is either masculinity or femininity. Accepting masculine characteristics as self-descriptive appears to be necessary for high self-esteem in *both* men and women. Moreover, women also seem to need some positive feminine characteristics for high self-esteem. In general, self-description in terms of feminine characteristics alone, or in combination with masculine ones, seems to present problems for the emotional adjustment of college males (Kaplan & Sedney, 1980).

The high level of masculinity that is so adaptive in the older adolescent male may not be as useful in later life when social relationships change.

Mussen (1961, 1962) found that high masculinity was associated with adjustment, high self-esteem, positive emotional state, and effective social functioning in adolescence. When the same men were tested 20 years later, however, high masculinity was associated with lower levels of self-acceptance, thoughtful self-understanding, sociability, self-assurance, perceived likelihood to be leaders, and dominance.

Traditional gender roles may be associated with the severity of midlife transitions. Cohen (1979) reviewed the literature on masculine gender roles and midlife crisis. The traditional masculine role requires men to be strong, aggressive, and unemotional. These characteristics begin to decline during middle age as men experience pronounced changes in themselves and in their families. Rigid adherence to stereotypically masculine characteristics may interfere with midlife adjustment. Cohen concluded that greater male involvement with androgynous values and behaviors may help resolve midlife conflicts.

It is important to emphasize that the North American culture provides little support for the development of androgyny. The media continue to supply models that emphasize pure gender-role stereotypes. People who display other-gender attributes may provoke disdain and ostracism in a culture that emphasizes rigid gender-role divisions. Gender-role stereotypes do provide structure and predictability in life. Androgyny can lead to a view of life that is at least temporarily ambiguous. A more complex world view invites a greater range of choices, and life is often more difficult when there are choices. However, this statement of the difficulties involved in change toward androgyny is not meant to discourage such change, but only to clarify the problems.

Change and adjustment   Individuals who attempt to achieve gender-role flexibility confront a good deal of opposition from those who support the status quo. In North American culture, the attempt by an individual to develop both masculine and feminine qualities can lead to conflict as easily as to integration. In two studies (Kaplan, 1979; Sedney, 1977) with small samples of clients in psychotherapy, the majority scored as androgynous on the BSRI. Feminine women were less likely to be in therapy. The development of both feminine and masculine characteristics may increase the probability of conflict within a person and between a person and society.

Adapting to our social environment in terms of our gender may be accomplished in a number of ways, as illustrated by Livson's (1976, 1978) research. She selected a group of women who were members of the longitudinal Oakland Growth Study in Berkeley, California. The study was started in 1932 when the participants were 11 years old. Livson studied 24 women and

21 men who had scored above the mean for their gender on an index of psychological health at the age of 50. In other words, the healthiest members of the original sample were studied to observe successful patterns of development in the middle years. Livson found two patterns of development: (1) a *stable* pattern, consisting of 7 women and 7 men whose psychological health remained high and stable between ages 40 and 50, and (2) an *improved* pattern of 17 women and 14 men whose psychological health was relatively poor at 40 but improved significantly by the time they were age 50.

The stable women were quite traditional. From adolescence on, they had developed and elaborated the "feminine," affiliative side of their personalities. At age 50 they were gregarious, nurturant women whose sociability had matured and become less self-oriented. They were conventional women with minimal conflict between their personalities and the traditional roles for women in North American culture.

The improved women did not conform as neatly to traditional gender roles. Although their family size and demographic characters did not differ from the traditional women, at age 50 the improved women were ambitious, intellectual, and unconventional. Livson called this group *nontraditionalists*. They relied on their intellect to deal with the world. They impressed others as interesting people with high intellectual ability, although they did not differ from traditional women in intelligence tests. Interestingly, at age 40 these women appeared to be having psychological difficulties. Livson proposed that these women experienced a great deal of stress because they suppressed their intellectuality and desires for achievement in order to fulfill the roles of wife and mother. By age 50, however, they had resolved their crises as they integrated the achieving, more conventionally masculine side of themselves. More androgynous by age 50, their psychological health rose to match the level of traditional women.

Traditional men, like their female counterparts, followed a consistent pattern. As adolescents, they were intellectual and competent, but lacked spontaneity. By age 40, their masculine orientation continued to evolve but was complemented by softer, more affiliative qualities. Their dominant characteristic continued to be rational, disciplined instrumentality, although they became more thoughtful, spontaneous, and likeable as they reached age 50.

Nontraditional men were more extroverted and less controlled than traditional men during adolescence. By age 40, they had suppressed their emotionality in favor of conventional masculine behavior. They were angry and defensive at 40, punitive and self-centered. Livson suggests that their problems stemmed from restraining their emotionality in the service of achievement.

By age 50, however, their power concerns diminished, and they integrated the emotionality of their youth into sociability and charm with a concomitant rise in psychological health. "Like nontraditional women, they reclaim opposite-sex characteristics suppressed since adolescence" (Livson, 1978, p. 14).

Thus, psychological adjustment can be attained through different coping strategies. Unfortunately, many aging individuals do not find social environments that allow them to develop their potential fully, as Lowenthal and her associates (1975) documented in a longitudinal study. Although gender roles were not studied directly, the attributes of the middle-class individuals studied are related to our discussion. A combination of many positive and many negative characteristics appeared to produce a sense of well-being and satisfaction in a group of people they labeled "complex." These individuals were deeply involved in their lives and coped well with the various stresses of life. People who exhibited both strengths and weaknesses adapted particularly well in early adulthood and middle age.

In the late middle age, however, it was the more "simplistic" people who reported themselves to be the happiest. The more complex among the late middle-aged grew older gracefully only if they had the opportunities that are usually restricted to the more privileged sectors of our society. As Fiske (1979, p. 114) notes,

> Sadly, the more complex and challenged people among the great middle-class majority often become deprived of the arenas in which they find satisfaction as they reach late middle and old age. They suffer for this, and so do the rest of us, because they become less visible as examples for the generations coming after them.

I do not mean to equate androgynous with "complex" and gender-stereotyped with "simple" in describing Livson's study, although there are conceptual similarities. The main theme is that the social environment that we shape and that shapes us is complex and demanding. It requires different roles at different stages of life. There is not an invariable sequence to aging and gender-role identity. To some extent, we can affect this process: it is possible to transcend the narrow limitations we have imposed on our conceptions of gender roles across the life span. As Riley (1978, p. 49) says,

> A sociology of age makes clear that the meanings we attach to age have power. They become age stereotypes, shaping our personal plans, hopes, and fears. They become age constraints, built into the social structure, molding the course of our lives, directing social change. They are continually affecting the way we grow up and grow old . . . modifying the

values attached to life and death, pressing toward societal conflict or integration. Because of this power, the sociology of age contains within it both responsibilities and opportunities."

THE DIALECTICS OF AGING

If we are to expand our conception of sexuality, people in the second half of life are the most likely to lead such an expansion. The tensions that occur during midlife crisis and on entry into old age provide an opportunity for both men and women to reexamine their traditional patterns of thinking and behaving. What was valued in youth may no longer appeal to the older individual.

Both the individual and the science that studies him or her need to broaden the constructs about middle and old age to account for the complexity of human beings. The social environment is constantly changing. An understanding of this process as it is related to gender roles and sexuality over the life span must be able to take into account the complexities and ambiguities faced by the aging individual. Just as we are affected by our environment, we also affect it. This constant interplay, with all its tension and the possibility of the integration of opposites, is the heart of dialectical psychology.

Dialectical interpretations of human development focus on change, instability, and crisis (Riegel, 1975, 1976; Rychlak, 1968, 1976; Sinnot, 1977). They deal with the tension among the biological, psychological, and social demands on a person that lead to conflict and growth. As elaborated by Riegel (1975, 1976), dialectical interpretations appear to offer the best fit between life span development and our understanding of sexuality and gender roles. Erikson's (1968) crisis resolution theory and Levinson's (1978) "stages of a man's life" can also be described in dialectical terms, and both Freud and Jung made use of the dialectic in their theorizing (Rychlak, 1968).

Beyond its theoretical implications, however, dialectical psychology offers a conception of life that most individuals intuitively experience. In such a conception, conflict is viewed as positive and as the main means through which individuals and social groups move toward more advanced developmental stages. Development is believed to occur continuously and simultaneously on biological, psychological, and social dimensions. When these dimensions are synchronized, development proceeds along the normative or socially prescribed course. When discontinuities arise on one dimension or between dimensions, crises occur. Although crises result from a host of complex factors, they are experienced by individuals in dialogues and debates with intimate friends (Riegel, 1975). The resolution of a crisis is a radical reconstruction of experience and represents a move to a more advanced developmental state. As the transcendence of the poles of masculinity and femininity, the development of an androgynous personality represents a radical reinterpretation and synthesis of gender-role conflict.

Shostrom (1967) maintains that individuals derive identity from reconciling and integrating the polarities (thesis and antithesis) within their personalities. This dialectical process leads to synthesis, or, as Shostrom would say, to self-actualization—the full development of one's potential. Dominance-submissiveness, dependence-independence, and masculinity-femininity all must be balanced in the individual's life if he or she is to avoid one-sidedness.

Finally, a dialectical approach provides a framework for understanding the ambiguities and conflicts that often envelop our sexuality as it develops over the life span. As I have pointed out, the meaning and limitations of one's concept of sexuality vis-à-vis reproduction are also intimately associated with gender roles. Many descriptions of stereotypic characteristics of the genders are youth oriented. Our language is rooted in historical periods in which few people reached late middle age and even fewer reached old age. Therefore, our descriptions of the genders are primarily based on the young at their reproductive peaks. This pattern may have served a purpose during most of our history. It may still be partially relevant among those in their "mating" years, given the clear differentiation of male and female and the implied synthesis or union between them. However, it now serves to obscure our vision of masculinity and feminity in the second half of the life cycle. No longer goaded by hypothetical "sex drives" and /or cultural imperatives to reproduce, the mature human can expand our notions of what it means to be a sensuous man or woman. Ironically, at the very time that we begin to sense a decline in our bodies, we are presented with the opportunity to become more sensuous and complete beings.

CONCLUSIONS

Earlier, I said that being male or female has a dramatic impact on the frequency of sexual activities. Most women end sexual activities at a younger age than men even though, from a strict biological viewpoint, their sexual functioning is less affected by aging than is that of men. Middle-aged and older women are less likely to have active sex lives than men of comparable ages, and the greatest differences occur after age 55 (Williams, 1977).

Cultural inhibitions, lack of partners for women, and the double standard of aging all contribute to this gender difference. The most overwhelming reason for differences in sexual activity, however, may be gender-role stereotypes. The stereotypes and roles that cluster around being male or female have a dramatic impact on how we conduct our sexual lives. Traditional masculinity is seen as active, dominant, and oversexed. Traditional femininity is seen as passive, submissive, and undersexed.

From both theoretical and commonsense viewpoints, sexual adjustment or satisfaction may be highest among androgynous individuals (see Chapter 4 for preliminary research supporting this viewpoint). The ability to express both feminine and masculine sexual behaviors when appropriate would appear to provide the most emotionally satisfying sexual experience. This speculation supposes that we all have the potential to be active or passive, coy or straightforward, dominant or submissive in some combination in our sexual lives. The ability to express this greater range of behavior and emotionality adds a flavor of variety to one's sexual life. And this variety is often sorely needed by long-term partners during the second half of life.

In a culture exploring sex for its recreational rather than procreational value, couples beyond the menopause have a distinct advantage. What we can learn from them is that a person whose genital functions have declined or become nonexistent is still not sexless unless we continue to equate sexuality with genital performance culminating in a penis in a vagina. As long as we live and despite our infirmities, we remain sensuous beings who must adapt to the often-conflicting demands of gender and sexuality.

P A R T   T W O

Contemporary Perspective

Contemporary society challenges our assumptions about the normality of prevailing norms for gender roles and sexual expression. On a daily basis, the mass media confront us with what seem to be an expanding variety of sexual lifestyles.

More heterosexuals are experimenting with the option of remaining single. Lesbians and gay men are becoming more open about their lifestyles. We are also aware that sexuality has become a product for mass consumption. In the marketplace, we can buy erotic materials to arouse us and contraceptives to prevent unwanted pregnancies that could result from acting on our arousal. Finally, as we raise our consciousness about the costs of living in today's world, we must acknowledge that some forms of sexual expression are blatantly harmful. Sexual harassment and sexual assault are grave problems.

How are gender roles and sexuality related in all these aspects of modern life? The picture is complex but not beyond our comprehension. The next six chapters consider the ways in which gender-role norms and gender influence contemporary sexual expression in a rapidly changing society.

In the past, biology was destiny. Because only the woman could become pregnant, she was usually expected to assume complete responsibility for child rearing and domestic duties. Chapter 7 points out the extent to which this situation is changing in response to modern contraceptive technology, the women's movement, and increasing numbers of women working outside the home. Predictably, egalitarian people use contraceptives with greater effectiveness and favor smaller families than do people with traditional gender-role attitudes. Nevertheless, many gender-role barriers remain. With the exception of those who marry egalitarian or androgynous men, working

159

mothers can expect little help with child care or household responsibilities from their husbands.

Sexuality in the workplace is not always welcome. Chapter 8 defines sexual harassment as giving unsolicited and nonreciprocal sexual attention. Marked gender differences exist. Men are much more likely to engage in sexual harassment; women are much more likely to be victims. Gender-role stereotyping of women workers and vocations play a crucial role in harassment. Women who are physically attractive and personable—those most likely to be hired, and those who best fit the "feminine" stereotype—are most likely to be victimized. Sexual harassment, salary and promotional inequities, and the added costs of child care make the working woman's life difficult.

Marriage is no longer the only option for heterosexual adults. Because many are postponing marriage and divorcing one another, single lifestyles have gained acceptance. As noted in Chapter 9, some single adults seem to be liberated from traditional gender roles and sexual constraints. Adults who chose to remain single are often androgynous; androgynous people are more liberal about living together without legally marrying. Nevertheless, not all single people escape the sticky appeal of gender-role norms. Couples who live together divide household duties according to traditional gender-role norms. Also, dating and courtship usually follow these expected patterns. Single people are faced with special problems. In a society that continues to be oriented toward couples and families, unattached men and women may experience difficulties in filling their needs for intimacy, sexuality, and community.

After discussing popular misconceptions, Chapter 10 describes well-researched similarities and differences between homosexuals and heterosexuals. Many of the differences between gay men and lesbians parallel gender differences among heterosexuals. Regardless of their sexual preferences, men are more comfortable with casual sex and somewhat less interested in sharing feelings with a partner than are women. Gender differences aside, many homosexuals are more liberated from traditional gender-role norms than are heterosexuals. Stressing equal power in decision making, gay and lesbian relationships are commonly modeled after friendship, *not* traditional marriage. In committed homosexual relationships, partners often value role flexibility and share household chores and financial responsibilities whenever possible.

Chapter 11 looks at the relationship between traditional gender roles and sexual violence. Forcible rape is at the extreme of a socialization process in which men are expected to dominate women. As a result, men who are uncertain of their manhood or who are victims of male peer pressure are especially likely to engage in sexual assault. Because of a tendency to confuse "normal" sexuality with male aggression and female passivity, outsiders, in-

160

cluding those in the criminal justice system, may perceive the victim as just as responsible for a rape as her male assailant. Feminist attitudes are changing our tendency to blame the rape victim. Already, these more progressive attitudes have facilitated positive changes in the legal and social organizations that attempt to prevent rape and serve rape victims. Nonetheless, the old saying "You can't legislate morality" is still cited. Despite the reform of rape laws in Michigan, for example, there are still many instances in which law enforcement officers fail to believe women who say they have been raped.

In an age in which sex sells and is sold, erotica is big business and men are the big consumers. Men are far more likely than women to purchase and report being aroused by erotic materials. However, as described in Chapter 12, experimental evidence points to an absence of gender differences in peoples' responses to erotica. With few exceptions, both men and women are equally aroused by the same erotic stimuli. In marked contrast with popular opinion, women find erotic content more stimulating than romance. If erotica is stimulating to women, why do few seek it out? Perhaps women are reluctant to expose themselves to erotic stimulation because they fear that such behavior would be "unfeminine." Marketing strategies, too, may help explain these gender differences. Although men are targets for products that are presented as enhancing their sexual arousal and functioning, women may be more likely to be sold "good looks" or products that promise to make them more arousing to men.

On a closing note, most of the chapters in this part of the book share one common feature. Each in its own way touches on the current political turmoil over gender roles, status of the family, and related issues. For example, some people advocate greater freedom for women, especially in deciding whether or not to work outside of the home or have children. Others prefer traditional gender roles and idealize families in which the husband works and the wife stays home with the children. According to these people, families should have serious misgivings about contraception—in particular, the option of abortion.

This bitter struggle continues on many other fronts. Some people are comfortable with a variety of sexual and affectional lifestyles outside of marriage. They have a positive attitude toward those who decide not to get married, divorce or separate from a spouse, or become involved with a sexual partner of their own gender. Other people are opposed to these alternative lifestyles and see them as eroding important religious and family values.

People in our society also hold very different opinions about erotica—products that are marketed to enhance peoples' sensual pleasures. Although feminists have misgivings about some pornography, especially materials that portray women as victims of sexual violence, many people are opposed to

161

censorship of erotic materials in general. In contrast, others feel that things have gone too far and prefer strict restrictions on the dissemination of erotic literature and materials.

Chapter 11, given its concern with sexual violence, is perhaps the only chapter in this section of the book that has only peripheral relevance to this struggle. Rape and sexual violence in today's society disturb people of all political persuasions. However, people have different ideas for solving the problem. Some people, for example, advocate more rigorous law enforcement as the solution. Others would probably perceive better law enforcement as only a beginning. Most people affiliated with the women's movement argue that changing gender roles are a necessary prerequisite for liberating society from sexual violence. In other words, they believe that women must free themselves from their traditional passivity and men must reject gender-typed notions of masculinity that make the words *sexuality* and *aggression* synonymous.

7 Reproduction, Roles and Responsibilities

ELIZABETH RICE ALLGEIER

This chapter could have been placed in Part One, where the focus was primarily on life span development. However, many of the changes in our ideas about what it means to be a man or a woman are related to changes in our ideas about the place of reproduction in our lives and the extent to which that capacity defines the roles of men and women. A description of reproduction and gender roles, therefore, introduces our focus on contemporary issues.

Elizabeth Allgeier discusses the enormous and very recent shift in definitions of the purpose of sexuality. The pressure of overpopulation and the development of reliable contraceptives have contributed to a redefinition in North American culture of sex not only as necessary for procreation but also as something to be cultivated and enjoyed in its own right. Along with these changes, there has been an expansion of important roles for women beyond motherhood. Allgeier describes the effects these changes are having on sexual and contraceptive behavior, marriage, family formation, and on the distribution of work within the family. Not all members of contemporary society accept shifts toward egalitarian marriage. Forces at the highest levels of government, in fact, continue to push for federal legislation to prohibit the funding of any programs that do not support women's traditional roles. As Allgeier documents, however, most women no longer completely conform to those traditional roles. The majority of American women are employed in paid work, including those women who have school-age children.

A major concern in contemporary society is the effect these changes are having on children, and Allgeier presents the available evidence. These shifts, from the traditional roles we were as children socialized to expect, toward more egalitarian relationships contain inevitable stresses for men and women alike. Allgeier is clearly optimistic, however, about the effects of these shifts on the quality of life for children whose parents choose to bring them into the world. Their parents also have greater flexibility regarding their parental roles and in their adult roles with one another. Sharing the results of their individual development and their joint responsibilities may finally provide an end to the conflicted goals and mutually exploitive relations that characterize many marriages of previous generations.

 As we near the end of the twentieth century, it is easy to believe that most gender differences are learned through exposure to cultural beliefs and regulations. This viewpoint permeates much contemporary writing on gender roles, and, in fact, most of the chapters in this book. This orientation assumes that because we have *learned* to differentiate—and, in some cases to discriminate—on the basis of gender, we can unlearn these habits. We can socialize both men and women to be nurturant, active, yielding, and assertive. These behaviors would then be expressed as a function of a given situation rather than as a function of one's gender.

Biological differences *do* have an enormous impact, however, on several aspects of our lives. As noted in the last chapter, differences in the sexual arousability of men and women appear to be diminishing. But when the mutually sexually aroused couple accidentally conceives, the fetus is in the woman's, not the man's body. Subsequent costs of "resolution"—whether the pregnancy is maintained or aborted—are greater for the woman than for the man.

Although a third of American brides (and one-half of teenage brides) were pregnant at their weddings during the 1970s (Alan Guttmacher Institute, 1981), many couples do follow the conventionally approved pattern. That is, they marry, and then decide if and when to have a child. These decisions may be made in the most mutually egalitarian fashion. Aside from the act that results in conception, though, all the direct responsibility for pregnancy and the birth process resides within the woman's body.

On the other hand, both men and women can take responsibility for contraception. If they choose to conceive, both parents can care for the child. The intent of this chapter, then, is to examine the interaction of gender roles both with the control of and with the exercise of our reproductive capacities. After briefly reviewing reproductive behavior and roles in the past, I examine contemporary research on contraceptive, reproductive, and family roles.

HISTORICAL AND CROSS-CULTURAL PERSPECTIVE

Traditional divisions of labor across most cultures and time periods have placed responsibility for the economic support (meat gathering or money making) of families squarely on the shoulders of men. The responsibility for the care and socialization of children has resided with women. Given the different biological capacities of man and woman and the precariousness of our species' survival throughout most of our history, this division of labor was highly adaptive.

In most cultures, the responsibilities of women for nurturing the young have extended far beyond those dictated by biological differences between men and women. High infant mortality rates, the danger of extinction of particular cultural groups, and the economic usefulness of offspring meant that the reproduction rate of one or two children per woman would have been inadequate to maintain the population base. Thus, women ideally had large numbers of children. Women's reproductive role was paramount, feared, revered, and all-consuming.

Within the United States as short a time as two centuries ago, each woman was still producing an average of 7.5 children (Coale, 1974). Innovations in medical technology, public health improvements, and an emphasis on the importance of personal hygiene reduced the number of children who died before they could grow up and have babies. In response to these survival-enhancing developments, the population expanded very rapidly. It took our species thousands of years to reach a population of 1 billion in 1800. However, it took us only 175 years to add an additional 3 billion people to our planet. We reached the 4 billion mark in 1975.

By the middle of the twentieth century, scientists were beginning to express alarm that the number of humans would soon expand beyond our planet's capacity to support us. Such slogans as "zero population growth" and "planned parenthood" became common, and increasingly, couples were asked to examine and justify decisions to have large families. Nonetheless, the assumption remains that there is something pathological about the person who desires *no* children, and we still pay homage to the "Mother of the Year."

Writers of the 1960s and 1970s offered many suggestions for methods of reducing the growth of the population. Prominent in many of the articles and books that appeared during those decades was the recommendation that women be encouraged to take roles other than those stemming from their capacity to reproduce (Davis, 1967; Russo & Brackbill, 1973).

CONTROL OF REPRODUCTIVE CAPACITY

Paralleling these recommendations by population scientists, several other developments altered our notions about sex and the role of women. Contraceptive technology was given a tremendous boost in the late 1950s and early 1960s with the development and marketing of oral contraceptives. The pill was soon followed by the marketing of a device that could be inserted in the uterus—the intrauterine device (IUD). Variations on both the pill and the IUD have proliferated. Prior to the 1960s, the only recourse for couples who wished to avoid conception was abstinence or the use of a barrier method—the condom or the diaphragm with jelly. Although the barrier methods are safe and highly effective *when used,* they require some advance planning. The diaphragm must be inserted in a woman's vagina shortly before intercourse takes place, and the condom cannot be donned until the man's penis is erect. Thus, a large number of people who didn't want (more) children, but who took "chances" from time to time because of the inconvenience and intrusive nature of the barrier methods, were faced with unwanted pregnancies. Development of coitus-independent methods "took the worry out of being close," as some ads of the 1970s put it.

Notions regarding the purpose of sexual intercourse were also shifting. Traditionally, sexual pleasure (especially for women) was viewed as a side effect of trying to make babies. The *purpose* of sex was to procreate. This view so dominated our thinking about sexuality that even enlightened (at the time) writers of sex manuals labeled certain acts as "perversions" if they didn't lead to the possibility of conception. For instance, oral sex was viewed as a legitimate part of pre-coital stimulation. But the act lost its respectability if a woman stimulated a man's penis with her lips and tongue and he ejaculated in her mouth rather than in her vagina. Almost anything could be done to increase sexual arousal as long as the man's penis made it to the woman's vagina to deposit sperm as the culminating event of lovemaking. In the 1980s, the Catholic Church still views reproduction as the primary purpose of sexual intimacy and continues to forbid the use of the most effective contraceptive methods. The rhythm method, or abstinence during the woman's fertile period, is permitted by the Catholic Church, but up to 21 out of every 100 women relying on the rhythm method become pregnant each year (Hatcher et al., 1980). However, the majority of married Americans,

Catholics and non-Catholics alike, now use reliable contraceptives in order to engage in sexual intercourse for purposes other than procreation (Westoff & Bumpass, 1973).

Consequences of Reproductive Capacity for Males and Females

Before they reach the end of their teenage years, the majority of today's adolescents begin having sexual intercourse (DeLamater & MacCorquodale, 1979; Zelnik & Kantner, 1980). Twelve million American teenagers are sexually active; 16 is their average age at first intercourse (Alan Guttmacher Institute, 1981).

Throughout the reproductive life span, the medical and social risks of engaging in intercourse are considerably greater for women than for men. Pregnancy can threaten a woman's life; pregnant teenagers are five times more likely to die of pregnancy-related causes if they use no method of birth control than if they use the pill. The relatively greater risk of death from pregnancy and childbirth versus death from the use of any contraceptive is maintained throughout a woman's reproductive life span (Alan Guttmacher Institute, 1981). However, the most effective methods of birth control are those used by women, and they do pose some risk to a woman's life and health.

Moreover, if the couple is not married, conception is far more costly socially for the woman than it is for the man. Because of the stereotypes regarding differences in male versus female sexuality (see Chapters 2 and 3), men are expected to attempt to have intercourse. After all, the stereotype says they have driving sexual needs and even suffer pain ("blue balls") when denied sexual outlet. Women, in contrast, are perceived as less sexually compelled. Their role is to place limits on men's impulses, determining the conditions (commitment, engagement, marriage) under which sexual intercourse may take place. Nonmarital pregnancy, then, is taken as evidence that the woman has failed to perform her role effectively. Her subsequent loss of status is far greater than the loss to the man who impregnated her.

Despite the risks associated with unwanted pregnancy, the majority of sexually active teenagers fail to use contraceptives when they begin having sexual intercourse (Zelnik & Kantner, 1977, 1978). In fact, many teenagers don't begin using contraceptives until after they have experienced an unwanted pregnancy. For an extensive overview of the research that has been done on the tendency of adolescents to engage in unprotected intercourse, see Byrne & Fisher's *Adolescents, Sex, and Contraception* (1982).

Birth Control and Gender Roles

One factor that has been blamed for the high rate of unplanned pregnancy has been adherence to traditional gender-role norms by both men and women.

Contraception and women   Women are taught in our culture to inhibit and/or control the time, place, and circumstances under which men's "urgent" sexual feelings are expressed. Such a view places the burden of sexual and contraceptive responsibility on the woman. Unfortunately, traditional gender-role norms regarding women's sexuality do not equip them for this responsibility very well. As a consequence, many adolescent girls engage in sexual intercourse while maintaining a perception of themselves as *not* sexually active (Lindemann, 1975). The connotation of sexual intercourse by an adolescent girl is quite different from that for the adolescent boy. Because young unmarried women are expected to be chaste, they are given few models or sources of advice regarding contraceptive acquisiton and use.

Fox's (1980) review of research on mother-daughter communication indicates that the majority of girls do not discuss sexual or contraceptive matters with their mothers. Given the state of our contraceptive technology, use of birth control by women requires that they actively acknowledge their participation in "bad" behavior to strangers and/or authority figures—pharmacists, doctors, or clinic personnel. Traditionally, women are socialized to be "nice" (Fox, 1977), and they have also been trained to be passive, as we've seen in earlier chapters. Therefore, women who identify with and support traditional gender-role norms should be less likely to acquire and use contraceptives than women who do not follow traditional gender-role norms.

Using a variety of different approaches, researchers have attempted to identify the impact of gender-role norms on contraceptive behavior. Two of the most extensively used measures are gender-role identification and profeminist attitudes.

In general, profeminist attitudes regarding the roles of women in society seem to be more predictive of effective contraceptive behavior than is gender-role identification per se (Garblik, 1978; Irons, 1977). However, Fox's (1977) questionnaire study of 700 college students suggests that pro-feminist attitudes may not be enough to guarantee effective contraceptive use:

> It has been suggested that feminist ideology leads to a greater valuation of one's self, one's potentiality, one's life. One indication of valuing oneself is ensuring one's own contraceptive protection. . . . It is significant that the alignment with feminist ideology (that is, nontraditional sex-role attitudes) had a substantial impact on contraceptive behavior only

for women who believed themselves to be personally in control of their lives. But the reverse is true, too: Unless accompanied by nontraditional sex-role attitudes, a woman's [sense of personal control] was not likely to have much impact on her contraceptive behavior. [p. 279]

Contraception and men   Men often report feeling "left out" by family planning agencies (Swanson, 1979). Acknowledging their neglect of men, some birth control agencies have begun active outreach campaigns to provide birth control information and condoms for men (Johnson & Staples, 1979). In the late 1970s, Planned Parenthood in Washington, D.C., culminated a "National Condom Week" with a "Rubber Disco" in which they offered reduced admission prices to the dance for those who had condoms in their possession, and 90 percent of the men attending the dance did, in fact, produce condoms at the door!

Researchers have also tended to ignore the male role in their investigations of variables related to contraceptive use. However, a few studies have explored men's contraceptive attitudes and behavior. Male contraceptive use was more likely among men who had had permissive parents and who were experienced in dating (Hornick, Doran, & Crawford, 1979).

Among sexually experienced male college students in Australia, Cole and Allen (1979) found a high incidence of contraceptive risk taking. Almost a fifth of the sample reported that they had been involved in an unwanted pregnancy, and a few had been involved in more than one. Two beliefs accounted for their poor contraceptive techniques. Males believed that contraception was a female responsibility, and they thought that sexual intercourse should be entirely spontaneous rather than planned.

Finally, Gough (1979) has examined the factors related to willingness to use a male contraceptive pill if it becomes available. Men who expressed greater willingness to use such a pill preferred smaller families and were more favorably disposed to population planning and abortion. They rated vasectomy (male sterilization), tubal ligation (female sterilization), and the female pill as acceptable birth control methods. Potential nonusers, in contrast, were more authoritarian, assertive, conventional, and self-centered than were potential users.

Contraceptive technology: A sexist plot?   As noted earlier, men often feel left out of family planning services. Acknowledging that problem, some representatives of the women's movement have complained that women are being forced to bear the entire burden of contraceptive responsibility and risk. This criticism, while valid, ignores historical reasons for women's greater contraceptive responsibility.

For a partial understanding of why only one of the half-dozen presently available temporary methods—the condom—is used by men, we need to go back in time almost a hundred years. In the 1800s, there were two methods available: the condom and the diaphragm. Both of these methods are highly effective *when used*, and neither causes unwanted physical side effects. At that time, however, contraceptive use was illegal, and considered by many to be immoral. In the early part of this century, Margaret Sanger, a pioneer in the birth control movement, endured fines and jail sentences because of her energetic involvement in the movement to make contraceptives legal and available. Her goal was to provide women with control over their own reproductive lives, because they bear the physical and many of the emotional consequences of conception. Therefore, she provided financial backing for research by Gregory Pincus, the so-called father of the pill. In other words, she felt that the provision of contraceptives for women would have the effect of liberating them, making reproduction a matter of choice.

That goal has been realized for a great many women, but there has also been a price to pay for this "freedom" in the form of unwanted side effects of more recent female contraceptives. The fact that only women bear these risks has led some to question why more resources haven't been devoted to the development of other male methods.

To some extent, neglect of male methods is due to a biological difference between women and men. Males are always fertile, whereas women are fertile for only a few days each month. Therefore, it seemed easier to intervene in the reproductive cycle of women than to tackle the constantly fertile male. For these and other reasons, far more money has been devoted to the search for female than for male contraceptive methods until quite recently. From 1966 to 1974, for instance, the Agency for International Development awarded over $35 million for research on fertility, of which only 5 percent was allocated to male fertility. In 1974, however, the federal government invested, for the first time, more money in male than in female fertility studies (Shapiro, 1977). For a good description of the issue of investment of resources into female fertility regulation, see Emily Moore's 1977 article, "Fertility Regulation: Friend or Foe of the Female?" As Moore notes, just because women want the choice of being able to control their own reproductive capacities doesn't necessarily mean that they want all the responsibility and risk every time they have intercourse between the time of puberty and menopause.

Gender, Unwanted Pregnancy, and the Law

Recent abortion rulings have favored female control in that men cannot restrain their wives (or girlfriends) from obtaining an abortion (Hayman, 1976). Two important U.S. Supreme Court decisions—*Roe v. Wade* (1973) and *Doe* v. *Doe* (1974)—have held that the mother's right regarding the fetus was more important than the father's right, whether or not they were married.

When the pregnancy is carried to term, the mother is assumed by law to be the natural guardian of the baby, and the father's potential rights over the child are denied (Hayman, 1976; Krause, 1972). As Aberg, Small, and Watson (1977) have pointed out, the legal position of unwed fathers has begun to improve, but basically these men are not given the rights accorded to wedded parents regarding visitation, or (in cases where the mother wishes to give the child up for adoption after birth) custody and adoption. Furthermore, unwed fathers tend to be discriminated against to punish them for their sins and to encourage them to marry the unwed mother (Schafrick, 1973). In most states, the parental rights of the unwed father can be terminated without his consent. This picture regarding both rights and responsibilities began to change in the 1970s, however, with the landmark case of *Stanley* v. *Illinois* (1973). The court held that unwed fathers should be considered in decisions regarding the guardianship of their offspring. In that same year, the U.S. Supreme Court ruled that unwed fathers should contribute to the support of their offspring. In their review of laws in this area Aberg and her colleagues (1977) believe that as equality between men and women increases, men will gain the legal option of taking on the parental role in many of the situations just described.

MARRIAGE AND FAMILY FORMATION

Historically, it has been assumed that the desire to reproduce is central to human existence. Women, in particular, have been perceived as seeking marriage and motherhood above all else, and even now, traditional men and women want to marry and begin having children at a younger age than do those who are less traditional in their attitudes toward gender roles (Wicks & Workman, 1978).

Those couples who are unable to conceive have tended to be the objects of pity by friends and family members. Currently, however, about 5 percent of American women *choose* to remain childless (Veevers, 1979). Many of these women perceive the role of "mother" as incompatible with other goals they have for education and occupational development (Kaltreider & Margolis, 1977). College women who intend to remain childless, compared to those who want children, are more likely to identify with the women's movement and are more optimistic about the effects of the women's movement for creating positive change in the status of women. In addition, women who don't wish to exercise their reproductive capacity are concerned with success in their vocational and other nonfamily roles to a far greater extent than is characteristic of women who want to have children (Houseknecht, 1978). As Kearney (1979) has pointed out, such voluntary childlessness challenges the concept that motherhood is central to adult feminine identity.

Among those people who *do* want to have children, the desired number of offspring is associated with their gender-role identities and attitudes. For instance, among working-class people, preference for small families is more characteristic of couples who tend to share family roles and decision making. Role relationships that are more segregated are found among those who prefer to have larger families (Rainwater & Weinstein, 1960; Rainwater, 1965). High school women with career plans and profeminist attitudes want smaller families than do more traditional women (McLaughlin, 1974). Similarly, smaller families are wanted by college students who hold egalitarian attitudes (Eagly & Anderson, 1974) and androgynous identities (Allgeier, 1975) than are wanted by more traditional and gender-typed college students.

What people intend to do at one point in their lives may be quite different from their actual later behavior. But the relationship between role attitudes and desired family size is consistent with that seen for actual completed family size. In the large-scale 1970 National Fertility Study, the *most* crucial factor in predicting the number of children borne by a woman was the extent to which the woman identified with the traditional roles of housewife and homemaker. Women with traditional gender-role definitions had more children than those with less traditional definitions (Thornton & Camburn, 1979). Among college women, members of women's organizations, Catholic woman, and married couples, those who endorse traditional roles produce more children than do those who favor egalitarian relationships (Clarkson et al., 1970; Falbo, Graham, & Gryskiewicz, 1978; Scanzoni, 1975, 1976).

Childbirth

Childbirth may be a process of relatively solitary confinement for the mother, or may be an event that includes the father and other relatives, depending on cultural norms or beliefs. Those women whose labor and delivery occurs in relative isolation because of cultural restrictions tend to have far more difficult and lengthy childbirths than do those women who are aided by their mates, family members, or friends (Newton, 1970). In Western industrialized countries in the twentieth century, women typically give birth in unfamiliar places, interrupted only by the occasional appearance of hospital personnel and doctors to check on their progress.

A rather dramatic shift in state laws, hospital policies, and maternity ward practices in the past few decades has resulted in the inclusion of expectant fathers in the process of childbirth. To date, however, there have been no systematic investigations of the extent to which gender-role identities influence expectant parents' choices relevant to the birth of their offspring.

Are traditional men more likely than egalitarian men to avoid exposure to childbirth by keeping their distance in a waiting room or bar instead of choosing to aid their wives during delivery? At this point we don't know. However, Resnick and her colleagues (1978) have suggested that the socialization of men has created a cultural barrier to participation in the birth of the baby, paternity leave, psychological preparation for child rearing, and active fathering. They conclude that educational programs are needed to involve fathers in their new role at a time that may be critical for developing attachments with newborn children. Accordingly, they have proposed an educational program to help expectant and new fathers gain support, knowledge, skills, and confidence in the fathering role.

Division of Labor Within the Family

Traditionally, men have been viewed as primarily responsible for providing the economic support of the family through paid work. Women are assigned family work (Pleck, 1975): child care, housecleaning, grocery shopping, meal preparation, and so forth. Socialized for one set of expectations regarding the functions and roles of men *versus* women, then, many of us have grown up in a world in which the "rules" changed after we started playing the game. The consequences are numerous.

Even for couples who are in comfortable agreement about contributing equally to the housecleaning, child care, and checking account, societal support for this pattern is still relatively skimpy. "Flex time," which may permit the couple to avoid overlapping time away from home, is now a practical reality in only one major institution: higher education.* Socialized to derive a sense of security from service functions, the physical impossibility of fulfilling all expectations based on *both* traditional *and* egalitarian role norms can be quite emotionally taxing on employed women. Televised commercials, such as those for Aviance perfume and other products, that portray a Superwoman who works all day, then cooks a fantastic meal, followed by dancing late into the evening and the seduction of her husband, present an impossible ideal. Although a working woman may, in fact, accomplish all that in one day, these commercials provide no hints on the likely quality of her work performance, cooking, dancing, and sexual interaction the *next* day.

---

*At a more trivial, but very aggravating level, regardless of the agreement of the couple regarding their division of labor, the inevitable neighbor or relative who compulsively conducts "white-glove" inspections attributes to the woman all responsibility for any deviation from spotlessness.

The price for men is also high. After observing their fathers in the traditional mode of arriving after work to be waited on and pampered by their mothers, they emerge into adulthood in the latter part of the twentieth century to be greeted by a very different set of expectations. They, too, must deal with multiple roles. For women, this transition offers an increase in status and economic freedom. For men, however, the transition, while potentially relieving them of some of their former economic burden, also places demands on them. Some of these demands are unpleasant. Although they no longer have to support their households all by themselves, they are also finding that it is no longer true that "A man's home is his castle." Not only are men being dethroned, but they are expected to do some of the drudgery—washing of dishes, clothes, floors, and so forth—to help maintain the castle. Given the increase in responsibility for mundane and boring tasks, it is not surprising that some men passionately resist the concept and reality of egalitarian gender roles.

Actually, what *is* surprising from the standpoint of the previous paragraph, is the number of men who do actively participate in egalitarian relationships. Despite the costs, the benefits for women are obvious. The benefits for men are less obvious, and are not often articulated except by those people in the newly emerging "men's liberation movement." What are these benefits? Traditional divisions of labor for men and women have tended to deprive men of many of the more rewarding aspects of contact with their children. The rewards of shared tenderness and vulnerability that characterize many mother-child relationships have been relatively inaccessible for fathers, who have been cast in the role of distant disciplinarian. A more egalitarian sharing of both the loving and the limit-setting aspects of child rearing is providing some men with the richness of a relationship with their children that they did not experience with their own fathers.

Traditional divisions of labor have also made communication between spouses difficult regarding the demands and frustrations of their separate roles. The utter aggravation and sense of entrapment in dealing hour after hour with a sick and exhausted 2-year-old who spits her medicine all over you and the floor can't be readily understood except by others (for instance, one's spouse) who have experienced it. Similarly, the sense of failure and frustration in spending months preparing a report or paper only to have it evaluated and rejected is difficult to convey to others who have had no experience with that sort of process.

The direct sharing of these kinds of experiences (as well as the more rewarding qualities inherent in both arenas) provides men and women with the opportunity to replace with empathic friendship the isolation associated with highly differentiated gender roles. The available evidence suggests that differences in perspective leading to gender conflict are more a function of differences in the roles traditionally assigned to men and women than to inherent differences in their biology (Chilman, 1967; Rainwater, 1965). What changes have occurred in men's and women's family roles, and what do we know about their effects?

Family work The majority of women with school-age children are now engaged in paid work (Glick & Norton, 1979). As noted, they generally find it impossible to work all day *and* greet other family members with cookies and cocktails as they arrive home from school and work to a spotless house. As women take on a portion of the "masculine" responsibility for providing the family with economic support, has there been a corresponding shouldering by husbands of some of the traditional roles assigned to women? Under pressure from the women's movement, Madison Avenue advertisers have begun to show men demonstrating the use of various kitchen products ranging from soups to microwave ovens. Several of these advertisements have portrayed a husband preparing dinner so that his employed wife may sit down to dinner rather than walking in the door to exchange her business attire and briefcase for an apron and frying pan. To what extent are men actually taking a larger role in such household tasks as cooking, washing, vacuuming, and child care?

Investigators in this area determine the contributions of men and women to family work in a very simple way: they ask men and women to report in diary fashion the amount of time they spend doing a variety of activities. From their reports, researchers are able to determine the number of hours spent in family work, including child care, and in paid work. Using such self-reports, Walker and Woods (1976) found that employed husbands engage in family work 1.6 hours per day. Housewives, in contrast, spend over 8 hours a day doing family work. From the traditional perspective, this discrepancy may seem reasonable if the man, but not the woman, is employed in paid work about 40 hours a week.

What happens in families where both parents are employed? Do husbands devote more time to family work? Apparently not, according to Walker and Woods' (1976) data. Employed women devote 4.8 hours a day to family work, but the husbands spend precisely the same number of hours in family work per day—1.6—regardless of whether or not their wives are employed. Thus, when women accept outside employment, they end up with a work overload. Men devote a total of 7.9 hours per day (averaged over a seven-day week) to paid work and family work. In contrast, women are employed, in paid and family work, an average of 10.1 hours per day.

Other researchers have found similar patterns (Meissner et al., 1975; Robinson, 1977). Furthermore, Robinson (1977) reported that employed women have less time for leisure activities and sleep than do their husbands.

It should come as no surprise that such women, compared to men, feel more time pressure and less sense of well-being.

The situation appears to be the same when women's goals, and therefore role behaviors, change during a marriage. Krieger (1977) examined the effect of mothers' return to school. She administered measures of gender-role orientation, gender-role behavior, and several other factors. All the women became less traditional in their role orientation during their first year after returning to school. In addition, the time they spent in family work decreased during that year. Did their husbands take up the slack? Apparently not. Husbands' performance remained the same before and after the women returned to school, except for those men married to traditional women. These husbands *decreased* their parental involvement. In addition, regardless of whether they were married to traditional or nontraditional women, husbands' perception of the ideal woman became significantly *more* traditional after their wives returned to school. In spite of this, decreases in family stress levels over the year led Krieger to conclude that the women's return to school may have had positive effects on the family.

Child care   One of the most important aspects of family work involves the raising of children. In a report of case studies of over 200 British mothers with infants and young children, Danyiger (1978) concluded that contemporary young mothers differ little from their counterparts of decades ago. She suggested that women continue to carry the brunt of responsibility for child care and household routines, while the fathers play peripheral roles in the care of their offspring.

The father who does wish to participate in the care of his children confronts a number of obstacles. DeFrain's (1979) research with androgynous parents indicated that the biggest difficulty they faced was in finding flexible work schedules. Some parents attempt to resolve this by taking turns with the major parental responsibility. For instance, one young father quit work for several years to permit his wife to complete her medical training (Rotbart, 1981). Although he had been successfully employed prior to taking on the homemaker role, he had a great deal of difficulty reentering the job market after being absent from it for several years while caring for their children. An executive of a Los Angeles employment firm estimated that men have three times the difficulty women do in returning to work (Rotbart, 1981). Precise reasons for employers' reluctance to hire such men are not known. Perhaps these men are victims of the same assumptions formerly held about women who cease employment while their children are young.

In spite of these difficulties, some parents are attempting to share the responsibilities for the care and socialization of their children. Evidence is beginning to emerge that men holding less stereotypic gender-role identities participate more actively in the parental role than do more traditional fathers. Androgynous fathers are more involved in caring for, as well as playing with, their children than are masculine fathers (Corradino, 1978; Russell, 1978). Furthermore, Russell (1978) found that those masculine fathers who are married to androgynous or masculine women are more involved in child care than are masculine fathers who are married to feminine women.

Effects of Changing Adult Roles on Children

What are the effects of changing gender roles on children's development and well-being? Do children who spend a portion of their time in day-care centers or in the company of their fathers while their mothers are involved elsewhere suffer by comparison to children who are cared for full time by their mothers?

Some studies have indicated that maternal employment may actually have positive benefits for family members. Hoffman (1960) found that employed mothers were more warm, helpful, supportive, and mild in their discipline of their children than were their nonemployed counterparts. She suggested that perhaps working mothers are more relaxed and satisfied people. Other research has indicated that the children of employed mothers are better adjusted than are the children of nonemployed mothers (Gold & Andres, 1978). As might be expected, the children of working mothers tend to have less stereotypic views of gender roles than do the children of nonemployed mothers (Hansson, Chernovetz, & Jones, 1977). Similarly, those fathers who actively participate in child care have children who are less likely to stereotype their parents and their peers along gender-role lines than are the offspring of fathers who participate in child care only in the presence of the mother (Baruch & Barnett, 1978).

On the basis of her extensive review of the research in this area, Etaugh (1980) reaches two conclusions: First, presently available evidence indicates "that high-quality nonmaternal care does not appear to have harmful effects on the preschool child's maternal attachment, intellectual development, social-emotional behavior, or physical health" (p. 313). Second, she agrees with other researchers that these conclusions must be considered as tentative given the problems in conducting research in the area. In any event, the position taken by opponents of day-care centers—that nonmaternal care is harmful for young children—is *not* supported by studies comparing children raised exclusively at home by their mothers with children who spend a portion of their day with nonmaternal caretakers.

As one example of the shift in our society's attitudes toward working women, it has been interesting to watch the transition in beliefs of one of the most popular and widely respected advisers on infant and child care, Dr. Benjamin Spock. From 1946, when the first edition of *Baby and Child Care* was published, and until 1976, he stated that the children of working mothers may be maladjusted. If a mother did have to work, he advised individualized care rather than placing the child in a day-care center. With the publication of the third edition of his book in 1976, his attitudes about gender-role responsibilities and maternal employment appeared to have changed considerably. Concluding that *both* parents have equal responsibilities in caring for offspring, he suggested that *both* parents have equal rights to careers if they want them. He went so far as to suggest that outside work may actually improve parent-child relationships. However, he still advocates *parental*—but, for the first time, not necessarily *maternal*—care during the first three years.

Clearly, adherence to Spock's advice is difficult for parents employed in most settings. Although academic positions provide adequate flexibility to permit employed parents to schedule their time so that they can take turns caring for infants, few other employment settings offer that advantage. Such flexibility in scheduling to permit joint parenting could be included in employee negotiations with management in a wide variety of employment settings.

Finally, North American culture has operated under a long-standing assumption that children need *both* a father and a mother in order to become healthy adults. Even more crucial than that, according to this assumption, is the presence of a parent of the same gender so that the child can develop an appropriate gender-role identity. A popular movie and book of the late 1970s, *Kramer vs. Kramer,* presented a very sympathetic view of the potentially positive effects for the child of awarding custody to the father. Whether or not tolerance for such judicial decisions has been increased by the success and publicity associated with that movie is not known. However, Stephens and Day (1979) examined the effects of divorce and subsequent awarding of custody of 39 girls to either the mother or the father. They compared those girls awarded to one parent with girls raised in families with both a mother and a father present. They found *no* negative consequences of awarding custody of the daughters to the fathers compared to the other two groups (custody awarded to mother, girl raised by both parents). The gender-role identity of the girls in adolescence was unrelated to which group raised them.

CONCLUSIONS

This chapter has focused on traditional versus egalitarian gender roles as they relate to reproductive roles and responsibilities. In reviewing the research, I have been impressed with Pleck's (1979) analysis.* Therefore, I will

---

*Although I am familiar with Pleck's earlier research on men's roles, I am indebted to Anne Peplau for calling my attention to his more recent work.

conclude this chapter with a brief summary of his perception of the three assumptions that have guided research on the division of labor within the family. I think that this approach is equally applicable to the initiation of relationships, sexual interaction, contraceptive responsibilities, and so forth (see the Afterword to this book).

Pleck suggests that investigators have held one of three sets of beliefs. He calls the earliest of these the *traditional perspective*. These researchers operated on the assumption that, because of men's economic contribution through paid work, men should not be expected to contribute to family work to any significant degree. More recently, a number of investigators have employed an *exploitation perspective*. These researchers argue that women—although they increasingly share economic responsibility for sustenance of the family—continue to carry most of the burden for family work (Mainardi, 1971; Farrell, 1974). In fact, Polatnick (1973–1974) concluded that men burden women with housework and child care in the deliberate attempt to maintain power over them.

Is that true? Is the behavior of men consistent with the old "Keep 'em barefoot, broke, and pregnant!" notion? The results of research on the amount of time devoted to family work by employed women versus employed men does not contradict that hypothesis. On the other hand, researchers haven't tapped the motivations of men. They have simply compared the behavioral contributions of men and women to family work.

Pleck (1979) goes on to describe a third and very recent assumption: the *changing roles perspective*. Adherents of this point of view reject the pessimism of the exploitation perspective. They acknowledge the disproportionate contribution of employed women to family work relative to the amount of family work done by men. However, this discrepancy is attributed to the more rapid change in women's roles than in men's roles. Pleck also suggests that an exploitation perspective does little to provide directions and support for men to increase their participation in family work. However, data from Quinn and Staines's (1978) research provide the first finding of nontrivial increases in husbands' family work associated with wives' employment. Specifically, employed husbands with employed wives reported spending almost two hours more per week in housework and almost three hours more per week in caring for their children than did employed men who were married to nonemployed wives. Citing these data as the basis for optimism, Pleck says,

> In contrast to earlier time use studies . . . men are beginning at last to increase their family work when their wives are employed. There is no question, of course, that wives continue to hold the primary responsibility for family work. But even as this reality is acknowledged, it is im-

portant to recognize that men's behavior is changing on an important social indicator. The pace of change may seem slow. Yet, it should not be dismissed or taken for granted. Change of this magnitude in a national sample actually represents a substantial phenomenon. Those working to facilitate future growth in men's family roles—researchers, educators, and clinicians—should take heart from it and build upon it. [1979, pp. 487–488]

To return briefly to the exploitation perspective (that men are deliberately trying to dominate women), there is a fascinating parallel in Mead and Newton's (1967) cross-cultural observations of the exclusion of men by women from the mysteries of reproduction. They report that in some cultures men harbor resentment toward women because they perceive women as barring them from reproductive experiences. Although men participate in the initial conception of life, they are prohibited from any further involvement. They cannot be pregnant, they are prohibited from attending labor and birth, and they are allowed very little contact with the infant for some time after its birth. In fact, recent data (Barry & Paxson, 1971) indicate that after childbirth, fathers are also prohibited from sexual contact with the mother for at least six months in 93 percent of the world's societies and for as long as two and a half years in 79 percent of societies!

On the basis of data reported by those adhering to the exploitation perspective, and those stemming from cross-cultural observations, two hypotheses might be entertained. Women may have prevented men from intimate experience with reproductive events in retaliation for women's exclusion from status and decision-making powers affecting society. Conversely, men may have prevented women from holding positions of status and power in retaliation for men's exclusion from the miracle of reproduction.

Because it is impossible to confirm either sequence, I will suggest a third. Until recently, one aspect of our potential as human beings—our respective reproductive roles as males or females—has determined our roles throughout our short life spans. Biology *was* destiny. Two centuries ago, a very short period of time from an evolutionary standpoint, the average woman died before the end of her potential to reproduce (35 years was the average life span). Within a relatively short period of time, women are living to an age in excess of 75 years. Therefore, for the majority of their years, they are incapable of reproducing. Although it is not generally included in the list of factors influencing our notions about changing gender roles, the influence of our increasing longevity on notions regarding the appropriate roles of men and women may be having its impact (see Chapter 6).

Frankly, when I began the process of examining the research relevant to this chapter, I was quite curious about the findings. I didn't hold very intense attitudes about the "best" lifestyle, and it is clear that we don't yet know all the costs and benefits associated with choices to adhere to traditional versus egalitarian roles. However, at this point, I share Pleck's (1979) optimism. I think that we are beginning to *share* the responsibilities and rewards of developing our human capacities—men and women together—as sources of emotional and economic resources to the children we *choose* to conceive, and as true partners to one another.

8 Gender Roles and Sexuality in the World of Work

BARBARA A. GUTEK
and
CHARLES Y. NAKAMURA

Until recently, the vast majority of employed people were men. As noted in the preceding chapter, the majority of women are now employed in paid work. Barbara Gutek and Charles Nakamura report that the influx of women into the workplace has produced both positive and negative results. With men and women working in close proximity, sexual attraction between co-workers sometimes occurs. Gutek and Nakamura are refreshingly broad in their overview of the place of sex at work. They point out that women and men alike may view their jobs as providing them with the potential of meeting someone for sexual and/or marital partnership. They also note that sexual attraction between co-workers may increase their mutual pleasure in carrying out their jobs.

Most of the emphasis of their research and that of others they review, however, is on unwanted sexual advances. Official recognition of sexual harassment is a very new phenomenon. Until recently, the only knowledge about the process was anecdotal. Behavioral scientists have just begun to examine the extent of the problem. Gutek and Nakamura were awarded one of the first federal grants to conduct surveys on sexual harassment. They have been studying the incidence of harassment and some of the personal and demographic characteristics of people who are harassed and of those who do the harassing. They discuss the costs of harassment both to individuals and to organizations.

Throughout the chapter, they consider the contribution of stereotypic gender-role norms to the existence of harassment, to the disproportionate number of women (compared to men) who are harassed, and to the disproportionate number of men (compared to women) who do the harassing. Those results may reflect gender-role norms. That is, men may be unaware that some of their behavior is offensive to women at work. In fact, they may be flattered by the same behavior from women that women dislike from men.

Finally, Gutek and Nakamura suggest ways in which harassment in the workplace may be reduced through changes in the work atmosphere and by the position on harassment taken by the employer. In particular, they note that two factors are necessary to allow co-workers to use work as a forum for meeting and getting to know people without engaging in sexual exploitation or harassment. A clear separation of traditional gender roles from work roles is one important factor, and they believe this is best accomplished by hiring equal numbers of men and women in a given workplace. Second, they suggest that organizations and individuals should prohibit the use of organizational resources to further individuals' inappropriate goals. For example, a supervisor may arrange an unnecessary business trip as a way to spend time with a colleague or subordinate whom he or she finds attractive.

 The workplace, where the majority of adults spend most of their waking days, is not insulated from the pervasive effects of gender-role socialization. Beliefs about masculinity, femininity, and sexual expression that were acquired during childhood and adolescence color workers' expectations of themselves, their co-workers, and their employers. Consequently, few people should be astonished to learn that issues of sexuality may occur at work.*

The power and status aspects of work and the fact that most people depend on their jobs for sustenance complicates the occurrence of sexuality at work. Research on sexuality at work, like the serious discussion of sexuality at work, has been a taboo topic. However, as shifts in gender-role norms continue, people are increasingly conscious of the need to recognize and understand the variety of sexual experiences that do occur. Men and women who work together flirt, date, fall in love, get married, have affairs, or exploit each other sexually. Sexuality is also a factor in other ways: within the workplace, people whistle at, notice, make comments, joke about, and engage in nonverbal behavior that is sexual in nature. At an even more subtle level, people in powerful positions (usually men) often surround themselves with sexually attractive people (usually women) who are generally young and in subordinate positions.

It is not surprising that all these behaviors occur: sexuality is everywhere in our society. People think of sex frequently at work as well as at play.

*This paper was written in part with the help of National Institute of Mental Health grant USPHS-MH-32606-01.

Furthermore, many jobs are sexy, according to Michael Maccoby, author of *The Gamesman* (1978). Athletes, flight attendants, movie stars, executives, authors, and others are sexually exciting people. Their work makes them more attractive because they do things and go places that many people admire or envy. Furthermore, many work roles overlap with gender roles. Women, for example, are often expected to dress seductively and act in a sexy or overly feminine manner. Like the adolescents described by Zellman and Goodchilds in Chapter 2, adults may stereotype women's seductive clothing as implying sexual readiness. And, as MacKinnon (1979) has noted, women are often expected to adopt "an ingratiating, flattering, and deferential manner which projects sexual compliance" (p. 22). The traditional male gender role complicates the situation. Men, too, may be expected to act in a "macho" manner on the job. Other men (and women) may encourage a man to flirt, tease women, and act as though he were eager to have a sexual relationship with women at work.

In this chapter, we discuss sexuality at work, what it includes, whether it is good or bad, why it happens, and when it happens. Where appropriate, we include data from three surveys we have conducted on the subject of social and sexual behavior at work. Each survey used half-hour telephone interviews with representative samples of working people in the Los Angeles area. All together, over 1,900 working men and women were interviewed (see Gutek et al., 1980; Gutek, 1981; Gutek, in preparation). All three surveys and this chapter are concerned with heterosexual behavior only, although we recognize that such encounters can be homosexual as well. In fact, in the first pilot study, in the absence of repeated statements that we were asking only about heterosexual experiences, men in particular tended to report homosexual social and sexual experiences. We have not studied dating or marriage among co-workers, although that is also an important and much neglected area.

IS SEX IN THE WORKPLACE ALWAYS UNDESIRABLE?

In considering what the role of sex should be in the workplace, it is necessary to look at the issue from two perspectives. One is the organization's point of view: what will the organization gain by flirtation or sexual activity between employees? The other point of view is the employee's: what can he or she gain by flirting, propositioning, or harassing another worker?

The Organization's Point of View

Organizations have generally viewed the consequences of sexual comments and encounters negatively. Problems resulting from introducing women into previously all-male workgroups or organizations are often discussed. The presence of women has been viewed as a distracting influence on male workers, who are assumed to occupy more responsible and valuable positions. Furthermore, organizations fear that relationships between a man and a woman at work may interfere with the man's allegiance to the company, that he may show favoritism toward the woman, and that they may spend too much company time on personal matters (Quinn, 1977). A general fear of female workers and female sexuality as a disruptive influence has been mentioned by various people in the military services, as well. A "love-sick" general might make a poor strategic move, for example. In addition, spouses of organizational members frequently prefer that their spouses not work with members of the other gender. In particular, housewives were assumed to fear that all working women were trying to seduce their husbands.

On the other hand, possible positive consequences for the organization have not been explored. For example, two workers who are sexually involved with each other might show an increased loyalty and commitment to their company.

The Individual's Point of View

Individuals are more likely than organizations to see the consequences of sexuality as positive. Traditionally, it was assumed that women took jobs in order to find a husband. Contemporary research (Schriesheim, 1980) suggests that men also view the work setting as an appropriate place to meet and get to know women. Contact at work can result in marriage, steady relationships, or affairs that may be viewed as positive by the people involved. And co-workers can also engage in sexual jokes or flirting that may enhance one's ego and fantasy life as well as making work more enjoyable.

But sexuality can also have negative consequences for workers. The general term *sexual harassment* describes unwanted sexual comments or behaviors. Farley (1978, pp. 14–15) defines sexual harassment as follows:

> Sexual harassment is best described as unsolicited, nonreciprocal male behavior that asserts a woman's sex role over her function as a worker. It can be any or all of the following: staring at, commenting upon, or touching a woman's body; requests for acquiescence in sexual behavior; repeated nonreciprocated propositions for dates; demands for sexual intercourse; and rape.

Sexual harassment, however, is not always easy to define, nor is it always experienced or evaluated similarly by initiator and recipient. For example, "his" expression of sexual interest may be "her" experience of sexual harassment. In order to understand sexual harassment, sexual behavior must be studied in the broader context of sexuality in the workplace, the influence of gender roles and work roles, and changing attitudes toward sexuality and gender roles.

The concept of sexual harassment, popularized by journalists (Farley, 1978; Lindsey, 1977), has also been viewed as sex discrimination by attorney MacKinnon (1979). These writers describe many clear-cut cases of sexual harassment. For example, Farley (1978) cites a case in which a 20-year-old woman, applying for a waitress position, was offered the job with the proviso that she regularly engage in sexual relations with the owner of the restaurant. MacKinnon (1979) cites a case of a secretary who was invited to lunch by her boss. She was physically detained against her will at a bar with him. He told her that willingness to engage in sexual relations with him "was necessary to their satisfactory working relations. When she tried to leave, he physically prevented her, implying that if she protested, no one [who worked] at the company would help her" (MacKinnon, 1979, p. 70). Most people would consider such cases to involve sexual harassment and would conclude that there were both undesirable psychological and economic consequences for the woman. Reports of such experiences in books, newspapers, and magazines, as well as in accumulating psychological research (Benson & Thomson, 1980: Gutek et al., 1980; Pope, Levenson, & Schover, 1979; Pope, Schover, & Levenson, 1980; Merit System Protection Board, 1981) have resulted in increased public awareness of the problem.

For the individual, sexuality at work is positive if it involves falling in love or having an exciting affair. It is negative if it involves sexual harassment. Other behaviors may be either positive or negative for the individual. Is being asked to have a drink after work positive or negative? How about being patted on the derrière? Or being whistled at? Some of these behaviors may be viewed as sexual harassment; others may be viewed as ego enhancing and enjoyable, or as the prelude to a more intimate relationship. We refer to all these as *social-sexual behaviors*. Social-sexual behaviors are non-work-related behaviors that have sexual content.

SOCIAL-SEXUAL BEHAVIOR AT WORK

A list of varieties of social-sexual behaviors can help to clarify the kinds of situations and interactions that constitute sexual harassment. We developed such a list in the process of conducting our surveys. We currently distinguish whether the behavior is intended just to get the attention of the recipient or whether it requires a response from the recipient, whether the behavior involves physical contact or not, whether the behavior is verbal or nonverbal, and whether the behavior was meant as a compliment or meant as an insult.

The most basic distinction we make is between attentional behaviors and behaviors requiring a response. Attentional behaviors do not require a response from the recipient. Examples are comments, catcalls, or whistling.

Other examples are sending sexual cartoons or obscene letters, notes, or advertisements to someone at work. Most such behaviors are meant to be insulting, but some are meant to be complimentary. Comments on one's physical attractiveness or sexual desirability may be intended as compliments, depending on the circumstances. In any case, none of these behaviors *requires* a response from the recipient, a fact that is sometimes interpreted, perhaps incorrectly, to mean that they are less objectionable to the recipient.

Other behaviors, however, do require a response from the recipient. This category includes sexual activity or dating as a requirement of getting or keeping a job, or getting a promotion or a desirable job. It also includes sexual activity to avoid being fired, demoted, or assigned an undesirable job. Most often, if a person is going to make such a demand it will be for sexual activity, but a supervisor or employer may sometimes just demand that an employee accompany him or her on social occasions. Other people may then think the two are sexually intimate. Because of the element of coercion and sometimes physical force, it is highly unlikely that these behaviors would ever be perceived as complimentary by the recipient or the initiator.

The attentional behaviors include several types. Some are verbal (such as comments, whistles, and laughing), and some are nonverbal (such as gestures, leering, and body language). Some involve physical contact and others do not. In the surveys, men and women often distinguished between touching and other nonverbal behaviors. Unwanted touching, besides being a nonverbal objectional behavior, also intrudes into one's personal space (Sommers, 1969).

Another way of looking at attentional behaviors is to determine if they were meant to be complimentary or insulting. This distinction focuses on the intentions of the initiator as interpreted by the recipient. An even finer distinction might be made between initiator intentions and recipient perceptions. That is, is the message received the same as the message sent? Current changes in expectations and beliefs about gender roles suggest that an initiator's intentions will differ from the recipient's evaluation of behavior. A man may intend his whistling to compliment a woman, but she may perceive it as an insult. The perceptual component seems to be important in the way in which men and women report social-sexual experiences. However, the present state of what we actually know does not allow us to make such detailed distinctions.

DEFINITIONS OF SEXUAL HARASSMENT

The term *sexual harassment* was initially conceptualized rather narrowly by the popular press and the law. It included sexual relations as a requirement for getting or keeping a job, but little else. In 1980, Equal Employment Opportunity Commission (EEOC) rulings on sexual harassment greatly expanded the definition to include any unwanted verbal or nonverbal sexual behavior. The EEOC's position is "that sexual harassment, like racial harassment, generates a harmful atmosphere" and that "employees should be afforded a working environment free from discriminatory intimidation whether based on sex, race, religion, or national origin" ("Rules and Regulations," p. 25024). If the behaviors negatively affect the work performance of the employee, the behavior can be considered sexual harassment. Furthermore, the EEOC has ruled that employers are responsible for seeing that employees work in a harassment-free environment. Thus an employer is held responsible when sexual harassment of employees occurs.

Keeping with both the spirit and the letter of the EEOC rulings, the U.S. government has issued guidelines for federal employees. Congress requested that a survey be conducted to assess the extent of sexual harassment within the Civil Service Systems (Merit System Protection Board, 1981). Federal guidelines define sexual harassment rather broadly. For example, the Office of Personnel Management (Campbell, 1980, p. 2) states that "Specifically, sexual harassment is deliberate or repeated unsolicited verbal comments, gestures, or physical contact of a sexual nature that is unwelcome" (see OPM's unpublished 1980 guidelines, Office of Personnel Management, 1900 E St. NW, Rm. 7540, Washington, D.C. 20415).

The position taken by the EEOC specifically, and by the federal government in general, is roughly consistent with the public's conception of sexual harassment. In a pilot study of sexual harassment in the fall of 1978 (Gutek et al., 1980), 19.9 percent of a randomly chosen sample of working people in the Los Angeles area defined even positive comments of a sexual nature as sexual harassment. In a second study, conducted in February 1980 (Gutek, 1981), 24.6 percent of respondents defined positive comments of a sexual nature as sexual harassment. Likewise, there was a slight increase in respondents who believed that being expected to date as part of the job was sexual harassment. Of people interviewed in 1978, 82 percent said that dating as part of the job was sexual harassment, compared to 90.4 percent of respondents in the 1980 study. There was no complete consensus among respondents in either survey about what constitutes sexual harassment. Although 84.4 percent of respondents in the first study thought sexual activity as a requirement of the job was sexual harassment, 15.2 percent did not. A smaller minority (5.3 percent) of people in the second study also thought that sex as a requirement of work was not sexual harassment.

These findings and the EEOC rulings suggest that, although sexual harassment can be identified with a specific set of behaviors, it cannot be defined exclusively by these behaviors. Some people may think being whistled at is sexual harassment; other people disagree. Furthermore, whether or not whistling is considered sexual harassment may also depend on who does the whistling, on characteristics of the recipient, and on the context of the event. In response to criticism that the EEOC is interfering in personal matters, spokespeople have emphasized that legal decisions will be made on a case-by-case basis. The context of the experiences is recognized as being crucial (Marcus, 1980). The task of defining the conditions under which people feel sexually harassed can be simultaneously studied within the legal profession and within the social science research community.

VICTIMS AND HARASSERS

Men's and women's behavior at work is patterned after the gender roles they acquired as children and adolescents (see Chapters 1 and 2). Essentially, men have been socialized to be powerful and sexual, whereas women have been socialized into compliance or being the targets of men's sexual advances. Therefore, work obligations, gender roles, and sexuality may become confused.

WHO IS BEING HARASSED?

In the workplace, men are more often in leadership positions than are women. Male supervisors may be tempted to generalize the aggression and control expected of them on the job to sexual aggression—the active pursuit of women they want. And women subordinates may carry their passivity too far. Some women, believing that sexual harassment is unavoidable, may permit men to sexually exploit them. These dynamics are similar to those Cherry describes in Chapter 11, on rape. As long as the normal masculine gender role teaches men to confuse sexuality with dominance, men are encouraged to be sexual aggressors and women to be sexual victims. Traditional gender-role socialization alone, however, cannot account completely for workers' experiences with unwanted sexual advances. Work roles—for example, how much authority men have on the job vis-à-vis women—must also be considered.

Together, gender roles and work roles interact to present men and women with very different opportunities. Men are in an excellent position to sexually harass women because of both men's training in sexual aggressiveness and their supervisory power over women employees. Women, on the other hand, have little opportunity to harass male co-workers because they are rarely either sexually aggressive or in a position of authority over men. Consequently, it should come as no surprise that women are more likely to complain about sexual harassment than are men.

Women are more likely to define various behaviors as sexual harassment. They are more likely than men to quit a job because of sexual harassment (17.3 percent, compared to 4.8 percent). They are more likely to file suit because of sexual harassment (Marcus, 1980) and are more likely to miss work because of harassment (7.1 percent, compared to 2.4 percent). The point that women are more likely to be harassed needs to be emphasized, because there is currently much media interest in sexual harassment of men. For example, the media have been reporting on the reverse "casting-couch" phenomenon (that is, female casting directors forcing attractive young male actors to engage in sexual activity in exchange for acting roles). Our own data have been "selectively reported" in this manner ("Executive Sweet," 1979). Sexual harassment of men does exist, but it is a rare phenomenon, currently affecting perhaps 1 or 2 percent of men in their working lives.

Our studies suggest that other demographic characteristics are much less important than gender, although age, ethnicity, and marital status of women are significant. Through their 30s, women are slightly more likely to report being targets of social-sexual behaviors in their current jobs than are older women. White women are more likely to report harassment than are minority women. Asian women report the fewest experiences. The relationship of marital status to reported harassment is surprising. In general, married women and widows report fewer experiences of sexual harassment than do single or divorced women. But the highest incidence is among women who are living with a man. These cohabiting women are twice as likely as women in general to report that they were touched sexually by a man at work (29 percent, compared to 15 percent). And they were almost twice as likely to report insulting sexual looks or gestures (32 percent, compared to 19 percent) than were women in general. These findings are consistent with results reported by Farley (1978), who cites instances of sexual harassment among professional women, older women, teenagers, minority women, and so on. She contends that sexual harassment can happen to any woman, not just certain small groups of women.

Physical attractiveness may be a factor in sexual harassment. Our research shows that people who label themselves as physically attractive were more likely to report that they were expected to date or engage in sexual activity as a part of their jobs than were people who did not see themselves as physically attractive. They were also more likely to report complimentary comments of a sexual nature than women who reported themselves to be less attractive. Women who rated themselves as physically attractive were more likely to report social-sexual behaviors in general than were less attractive women. Of the women who rated themselves very attractive, 73 percent reported at least one social-sexual incident, compared to 33 percent of the other female respondents. These relationships are fairly consistent, but it is not true that, as popular opinion suggests, sexual harassment is a problem that affects only young, attractive women.

Ratings of personality may be more important than physical attractiveness. In both pilot studies, women who reported having attractive personalities reported more of all types of social-sexual behaviors. This finding is consistent with MacKinnon's (1979) hypothesis that women are chosen for jobs on the basis of sexual appeal and friendliness and are then subjected to sexual harassment.

An interesting finding is that defining a behavior as sexual harassment is not affected by whether one has or has not experienced that behavior. One might suspect that, unless they experience it firsthand, people may not give a great deal of thought to sexual harassment but may dismiss it as a trivial complaint (see MacKinnon, 1979). This does not appear to be the case. People who are approached with behaviors we have mentioned are not more likely than others to label those behaviors as sexual harassment.

In sum, sexual harassment happens mostly to women, particularly attractive, personable women who are living with a man. However, others may experience harassment or complimentary sexual comments or both.

WHO PROPOSITIONS OR HARASSES WORKERS?

The vast majority of sexual harassment behaviors are initiated by men. As MacKinnon (1979) and others point out, women have been socialized to be subservient, submissive, and passive in relations with men (see Chapters 3 and 4). In the workplace, traditional gender-role socialization is salient because men are more likely to be in dominant positions relative to women. As a result, in the workplace just as everywhere else, women are less likely than men to initiate any kind of sexual encounter (see Chapter 3).

Other demographic characteristics of the initiator (besides gender role) are no more important than the demographic characteristics of the recipient. Women report that male initiators span the age spectrum. Initiators are more likely to be married than not, but this probably reflects the higher number of married men in the population. And initiators vary in physical attractiveness.

One factor that has been given a great deal of attention is the organizational position of the initiator. A narrow definition of sexual harassment — that is, sex as a condition of work — would suggest that only supervisors could initiate harassment. Although supervisors are the most likely initiators according to many reports (for example, see Benson & Thomson, 1980; Farley, 1978; Gutek et al., 1980), even a narrow interpretation of harassment could include others as initiators. Many groups of people in the work situation are in positions to coerce or pressure people into engaging in sexual relations. One group is people on whom one depends at work; for example, people who provide one's work supplies, or who are valued customers or clients. Another group is people with whom one is interdependent at work; for example, a teammate on an assembly-line job, or a partner in a police squad car.

A broader definition of sexual harassment suggests that people at virtually all positions within an organization could be initiators of sexual harassment. If harassment includes being the target of obscene jokes or catcalls, or being expected by members of a workgroup to do, or being coerced into doing, demeaning tasks, then people at all levels can be initiators. The legal guidelines, however, state that where a lower-level person is the actual initiator of an objectionable behavior (for example, bombarding a co-worker with obscene pictures and letters), the supervisor is also responsible. This provision suggests, of course, that the atmosphere of the workplace is an important factor in sexual harassment (and this suggestion is covered in a later section of this chapter).

Not all people in supervisory positions sexually harass their employees, of course. The personality of the supervisor involved is also important. People with a high need for power or dominance, besides using an overbearing or heavy-handed style of leadership, often try to use sex to control their employees. For example, one secretary noted that her boss wanted to dominate his subordinates in all aspects of work; and, in her case, that extended to a wish to dominate her sexual life as well.

WHEN DO WORKERS FEEL HARASSED?

In general, if you were asked by a man (or woman) at work to engage in sexual activity, would you feel flattered or insulted? One possible response to such as question is "It depends on the person." Sexual overtures from a person who is perceived as attractive may not be viewed as sexual harassment, whereas attention from someone perceived as unattractive, undesirable, or an inappropriate companion may be viewed as harassment. In studying third-person reports of office romances, Quinn (1977) found three possible goals of men and women who become sexually involved. The first set of goals and motives involves *job motives*. That is, people felt the relationship would increase job security, financial rewards, job efficiency, or result in easier work, or job advancement. This motive is predominantly used by women, because few women are in a position to offer these organizational rewards to men. The second set of motives involves *ego motives:* people felt the relationship would offer excitement, ego enhancement, adventure, and sexual experience. The third set of motives involves a *love motive* —a feeling of sincere love and companionship.

A man and a woman may have different motives for getting involved with each other. Quinn (1977) found three common patterns or combinations of motives. When a woman is job motivated and a man is ego motivated, he called the relationship *utilitarian*. When both are motivated by ego motives, the relationship is labeled the "Fling," and when both are motivated by love motives, the relationship is called "True Love." The utilitarian relationship might or might not be considered sexual harassment by the woman involved. The position of the man, rather than his personal characteristics, determines the utilitarian relationship, whereas the personal characteristics of the individual are factors in both the Fling and True Love.

Regardless of whether one is motivated by job factors, ego factors, or love factors, sexual overtures from a person who can supply one or more of these may be viewed as less offensive than overtures from someone who cannot supply such rewards. On the other hand, the ability to grant job rewards may make the initiator's actions more objectionable, because the power to reward is usually accompanied by the power to punish. People who are willing to use job rewards in order to achieve personal gains may be just as willing to use job sanctions in response to rejection. In our research, for example, one woman pointed out that after she rejected a foreman's overtures she was put on an extremely difficult job requiring heavy lifting. She eventually quit the job.

Although a woman might feel sexually harassed even though she is motivated to be involved, she is more likely to feel harassed if she is not motivated to be involved. For example, if a man is motivated by love motives but the woman is not interested, she may feel sexually harassed, especially if he uses his position at work to advance his cause. Whether a woman will feel more harassed if a man is motivated by love motives or ego motives is not known but could be easily researched.

A man also may feel harassed if a woman is motivated by love motives or ego motives and he is not interested. Because of the kinds of positions women occupy in organizations, however, women are less likely to be able to use organizational resources to pursue a man. Perhaps the situation most like harassment for men is when a woman is motivated by job motives and he is not interested. In our studies, some men who were in supervisory positions labeled sexual comments and gestures that were meant to be positive as sexual harassment, presumably because they encountered women who engage in seductive behavior in an attempt to get a job or get a better job. This annoyance might be considered sexual harassment although the job consequences to the man are relatively minor. Fuller (1979) prefers to call this behavior "enticement" rather than "harassment." Clearly, this situation is different from having to engage in sexual relations to get or keep a job.

One general hypothesis about sexual harassment that emerges from Quinn's (1977) research is that the greater the discrepancy between a man's motives for interacting with a woman at work and a woman's motives for interacting with a man at work, the more likely one of them is to feel sexually harassed. For example, if co-workers arrange a lunch and the woman is motivated to learn more about her job while a man is motivated to start an affair, the woman may feel disappointed, frustrated, and harassed.

Several conditions at work can contribute to a person feeling sexually harassed: the proximity of men and women, the percentage of women in the workgroup or job, powerlessness, and the general atmosphere.

Proximity of Men and Women

Quinn (1977) pointed out the importance of proximity in the formation of office romances. There are three types of proximity. First, workers may be in geographical proximity (such as secretary and manager). Second, workers may have ongoing, work-related proximity (such as a group of telephone operators, or police squad partners). Finally, workers may have occasional contact at the water cooler or in the lunch room. Proximity is a well-documented factor in the formation of relationships in general (for example, see Freedman, Sears, & Carlsmith, 1978), and sexually harassing relationships are no exception.

Percentage of Women in the Work Group

The percentage of women in the job or workgroup is also likely to affect sexual harassment. We believe that sexual harassment occurs the most in jobs which have been traditionally held by men (such as welder or accountant). In addition, sexual harassment also occurs in jobs that are predominantly female (such as secretary or flight attendant). The reasons for such behaviors, however, are quite different (Gutek & Morasch, 1982). In the case of the traditionally male job, sexual harassment is probably a response to resentment about women "invading" male turf. Part of the mythology surrounding many traditional male jobs, from construction worker to corporate lawyer, is that women are not "fit" for the job. Men, especially men in male-dominated occupations, are quite likely to say that women could not handle their job as well as they, whereas women are not as likely to say that men could not handle traditionally female jobs (Staines et al., 1979). When women are hired and perform as well as men, men are forced to face the fact that their beliefs about female inferiority are myths. One response is to try to prove that women are inadequate for the job by making the job more difficult through sexual insults and harassment. Recent newspaper stories have noted that the military in particular has had a real problem integrating women into male jobs ("Army Begins to Confront Sexual Harassment Problems," 1979; "Women Officers Cite Widespread Sexual Harassment," 1980). It is difficult to integrate women into an organization that has traditionally used, as the ultimate insult, the charge that "You act like a bunch of girls."

In the case of predominantly female jobs, the mechanisms involved in sexual harassment are probably different. "Women's jobs" often have a large component of female gender role, a point emphasized by R. M. Kanter (1977) in the case of secretaries and by MacKinnon (1979) in general. In an atmosphere in which a woman is expected to cater to a man's ego and personal maintenance needs, it is not too surprising that she may be expected to cater to his sexual needs, too. This point is elaborated later in this chapter.

Powerlessness

Another working condition that contributes to feeling sexually harassed is a lack of control over one's work environment. A person who has enough control over the work situation to rebuff sexual overtures without reprisal, or who does not have to tolerate lewd or obscene comments, gestures, or sexual touching, is less likely to feel sexually harassed than the powerless worker.

People can be powerless in two ways, and the two often go together. One is powerlessness on the job. The person at the bottom of the organizational heap can be ordered about by lots of people and has little recourse except to quit the job. These people are undoubtedly insulted in many ways; sexual insults are probably just one of the kinds of putdowns they receive. In our studies, respondents who reported being treated disrespectfully at work in general were also more likely than other respondents to receive insulting sexual comments. Powerless workers may also be expected to engage in a variety of demeaning or humiliating activities; sexual demands are one way to demean and humiliate. Farley (1978, pp. 108–109) described the case of a waitress:

> One day I was pouring a cup of coffee from the urn which is right in front, and a man came up to the urn to get his own coffee. As he was doing that he reached around me and started rubbing my back. I said, "Let's cut it out." He said, "I was just feeling the fruit." I said, "Not this fruit." That was all, no need to get heavy about it. The next moment he turned around and he started yelling at me and calling me a bitch. He was cursing me in front of everyone.

The second kind of powerlessness is broader and concerns the job market and one's work options. If a person has other job options, she or he can quit and find another job. Most of the people in powerless jobs are also relatively powerless in the job market. If the person also has family responsibilities, as do many single parents, the powerlessness is compounded. Women who are divorced and have small children, minority women, women who don't speak English, and uneducated women may all be especially vulnerable to sexual harassment because they lack control over their lives.

General Atmosphere

A final group of factors that we believe contribute to feeling sexually harassed involves the general atmosphere at work An environment in which there are frequent sexual jokes and comments constantly calls attention to male and female sexuality. Clothing is another factor in organizational atmosphere. An environment where women are expected to wear skimpy or sexually revealing clothing (for instance, cocktail waitresses) accentuates their sexuality and encourages sexual comments and propositions. A current court case (Marcus, 1980, p. 12) involves "the case of a woman who was fired from her job as a lobby attendant in an office building when she refused to wear a skimpy outfit that she said led to intolerable harassment." In another case, waitresses are suing a Michigan company because they were required to wear short, revealing uniforms that they said encouraged customers to harass them sexually.

An environment in which a macho image is encouraged in men (for instance, the military) or a helpless vulnerable image is encouraged in women, may also increase the probability of sexual harassment. Some work environments (such as some factories) encourage men to engage in exaggerated masculine behavior, to make comments about women in both their presence and their absence, and to present an image of constant readiness for sexual activity. Some environments (such as some offices) also encourage women to flirt with men, to flatter men's egos, and to behave in a subservient manner.

The employer, foreman, supervisor, or workgroup leader can control the general atmosphere at work. A supervisor who encourages a sexualized environment is likely to find that sexual harassment occurs. In this environment, female victims are not likely to feel they can approach the supervisor for support. On the other hand, a supervisor who does not tolerate or permit people to be treated as sexual objects or does not encourage flirting is less likely to have employees who are harassed. The new Equal Employment Opportunity Commission rulings make the supervisor responsible for sexual harassment that occurs among employees. The supervisor can no longer ignore sexual harassment; therefore, it may behoove supervisory personnel to eliminate the sexually charged environments in which some people work.

NEGATIVE EFFECTS OF SEXUAL HARASSMENT ON WOMEN WORKERS

One effect of being sexually harassed is that the victim may become generally disillusioned with male workers (Benson & Thomson, 1980). A woman secretary who previously admired her boss may be extremely disappointed if he tries to coerce her into sexual relations. According to Benson and Thomson

(1980), a second effect is that sexual harassment lessens contact between men and women. In their study, they noted that female students harassed by male faculty at colleges or universities avoided the faculty member, even when help was needed, or avoided classes where the instructor had a reputation of harassing students (Dolan, 1977). In the workplace, women may avoid contact with harassing male workers even though the contact is desirable or necessary to do the job.

Other, more general effects are felt by all women. For example, sexual harassment hinders the integration of women into traditionally male jobs. Men may use sexual harassment as a conscious or unconscious strategy to discourage women from pursuing such careers, and the strategy is successful unless women receive support from their supervisors at work as well as from the law. Moreover, men who are not used to working with women do not have a sense of women's work roles. Because they are used to dealing with women's gender roles but not work roles, they may treat women in the work environment the same way they would outside the work environment, which may be inappropriate. Bass, Krusall, and Alexander (1971) found that the most important factor influencing male managers to think that women would be inappropriate in managerial positions was a sense of deference for women. They expected this deference to conflict with work requirements. When women workers react negatively to deference, men may overreact by making lewd and obscene comments or by otherwise subjecting women to sexual harassment. Several female student interviewers received such treatment from male respondents in one of our surveys. The respondents viewed the survey instrument as inappropriate and responded by making sexual comments to the interviewer. One respondent also called one author (Gutek) and, after saying that he thought sex was not an appropriate topic for a survey, added "If you want to hear about sex, I'll tell you about sex . . . "

A general effect of sexual harassment mentioned by Benson and Thomson (1980), MacKinnon (1979), and Nieva and Gutek (1981) is that sexual harassment reinforces job inequality. An example is in factory settings, where men may encourage (and women may go along with) trading work for sex. The man uses his lunch and break time to do the woman's job in exchange for sexual favors. Men view such behavior by women as proof of women's inability to handle a job. Thus, sex does have an exchange value but using sex in that manner does not improve work conditions for women. Gender inequality in the workplace remains.

Over the long run, sexual harassment reduces women's career commitment (Benson & Thomson, 1980). If women believe that they are not rewarded for their efforts and achievements and instead are rewarded for their sexuality, they are not motivated to achieve or exert effort on the job. Furthermore, because our society values youth in women, a woman's source of reward—her sexuality—loses its value as she grows older. It is well documented that women have lower career aspirations compared to men (Nieva & Gutek, 1979; 1981). How large a role sexual harassment plays in this phenomenon is not clear.

NEGATIVE EFFECTS OF SEXUAL HARASSMENT ON ORGANIZATIONS

One negative effect of sexual harassment on organizations is increased absenteeism and turnover among female employees. Our studies show that up to 17 percent of women have quit jobs because of sexual harassment and 7 percent have missed work because of it (Gutek et al., 1980). A second negative effect concerns women's career commitment. Women are not the only ones who suffer as a result of their own lower career aspirations and career commitment. Organizations do, too, because they lose the energy and creativity of which women are capable. Organizations may also be hampered in fulfilling their affirmative action programs. Women may be hired into traditionally male jobs, but unless the employer sees to it that they work in a harassment-free environment, they may leave at the first opportunity. Finally, the latest EEOC regulations make employers responsible for sexual harassment. Marcus (1980) estimates that over 50 sexual harassment suits have already been launched and that number is likely to rise dramatically. Thus, there are both internal and external pressures on organizations to be concerned with sexual harassment and to try to eliminate it.

CONCLUSIONS

We indicated earlier that it would be surprising if sexual exchange did not occur in the workplace. Our concern is not so much with why it emerges, but rather with the various forms in which, and conditions under which, it happens. We need to know which kinds have positive consequences and which have negative consequences for individuals, organizations, and social institutions. Knowing more might allow people to encourage the positive aspects of sexuality and inhibit the negative at work, to the benefit of both workers and organizations.

On the one hand, people learn that behavior should be appropriate to the situation. Work roles call for certain kinds of behavior, and that behavior should be the same regardless of personal factors—whether two workers know each other or not, are sexually intimate or not, are brother and sister or not. A husband and wife who work together should not behave at work the same as they behave at home (although one of our subjects said she was frequently touched sexually at work, because she works with her husband).

But even among strangers at work, these situationally defined roles become blurred. The fear that people cannot or will not separate work role and gender role has led to a variety of rules and hiring practices (such as forbidding two members of the same family to work together) and may be one reason for resistance to gender desegregation of the labor force.

Some research shows that people do not distinguish situation-appropriate gender roles from work roles. For example, Goodchilds (1980) reported that teenagers, in a Los Angeles study in 1979, did not evaluate forced sexual relations any differently if they occurred at a party or if they occurred at work. Those young people thought that what was permissible at a party was also permissible at work; they did not make a distinction between the two settings.

The socialization of gender roles is so predominant throughout life that gender roles are fused with all other roles and, for most people, override the work roles that are learned and that are defined by the work situation. Masculine and feminine roles are deeply ingrained. Gender-defined characteristics such as dominance, aggressiveness, and independence in men, and gentleness, nurturance, and supportiveness in women, are carried into the workplace. Furthermore, the male value system governs the workplace in most instances (Levin, 1980; Nieva & Gutek, 1981). Under these circumstances, men are most likely to be in the powerful and controlling positions, and women may easily fall into the "ingratiating, flattering, and deferential manner which projects sexual compliance" (MacKinnon, 1979, p. 22). It is highly probable that the combination of these gender-role and work-role norms at least partly determines the forms of sexuality at work. In negative forms of sexuality such as harassment, men openly initiate. Women are restricted to more subtle routes, such as enticement, to try to get their way.

This blending of work and gender roles is further facilitated by the fact that, in many traditionally female jobs, work role *is* gender role. If we look at the evolution of a job such as bank teller from a male-dominated job to a female-dominated job, we can see how aspects of the female gender role now enter into the bank teller role. The bank teller was originally the guardian of one's money, and bank tellers were men. The teller was viewed as a symbol of the security of the bank. As tellers' salaries declined in relation to other jobs and as more women became tellers, the symbolism of the job changed. The bank teller today is a symbol of the courteous service that the bank provides to customers, and bank tellers are women.

Another reason for the blending of work and gender roles is that people generally want to feel sexually attractive and desirable, and sometimes this may be more important than wanting to feel like a capable worker. Work is a setting where people can test out their "sexual worth." Sometimes a person may be more interested in being perceived as sexually desirable than as a good worker, especially if work is boring, meaningless, or only temporary.

Many people prefer to interpret social-sexual behavior they receive — such as comments, looks, or even propositions — as an indication of their physical attractiveness or sexual desirability. Our surveys indicate that both men and women, but especially men, explained overtures and propositions by workers of the other gender in terms of their own attractiveness. For example, in response to a question about why women at work had touched them sexually, some men reported that they were attractive to the woman:

> I asked her out and showed I liked her. I may have touched her first.
>
> It was a customer who I talked to a lot. We were fooling around.
>
> She stepped on my foot, and that told me she was interested in sexual relations. Then we talked about things and started to date.
>
> She was attracted to me.
>
> She liked me.

Women also report such comments but with less frequency.

> It was physical attractiveness. I have physical assets that are advantageous to the attraction of men. I have always had the problem of men coming on to me.

These kinds of responses indicate that these people were flattered by sexual attention; such responses further blend work roles and gender roles.

Although some social-sexual behavior is viewed as flattering to the recipients, this kind of behavior as well as serious sexual harassment interferes with effectiveness and productivity at work. Margaret Mead (1978) proposed that such behaviors be terminated. She felt that a general work taboo, similar to an incest taboo, is necessary to ensure women equal opportunity and equal treatment at work. However, eliminating sexuality in the workplace may not only be impossible but may also remove many benefits. Many people meet their spouses or begin enduring social relations in a work context. Others obtain mutual gratification from associations with opposite-sex workers. A more reasonable objective is not to establish a taboo on sexuality at work but to develop the conditions that permit relationships based on mutual attraction and eliminate sexual harassment.

At least two factors are necessary to allow people who work together to use work as a forum for meeting and getting to know people without engaging in sexual exploitation or sexual harassment. One is a clear understanding of gender roles and work roles and a commitment to separate the two. This is done most easily when occupations and work groups consist of about half men and half women. Jobs that are exclusively occupied by one gender are likely to be based on and to perpetuate gender-role stereotypes. Traditionally, for example, the images of construction worker, truck driver, and corporate executive are resoundingly masculine, and the images of secretary, nurse, and cleaning "woman" are feminine. Ickes and Barnes (1978) found that men and women feel more alienated and communicate less when they behave in a stereotyped manner according to gender role, as they do in a job dominated by one gender.

The second factor is a commitment on the part of organizations and individuals to avoid using organizational resources to further an individual's inappropriate personal goals. A person in a position of power may use that position, for example, to wine and dine an employee or co-worker who is the object of sexual interest. If rewards do not work, the person may easily resort to sexual harassment or other forms of punishment. Sexual harassment is bound to occur when people make a practice of using organizational resources of various kinds to achieve personal goals.

If sexual harassment is not tolerated, and if employers make a concerted effort to enforce a distinction between appropriate work roles and gender roles, perhaps sexual harassment and sexual exploitation will be eliminated. This is not easily accomplished. Years of gender-role socialization will not be changed overnight. In the short run, offering workshops for managers, supervisors, and new employees—both men and women—will help. In the long run, the educational process must start at a much younger age. Parent education and changes in public schools and children's literature will be necessary. Otherwise, children will continue to grow up thinking that women take jobs mainly to find husbands. As long as this stereotyped belief persists, the workplace is fertile for sexual harassment.

9 Sink or Swing? The Lifestyles of Single Adults

DIANE E. PHILLIS
and
PETER J. STEIN

One contemporary change in the boundaries of traditional gender roles and sexual lifestyles has been the growing numbers of single adults. Singles now represent over a fifth of all American households, and there has been a 40 percent increase in single households just in the decade from the beginning to the end of the 1970s. Two decades earlier, only 7 percent of households were headed by a single person.

Diane Phillis and Peter Stein describe some of the factors that have contributed to this startling increase in the proportion of adults choosing to remain single. They also discuss the demise of some of the formerly held stereotypes of singles. For example, the unmarried woman was particularly disparaged as a sexless spinster. Phillis and Stein examine the costs and benefits of marriage versus single status, and the influence of gender roles on adults who choose to avoid legal marriage.

Phillis and Stein then focus more closely on particular groups of singles. They describe singles who choose to live together, their roles with one another, and the quality of their sexual lives. Divorced and widowed people and single parents also receive attention. In particular, the authors discuss the ways in which gender-role expectations affect the sexual opportunities and experiences of these groups.

The authors also examine some of the special problems of single adults. Social interactions among adults are still dominated by married couples, and their attitudes toward singles sometimes result in the exclusion and isolation of single adults. Friendship and social support are clearly very important for the well-being of single adults. Phillis and Stein conclude that shifting gender-role norms have been particularly beneficial in two respects. First, they have reduced the stereotype that the single woman is unmarried primarily because she is sexually or maritally undesirable. Second, changes

203

9 Sink or Swing? The Lifestyles of Single Adults

in gender-role norms allow more freedom for the single man to develop closer emotional ties to other male friends, and to relate to women as friends as well as lovers.

 An appreciation of singlehood as a respectable and fulfilling lifestyle has not always been present in our culture. Consider the following opinion, voiced by a nineteenth-century superintendent of an insane asylum:

> We remember that the unmarried so often give unbridled indulgence to the feelings, propensities, and passions of depraved human nature, and that uninfluenced by the wholesome and purifying restraints of matrimony, they plunge recklessly into dissipation and vice, reaping as their reward, a broken constitution, ruined fortune, and blasted reputation. We must cease to feel surprised, that in so many instances, they present the pitiable spectacle of "mind in ruins" and become the tenants of our asylums for this afflicted class of citizens [Stribling, 1842, pp. 15–16].

When I (D. E. Phillis) try to recall my impressions of unmarried adults as I was growing up, several neighborhood eccentrics come to mind. Our kickball games would often pull us into the territory of two (or was it three? We never really could tell for sure how many were in there . . .) middle-aged women who lived in the corner house on our block. For a while, they were simply women we didn't know, who had no children to join our games. By the time we were in high school, our nonchalance had turned to intrigue and innuendo. Who were these strange, unrelated women who lived together? The fact that they even owned their house gave us further evidence of the permanence of their perversity. Why weren't they married? we all wondered. (We felt sorry for them—"They must be so lonely and sad without husbands or children.") Why wasn't each of them living alone? ("They *must* be lesbians, but they don't look like lesbians.") Although they were nice to us the few times we actually met them, we simply couldn't grasp the idea that perhaps there was nothing suspect about their lives. Sometimes on Halloween we'd trick-or-treat at their house twice, trying to glimpse any internal clues to their identities.

Several blocks away, a large house was purchased by three single adult men. They were even more sexually suspect to us than were the three women. Within a week, gossip informed us of what we already *knew:* These men must be homosexuals. Men just don't remain single in their 30s, much less "shack up" together unless there's something wrong with them. During the next few months we were consumed by fantasies of introducing these six lost souls to each other. They would meet, pair off, and fall in love. Then, of course, they would get married and live happily ever after. We were desperate for them to be normal.

How accurate are these perceptions regarding the sexual preferences, life satisfaction, and psychological health of single adults? Although some single adults are gay or bisexual (see Chapter 10), the vast majority are heterosexually inclined (Hunt, 1974). The reasons for being single are quite varied, as are the implications of singlehood for a person's sexuality.

Today, when ideas concerning sexual behavior and gender roles are becoming liberalized, the stereotype persists of the single individual either as a carefree swinger or as a frustrated, lonely person. In reality, single men and women are increasingly experiencing singlehood as a positive and fulfilling sexual lifestyle. There is growing societal legitimization of sexual expression outside of marriage. Singles are capitalizing on the variety of options available to them.

INCIDENCE OF SINGLEHOOD

In 1979, 36 percent of the U.S. population over 18 years of age were unmarried, for one reason or another (U.S. Bureau of the Census, 1980). This figure may surprise those of us used to thinking of marriage as normative during adulthood. Just who are all these unmarried people?

The never-married account for the largest proportion (55 percent) of single adults (U.S. Bureau of the Census, 1980). Separated and divorced people account for 23 percent, and the widowed account for 22 percent of single people over age 18. Singles now comprise about 23 percent of all households. This rise represents a 40 percent increase between the beginning and end of the 1970s in the number of unmarried people heading a home (Glick & Norton, 1979). In 1949, a mere 7 percent of households was headed by single people. The growth of singlehood is obvious.

A number of demographic factors contribute to this increase in the number of single people. These include increases in age at first marriage, the divorce rate, number of widowed people, and number of people who cohabit.

Young men and women are waiting to marry until they are older than was formerly the case. The median age of marriage is now 24.4 for males, and 22.1 for females (U.S. Bureau of the Census, 1980). The divorce rate is notoriously high; close to 40 percent of first marriages end before the death of a spouse (Glick & Norton, 1979). Among older Americans, the death of a spouse is the most common reintroduction to being single. Finally, the number of couples living together without a marriage license (cohabiting) has shown a marked increase over the last 20 years.

205

9 Sink or Swing? The Lifestyles of Single Adults

Singles share one common characteristic—their unmarried status. There are, however, many differences among single individuals. This chapter discusses the following groups of single Americans: the never-married, the divorced, the widowed, and the cohabiting. The lifestyles of single parents are also described. We discuss some general characteristics of those who are single, and their reported reasons for being single. We then consider how changing gender roles may affect the lives of singles, and how singlehood influences their sexual behavior and intimate relations with others. Because most research on singles has been done on predominantly white, middle-class groups, the information in this chapter best represents members of such groups. We do not discuss those who remain single for religious reasons, single adults in institutions such as prisons or hospitals, single gay adults, or those individuals who pursue a single lifestyle although they may be married or separated.

NEGLECT OF SINGLES IN SOCIAL SCIENCE RESEARCH

Singles are an overlooked minority, as shown by the amount and nature of research that has been done on various aspects of their lives. Single men are particularly neglected. (The disproportionate amount of research on single women has occurred over the last 10 to 15 years, paralleling the increased interest in feminism and women's concerns in general. As interest in non-traditional lifestyles of men increases, we may see more research on single men.) The same is true of singles who are black, or hold other minority group membership (for two recent exceptions, see Higginbotham, 1981, and Staples, 1981). The information available on singles generally consists of journalistic or descriptive surveys and interview data from nonrandom samples.

Information on the sex lives and gender roles of singles is especially scant. (For an exception, see R. W. Libby, 1977, for a discussion of single-hood as a sexual lifestyle.) Racy activities in the swinging singles' scene are probably the most frequently reported. The void in describing the range of singles' sexuality beyond this highly popularized segment suggests that a single adult either sinks or swings: without participating in singles' cruises, get-away weekends, or bar-hopping, it is assumed, loneliness and quiet desperation must await the unmarried.

Through this sensationalized focus on one option open to singles, the diversity of backgrounds and lifestyles of the unmarried is obscured. What about all those unmarried individuals who don't look like Farrah Fawcett or Burt Reynolds, or make at least $40,000 per year? What do they do for fun on a Saturday night? Although we recently ran across a "Coloring Book for Bawdy Bachelors" (with rather revealing poses of women in various stages of undress), we assume that there must be other entertainment available to singles. But the activities of singles over age 40, or with low incomes, or with children living at home, or from other than a white, middle- to upper-class background, or living in small towns or isolated areas have rarely been studied.

It is important to keep in mind that there are as many individual differences among singles as there are among married people. The fact that singles happen to be unmarried at a particular time in their lives does not imply a pervasive group unity among them, or even consistency in their own lifestyles over time. It is predicted that only about 3 to 4 percent of today's young will never marry (Glick & Norton, 1979). However, at a given time nearly 35 percent of adults are unmarried. Singlehood, therefore, is most commonly a transient state, and one that can be experienced more than once in a lifetime. Variety of lifestyle and diversity among single individuals is at least as rich as within a group of the married.

TYPES OF SINGLES

Popular impressions of unmarried people who are over age 25 are basically of two types. One stereotype of the never-married is of a person who has some fault or deficiency sufficiently serious to warrant a life of rejection, frustration, and lonely masturbation. The men described in George Gilder's *Sexual Suicide* (1973) and *The Naked Nomads* (1974) exemplify this conception. Never-married older women are regarded as slightly amusing and pathetic spinsters, characterized by a total lack of sexual attractiveness (remember the card game "Old Maid"?).

The other stereotype is that of the swinging single who hops from one bed to the next, not wishing to make a commitment to a meaningful relationship lest it dampen the variety of sexual experiences available. The recent popularity of Judith Rossner's novel *Looking for Mr. Goodbar* (1975) typifies our fascination with this lifestyle. Single men, unless obviously homosexual, physically repulsive, or abhorrent in character, are commonly regarded as carefree bachelors (for example, Hugh Hefner). They have somehow eluded the clutches of scores of women to pursue an exciting life of freedom and varied romance. Such men usually are regarded as charming companions and have no shortage of social invitations.

Young single women, on the other hand, are often considered to be threatening. Because promiscuity is assumed to typify the lives of such young women, it is assumed that married women should beware of them. Their search for romantic adventure never ends; even the wedding rings on married men's fingers have lost the power to repel the advances of such hussies.

207

9 Sink or Swing? The Lifestyles of Single Adults

The Never-Married

The first group of singles we will discuss are those individuals who have never been married. After describing various characteristics of this group, we discuss the decision-making process of whether to remain single or to marry, the gender roles of never-married adults, and how these roles affect the sexuality of singles.

Who are these never-married adults?   Between 1960 and 1975, there was a 50 percent increase in the number of never-married adults between the ages of 20 and 34 (Glick, 1975). In 1979, 30 percent of 25 to 29-year-old men and 20 percent of 25 to 29-year-old women had never been married. At ages 30 to 34, 15 percent of men and 10 percent of women were still single. At ages 35 to 39, 8 percent of men and 7 percent of women had not been married (U.S. Bureau of the Census, 1980). Hence, the years between age 25 and 30 appear to be the most likely time to decide whether to remain single or not.

There is no one particular type of person who remains single. However, there is a general tendency for people with little education (less than five years) and for women who pursue graduate training to contribute more heavily to the ranks of the never-married (U.S. Bureau of the Census, 1978). People with little education are more likely to have a variety of handicaps that would decrease their marital desirability. Mental and physical problems, low income, and geographic isolation are all correlated with having little education. Women with graduate training may regard marriage as conflicting with their career plans and personal freedom. Or such highly educated women may intimidate men.

Unger (1979) speculates that highly educated single women may pose a threat to male dominance. By ostensibly rejecting traditional gender roles (of feminine subservience and inferiority, to masculine protectiveness and dominance), they may elicit hostility and defensiveness from men. Although there is no empirical evidence that single women are more assertive or domineering than their married peers, they are higher achievers. In this sense, men may be intimidated by their superior earning power and career success (Doudna & McBride, 1981).

Why stay single? Singlehood versus marriage   Peter Stein (1981a) states that

> The emergence of singlehood as a lifestyle is seen as a developmental phenomenon in response to the dissatisfaction with traditional marriage. As such, it represents an important change in social values and cultural expectations regarding the 'naturalness' of marriage and the cultural expectation that one must marry to be an adult.

In 1973, Stein compared women's attitudes in their first and last college years. He found that in 1969 only 3 percent of his first-year sample did not expect to marry. In comparison, by 1973, 8 percent of women in their senior year did not expect to marry. Of the seniors, 40 percent voiced doubts about whether or not they should marry. And a full 39 percent of seniors said they believed that traditional marriage was becoming obsolete. Most of these women did go on to marry, but they tended to question marriage as an institution and tended to marry later than did earlier generations.

Why is marriage being questioned and examined with much greater intensity by current generations of young people? Several authors have suggested that changes in sexual standards and the increased earning ability of women are fundamentally responsible. Men no longer must marry to ensure a sexual partner (nor must women). Women no longer need marriage to guarantee economic security (Bird, 1972; Safilios-Rothschild, 1977).

The women's movement has tried to show women the multitude of avenues available for self-fulfillment beyond the roles of wife and mother. Traditional marriage has, by some, been described as socially acceptable slave labor (Greer, 1971). Others have cited statistics suggesting that, although married men have greater longevity and mental and physical health than single men, the reverse is true for women (Bernard, 1972; Gove, 1972). Women have fewer physical and psychological problems when single than when married.

The contemporary separation between sex and reproduction has also challenged the institution of marriage. As marriage and the goal of having babies become less important reasons for having sex, more people are encouraged to remain single. Organized support has been lent to this position by such groups as Zero Population Growth, Planned Parenthood, the National Organization of Non-Parents (NON), and the women's movement. The media's discussion of the recreational aspects of sex enhances these changing values.

This contemporary liberation of sex from the sole province of marriage and reproduction stands in sharp contrast to earlier views. For instance, the quote that began this chapter was from a nineteenth-century superintendent of the Western Lunatic Asylum in Richmond, Virginia. He was attempting to explain why he believed that singles and widowed people were more likely candidates for insanity.

The awareness that marriage is not always a satisfying, permanent lifestyle can be both frightening and painful. Traditional marriage is founded on conventional roles for men and women. Although these roles (that is, dominant breadwinner for men and homemaker or secondary breadwinner for women) may seem constraining to some, there is a certain reassurance in knowing such roles are considered "normal." Diminishing

209

9 Sink or Swing? The Lifestyles of Single Adults

access to or respect for these roles may leave some young people confused about what being a normal adult means. Perhaps the failure of marital roles to keep pace with the increased flexibility of contemporary standards is responsible for our loss of faith. In any case, singlehood is enjoying newfound respectability as more and more people live this way.

Stein (1978) has conceptualized one way to understand the process of deliberation to marry or to be single (see Table 9-1). As our experiences and needs vary across the life span, each lifestyle's attractiveness may change. For example, some young people might find that the need to leave home, fear of independence, and a romanticized view of marriage encourage them to get married. Later in their lives, however, they may perceive stronger pulls toward self-sufficiency, career goals, and the exploration of new friendships, which appear more feasible if they were not married.

Gender roles of never-married adults   Little information is available on the gender roles of never-married adults. What information does exist suggests that many never-married adults tend to have androgynous gender identities. Kanter (1978) found that most never-married women ages 24 to 34 were gender-typed as androgynous or masculine. Similarly, Kelly (1978) found androgynous gender-typing in single men and women ages 25 to 37. In fact, few gender differences on any measures were found. Both men and women tended to have high needs for achievement and autonomy. They scored high on measures of self-reliance and self-perception. Their desire to maintain a high degree of independence was mentioned repeatedly. These men and women also were very concerned with maintaining friendships and intimacy with people of the other gender. Indeed, almost all men and women in this study reported their relationships with others were the most meaningful parts of their lives. They were aware of ambivalent feelings over their competing career versus intimacy goals. For this reason, their hesitancy to consider marriage was strong.

It is not surprising that singles score high on measures of androgyny. The versatility of their personalities would be an asset to their lifestyle. Role constraints of traditional marriage might be less desirable to an androgynous person, resulting in a lower likelihood of getting married.

Although some researchers have found singles to be more androgynous, other evidence contradicts these findings. Gender-role stereotyping seems to flourish in parts of the singles' world. The persistent role playing that occurs in singles' bars is an obvious example (Allon & Fishel, 1981).

How do gender roles affect the sexuality of singles?   One problem frequently mentioned by singles is in regard to the role demands of dating. The double standard for male and female sexuality is evident to many. Even

TABLE 9-1

Attractive and Deterrent Features of Marriage and Singlehood

TOWARD BEING MARRIED	
Pushes (drawbacks in present situation)	*Pulls* (attractive aspects of potential situation)
Economic security	Influence of parents
Influence from mass media	Desire for family
Pressure from parents	Example of peers
Need to leave home	Romanticization of marriage
Interpersonal and personal reasons	Love
Fear of independence	Physical attraction
Loneliness	Emotional attachment
Alternatives apparently not feasible	Security, social status, prestige
Cultural expectations, socialization	
Regular sex	
Guilt over singlehood	

TOWARD BEING SINGLE	
Pushes (to leave permanent relationship)	*Pulls* (to remain single or to return to singlehood)
Restrictions	Career opportunities
Suffocating one-to-one relationships, feeling trapped	Variety of experiences
Obstacles to self-development	Self-sufficiency
Boredom, unhappiness, and anger	Sexual availability
Role playing and conformity to expectations	Exciting lifestyle
Poor communication with mate	Freedom to change and experiment
Sexual frustration	Mobility
Lack of friends, isolation, loneliness	Sustaining friendships
Limitations on mobility and available experience	Supportive groups
Influence of and participation in the women's movement	Men's and women's groups
	Group living arrangements
	Specialized groups

SOURCE: Adapted from Stein, P. The lifestyles and life chances of the never married. *Marriage and Family Review*, 1978, 1, 4. Reprinted by permission of Haworth Press, Inc., and the author.

211

9 Sink or Swing? The Lifestyles of Single Adults

the ostensibly liberated, swinging singles' scene is actually quite supportive of traditional gender-role stereotypes. Unrestrained sexual desire (and activity) is acceptable for men, but women are expected to show at least a modicum of coyness and modesty (Proulx, 1976).

Note that these traditional role demands put a burden on both the man and the woman. A man may not relish the role of a superstud. However, he may feel that if he did not press for sex with a woman he might be less of a man in her eyes and might let himself down as well. The possibility that he might insult his date by not wanting to have sex with her—thus implying that he finds her unattractive—may cross his mind. It may also cross hers.

The role constrictions placed on single women are equally awkward. Their age and physical attractiveness are repeatedly evaluated as more important than their personality or intelligence. They should be flirtatious and dressed to kill, yet not seem too "easy." If they appear interested in marriage, it might scare away their dates; if they espouse disinterest in marriage, they are assumed to be "castrating women's libbers" whom men avoid before giving friendship a chance (Adams, 1976).

Another way in which gender roles affect the adjustment of singles is in the traditional expectation that people—especially women—should marry. Particularly before age 30, a woman who is single is continually confronted with evidence of her deviancy from the norm. Everyone around her is getting married and having children. She must repeatedly defend her single status against inquiries by concerned relatives and friends: "So, who's the special man in your life now?" "Any sign of wedding bells in the future?" The attrition of her social circle to married life leaves her feeling left out and conspicuous. Her singleness is seen as unfortunate; it is assumed that if given the opportunity she would certainly marry. When she defends her choice to be single, it is interpreted as rationalization. The ultimate insult is to accuse her of denial. Through the defense mechanism of denial, she supposedly represses the conflict and the unfulfilled sexual energy stereotypically attributed to the single woman (Adams, 1976).

For men, the pressure to follow the traditional role toward heterosexual commitment through marriage is present, although not as great. Just as in adolescence, society tolerates a great deal more sexual experience and rambunctiousness in males than it does in females. The ultimate insult to a single adult male is to accuse him of avoiding marriage because of latent—or active—homosexuality. Fear of homosexuality is so pervasive in our society that thoughts about this may occur to him as well as to concerned others.

Although such attributions of homosexuality may be made more often about single men, it is also not unknown to unmarried women: "When I tell people I'm 28 and not married, they look at me like there's something wrong with me—they think I'm a lesbian. Some just feel sorry for me. What a drag" (Stein, Richman, & Hannon, 1977, p. 389).

Insinuations of homosexuality are one way society exposes its inflexibility regarding acceptable gender-role behavior. To conclude that the unmarried person must be either homosexual or unattractive is more reflective of our lack of knowledge about singles than of actual fact. Limited understanding of platonic relationships—friendships devoid of sexual overtones—makes it difficult to appreciate that one may achieve emotional closeness with someone of the other gender and not be inclined to marry. People still hold marriage as the proper outcome of a close, loving relationship. And finally, marriage is still regarded as the sanctioned domain of sexual expression. Although the majority of people now engage in sex outside of marriage (Hunt, 1974; Reiss, 1980), the legitimacy accorded marital sexuality over nonmarital sex is undeniable.

Yet nonmarital sex does have a certain appeal all of its own. This appeal is amplified through the pandering of the advertisers of singles' bars, cruises, get-away weekends, and so on, to the sexual and social needs of singles. Sexual opportunity is heavily promoted, giving singles perhaps an exaggerated impression of its satisfaction. The message that all "in" singles are eager for sex has some unwanted side effects for many singles. Such perceptions may leave those who are more reserved, or who feel they cannot compete, feeling inadequate or excluded (Starr & Carns, 1972). The interesting twist in this sort of promotion is the unspoken suggestion that a relationship sparked from such a meeting might culminate in marriage. Eligibility and attractiveness of the clientele are advertised in no uncertain terms. Singles may end up feeling disappointed due to the unfulfilled promises suggested by the advertisements. Or they may worry about what they are missing if they don't give such activities a try (Adams, 1976).

Despite these problems, many people who have never been married experience single life as quite positive. Many achieve satisfaction through work and career goals, friendships, and sexuality (Adams, 1976; Libby, 1977; Stein, Richman, & Hannon, 1977).

Cohabitation

In the last 20 years, the proportion of people who cohabit has increased dramatically. In 1960, approximately 34,000 unmarried people of the opposite gender were living together. Today, nearly 2 million single men and women share living quarters. This figure does not necessarily indicate ongoing sexual relationships, because boarders and live-in employees are included in these numbers (Glick & Norton, 1979). The number of unmarried couples living together increased by 20 percent between 1977 and 1978 alone.

213

9 Sink or Swing? The Lifestyles of Single Adults

Who cohabits?   Although most of the studies have involved college-age couples, cohabitation is by no means confined to this age group (Glick & Spanier, 1980). In a nationwide random sample of over 2,000 men between the ages of 20 and 30, 18 percent reported that they had cohabited with women for a period of six months or longer (Clayton & Voss, 1977). The educational backgrounds of those who had cohabited revealed that this phenomenon is not restricted to campus communities. Men who were not attending college, and those who had less than a high school education, were more likely to report having engaged in cohabitation. Elderly and middle-aged couples also are increasingly choosing to live together outside of marriage (Glick & Norton, 1979).

Attitudes toward cohabitation   Eleanor Macklin has recently compiled an excellent review of the literature on cohabitation (1978). In examining the research on attitudes toward cohabitation, she concludes that the majority of college students approve of such living arrangements outside of marriage and would themselves consider cohabiting under the right circumstances. Most do not think long-term commitments such as being engaged are a prerequisite to cohabit. Cohabitation appears to be acceptable given a strong, affectionate, and preferably monogamous relationship between the partners: it is seen as a relevant step toward marriage rather than as a permanent alternative. Students repeatedly emphasize the educational and preparatory value of cohabitation, and describe living together as successful and enjoyable. They also regard it as a valuable learning experience that has helped them to become more mature and to evaluate their degree of commitment to their partners and to eventual marriage.

Some interesting differences between men's and women's attitudes toward cohabitation have been noted. Men appear to be somewhat more accepting of cohabitation than women. This difference may reflect the typically more liberal attitudes of males in general toward sex. Data also suggest that men may not feel the need for as strong an emotional involvement before entering into such living arrangements. This difference suggests that some cohabiting women have different expectations about the depth of commitment than their male partners. Therefore, the possibility of feeling exploited is greater for women in such circumstances (Macklin, 1978).

Why might a woman desire a stronger degree of commitment before living with a man? A woman traditionally has been socialized to believe it would look and feel more respectable not to share such a high level of intimacy with a man unless she cares deeply about him. She also may be more aware of the work it takes to run a household as well as a relationship. In this sense, a woman may be more willing to engage in cohabitation with a man she knows is more committed to her and willing to share the responsibility for making their relationship work.

Gender roles and cohabitation   Women who were more accepting of cohabitation tended to be more androgynous than those who did not approve of such living arrangements (Strong & Nass, 1975). They also tended to perceive their mothers as being more rejecting toward them and as less satisfied with their marriages. This finding is consistent with the conclusion of Arafat and Yorburg (1973): women who approved of cohabitation were more likely to describe themselves as independent, aggressive, and outgoing. Others have noted that cohabiting women tend to view themselves as more competitive, aggressive, managerial, and distant from their mothers than do noncohabiting women who were engaged (Guittar & Lewis, 1974). In contrast, cohabiting men described themselves as less managerial and autocratic, and less competitive and exploitative than did engaged, noncohabiting men. They also view themselves as warmer and more supportive. As Macklin (1978, p. 221) states,

> It has frequently been hypothesized that women who are more independent, have more need to achieve, and are less accepting of traditional femininity tend to see their mothers as colder and less supportive. It would make sense that these less traditional women would more easily accept nontraditional courtship patterns.

Whether these personality characteristics were encouraged through the process of cohabiting, or whether they preceded it, is at this point very difficult to determine. It does seem that such relationships are not necessarily more egalitarian than most marriages. For cohabitors, decision-making power, division of labor, ease in communication, and satisfaction with the relationship were not significantly different from a married sample (Yllo, 1978). Both married and cohabiting couples were fairly traditional in terms of dividing household chores along gender lines.

In summary, research consistently indicates more similarities than differences between people who cohabit and those who do not. One might have expected that the gender roles of cohabitors would be more liberal (that is, androgynous) than those of married couples. But gender-role measures fail to distinguish cohabitors as consistently being much more androgynous than married men and women. Cohabiting couples reflect predominant societal values and gender roles as much as the rest of the population (although there is a tendency for both cohabitors and noncohabitors to be slightly more androgynous today than in previous decades). Stafford, Bachman, and diBona (1977) conclude that gender-role norms, modeled by parents throughout childhood and adolescent socialization, preserve traditional gen-

215

9 Sink or Swing? The Lifestyles of Single Adults

der roles in cohabitors as well as the rest of us. We should not be surprised, therefore, to learn that couples who live together act very much like their married neighbors.

Sex and cohabitation Do cohabitors have more exciting sexual lives than their marital counterparts? Newcomb and Bentler (1980), discovered that couples who lived together were more likely to engage in oral sex and different coital positions than were married couples who had not cohabited. Although this finding hints at the possibility that cohabitors may have more varied sex lives than married couples, there is little research to further substantiate this suggestion. Cohabitors do engage in sexual relations outside of their primary relationships about as much as do married people. Bower (1975) found that 19 percent of the women and 31 percent of the men in his study of cohabiting college-age individuals had had sex with one or more other people during the time they were cohabiting. These figures are similar to Hunt's (1974) report that 24 percent of young married women and 32 percent of young married men had engaged in extramarital sex. Perhaps this situation reflects the differential commitment to the relationship noticed between men and women. In general, however, couples who lived together expressed as much satisfaction with their sex lives as did married couples.

Divorced People

Another group of people find themselves reintroduced to singlehood following divorce. After describing the incidence of divorce, we turn to the major concerns divorced people have expressed about sexuality and to the incidence of sexual activity among those who are no longer married.

Incidence of divorce Because approximately one out of three marriages currently ends in divorce, usually within seven years, a large number of people will rediscover singlehood between their late 20s and early 40s. Although a large proportion will eventually remarry (about 75 percent of women and 80 percent of men), the average number of years spent between marriages has increased slightly in recent years. Today, most divorced people spend three years reacquainting themselves with singlehood before they remarry (Glick & Norton, 1979).

The last year or two has shown a tenuous stabilization in divorce rates (Glick & Norton, 1979), but the marked increase in divorce until this time has been quite dramatic. A hundred years ago, one's chances of ever being divorced were 1 in 1,234; in 1900, 1 in 500; in 1920, 1 in 20; in 1940, 1 in 6; and the present rate nationally is slightly greater than 1 in 3 (Bardwick, 1979). Obviously, for a large proportion of Americans, the permanence and security of marriage is not all it's cracked up to be.

Divorce and sexuality: major concerns   Although people who have regained single status through divorce share many of the same characteristics of the never-married, there are several differences in their sexual adjustment. First, we discuss the impact of divorce on the sexuality of those who do not have children. Then we examine the special adjustment of single parents.

Perhaps the most common social concern over becoming single after a divorce is not knowing how to go about meeting others. Anxiety over arranging dates, whether and when to have sex, and the general procedural etiquette of dating once again are all concerns newly divorced people have not had for quite a while. Because these demands are generally awkward for both genders, stereotyped role playing may seem a welcome guide when uncertain about how to act (Gagnon, 1977).

Reliance on role playing is common when we are not sure what is expected of us. Many social establishments available to singles—loud bars, dances, and parties—do not provide atmospheres conducive to relaxed, open conversation. It is no surprise, then, that singles might behave in a role-stereotyped fashion in these settings. Appearing at a party in sexy clothing, for example, may provide the recently divorced with reassurance that they are still attractive. Commanding admiring glances on the dance floor in a tight, V-neck shirt may help a divorced man to regain the confidence he needs to date again. Or, a divorced woman's self-image might be reaffirmed by playing the vamp for a night or two.

Hence, finding oneself again in a state of sexual availability may be a welcome change. It can also be traumatic. The liberal world of nonmarital sex can be especially anxiety provoking to those who had been faithfully married or who had had little or no premarital sexual experience. (Likewise, such anxiety may occur in a person who had just ended a long-term, nonmarital relationship.) They may have little idea of current sexual mores, and it may take some time to determine standards of single sexual behavior for themselves again (Hunt, 1974). Guidelines from high school or college may be outdated. Mixed feelings over re-entry into a single sexual lifestyle seem particularly characteristic of women:

> [*Female, age 34:*] I was nervous enough on my first date after ten years of marriage, just wondering whether I'd have any problems later on, or how I'd handle it, when this clod asked me straight out—even before dinner was over—"how about it?" I was so dumb, and so unsure of what was happening, that I actually said "How about what?" Oh, God, I was so embarrassed! And then there were all the gropers, the grabbers, the smoochers, the dirty-talkers, the guys who swore they were in love with me after an hour or two. I was no prude, and I was plenty frustrated, but I was damned if I'd trade my bod' for dinner. I didn't come that cheap. [Hunt, 1974, p. 249].

217

9 Sink or Swing? The Lifestyles of Single Adults

The world of postmarital sex may be trying for men as well. It is not necessarily easy—or satisfying—to live up to the image of the playboy bachelor:

> [*Male, age 35:*] It took me three years to get it through my head that I didn't have to screw every woman I took out. I used to make an all-out try with every one of them—and let me tell you, if I didn't find the gal appealing, it could be a rough trip, and afterward I'd be furious with myself. But somehow I *had* to. I felt that if I didn't come on like the superstud of all time, they'd think I was a fag, or hung up, or something. [Hunt, 1974, p. 251].

Incidence of sexual activity among the divorced   Very few divorced people refrain from sexual activity. Gebhard (1968) found that between 1939 and 1956, 82 percent of divorced women were sexually active. This percentage increased to 90 percent in 1972. Divorced women average four sexual partners per year, and most have a higher incidence of orgasm than when they were married (Hunt, 1974).

Similarly, almost all divorced men are sexually active, averaging eight partners over a year's time (Gebhard, 1968; Hunt, 1974). Interestingly, divorced as well as widowed men do not report lacking spouses limits their sexual behavior. They have sex slightly more often than do married men their age.

Both men and women report that postmarital sex is more enjoyable than sex was when they were married. Hunt (1974) also found that divorced people are more varied in their sexual activities and positions than are most young married couples. Perhaps we should suggest short separations on an annual basis for husbands and wives so that their sex lives could be regularly rejuvenated!

Single Parents

Single parents share some special concerns about their sexuality. As single parenting has become more common, attention has been drawn to the possible influences of such parents' sex lives on their children.

Incidence of single parenting   A significant proportion of separated and divorced people have children living at home. In 1978, 14 percent of white children lived with one parent. Despite recent media attention to the growing number of single fathers (see the movie *Kramer vs. Kramer*), less than 2 percent of white single-parent families are headed by fathers. Single parenting is even more common among blacks. In 1978, 44 percent of black children were living with one parent: 42 percent lived with their mothers, and 2 percent with their fathers. It is estimated that approximately half of all children will at some time in their lives live with only one parent (U.S. Bureau of the Census, 1978).

Single parenting and sexuality: major concerns Single parents, of course, share many of the same concerns about sexuality as divorced people in general. After a divorce, accepting their sexual needs may be hard both for them and for their children. Adolescents do not easily picture their middle-aged parents as sexual beings (Pocs & Godow, 1976). And many parents are hesitant to express this side of themselves in front of their children. Parents resent their children's questioning them about their dates, not to mention their open disapproval of particular people. Kids can also feel resentful of their parents' dates because of competition for time and attention (Cleveland, 1981).

Rockwell (1976) notes the three questions that seem to be asked by single parents most often:

1. How do I become available again?
2. How will my children react to my being sexually active?
3. How do I cope with my own sexuality?

In regard to the first question—"How does one reenter the social and sexual world of singles?"—the process is much the same as described for divorced people without children. Introductions from friends, parties, bars, dances, or interest groups are all ways of meeting new people. There are a number of formal organizations for single parents. Parents Without Partners is probably the best known. It is over 30 years old, and has a broad base of community acceptance and participation.

Access to social activities may be more difficult for the divorced person who is also a parent. He or she must arrange for child care while out, and sometimes it is simply not a good idea to leave a child for an evening (when the child is ill, for example). Babysitting expenses also may be a strong deterrent, especially to low-income parents. And since pay scales for women continue to be lower than for men in the United States, single mothers may be less able to afford an evening out than their male counterparts.

Many single parents express trouble finding desirable partners with whom they would like to become sexually involved (Greenberg, 1979; Rockwell, 1976). This problem seems to be greater for women. Age is an apparent handicap; it is not socially acceptable for women to date men more than a few years younger than themselves, whereas no such social stigma is attached to a man dating a much younger woman. It is also clear that the older a woman is and the more children she has, the longer time she will spend between divorce and remarriage (Glick & Norton, 1979). Divorced white men have the highest remarriage rate and tend to remarry earliest.

219

9 Sink or Swing? The Lifestyles of Single Adults

Black women are the least likely to remarry (U.S. Bureau of the Census, 1980).

The second big concern of single parents—how their children will react to their sexual activity—has been studied extensively by Greenberg (1979). The majority of single parents felt that nonmarital sex was fine as long as they engaged in it discreetly. They worried about the potentially negative effects it might have on their children. Specifically, they were concerned that their sexual behavior might set a bad example or produce emotional upset in their offspring.

The double standard was evident in the sexual behavior and concerns of single parents. More mothers than fathers were worried about the impact their sexuality would have on their children. Because motherhood is so often associated with asexuality, both mothers and children may have felt the need to create a maternal image that confirmed this stereotype. Dates spent the night more often if the child was a son, not a daughter. Both mothers and fathers, however, expressed concern over the impact having a date stay all night might have on their children (Bequaert, 1976; Greenberg, 1979).

Two studies of single fathers indicated that although they were uncomfortable about being open with their children when dates remained all night, they perceived this as more permissible than engaging in open cohabitation (Orthner, Brown, & Ferguson, 1976; Rosenthal & Keshet, 1978). In general, it appears that single fathers are slightly more willing to let their children know they are engaging in sex, especially if the child is a boy.

The third major concern of single parents is how to deal with their own sexuality. Most single mothers did not see remarriage as a prerequisite to resuming a satisfying sex life (Bequaert, 1976). Hunt and Hunt (1976) found that sex was often considered on the first date—and the majority acted on this consideration. It seemed to be acceptable to ask and to consent or to refuse. They also noted that in contrast to Kinsey's data, churchgoers were just about as sexually active and experimental as were single parents who never went to church. No data were available on how long the lines were at the confessional, however. (Given the consistent correlation between frequency of church attendance and sexual conservatism, we might assume that although these churchgoers were as active and varied in their sexual behavior, they were not as free of guilt over being so).

In summary, single parents share many of the same concerns over sexuality as do divorced and single people in general. The presence of children seems to make them more aware of cultural mores in regard to sex. Both mothers and fathers convey the gender-role norm that it is more acceptable for males to be sexually active. They do not want to set a bad example for their children. Problems of isolation and restricted opportunity to socialize are common. Women, in particular, have more trouble finding the extra time and money needed for going out.

Value of friendship   For women, friendships with other women are valued sources of companionship and emotional support, especially with single mothers like themselves. In contrast, single fathers indicate that male friends are rarely the main source of such support. Women, with whom the single fathers are often romantically involved, fill this role (Greenberg, 1979).

Lauralee Rockwell (1976) advises single parents to develop and enjoy platonic friendships to ease the readjustment to a single lifestyle. She feels that such relationships may have much to offer beyond the normal benefits that friendship affords. They may provide the person with the viewpoint of the other gender, freed of the complication of sexual overtones. A man does not have to prove to himself or his woman friend that he is a heterosexual superstud. A woman can be reassured that she is more than just sexually appealing to a man. Platonic friendships help diffuse the driving desire to search for a new mate, by providing many of the same sorts of emotional and social supports the person may feel lacking since his or her divorce. For similar reasons, such friendships are also valued very much by never-married singles, cohabitors, and widowed people.

Widowed People

As we stated earlier in this chapter, singlehood is a transient state for most people. The last passage into this stage is through widowhood. Unless both husband and wife die at the same time, one of them will again become single.

Incidence of widowhood   It is much more likely that the surviving spouse will be the wife. There are approximately five times as many widowed women as widowed men (Kimmel, 1980). Because of the gender differences in life expectancies, three out of four married women can expect to be widowed by age 56 and can expect to live 20 years following the death of their husbands. Only one out of four will remarry during that time (Lopata, 1973; U.S. Bureau of the Census, 1978). Other factors contributing to the greater proportion of widowed women are the tendency of women to marry men who are older than themselves and the higher remarriage rate among widowed men (Kimmel, 1980).

Persons widowed at older ages seem to have less opportunity to form new sexual and social relationships. Beyond age 65, remarriage is not common. Widowed people who marry after that age may lose pension payments from the deceased spouse, and some fear losing control over their personal financial holdings. Some are discouraged from taking another husband by their children, who imply this would detract from the loyalty due their father's memory. And others mention they do not want to relinquish their independence or undertake the role of wife again (Lopata, 1973).

221

9 Sink or Swing? The Lifestyles of Single Adults

Sex among the widowed Fewer widows than divorcees have been found to engage in sexual activity, even when their ages are the same. About half as many widows engage in sex compared to divorced women (that is, 82 percent of divorced women and 43 percent of widows engaged in sex, according to Gebhard, 1968). Gebhard did notice that those widows who resumed sexual activity, like their divorced counterparts, reported more enjoyment during sex than when they were married. Hunt (1974) found that when comparing divorced and widowed men, those who were widowed also were less likely to resume sexual activity.

Why should there be such a large difference between the sexual activity of divorced and widowed people? Perhaps the trauma of their spouses' deaths has an overriding effect on the sexual desires of the widowed. Their lack of sexual interest is reinforced by pressures to be "faithful" to the deceased. There is no evidence to indicate that the widowed are not offered opportunities to engage in sexual relationships. Widowed women have been frightened by the abundance of sexual advances they receive, and widowed men report being angered by frequent propositioning (Datan & Lohmann, 1980).

What sexual options are available to older singles? Since so many women outlive their spouses and are not encouraged to remarry younger men, they are not all able to satisfy sexual needs through marriage. Klemmack and Roff (1980) have investigated social support for alternative forms of intimate relationships among older persons, such as living together. How much approval exists for older people to enjoy such sexual alternatives? These researchers found that most of their middle-class, middle-aged, married sample did not view the aged as asexual. They voiced support for them to experiment with alternative sexual outlets to marriage. In general, the younger and more liberal the respondents, the greater was their support. But the noticeably lower support for such alternatives among the elderly person's peers shows why such alternatives might be difficult for him or her to enjoy.

FRIENDSHIPS AND SEXUALITY OF SINGLES

Important influences on the potential satisfaction of a single lifestyle are the friendships and sexual opportunity open to the unmarried. First, we note the reliance of singles on strong friendships as a means of social support. Second, we look at the impact and/or expectation of sexual availability on the satisfaction of singles with their lifestyle.

Friendships and Social Support Systems for Singles

The importance of social support in people's lives has been extensively documented in the sociological and psychological literature. By social support systems, we mean those interpersonal patterns and social services that lead to an improved quality of life. These may be informal or highly organized, continual or sporadic, led by a peer or by a professional, easily available to most people or only available to a few.

Although work, marriage, and parenthood have constituted duty-bound adult social roles in our culture, friendship has constituted an optional social role. The judgment of our success or failure as adults has not rested on the number of friends we have nor on the quality of our friendships (Blau, 1973). Yet for unmarried adults, friends and friendship networks constitute a major source of social support (Adams, 1976; Hiltz, 1977; Ramey, 1976; Schwartz, 1976; Starr & Carns, 1972; Weiss, 1975).

The importance of close, caring friendships, based on free choice and a sense of mutuality, has been emphasized by single men and women (Stein, 1976, 1978). In their departure from traditional family structures, these single adults express a strong need for substitute networks of human relationships that provide the basic satisfactions of intimacy, sharing, and continuity.

Interestingly, it has been suggested that friendship between a man and a woman, when one of them is gay, is often a very satisfying, comfortable combination (Adams, 1976). The ubiquitous pressure for sex is absent in such friendships, allowing the friends to relate more freely as individuals divorced of sexual availability.

A number of adults indicate that the same freedom in male-female friendships is not as easily achieved when both are heterosexual. One likely place for this sort of friendship to occur is at work. The close collaboration required between co-workers lends itself naturally to the development of friendship. On this point, Margaret Adams (1976, pp. 183–184) incisively comments,

> Given the sex-based expectations in any male-female relationship today, the fact that legal marriage presupposes exclusive possession of the spouse . . . it is almost a foregone conclusion that a close professional involvement between sexes will be imbued with the taint of psychological adultery, disloyalty, and treachery—on the part of the man toward his allegedly wronged wife and of the women toward another member of her already exploited sex.

The same situation could, of course, occur between a married woman, her allegedly wronged husband, and her single male co-worker.

Singlehood and Sexuality

Singlehood as a sexual lifestyle implies a state of availability. It is the freedom and variety of sexual experiences that makes staying single so appealing to some. Indeed, research has shown that sexual availability can be an im-

223

9 Sink or Swing? The Lifestyles of Single Adults

portant motivation for remaining unmarried or unattached (Libby, 1977; Proulx, 1976; Stein, 1976, 1978, 1981b; Stein, Richman, & Hannon, 1977).

Many singles experience sexual availability as part of their social identity and enjoy a variety of relationships. Some singles do not. Singles may experience sexual experimentation as a stage leading to marriage or to a choice of a primary sexual partner. Alternatively, they may be committed to experimentation as a lifestyle. Commitment to one primary partner may be precluded for a variety of reasons. Other commitments, to career, personal growth, or social mobility, may be seen as more important and require greater attention. A person recovering from the pains of a broken relationship may choose to withhold personal commitment. Many prefer the pleasure of variety in their experience. Simultaneous relating offers the possibility of getting to know a range of people, providing information about the world and oneself.

Some set up a hierarchy of relationships. A single may have a primary relationship with one partner and secondary relationships with several others. This arrangement involves special obligations to that primary other and less responsibility to the secondary relationships.

Availability presents opportunities and problems. Personal enrichment, access to a variety of ideas and types of encounters, the opportunity to identify oneself by one's own needs and goals are obvious advantages. Problems occur in the form of limited access to the world of the married, the stress of juggling ever-shifting emotional commitments, uncertainty of the commitment of others, and lack of role clarity and social endorsement.

Sexual experimentation does not necessarily imply rampant promiscuity, however. Although there are such individuals (see Proulx, 1976), the majority of singles are coping with the same problems of living and relating to others as the rest of the population. A life of wild abandon is no more real for them than for the average person on the street (Starr & Carns, 1972). Rather than finding singles' bars and so forth opportune for establishing dating relationships, many singles find such locations undesirable due to the strong role-playing demands and exploitative atmosphere there. They report that their dates primarily develop from introductions through fellow workers.

Another source of sexual satisfaction for singles, as well as married people, is masturbation. Although there are no data on whether or not singles masturbate more or less than the general population, we could assume that its incidence approximates the adult average; that is, 95 percent of men and 63 percent of women report having masturbated, most doing so once or twice a month (Hunt, 1974).

However, masturbation does not command the same degree of respect as does being seen in the company of an attractive date. Is the second-class status of masturbation reflective of our couple-oriented values once again? Must it always imply that one was unable to have sex through normal interpersonal channels, that it is a last resort for sexual "release" (suggesting that libido can be backed up in the plumbing until it might burst)? Certainly, the devaluation of masturbation as a desirable and pleasurable activity can increase the singles' sense of low social regard. It may also make people more self-conscious of their unattached (read "unfulfilled") social position (Adams, 1976).

CONCLUSIONS:
CHANGING GENDER ROLES AND SINGLEHOOD

The stereotypes of the carefree bachelor and lonely spinster imply several gender differences in adjustment to being single. One implication is that men may be single by choice and women only by default. A second message is that singlehood is more healthy for men than women: men, although single, can be carefree and can have a ball, while women are caricatured as sad, neurotic, suffering souls when deprived of male companionship. The supposedly greater need of a woman to find a mate is the topic of endless joking in fiction, cartoons, television, and films. During college, people joke, a man strives to obtain his B.A. degree; a woman envisions receiving her "Mrs." degree. In an analysis of women's magazine fiction (Franzwa, 1975), the following themes were repeatedly stressed: every normal woman gets married; the widow and divorcee are unable to cope with life without men; and the spinster is invariably lonely, useless, and unfulfilled without a mate. Although spinsters more often were described as having careers, their jobs were portrayed as boring, meaningless, and trivial when compared to the rewards of being married.

Such folk wisdom concerning the emotional adjustment of single men and women stands in striking contrast to what research in this area actually reveals. Single women appear to be happier than single men, and single, divorced, and widowed women have lower rates of mental illness than do unmarried men (Bernard, 1972; Gove, 1972; Macklin, 1980). Divorced men appear less productive and more unhappy than are both married men and divorced women (Feldman, 1973). And widowed men have more difficulty adjusting to the death of their spouse than do widowed women (Schaffer, 1981). Schaffer concludes, "In our society both women and men are usually willing to pretend that it is women who need men, rather than the other way around" (p. 106).

How might we account for the higher incidence of mental illness and unhappiness among unmarried men than women? Perhaps these indicators of maladjustment are what prevent such men from marrying in the first

225

9 Sink or Swing? The Lifestyles of Single Adults

place. The higher incidence of psychological maladjustment among married women (as compared to unmarried women and married men) is intriguing. Because most women marry, it is unlikely that "sicker" women are more likely to marry. Rather, marriage, especially for those who assume the homemaker role, does not seem to agree with women's mental health (Chesler, 1972; Schaffer, 1980).

Traditional gender roles, which restrict masculine behavior, also could account for single men's greater susceptibility to psychological disturbance. Gender roles have typically allowed women to be more emotionally expressive and support seeking than are men. Companionship and reassurance may more easily be sought by women in times of need. In contrast, single men may feel more isolated and unable to reach out to friends or family for emotional and social support. Stoicism, self-sufficiency, and bravado may have helped win the West, but these qualities can't take every man through moments of loneliness or the need to share one's thoughts with another human being. How many men grew up hearing, "Never burden other people with your own troubles"? The unmarried man, without an immediate family to turn to, may not be as able to find the support he needs through the help of his friends. Nor are men as likely to seek professional counseling as are women (Unger, 1979).

The evolution of gender roles into more androgynous standards of acceptability for both men and women may be one way to offset the gender imbalance in mental health. Adults, regardless of gender, would then be free to ask for and offer emotional nurturance, and to admit weaknesses, ignorance, and insecurity. The ability of friendships to weather times of personal crises and requests for emotional support would be more familiar to men. Close friendships between men in which such openness and sharing could occur are especially in need of development.

Changes toward greater equality in gender roles may also help to reduce many problems in dating that are described by singles. A man would be relieved of the need to prove himself sexually and could become free to relate to a woman as a person without compromising his sense of masculinity. A woman could more actively select the partners she would like to date, rather than waiting alluringly to be chosen. People could be more able to express their sexuality in accordance with individual needs and desires. Relieved of the pressures to demonstrate sexual prowess or appeal, unmarried people might increasingly find single life to be full of opportunities for the growth of varied interpersonal relationships. Increased gender-role equality might also allow greater contentment with one's chosen lifestyle for those who decide to remain single for a while or for a lifetime.

10   The Intimate Relationships of Lesbians and Gay Men

LETITIA ANNE PEPLAU
and
STEVEN L. GORDON

The problems generated by societal attitudes toward single adults are compounded for those whose sexual preference is toward people of the same gender. Letitia Anne Peplau and Steve Gordon begin their consideration of gay relationships by pointing out how popular stereotypes about gays demonstrate our assumptions about the centrality of gender roles in governing a couple's relationship. The knowledge that two single people who are living together are also sexually intimate raises questions in many naive observers regarding who plays the "man" and who plays the "woman." This area provides a clear demonstration of how intimately linked in many people's minds sexuality and gender-role behaviors are.

Several issues of importance in both gay and heterosexual relationships are explored in this chapter: what people want from relationships, the part played by love and commitment, satisfaction, and the issue of sexual exclusivity versus openness. Many commonalities are found in the relationship values of gays and heterosexuals: most people seek an intimate and relatively enduring partnership. One major difference has been found, however. Unlike the majority of heterosexual couples who emphasize traditional masculine-feminine role behavior, most gay couples reject such roles. In gay relationships, a more flexible division of labor occurs resembling a "best friend" pattern more than a traditional marriage. In fact, along with the examples provided by some of the elderly couples described earlier by Rick Allgeier, gay relationships may offer models of more egalitarian relationships.

One impact of gender-role socialization can be seen by comparing lesbian relationships to the relationships of gay men. Long-term bonding and fidelity are somewhat more characteristic of lesbian than of gay male relationships. Sexual variety and nonexclusivity is more valued by gay males.

226

Emotional intimacy and equality are values that are very strongly held among lesbians, perhaps more so than is characteristic of gay males or of heterosexual relationships. As the authors emphasize, however, there appears to be as much diversity in the lifestyle patterns of gay people as exists among heterosexual people.

Finally, regarding sexual interaction per se, homosexuals appear to be more sexually satisfied in their relationships than is characteristic of some heterosexuals. Perhaps this is to some extent a function of the absence of rigid patterns regarding who does what to whom. With greater flexibility and variety, there may be greater pleasure. There may also be a greater possibility for understanding the physical feelings of someone of the same gender. This understanding is, of course, theoretically also possible for heterosexual couples, but the communication needed to facilitate it may be easier for gays than for traditional heterosexuals.

 Confusion about gender roles and sexuality is perhaps greatest in response to homosexuality. Stereotypes often depict gay men and lesbians as individuals who are uncomfortable with their gender identity and who want to change their gender. Cultural images of the effeminate gay man and the masculine, "butch" lesbian are common. In relationships, homosexuals are thought to mimic heterosexual patterns, with one partner acting as the "wife" and the other partner playing the "husband." But current research shows that these stereotypes are inaccurate and misleading. Although these stereotypes may characterize a small minority of homosexuals, they fail to fit the lifestyles of most gay men and lesbians.

Where do these stereotypes come from? In part, they stem from the faulty assumption that three components of human sexuality are inseparable. These components are *sexual orientation* (attraction to same-gender versus other-gender partners), *gender identity* (our belief that we are male or female) and *gender-role behavior* (acting in traditionally "masculine" or "feminine" ways). Many people wrongly believe that, if an individual differs from the norm on one of these components, he or she must differ on the others as well. In North American culture, a typical heterosexual woman is attracted romantically and sexually to men (sexual orientation), she knows without doubt that she is female (gender identity), and she frequently enacts the roles or behaviors that society defines as appropriate for women. A lesbian differs from this pattern in that her sexual and romantic attraction is to women. The stereotype assumes that the lesbian must also differ in her gender identity and gender-role behavior. This assumption is wrong.

Homosexuals are not confused about their gender identity: lesbians are not different from heterosexual women in their sureness of being female, nor do gay men differ from heterosexual men on this dimension. In terms of behavior, research indicates that most gay men are not effeminate in dress or manner, nor are lesbians usually "masculine" in their behavior (see DeLora & Warren, 1977; Gagnon, 1977; Gagnon & Simon, 1973; Warren, 1974).

This chapter reviews research findings about the love relationships of lesbians and gay men. We begin by asking what people want in love relationships and by examining how relationship values are affected by sexual orientation. We next look at the question of whether homosexuals adopt heterosexual scripts for relationships (see Chapter 1 for a description of the use of scripts in our lives). Are homosexual relationships more similar to heterosexual "marriages" or to same-gender "best friendships"? We then consider love and commitment in the relationships of lesbians and gay men. Finally, we investigate sexual behavior and the issue of sexual exclusivity in gay relationships.

METHODOLOGICAL ISSUES AND LIMITATIONS

Before beginning our investigation of homosexual relationships, however, a few methodological issues deserve mention. First, terms need to be defined. The term *homosexual* is appropriately used to refer to both men and women whose primary sexual and affectional orientation is toward same-gender partners. But many gay men and lesbians dislike the term, believing that it overemphasizes the sexual aspect of their lifestyle. Instead, most prefer "gay" (for both men and women) or "lesbian" (for women).

Second, research on gay relationships, like studies of heterosexual relationships (see Hill et al., 1979), is limited in several ways. Most research uses questionnaires or interviews. Self-report responses can be biased because people lack insight into their relationships or because they want to present a favorable image to researchers. Whatever their sexual orientation, people are not always truthful in describing their relationships to themselves or to researchers. People who volunteer for studies may differ from nonvolunteers in being more interested in social science research, more liberal or permissive in their views, or more trusting of psychologists. In addition, studies of gays or of any partially hidden population encounter special problems. There is no such thing as a representative sample of lesbians and gay men (Morin, 1977). Some gay people are secretive about their sexual orientation and would not volunteer for psychological research. Those gays who have participated in research tend to be younger, educated, middle-class, white adults. Because of these limitations, we can place greatest confidence in findings that have been replicated in several different studies. And we need to be cautious in assuming that research findings adequately describe the entire gay popula-

tion in America. In this chapter for instance, our primary focus is on voluntary relationships. Generalizing our conclusions to forced sex in institutions
(for example, prisons or the military) would be inappropriate. With these
warnings in mind, we turn to the questions of what gay men and lesbians
are looking for in an intimate relationship.

VALUES ABOUT INTIMATE RELATIONSHIPS

What do lesbians and gay men want from their close relationships? Do gays
want a long-term relationship with a single partner, or do they prefer to live
pretty much in the present? Is their view of love romantic or cynical? Do
homosexuals have a distinctive set of values about relationships unique to
lesbians and gay men, or do gays and heterosexuals seek similar goals in
relationships? Research is beginning to answer these questions.

Most gays want to have steady love relationships. Few would be satisfied
to have only casual liaisons. One study (Bell & Weinberg, 1978) asked homosexuals how important it was to them to have "a permanent living arrangement with a homosexual partner." Of the lesbians, 25 percent said this
was "the most important thing in life," and another 35 percent said it was
"very important." Less than one woman in four said that a permanent
relationship was not important. Gay men showed a similar pattern: 15
percent said a relationship was the most important thing in life; 22 percent
said it was very important; and only a third said it was not important at all.
Thus a somewhat higher proportion of women than men said that having a
permanent relationship was extremely important.

Most gays, like most heterosexuals value steady love relationships (for
example, see Hill, Rubin & Peplau, 1976). What are the characteristics that
gays seek in such partnerships? Lesbians, gay men, and heterosexuals were
asked to rank nine possible relationship goals (Ramsey, Latham, &
Lindquist, 1978). All groups ranked affection, personal development, and
companionship as most important; least importance was given to having "a
place in the community" and to religion. Other goals such as economic
security and having an attractive home were ranked in the middle. Lesbians,
gay men, and heterosexuals have also been asked to rank the qualities that
they seek in partners (Laner, 1977). All groups gave greatest importance to
honesty, affection, and intelligence; these traits ranked above having "good
looks," a sense of humor, and money.

Matched samples of lesbians, gay men, and heterosexual women and
men rated the importance of various features of love relationships (Peplau &
Cochran, 1980). These included such issues as revealing intimate feelings,
spending time together, holding similar attitudes, having an equal-power
relationship, and having sexual exclusivity. Participants gave varied answers.

For example, although some considered it essential to share many activities with a partner, others viewed joint activities as relatively unimportant. Despite such individual differences, remarkably few overall group differences were found between heterosexuals and homosexuals. For example, on average, both groups gave greatest importance to "being able to talk about my most intimate feelings" with a partner.

One major difference between homosexuals and heterosexuals did emerge, however. Sexual exclusivity in relationships was much more important to heterosexuals than to homosexuals. Lesbians and gay men gave sexual fidelity an average rating of somewhat more than 5, compared with a rating of just over 7 for the heterosexuals (the highest possible importance rating was 9). Homosexuals were less likely than heterosexuals to endorse monogamy as an ideal for relationships. Two interesting gender differences also emerged. Whatever their sexual orientation, women gave greater importance than men did to emotional expressiveness and the sharing of feelings. This finding is consistent with the emphasis in North American gender-role socialization that men should conceal their feelings and present a tough exterior (David & Brannon, 1976). Second, lesbian and heterosexual women cared more than did men about having egalitarian relationships. Perhaps because of the women's movement, women showed greater sensitivity to equal power in love relationships.

Finally, Peplau and Cochran (1980) examined how "romantic" gays were in their attitudes about love. Participants were asked how much they agreed or disagreed with statements about love such as "Lovers ought to expect a certain amount of disillusionment after they have been together for a while" and "To be truly in love is to be in love forever." No differences were found in the answers of lesbians, gay men, and heterosexuals; most people took a middle-of-the-road position. Homosexuals and heterosexuals were equally likely to be starry-eyed romantics or cold-hearted cynics. In sum, the picture that emerges from these studies is that most people, whatever their sexual orientation, want much the same things from love relationships; namely, affection and companionship.

RELATIONSHIP SCRIPTS: MARRIAGE OR BEST FRIENDSHIP?

Of the myths about homosexual relationships, none is more persistent—or wrong—than the belief that in gay partnerships one person adopts the role of "husband" and the other the role of "wife." According to this stereotype, gay partners "make believe," in some sense, that one of them is male and the other female. One partner is the breadwinner, takes the initiative in sex, and generally assumes the conventional role of dominant male. The other partner keeps house and acts the part of the submissive female.

Scientific research refutes this stereotype. More typical of actual gay relationships are the following personal descriptions:

> [*Gay man:*] My involvement with other men is always like we are buddies, or at least that's what I strive for. . . . I very much want to have a man-to-man relationship with my friend and I value this element of masculinity. . . . I believe masculinity can be realized as readily through another man as it can through a woman. [Quoted by Spada, 1979, p. 168]

> [*Lesbian:*] In a heterosexual relationship, you are playing a role . . . in a gay relationship, you don't have that. You have two people on an equal level living together, sharing responsibilities. In a heterosexual relationship you are not going to get it 50:50 (division of labor). You'd be lucky if you get it 60:40, so there is a certain amount of role playing that you are going to have in a heterosexual relationship that you don't have in a gay relationship. [Quoted by Tanner, 1978, pp. 90–91]

Most lesbians and gay men actively reject traditional husband-wife roles as a model or script for love relationships. One study (Jay & Young, 1977) asked lesbians and gay men their feelings about "role playing." Most of the lesbians and half of the men said they felt negatively about role playing. One lesbian explained, "I don't like role playing because it copies the traditional male-female relationship. I'm proud I'm a woman. And I love women, not pseudo-men" (cited in Jay & Young, 1977, p. 320). Many gays value their relationships precisely because they feel freed from the restrictions imposed by gender roles in traditional heterosexual relationships. A gay man commented, "Role playing seems to me by nature to involve dominance and control, both of which make me feel uncomfortable" (cited in Jay & Young, 1977, p. 369). Three possible areas of masculine-feminine role playing in gay relationships have been investigated: the division of household tasks, sexual behavior and decision making (Bell & Weinberg, 1978; Caldwell & Peplau, 1980; Cardell, Finn, & Marecek, 1981; Harry & DeVall, 1978; Jay & Young, 1977; Saghir & Robins, 1973).

In most heterosexual marriages, clear distinctions are made between the husband's work (for example, being the breadwinner, doing household repairs) and the wife's work (for example, doing the cooking and other domestic chores). Is there a similar division of household tasks among gay couples who live together? Research finds little evidence for this idea. For example, Bell & Weinberg (1978) asked gay men and lesbians which partner in the relationship does "the housework"; 61 percent of gay men and 58 percent of lesbians said that housework was shared equally. When asked if one partner consistently does all the "feminine tasks" or all the "masculine tasks," about 90 percent of the gay men and lesbians said no. As one gay man commented, "When I am asked who is the husband and who is the wife, I would say we're just a couple of happily married husbands" (quoted by Saghir & Robins, 1973, p. 74). The predominant pattern is one of role flexibility, with partners sharing in housekeeping and financial expenditures. Because it is common in gay relationships for both partners to have jobs, both are usually able to contribute financially to the relationship and neither can devote all their time to homemaking (see Chapter 7 for a description of the effects of the employment of both partners in heterosexual marriages).

In the area of sexual behavior, role playing might be reflected in which partner initiates sexual interactions or in personal preferences for particular sexual activities (see Chapter 3). Some studies have asked gays which partner is more "active" or "passive" in sex. A majority of lesbians and gay men say that both partners are equally active or that partners alternate from situation to situation (Califia, 1979; Harry, 1976; Marmor, 1980; Saghir & Robins, 1973). Jay and Young (1977) asked gays if they role played sexually when they were sexually intimate. Only 12 percent of gay men and 8 percent of lesbians said they did this frequently; some said they took an active or passive role occasionally, and the largest group responded "never." Studies of gay men have investigated men's preferences for particular sexual activities, such as receiving versus giving anal intercourse. Again, many men indicate enjoying both roles. When a man does have a preference for one kind of sexuality, this preference is not linked to more general dominance in decision making in the relationship (Harry & DeVall, 1978). Few homosexuals consistently engage in sexual role playing. When role playing does occur, it may be more common among gay men than lesbians.

A third component of traditional marriage is the idea that the masculine partner should be the "boss" and leader in decision making. Gay men and lesbians largely reject this model, preferring a relationship in which partners share equally in power (for example, see Harry, 1979; Spada, 1979). One study (Peplau & Cochran, 1980) asked matched samples of heterosexual and homosexual college students about power in their current love relationship. Virtually everyone (over 95 percent in each group) said that ideally both partners should have "exactly equal say" in their relationship. Unfortunately, only about half the lesbians, gay men, and heterosexuals thought that their current relationships lived up to this ideal.

What are some of the factors that tip the balance of power away from equality in gay relationships? In gay relationships, power is more likely to be wielded by the partner who has greater personal resources, in terms of greater education, income, age, or other characteristics (Caldwell & Peplau,

1980; Harry & DeVall, 1978). In addition, when there is an imbalance of involvement or commitment in a relationship, the partner who is less interested often has greater power. Gay relationships, like heterosexual ones (Peplau, 1979; see also Chapters 3 and 5), seem to have the greatest chance for equality when partners have similar resources and commitments to the relationship.

Although most lesbians and gay men do not engage in gender-role playing, a small minority does. One lesbian described her experience: "When I am with a younger girl, I like to act 'male'—that is, protect her—and I like it very much if she lets me buy drinks, etc. . . . What I like best about the 'male' or 'butch' role is the protective angle, even though I realize intellectually that this is a lot of sexist shit" (quoted by Jay & Young, 1977, p. 322). A gay man expressed these views:

> I put strong emphasis on roles, more sexually than nonsexually. But, and this is the distinctive part, I can feel perfectly comfortable in either set of roles . . . but I like to keep these roles clearly defined with any given person. . . . I like the stability and clarity of it, the ease of prediction and minimal conflict it provides; the communications are so much easier, more familiar. [Quoted by Jay & Young, 1977, p. 367]

For a minority of homosexuals, some elements of gender-role playing are an important and comfortable part of relationships, just as they are for many heterosexuals (see Peplau, Rubin, & Hill, 1977).

Because a few gays do engage in some gender-role playing, it is informative to examine factors that may affect the adoption of these patterns. It appears that such role playing was more common in the "old gay life" prior to the recent evolution of homophile organizations, gay liberation, and the women's movement. One older lesbian commented, "I was 'butch' in experience prior to 1960, but never heavy butch. Just a wee bit more the aggressor, paying the way of my partner, for example. . . . Since 1964 I haven't engaged in role playing. [Now] we are equal women together" (cited in Jay & Young, 1977, p. 321). There has been a historical decline in gender-role playing in the United States. One possible consequence is that such role playing may be more common among older gay men and lesbians than among younger ones.

Gender-role playing may be more common among gays and lesbians from lower socioeconomic and educational levels (Gagnon & Simon, 1973; Harry & DeVall, 1978; Wolf, 1979). It has also been suggested that role playing is part of the "coming-out" experience of some gays (Gagnon & Simon, 1973; Saghir & Robins, 1973). For example, a young woman new to the lesbian community may initially dress in a "butch" manner in order to be more easily identified as lesbian (Wolf, 1979).

In some cases, gender-role playing may result from temporary situational factors. Saghir and Robins (1973) found that only 12 percent of lesbians and 17 percent of gay men had engaged in domestic role playing for a period of three months or longer. Role playing usually occurred because one partner was temporarily unemployed or attending school. Finally, role playing occurs in prison settings; prison culture sometimes defines masculine-feminine roles as the acceptable form for sexual or love relations between same-gender prisoners (for example, see Gagnon & Simon, 1973).

The idea that most lesbians and gay men engage in masculine-feminine role playing is a myth. Although a small minority of homosexuals does show these patterns, the vast majority does not. Why, then, does the role playing stereotype persist? One reason is that this, like other common stereotypes, is seldom subjected to careful scientific scrutiny. In addition, those gays who do engage in role playing may be much more visible to the general public than the majority of gays who do not. Movies and television often perpetuate the stereotype. Finally, in North America, heterosexual marriage is so powerful a script for love relationships that many people find it difficult to imagine an intimate relationship that does not involve husband-wife roles. In North American society, the imagery of romance, love, and "living happily ever after" is heavily colored by the symbolism of marriage.

Although most gays reject husband-wife roles as a model for intimacy, they do want a loving, committed relationship. Therefore, lesbians and gay men must find or create alternate scripts for relationships. Harry and DeVall (1978) suggest that gay relationships are often modeled after friendship, with the added component of erotic and romantic attraction. As such, gay relationships may most closely resemble best friendships.

A friendship script fosters equality in relationships. The norms or rules for friendship assume that partners will be relatively equal in status and power; this contrasts sharply with the institution of marriage, in which the husband is traditionally expected to be the "boss" or leader. Friends also tend to be similar in interests, resources, and skills. In contrast, spouses have traditionally brought different gender-linked qualities to a marriage. For heterosexuals, these differences often foster male dominance rather than equality. As one sociologist has observed,

> Take a young woman who has been trained for feminine dependencies, who wants to "look up" to the man she marries. Put her at a disadvantage in the labor market. Then marry her to a man who has a slight advantage over her in age, income, and education, shored up by an ideology with a male bias. . . . Then expect an egalitarian relationship? [Bernard, 1972, p. 146]

Because of the divergent socialization of males and females in our society, partners in heterosexual relationships often find it difficult to break out of traditional patterns. Research on same-gender relationships suggests that when partners are more similar in their interests and abilities, equality between partners is more easily (although not inevitably) achieved. Feminists have long argued that heterosexual couples *should* abandon gender-based differences in behavior and power. Studies of homosexual relationships demonstrate that successful love relationships *can* be built on models other than traditional marriage. We now turn to studies describing what gay relationships are actually like.

LOVE AND COMMITMENT IN GAY RELATIONSHIPS

A starting point for our discussion is the question of how many lesbians and gay men are actually involved in steady relationships. Although stereotypes often portray gays as unable to develop enduring relationships, empirical evidence argues to the contrary. In studies of lesbians, between 45 percent and 80 percent of the women surveyed were currently in a steady relationship (for example, see Bell & Weinberg, 1978; Jay & Young, 1977; Peplau et al., 1978; Raphael & Robinson, 1980; Schäfer, 1977). In most studies, the proportion of lesbians in an ongoing relationship was close to 75 percent. Studies of gay men show that between 45 percent and 60 percent of the men surveyed were currently involved in a steady relationship (for example, see Bell & Weinberg, 1978; Jay & Young, 1977; Peplau & Cochran, 1981; Spada, 1979). The best estimate about the proportion of gay men in such relationships is about 50 percent. Many lesbians and gay men in steady relationships live with their partners. Although these figures should not be taken as representative of all lesbians and gay men, they do suggest that at any particular point in time a large proportion of homosexuals have stable love relationships. It appears that relatively more lesbians than gay men are involved in steady relationships.

We should emphasize that those lesbians and gay men who do not currently have steady relationships are a diverse group. They include people who have recently ended relationships through breakups or the death of partners, people who are eager to begin new relationships, and others who do not want committed relationships.

Love and Satisfaction

We saw earlier that most homosexuals want close love relationships. How successful are lesbians and gay men in achieving this goal? Unfortunately, information about love, satisfaction, and commitment in gay relationships comes from a few studies based on fairly small samples. So the following results are presented cautiously. They suggest that gays do find their relationships highly rewarding.

One study (Cardell, Finn, & Marecek, 1981) compared lesbian, gay male, and heterosexual couples on a standardized measure of couple adjustment. Most couples were very satisfied with their relationships, and gay men and lesbians did not differ significantly from each other or from the heterosexuals. Another study (Ramsey, Latham, & Lindquist, 1978) compared lesbian, gay male, and heterosexual couples on the Locke-Wallace Scale, a widely used measure of marital adjustment. All couples scored in the "well-adjusted" range, and the homosexuals were indistinguishable from the heterosexuals.

Only recently have social psychologists attempted to measure love systematically, spurred by Rubin's (1973) development of scales to measure "love" and "liking" for a romantic partner. Peplau and Cochran (1980) compared matched samples of lesbians, gay men, and heterosexuals on these measures. Lesbians and gay men reported high love for their partners, indicating strong feelings of attachment, caring, and intimacy. They also scored high on the liking scale, reflecting feelings of respect and affection toward their partners. On other measures, lesbians and gay men rated their current relationships as highly satisfying and very close. When comparisons were made among lesbians, gay men, and heterosexuals on these measures, no significant differences were found.

Peplau and Cochran also asked lesbians, gay men, and heterosexuals to describe in their own words the "best things" and "worst things" about their relationships. Consider these observations by people listing the best aspects of their relationships: "The best thing is having someone to *be* with when you wake up" and "We like each other. We both seem to be getting what we want and need. We have wonderful sex together." Or these descriptions of the worst aspects of relationships: "My partner is too dependent emotionally" and "Her aunt lives with us!" All these remarks could have been made by heterosexuals, but they are actually all responses made by lesbians. Systematic analyses (Cochran, 1978) found no significant differences in the responses of lesbians, gay men, and heterosexuals—all of whom reported similar joys and problems. To examine the possibility that more subtle differences among groups existed that were not captured by the coding scheme, the "best things" and "worst things" statements were typed on cards in a standard format, with information about gender and sexual orientation removed. Panels of judges were asked to sort the cards, separating men and women and separating heterosexuals and homosexuals. The judges were not able to identify correctly the responses of lesbians, gay men, or heterosexual women and men.

Taken together, these findings suggest that many gay relationships are highly satisfying. Lesbian and gay male couples appear, on standardized measures, to be as "well adjusted" as are heterosexual couples. This does not mean, of course, that gays have no difficulties in their relationships. They undoubtedly have many of the same problems as heterosexuals in coordinating joint goals, resolving interpersonal conflicts, and so on. In addition, lesbian and gay male couples may have special problems arising from the hostile and rejecting attitudes of many people toward homosexuals (see Mendola, 1980; Silverstein, 1981). Overall, however, existing research shows that homosexual relationships can be as personally satisfying as heterosexual ones.

Commitment

It is a sad truth that love is no certain guarantee that any relationship will endure. In homosexual relationships, as in heterosexual ones, relationships begun hopefully and lovingly can and do fall apart. Do homosexual relationships last as long as heterosexual ones?

There is no easy answer to this complex question. The U.S. Bureau of the Census records with considerable accuracy the proportion of the population who are heterosexually married and divorced, but no comparable statistical information exists describing any aspect of homosexual relationships. We simply do not know how long the "average" lesbian or gay male relationship lasts. It is useful to remember that for an adolescent, whether lesbian or heterosexual, a relationship of three months may seem "long"; for a 25-year-old, a relationship of 2 years may be relatively "long"; for a 50-year-old, a relationship of 20 years may be long. In other words, a person's age determines to some extent the length of time that it is possible or likely for a relationship to endure.

A recent study of homosexuals in San Francisco (Bell & Weinberg, 1978) inquired about the length of people's *first* homosexual relationships. On the average, lesbians in this sample were 22 years old when they had their first "relatively steady relationships." Nearly 90 percent said they had been "in love" with these first woman partners, and the typical relationship lasted for a median of one to three years. For a third of the lesbians, these relationships lasted four years or longer. Gay men in this sample were, on the average, 23 years old when they had their first steady relationships. About 78 percent said they had been in love with these first male partners, and the typical relationship lasted for a median of one to three years. For 22 percent of the men in this sample, the first steady relationship lasted four years or longer.

Several studies have asked homosexuals to describe the length of their current love relationships (for example, see Bell & Weinberg, 1978; Jay & Young, 1977; Peplau & Amaro, in press; Saghir & Robins, 1973). In these studies, most participants have been young people in their 20s. The typical length of relationships is about two to three years for both men and women. Studies of older gays would be especially useful in understanding the length of homosexual relationships, but such research is strikingly absent from the available literature. A few studies that have included older lesbians and gay men document that relationships of 20 years or more are not uncommon (for example, see Mendola, 1980; Raphael & Robinson, 1980; Silverstein, 1981). Finally, although it is sometimes thought that lesbians have more long-lasting relationships than gay men, evidence about gender differences in the duration of gay relationships is inconsistent (for example, see Bell & Weinberg, 1978; Jay & Young, 1977; Schäfer, 1977).

What factors influence the permanence of gay relationships? Probably many of the same forces that operate in heterosexual relationships. Permanence is affected by two separate factors (Levinger, 1979). The first concerns the strength of the positive attraction that make a particular partner and relationship appealing. We have seen that homosexuals do not differ from heterosexuals in the love and satisfaction they feel in steady relationships. But the possibility always exists that attractions may wane and that people may "fall out of love." Thus, a decrease in attraction can lead to the ending of a relationship.

The second set of factors affecting the permanence of relationships consists of barriers that make the ending of a relationship costly, in either psychological or material terms. For heterosexuals, marriage usually creates many barriers to the dissolution of a relationship, including the cost of a divorce, a wife's financial dependence on her husband, joint investments in property, children, and so on. Such factors may encourage married couples to "work" on improving a declining relationship, rather than ending it. In some cases, these barriers can also keep partners trapped in an "empty-shell" relationship.

Gay men and lesbians probably encounter fewer barriers to the termination of relationships, as these quotations illustrate:

[*Gay Man:*] I see differences and I see similarities between gay and straight couples. A big difference is that gays are less frequently obliged "to stay together." Ed and I don't have the kids, the high cost of divorce, the in-laws, and the financial entanglements to keep us together. We also don't have all the support systems that straights enjoy. [Quoted by Mendola, 1980, pp. 122–123]

[*Lesbian:*] Marje and I are no different from any straight couple. We've got a lot of problems to work out. And the problems aren't any different from the problems straights have: financial, sexual, in-laws. . . . However, what's different is we don't have a lot of the structures straights have to help them solve their problems. We have to do it on our own, and so it's harder for a gay couple to stay together and make their relationship work. [Quoted by Mendola, 1980, p. 123]

Because of weaker barriers to relationship dissolution (Lewis et al., 1980), lesbians and gay men are less likely to become trapped in hopelessly unhappy relationships. They may also be less motivated to rescue deteriorating relationships.

SEXUAL BEHAVIOR IN GAY RELATIONSHIPS

Most people view gays largely in terms of their sexuality. Stereotypes sometimes depict lesbians and gay men as "highly sexed" people whose lives are organized around the pursuit of sexual pleasure to a much greater extent than is true for heterosexuals. Such a characterization is both far-fetched and wrong. Few of us, whether gay or heterosexual, have sexuality as the organizing principle in our lives (Gagnon & Simon, 1973). For most of us, sex is only one aspect of our lives, along with work, friendship, and other activities. Research suggests that, when it comes to sexuality, differences between men and women are much greater than differences between heterosexuals and homosexuals.

The Physiology of Sexual Arousal

Studies of the physiological aspects of sexuality (Kinsey et al., 1948, 1953; Masters & Johnson, 1979) have found no major differences in the pattern of sexual response of lesbians and heterosexual women, nor in the response of gay and heterosexual men. This should not be surprising. The physiological mechanics of sexual arousal and orgasm are human characteristics, unaffected by sexual orientation.

Heterosexual Experiences

Before considering sexuality in steady relationships, it is useful to provide some background about the more general sexual experiences of gay men and lesbians. Only a minority of lesbians and gay men have had exclusively homosexual experiences throughout their lives. Most homosexuals have had sex with other-gender partners, often before they adopted a homosexual lifestyle (Gundlach & Reiss, 1968; Jay & Young, 1977; Kinsey et al., 1948, 1953;

Saghir & Robins, 1973). For example, a recent study (Bell & Weinberg, 1978) found that 83 percent of lesbians and 64 percent of gay men had had heterosexual intercourse. For many people, these heterosexual experiences occurred in the context of dating relationships (Peplau et al., 1978; Peplau & Cochran, 1981). A significant minority of lesbians and gay men have been married. Bell and Weinberg (1978) found that 35 percent of the lesbians and 20 percent of the gay men surveyed had been in heterosexual marriages. Research findings lead to two conclusions. First, most homosexuals have had sexual experience with other-gender partners. Second, a greater proportion of lesbians than of gay men have had heterosexual experiences, including marriage.

Sex in a Steady Relationship

For most lesbians, sex is an enjoyable part of a steady relationship. In one study (Peplau et al., 1978), 75 percent of lesbians reported that sex with their steady partners was extremely satisfying, and only 4 percent said that it was not at all satisfying. One factor contributing to satisfaction was the reported lack of guilt among lesbians; 80 percent said they never felt guilty about their sexual activity with their partners, and only 4 percent said they usually or always felt guilty. Another major factor was the frequency with which lesbians experienced orgasms with their current partners. Over 70 percent of women said they almost always experienced orgasms; only 4 percent said they never had orgasms. Other studies (Jay & Young, 1977; Kinsey et al., 1953) confirm that most lesbians do not usually have difficulty in having orgasms during sex.

Comparative studies suggest that lesbians may have orgasms more regularly during sex than do heterosexual women (for example, see Hunt, 1974; Jay & Young, 1977; Pietropinto & Simenauer, 1979; Tavris & Sadd, 1977). Kinsey researchers (1953) compared heterosexual women who had been married for five years with lesbians who had been sexually active for an equal number of years. Among these women, 17 percent of the heterosexuals compared to only 7 percent of the lesbians had never had an orgasm. And only 40 percent of heterosexual women had orgasms consistently (that is, 90 to 100 percent of the times they had sex), compared to 68 percent of lesbians. These differences may, as Kinsey suggested, reflect differences in the knowledge and sexual techniques of women's partners. But differences in the emotional and interpersonal aspects of lovemaking may be equally important. Schäfer (1976) asked 57 lesbians who had had sexual relations during the past year both with women and with men to compare these experiences. Most lesbians said that compared to sex with men, sex with women was more tender (94 percent), intimate (91 percent), considerate (88 percent), partner related (73 percent), exciting (66 percent), and diversified (52 percent).

Lesbian couples have sex about as often as do heterosexual couples of the same age. Among the younger lesbians typically studied by researchers, the average frequency of sex is about two to three times per week. This figure varies widely from couple to couple, however. Among the lesbians surveyed by Jay and Young (1977), only 5 percent reported having sex with their partners daily. Most women (57 percent) had sex two to five times per week; 25 percent had sex once a week, and 8 percent had sex less often. Little is known about factors that influence the actual or desired frequency of sex in lesbian relationships. The picture that emerges from these statistics is that most lesbian couples find sex an enjoyable and rewarding part of their relationships.

Research on sexuality in gay men's relationships presents a fairly similar picture. In general, gay men report high satisfaction with sex in their relationships (Peplau & Cochran, 1981). Gay men have sex with their steady partners as often or more often than do heterosexual couples (Lewis et al., 1980; Schäfer, 1977). Among gay men studied by Jay and Young (1977), 11 percent reported having sex with their partners daily, 38 percent had sex three to four times per week, 40 percent once or twice a week, and 11 percent less than once a week. Researchers assume that sex usually leads to orgasm for men, and so questions specifically about orgasms have not been included in most studies of gay men's relationships.

It has been suggested (for example, by Saghir & Robins, 1973) that long-term gay men's relationships often decline in sexual activity and interest. Adequate empirical evidence on this point is, however, lacking. We do not know how often such sexual "devitalization" occurs in gay men's relationships, whether it is any more common among gay male couples than among lesbian and heterosexual couples, or what factors might create such a situation.

Sexual Exclusivity

Today many couples, both heterosexual and homosexual, are questioning whether it is better for relationships to be sexually monogamous or sexually "open." As we discussed earlier, Peplau and Cochran (1980) found that more heterosexuals than homosexuals strongly valued sexual exclusivity in a steady relationship. It is important to emphasize, however, that gays are a diverse group with varied views about sexual behavior. Some gays are strong advocates of sexual exclusivity, as this quotation from a gay man illustrates: "I want my lover to be mine and only mine, and I want to be his and only his. He is my life, and I am his life, and that's the way I want it to be" (cited in

Silverstein, 1981, p. 141). Other gay men and lesbians reject the idea of sexual exclusivity. One gay man explained,

> I still feel that a commitment to a relationship . . . has very little to do with what I choose to do with my body. My commitment is more intellectual and in the heart. I differentiate between sex and making love. . . . When I feel strongly toward a person, I make love. When I don't, I have sex. And I can enjoy both of them very much. [Quoted by Silverstein, 1981, p. 143]

Although these two quotations are from gay men, it is easy to imagine lesbians and heterosexuals who would agree with these views.

In actual practice, the relationships of gay men are less likely to be sexually exclusive than are those of lesbians or heterosexuals. Studies suggest that most gay men who are in a steady relationship also have sex with men other than their primary partner (for example, see Bell & Weinberg, 1978; Blasband & Peplau, 1980; Harry & Lovely, 1979; Plummer, 1978; Warren, 1974). In some studies, all the men whose relationships had continued for several years reported having had outside affairs. Why is sexual openness so common in the relationships of gay men? Several factors are relevant.

First, gender-role socialization in America teaches men to be more interested in sex and sexual variety than are women. One gay man suggested that "Promiscuity is inbred in all boy children, and since most boy children don't find out they're gay until later in life, their promiscuity has nothing to do with their gayness. It has to do with their *male*ness" (quoted by Mendola, 1980, p.55). In contrast, for many women, whatever their sexual orientation, sex and love are closely linked; thus casual sex may be less appealing.

In Jay and Young's survey (1977), 97 percent of lesbians said that emotional involvement was important to sex, and 92 percent said that emotional involvement always or very frequently accompanied their own sexual relations. In comparison, 83 percent of the gay men said that emotional involvement is important in sex, and 45 percent said that involvement always or usually accompanied sex. Gay men more often than lesbians separate sex and love and can enjoy casual sex for its own sake, without emotional involvement. In Schäfer's (1977) survey, gay men were more likely than lesbians to say that many of their sexual partners were people they had never met before (70 percent of gay men, 26 percent of lesbians) and were partners with whom they had sex only once (64 percent of gay men; 18 percent of lesbians). Gay men were less likely than lesbians to say they were in love with most of their sex partners (19 percent of gay men, 64 percent of lesbians).

Basic differences in men's and women's orientations toward love and sex may be more important here than sexual orientation. Equal proportions of lesbians and heterosexual women (64 percent) told Gundlach and Reiss

(1968) that they could have sex only if they were in love with their partners. Similarly, just as gay men are more likely than lesbians to have sexually open relationships, so too are heterosexual husbands more likely than wives to have extramarital affairs (Hunt, 1974; Kinsey et al., 1948, 1953; Pietropinto & Simenauer, 1979). Gender has a major influence on the kind of relationship people want. Whereas most men and women want a steady relationship with one special partner, men are more likely to want—and to have—sexual relations with other partners as well.

For gay men, the norms of the gay community may also encourage sexual openness rather than exclusivity. Especially in urban centers, the gay men's community provides many opportunities for casual sex. Gay men can find new partners at gay bars, public baths, and other places. The important point to remember is that for many gay men, as for many heterosexual men, casual sexual affairs are a complement to a steady relationship, not a substitute for it.

In growing up, men and women learn different lessons about sexuality. As adults, the genders are exposed to different opportunities for sexual exploration, and men continue to receive greater social support for sexual experimentation. Thus, we believe, differences in the sexual attitudes and behaviors of men and women are largely a result of socialization. But others attribute these gender differences to biology. For example, sociobiologist Donald Symons (1979) proposes that evolutionary pressures have encouraged a desire for sexual exclusivity in females and a desire for sexual diversity in males. In Symons' view, "the sex lives of homosexual men and women—who need not compromise sexually with members of the opposite sex—should provide dramatic insights into male sexuality and female sexuality in their undiluted states" (1979, p. 292). Symons is referring to the fact that heterosexual relationships are, in some measure, a compromise between the goals and desires of the male and female partners—a compromise that can obscure underlying gender differences. In relationships with same-gender partners, individuals may be able to express their personal dispositions more fully.

For gays as for heterosexuals, decisions about sexual exclusivity can have varied consequences for a love relationship. For some people, sexual exclusivity is a sign of love and commitment to their partners. For such individuals, sexual exploration with other partners might only occur if there were problems in the primary relationships. For others, however, secure and rewarding primary relationships are enhanced by the excitement and novelty of outside liaisons. Indeed, some people view sexual fidelity as excessively restrictive and unnecessary (see Harry, 1977; Jay & Young, 1977; Silverstein, 1981; Warren, 1974). In other words, the meaning of sexual openness and its implications for the continuation of a relationship can be quite diverse.

Research on the relationships of lesbians and gay men leads to several broad conclusions. There are many similarities between the relationship values of homosexuals and heterosexuals. Few significant differences have been found between gay and heterosexual couples on measures of relationship adjustment, love and satisfaction, or sex with one's partner. There appear to be many commonalities among intimate relationships, regardless of sexual orientation. However, a major difference between gay and heterosexual relationships did emerge. Heterosexual relationships usually emphasize gender-based differences between partners and adopt husband-wife roles as a relationship script. In contrast, lesbians and gay men usually reject traditional marital roles. Instead of treating one another as husband and wife, homosexuals treat their partners like best friends. The patterns of interaction that develop in gay couples are more likely to be based on the unique individual characteristics of the partners than on predetermined cultural scripts.

Our review has also highlighted several gender differences between the relationships of lesbians and gay men. Homosexuals are not a unitary group; it is unwise to assume that all homosexuals, regardless of gender, are necessarily similar. Lesbians are more likely than gay men to be in stable relationships. Lesbians give greater emphasis to emotional intimacy and to equality in relationships than do gay men. Lesbians are more likely to view sexuality and love as closely linked, and to prefer having sex only with partners they care about. Gay men, in contrast, are more likely to separate sex and love. Gay men enjoy sex with loved partners, but they are also more likely than gay women to enjoy recreational sex with casual partners. Gay men are more likely than lesbians to be in a sexually open relationship and to have had sex with a considerably larger number of partners. Cultural gender-role socialization undoubtedly touches all of us, regardless of sexual orientation. Gay men and lesbians bring to love relationships many of the same expectations, values, and interests as heterosexuals of the same gender.

11 Gender Roles and Sexual Violence

FRANCES CHERRY

In this chapter, Fran Cherry examines the relationship between increases in sexual assault (rape) and a number of factors including violent pornography, gender-role socialization, and reactions to the women's liberation movement.

The fusion of sex, dominance, and aggression that accompany sexual assault makes it difficult to disentangle the motivation of rapists. Cherry explores the socialization of men for sexual and aggressive behavior as one possible source of sexual assault. She also considers women's failure to communicate their feelings assertively. This problem is inherent in the traditional socialization of women. Although the lack of such skills probably contributes little to stranger rape, it may play some role in date rape.

Cherry devotes considerable space to the tendency of society as a whole, and rape victims in particular, to place responsibility for rape on the victim. Given societal attitudes toward rape victims, it is not surprising that many of these women fail to report rape; they blame themselves for their own victimization. Relying on the important work of Burgess and Holmstrom, Cherry describes the long-term effects of sexual assault.

Changes in gender-role norms in concert with other factors appear to be increasing the capacity of women to cope with rape in a more adaptive fashion. Such changes include learning self-defense techniques and showing an increased willingness to seek prosecution of the offender.

It is reasonable to be alarmed at what appears to be an increase in the incidence of rape. However, it is not clear what the source of that increase is. One possibility is that the rate is not increasing, but more women are perceiving assaults as rape and are willing to report rapes to authorities. Cherry describes legal reforms that are reducing (if not eliminating) the extent to which, having been raped, the victim must go through several more ordeals if she reports the crime. Finally, Cherry presents very interesting information on at least four significant changes that have accompanied the new rape reform laws in Michigan.

 The gender and sexual identities of men and women begin in the socialization process that molds each to a separate but complementary reality. As described in Chapter 3, men are expected to be dominant and sexually aggressive. In contrast, women have been socialized to be submissive and less sexual, either refusing to have sex or passively going along with men's efforts to initiate coitus. Forcible rape, or coercing an unwilling person into having sex, may be the extreme of this socialization process.

As considered in this chapter, "rape is the logical and psychological extension of a dominant-submissive, competitive, sex-role stereotyped culture" (Burt, 1980, p. 229). The extent of rape is examined first. Second, two aspects of gender roles, aggression and passivity, are considered in relation to rape. Finally, I look at how the changing expectations about gender roles are altering the definition of the crime of rape and its treatment in society. Much more has been written about rape than is presented here; the interested reader is referred to more extensive works for further information (Chappell, Geis, & Fogarty, 1974; Clark & Armstrong, 1979).

THE EXTENT OF RAPE

The number of rapes has doubled between 1967 and 1977 (Federal Bureau of Investigation, 1977). Rape is still underreported, however, when compared with many other serious crimes such as murder, robbery, and aggravated assault. An estimate of the ratio of rapes committed to those reported is difficult to determine, but we begin to get a picture of the serious underreporting by comparing police reports with survey data on unreported crime. A conservative estimate suggests that 50 percent of rapes go unreported (Law Enforcement Assistance Administration, 1974). Other estimates set the percentage at 75 percent or higher (Brownmiller, 1975). Based on data available from 13 U.S. cities, Johnson (1980) estimated that a girl who is now 12 years old has a 20 to 30 percent chance of being the victim of a violent sexual attack during the course of her lifetime. He used a conservative estimate that 50 percent of rapes and attempted rapes go unreported. His figure also does not include attacks on girls under 12 years of age or on married women. Not surprisingly, he concludes that "sexual violence against women is part of the everyday fabric of American life" (p. 146).

The increase in reported rape has two possible explanations. Either women are more likely to report rapes than in the past, or greater numbers of women are actually being raped. Both of these explanations are worth considering. Perhaps more rapes are reported because the women's liberation movement has encouraged women to reject their prescribed role of passivity when attacked. More concretely, women currently have access to improved services for handling rape among police, medical, and psychological personnel. Rape crisis centers across the country have formed links and provide support for women who want to obtain these services. However, on the negative side, more women may be being raped than ever before. Why might this be true? For one thing, the trend toward increased sexual freedom for women may be threatening to men. Men with fragile self-esteem, in particular, may be more likely to use sexual violence as a way of proving their "masculinity" or of reassuring themselves of their sexual adequacy when confronted by an unequivocal "no" from a female (Russell, 1975; Weis & Borges, 1973). Finally, both women's greater reporting and men's increased use of sexual assault could also account for the current statistics on rape.

The increase in concern about rape can be viewed to some extent as a reflection of the growing tensions resulting from the changing boundaries of our gender and sexual roles. When I have introduced the topic of rape in my classes, students often snicker when I raise the possibility that a man can be raped by a woman. Some of the men have sat back in their desks, opened their arms, and sighed, "rape me." When I further suggest we consider that men are raped by men, the men's chortles and sighs abruptly turn to nervous laughter, downward turning of the head and closing of the legs and arms. I have found this a very useful technique for acquainting students with their feelings about rape. First, they begin to examine their commonly held belief that rape is primarily sexual. They begin to look at the intent of the rapist not to seduce but to overpower and physically assault another person. Second, as the life-threatening aspects of rape become more real, students begin to question their acceptance of the idea that women are responsible for rape and are legitimate victims of rape. Unquestioned assumptions about male aggression and female passivity become more salient in the light of these considerations.

WHY DO MEN RAPE?

There are several answers to the question "Why do men rape?" In her review of past research on offenders, Albin (1977) concludes that the predominant view is that the rapist is either someone sexually aberrant, or someone generally well adjusted but the victim of a woman who has conscious or unconscious desires to be raped. Cohen, Garofalo, Boucher, and Seghorn (1971) view rape as primarily sexual for some rapists, but primarily aggressive for others, and a combination of sexual and aggressive needs for still others. Gebhard, Gagnon, Pomeroy, and Christenson (1965) classified about one-third of rapists as acting on aggressive rather than sexual desires. Whether the victim is female (Groth, Burgess, & Holmstrom, 1977) or male (Kaufman et al., 1980), these authors found that the majority of rapists are motivated by a desire to overpower, dominate, or express hostility rather than to achieve sexual gratification. These findings support the feminist view of rape as a mechanism of control and domination in women's lives (Brownmiller, 1975; Russell, 1975). However, it may be quite difficult to disentangle the motivations of rapists, largely because the male gender role encourages a fusion of sexuality, dominance, and aggression.

SEXUALITY AND AGGRESSION IN MEN'S LIVES

There are several excellent accounts of masculine and feminine gender and sexual roles and their relationship to rape (Brownmiller, 1975; Gross, 1978; Russell, 1975; Weis & Borges, 1973). Each of these suggests a fusion of masculinity and sexual dominance in men's lives. For example, Russell (1975, p. 261) writes, "Being aggressive is masculine; being sexually aggressive is masculine; rape is sexually aggressive behavior, therefore, masculine behavior."

Differences in aggression between boys and girls begin early and under some circumstances continue into adulthood. Unfortunately, much of the research on adult aggression is conducted with males only. However, when women are used as the targets of aggression, they receive less aggression than males except when men perceive women as behaving outside the boundaries of the female role (for example, when women initiate aggression, or when other men are expressing aggression against a female). Under such conditions, men will attack women as strongly as they would attack other men (Frodi, Macaulay, & Thome, 1977). This finding is in keeping with Weis and Borges' (1973) suggestion that women who say no to men's sexual advances are displaying an assertiveness that may well be perceived as provocation and may well result in attack. If saying no to a male can be thought of as annoying or provoking to men, Zillman's (1979) summary of much of the physiological research on the ways males and females handle annoyance is pertinent:

> Data show the female to be an effective minimizer of annoyance. It is the male, then, rather than the female who often behaves in what may be considered *nonintelligent* ways. . . . The annoyed male is forced into efforts "to get even" regardless of whether retaliatory action constitutes intelligent behavior. If the minimization of aversion is employed as a

yardstick of adaptive intelligence, it is not the behavior of the female but the hostile and aggressive modes of reaction of the male that are questionable and that call for correction. [p. 358]

In studies conducted by Kanin and his colleagues, between 10 percent and 30 percent of the college women studied reported themselves the victims of male sexual aggression. Women in these studies were not raped but felt that their partners, often casual dates, came very close to rape, tearing off their clothing, pinning them down, and threatening them (Kanin & Parcell, 1977; Kirkpatrick & Kanin, 1957). In keeping with the pressure on men to prove their masculinity in sexual terms, men report using sexual aggression quite frequently to initiate coitus. Men who have been sexually aggressive report that friends pressured them to seek sex and that admitting their virginity would likely result in a lowered status among their peers (Kanin, 1967; Kanin, 1969). Certainly, if a man bases his self-definition on behaving aggressively and sexually, we might expect that in situations where he feels threatened he will be more prone to use sexual assault to restore his esteem. This might help to explain Clark's (1980) recent finding that many rapes are committed as "gang rapes," despite the fact that only one offender is reported. Multiple-offender rapes provide another example of the peer pressures on men to prove their masculinity in sexual and assaultive terms.

Further evidence of the fusion of sexuality and aggression in men's lives comes from a growing body of research on sexual arousal. Some research has found that known rapists are more aroused by depictions of rape than are nonrapists. In fact, it has been shown that erection responses can discriminate among rapists who have repeated the offense many times, rapists who have chosen very young or old victims, and rapists who require aggressive stimulation to achieve an erection (Abel et al., 1978).

The low arousal response of nonrapists to depictions of rape has been challenged by research showing that the response is somewhat dependent on the fact that the victim is portrayed as being disgusted and nauseated by the actions of the rapist. When the victim is presented as being sexually aroused, and even experiencing pain, as is often the case in pornographic depictions of rape, men who have not raped are sexually aroused (Malamuth & Check, 1980; Malamuth, Heim, & Feshbach, 1980). These investigators have also found that exposure to depictions of violent sexuality increases men's fantasies about rape (Malamuth, 1981), their beliefs that violence against women is acceptable (Malamuth & Check, 1981a), and their reports that they might use force themselves (Malamuth & Check, 1981b; Malamuth, Haber, & Feshbach, 1980).

Research then shows that rape depictions are arousing to men in general, and not just to rapists. Furthermore, rape depictions may support some inaccurate beliefs regarding women's response to sexual assault. These facts are likely to figure prominently in discussions over the easy availability of this type of pornography. Pornographic material hostile to women has increased during the 1970s in such "soft-core" magazines as *Playboy* and *Penthouse* (Malamuth & Spinner, 1980), and a wave of sadomasochistic material is widely in evidence. Furthermore, there is evidence from a 10-year-long study in Copenhagen that the easy accessibility of pornography failed to reduce the rate of rape despite the fact that it did reduce other forms of sexual offense against women (Kutchinsky, 1973). The impact on rape of an increase in explicitly hostile pornography is a matter of current concern to those seeking to prevent violence against women.

So far, the fusion between sexual arousal and dominance-aggression in men's lives has been described. Yet there is no clear causal link between this aspect of gender-role socialization and actual rape behavior. Donnerstein (1980) summarizes his program of research on sexual arousal and nonsexual aggression with college students as indicating that aggression against women is at its height when men have been angered and then exposed to films depicting rape. Perhaps such films sanction aggression and free men who feel provoked from their usual inhibitions against expressing aggression against females in the laboratory. The aggression Donnerstein studied is nonsexual, and we can only speculate that it might be sexual if men were given the opportunity.

THE FEMALE RESPONSE TO RAPE: PASSIVITY AND SELF-BLAME

If men rape because their gender role prescribes sexual aggression, it is also possible that women remain silent about rape because their traditional gender role prescribes passivity and privacy regarding their sexuality. In this section, I examine women's response to their sexual victimization and to the reactions of others in society.

Burgess and Holmstrom (1974) have identified two phases of the woman's response in the aftermath of rape. The acute phase is marked by disorganization of her life, followed by a longer-term phase of reorientation. Immediately following rape, some women are highly emotional, while others are controlled. Several weeks following the rape, women often develop strong physical reactions; for example, persistent soreness, tension headaches, and stomach pains. The victim's emotions range from fear and anger to humiliation and self-blame. In long-term efforts to cope with rape, women often change their residences and telephone numbers and increase their contact with family and friends. Long after the rape has occurred, some women continue to experience nightmares and to fear situations that remind them of the rape (for example, being indoors, having sexual intercourse, and being alone). Clinicians have been alerted to the possibility that some of their clients who experience sudden fear reactions or a persistent loss of self-esteem may be experiencing a "silent rape reaction." These women are experiencing aspects of the rape trauma syndrome described by Burgess and Holmstrom, which were found to resurface in women who had remained silent about a rape in childhood or adolescence but who had experienced a second rape in adulthood.

Some women tell their families and friends about being raped, although some are very resistant to doing so. In a long-term follow-up study of rape victims (Burgess & Holmstrom, 1979), it was found that 25 percent of the women had not told family members four to six years later and were still satisfied with that decision. Most women told their families about the rape within days or months largely because they wanted to. In some cases, however, they felt it was expected of them, or were pressured to do so, or were simply overwhelmed by their feelings. Those who did not disclose the rape felt a need to protect their families from embarrassment or felt it was necessary to keep some distance between themselves and their families. It is important to help women choose the best course of action for themselves and to help mates and families (those who are told) to handle the traumatic aftermath of rape (Burgess & Holmstrom, 1979; Silverman, 1978).

Whether women report the rape in the early phase, when it will be taken more seriously by the police and judicial system (Bohmer, 1974; Brodyaga et al., 1975), depends on the woman's expectation that the police will be concerned, considerate, and efficient in handling the complaint. Reporting also depends whether the woman fears that the rapist or his friends will harm her again and on whether she is embarrassed about her family's reactions (Dukes & Mattley, 1977).

In addition to the subjective feelings women have about reporting rape, there are also more objective concerns regarding the handling of rape cases. Many rape reports are considered "unfounded" by the police, and the victim is advised not to prosecute. Reasons include instances in which the victim was intoxicated, refused to submit to a medical examination, did not report the rape immediately, was acquainted with the offender, was not severely bruised or wounded, or was too embarrassed or fearful to continue with the investigation (Clark & Lewis, 1977). The working definition of rape by the police is not based on whether the rape in fact occurred as legally defined but on whether the victim has a chance of successfully prosecuting the case. Weis and Borges (1973, pp. 71–72) suggest that "It is deemed as rape only if the assailant is a violent stranger, if the victim reports the rape immediately after it occurred, and if she can provide evidence of the attack and her active resistance."

Many rapes that are reported do not end in the arrest of the offender. If they do result in arrest, the offender is often convicted of a lesser, nonsexual offense, or the case ends in acquittal or dismissal. Not surprisingly, rape victims perceive the criminal justice system as increasingly ineffective over the months of their contact with it, because rarely do they see the offender apprehended and imprisoned (Ashworth & Feldman-Summers, 1978).

UNRECOGNIZED RAPES

In some instances, rapes literally "don't exist" because the victim sees the coercive sexual experience as natural and legitimate in the context of a structured power relationship between a man and a woman. Here, the failure to report rape stems largely from the relative legal and psychological powerlessness of the women—as, for example, in marriage, in a dating relationship, or as a subordinate in a work setting.

One of the most difficult attitudes to confront is the myth that rape is a statistically rare event involving people who are strangers to one another. Although the degree of intimacy varies, rape often takes place in an ongoing dating courtship relationship, and victims and assailants are known to one another in over 50 percent of all sexual assault cases (Amir, 1971). As we come to know more about sexual coercion and harassment in the workplace (see Gutek and Nakamura, Chapter 8), the incidence of rape in that area will become clearer, but as yet few data are available.

We are, however, coming to know more about marital rape despite the fact that it is rarely reported to police (Groth, 1979; Frieze, 1980; Martin, 1976; Russell, 1975). Less than 1 percent of rapes reported to rape crisis centers or family planning centers are allegedly committed by husbands (Gelles, 1977). The marriage contract and the rape laws both reinforce the notion that women are obliged to provide sex and that rape does not exist within marriage. It is not surprising, then, that wives do not necessarily view their abusive treatment as violent or as being rape. In fact, women often blame themselves for their husbands' use of sexual violence (Gelles, 1977; Russell, 1975).

Sexual violence and battering are often linked in marriages. Frieze (1980) found that over one-third of the women who were battered reported being raped, and over two-thirds reported that their husbands pressured them into having sex. These data lend some support to the previous examination of the fusion of sexuality and aggression in men's lives, particularly when men are in the powerful role of "husband" or "father." The legal and psychological powerlessness that women and children experience in the context of the family can result in rape and incest continuing privately and going unreported for many years (Sanford, 1980). In my reading of accounts of women who had been raped by their husbands, the following articulate account (Gelles, 1977) helped to clarify the way in which marital sexual violence is sometimes seen:

> Almost 14 years ago, my first husband attempted to rape me. At the time, we were very close to being separated, and I think he wanted to attempt to bring us closer, back together through a sexual act—he always maintained that that was his prime means of communication, how he felt the closest. At first I fought, and when he attempted to smother me with a pillow, I panicked and became only concerned with how to get him to stop—I was afraid he was going to kill me. So I became totally unresponsive to him—wouldn't talk or anything—and he eventually stopped tearing my clothes and pulling me, and there was no intercourse. Because it happened in the context of a whole lot of bad things in our marriage (he had been violent to me once or twice before, but not sexually so), I didn't have any particular feelings at the time except relief that it was over. Very shortly thereafter, I left him. I never thought of the incident as attempted rape until almost 10 years later when I was walking away from a session of a women's group I was in wherein we had been talking about specific rape incidents that had occurred to some of the members. Until that time, I think I felt rape was of the stereotypic type of the stranger leaping out of the bushes and never thought of an incident like that occurring between people who knew each other—especially husband and wife, as rape. I think that is true of many married women—they have accepted society's dictum that a man has sexual access to his wife whenever he wants, whether she does or not. Thus, it never occurs to them that this could be a crime, a felonious assault, that this is, indeed, rape. [p. 343]

BLAMING THE VICTIM

Women who are raped tend to blame themselves for the assault. In addition, women perceive that family members, friends, and helping agencies are also likely to blame them. Women's tendency to remain silent about rape reflects, in part, their perception that others will assume they themselves were responsible for the rape. They are not completely mistaken. Burt (1980) has found that over 50 percent of men and women still agree with statements such as "in the majority of cases, the victim is promiscuous or has a bad reputation" or "a woman who goes to the home or apartment of a man on their first date implies that she is willing to have sex." Burt has developed a "rape myth acceptance" scale including such statements.

People seem to organize their attitudes about rape and rape victims around the role the victim plays in preventing or precipitating rape (Feild, 1978; Selby, Calhoun, & Brock, 1977), when in fact only about 4 percent of all rapes are found to be precipitated by the victim (National Commission on the Causes and Prevention of Violence, 1969). One researcher (Janoff-Bulman, 1979) sees the connection rape victims make between their behavior (for example, hitchhiking, walking alone, leaving the car unlocked) and the rape as a positive attempt to regain control of one's life. However, in counseling rape victims it is equally important to acquaint them with the fact that their behavior rarely precipitates the rape.

Blaming the victim is only one of a set of beliefs commonly held about rape victims and offenders. Belief in the victim's blame for rape is stronger among those who hold more traditional attitudes about women's roles (Burt, 1980; Feild, 1978). Blaming the victim is also more likely among those who believe that sexual relationships are primarily exploitive—rape being the extreme of exploitation—and who believe that violence and coercion are legitimate means of obtaining sex (Burt, 1980).

Laboratory investigations of how much the victim of rape is blamed (termed "attributions of responsibility") have found several interesting and often complicated results. In general, people tend to blame the victim less for rape to the extent that she is someone they can respect, like, or is someone with whom they can identify; for example, another college student or someone in the same occupation (Feldman-Summers & Lindner, 1976; Fulero & DeLara, 1976; Smith et al., 1976). However, there are circumstances that lead people to blame her more for the rape, such as her refusal to talk about her sexual experiences, the perception that she has been provocative, or the rapist being a stranger to her (Calhoun, Selby, & Warring, 1976; Cann, Calhoun, & Selby, 1979; Smith et al., 1976).

People's perception that a woman is to blame for rape is also influenced by whether she was passive during the rape or actively resisted the attacker. Males tend to blame the victim more and punish the offender less when they learn that the victim did not resist the attacker. In fact, they are even less certain that a rape occurred when there is no resistance; they assume that the female is consenting and the male is not acting forcefully. As I have suggested earlier, women are expected to go along with men's sexual advances and failure to resist is within gender-role expectations. However, females will blame the victim less and penalize the attacker more when there is no resistance. They are more certain that a crime occurred, perhaps inferring that the rape victim was extremely fearful and in a life-threatening situation (Krulewitz, Nash, & Payne, 1977; Scroggs, 1976). Women's passivity signals sexual assault to women but signals consenting sexuality to men—a finding that is quite consistent with different perceptions men and women have of rape victims in general. Perhaps because they identify more with the victim of rape, women generally tend to blame women less for rape than do men (Cann, Calhoun, & Selby, 1979; Calhoun, Selby, & Warring, 1976; Feild, 1978; Fulero & DeLara, 1976; Selby, Calhoun, & Brock, 1977). It is not surpris-

hat they would also see her resistance in a different framework from
of men. Women's support for the rape victim depends also on the extent
.neir own feminism, feminists being more supportive (Krulewitz & Payne,
.978).

CHANGING GENDER ROLES AND COPING WITH RAPE

There is no one correct or completely effective strategy for preventing and
coping with rape. Riger and Gordon (1979) have found that attitudes toward
rape prevention fall into two distinct strategies. One strategy is labeled "restrictive," in that rape prevention is seen as being achieved best by such things
as dressing more modestly, not talking to strangers or going out alone at
night, and moderating the fight for women's rights. A second strategy is
labeled "assertive" and includes such techniques for rape prevention as self-
defense training in judo or karate, fighting off an attacker, publicizing the
names and pictures of known rapists, increasing men's respect for women,
and providing treatment for rape offenders. These two strategies seem to
differ in part on whether they advocate that women remain within or ven-
ture outside of the prescribed gender role of passivity.

Women experience anxiety about aggression (Frodi, Macaulay, &
Thome, 1977) and therefore may indeed find some of the assertive strategies
difficult to carry out. To some extent, the strategy people advocate depends
on their age, their gender, and their racial or ethnic group. Black women, for
example, who are brutalized by rape to a much greater extent than white
women (Hindelang & Davis, 1977; Johnson, 1980), tend to advocate greater
restrictiveness as a strategy for coping with rape (Riger & Gordon, 1979).

Strategies depend also on whether people are looking at long- or short-
run solutions to the problem of rape. In her discussion of strategies for
preventing rape, Burt (1980) argues that the best long-range strategy is
"fighting sex-role stereotyping at very young ages, before it is complicated by
sexual as well as sex-role interactions" (p. 229). By the time of adolescence,
the view of sexual interaction as a "battlefield" may mean that it is too late to
offset the fusion of sexuality and aggression in men's lives. Indeed, in Chapter
2, Zellman and Goodchilds point out the way in which adolescent boys
project their own desires for sexuality to mean that girls ask for it.

Many of the anti-rape efforts at present are directed at short-run efforts
to increase the threat of retaliation for engaging in sexual violence, as a
deterrent to rape. This trend is not surprising given what may be a real
increase in violence against women and given the fact that many reported
rapes do not currently end in conviction for the offense. The importance of
these efforts is even clearer when one notes that over half of the males in one
study indicated that they would rape if they thought they would not be
punished for their actions (Malamuth, Haber, & Feshbach, 1980). Several

avenues of change have been undertaken, including the establishment of rape crisis centers, self-defense training for women, and reform of the criminal justice system. All these areas of change serve to alter the societal perception from women as passive to women as prepared to actively retaliate against assault.

Advocates of self-defense training for women argue that this approach is a somewhat short-range solution but an effective one for combatting the myth of women's defenselessness (Connell & Wilsen, 1974). Police often caution women against resisting attack, while courts expect evidence of resistance to prove rape (McTeer, 1978). We have already seen the bias in men's perceptions of the victim who does not resist—in effect, she is considered to have consented to the rape. Of course, men holding such attitudes frequently are called for jury duty. Legal reformers generally agree that women should not have to put their lives in jeopardy to resist rape and have worked to develop laws requiring that women need only prove that force was threatened and could be used. Still, radical feminists argue that self-defense, even if never used, can provide women with more control of their bodies, help them to overcome the myth that it is unfeminine to fight, and provide them with a sense of psychological preparedness. It may also help reduce rape by establishing in men's minds that at least some women can and do retaliate with effective physical violence.

Another avenue of change has involved the women's helping network through the establishment of rape crisis centers and, more recently, homes for battered wives, who are often sexually abused as well. There is evidence that rape crisis counselors have more positive attitudes toward rape victims and blame them less for the rape than do police (Feild, 1978). Such counselors are also more sensitive to the traumatic aftermath of rape than are emergency room physicians (King et al., 1978). Counselors in these centers provide a useful link between the victim of rape and the other agencies that will deal with the victim should she decide to pursue her case. Their effectiveness may be largely due to the fact that they emphasize social change programs and do not blame the victim for her rape (Kasinsky, 1978). They have been instrumental in programs for police and medical personnel, sensitizing them to the traumatic aftermath of rape and assisting them with tactful ways of obtaining medical and personal evidence required for pursuing a rape case in the courtroom (Bard, 1976).

Legal reform is also viewed as particularly important in changing attitudes toward rape, rapists, and victims. Legal reform can provide greater opportunities for women to obtain justice. It is interesting that many women say they decided to report a rape out of the desire to prevent the rapist from committing the action again (Dukes & Mattley, 1977). They are thus using legal action to prevent others from being raped.

Rape is a legally unique crime in several ways (Brooks, 1975). The law places a heavy emphasis on the woman's proof of her resistance and the fact that she did not consent to intercourse. Sexual history information is routinely a part of the allowable testimony, and defense lawyers typically use such information to discredit the victim's character and imply her consent to intercourse. Judges tend to admit the information to the courtroom and further to warn the jury that testimony provided by the victim is uncorroborated and should be regarded with suspicion. All these tendencies have led feminist writers to argue that it is really the victim who is placed on trial rather than the defendant (Brownmiller, 1975).

Legal reform has several areas of impact. A change in rape laws could potentially increase reporting by victims and alter police behavior in labeling reports of rape as founded or unfounded. Reformed rape laws could also alter the behavior of prosecutors, judges, and jurors. Rape reform legislation in Michigan, implemented in 1975, has redefined the crime of rape and the treatment of the victim in the criminal justice system. First, the new laws reflect a range of sexually assaultive behaviors varying in terms of severity of damage to the victim and carrying penalties that reflect the seriousness of the assault. The range of penalties is from two years or a fine, to life imprisonment. Second, the law has been changed to focus more on the rapist's use of coercion than on the victim's resistance to the attack. Evidence of coercion is taken to mean that the victim did not consent. Third, the law now covers males and legally separated spouses. And finally, the victim's previous sexual history can be introduced as evidence only under special circumstances.

An evaluation of the impact of this law reform has been undertaken (Marsh et al., 1980). Following implementation of the new reform laws in Michigan, reports of rape and arrests and convictions of offenders appear to have increased. However, there is some indication that the new laws have only reflected already changing opinions toward rape—there was already more public concern about rape and greater willingness of victims to report the crime. Interviews with people involved in the criminal justice system provide some interesting results. Police and prosecutors continue to show concern with the credibility of the victim and use polygraph tests more often in rape cases than in equally serious cases involving other crimes. The tendency to see the victim as fabricating her story remains, despite the changes in the law that have addressed this problem. The findings stress the fact that many officials involved in processing rape cases can still use their discretion in interpreting "founded" or "unfounded" rapes. And as we have seen earlier, in many cases a woman still is simply not believed when she charges rape.

Researchers also found a perception among prosecutors and defense attorneys that jurors were now more likely to convict, but this perception was seen as a result of changing public opinion rather than of implementing the law. In many cases, however, the change in conviction rate has been attributed to the absence of sexual history information about the victim. Judges report that they are no longer tending to admit this information, and defense attorneys are focusing less on the "worthiness" of the victim and concentrating more on the facts of the case.

The admission of prior sexual history information is of particular significance because it tends to be one of the most biasing factors against the victim, and in favor of acquitting the defendant. Most legal reformers argue that the information is usually irrelevant and should be either inadmissible, heard privately by the judge and brought in at his or her discretion, or sought routinely from both defendant and plaintiff. Borgida (1978) has found that biasing sexual history information when excluded results in an increase in guilty verdicts. Sexual history information encourages jurors to blame the victim for rape, and to the extent that they do blame her the defendant is acquitted. Such biases are powerful and will not change solely by repealing rape laws.

In fact, changes in rape laws may follow rather than precede shifts in public opinion about rape. It seems important to combine the long-range strategy for change—namely, that we alter the gender socialization process early enough to see changes in attitudes and behavior toward women—with the more immediate repeal of the rape laws that do not reflect these changes. Repealing out-of-date rape laws both reflects changing public opinion and changes public opinion about rape by deemphasizing the sexual aspects of the crime of rape and increasing our awareness about rape as an assaultive and power-related crime. This type of awareness may develop through workshops with police who handle rape cases or through the media who present information to the community.

Many other important areas of judicial reform can be assessed through research. For example, it is important to understand the impact of judges' instructions to jurors on the perception of guilt and verdicts. As mentioned earlier, in rape cases, the judge very often acts to reduce the credibility of the victim. Laboratory investigations of the impact of judicial changes, far from being trivial and removed from the real world, have in the past proved quite useful to actual cases. Readers might remember the case of Joanne Little, who was accused of killing a jailer who had been attempting to rape her. Little was black, and the jailer was white. Many observers saw the case as a combination of the prejudicial attitudes toward women and blacks in America and questioned whether Little would receive a fair trial where the incident occurred. Research investigations were used to convince the trial judge to move Little's trial to a county that was less prejudicial to blacks and women (Vidmar, 1981). Such research may be quite helpful to the success of rape complainants in the courtroom.

In any discussion of rape, differences of opinion always arise about the role of the woman. Hence, differences of opinion also arise about how to change the extent of sexual violence against women. As I was finishing this chapter, I wondered about the connection between physical battering and sexual violence—is rape really something separate and apart from physical brutality, a violation quite different than anything else? That same day a friend of mine told her mother about a co-worker who went to a job interview. A man, who met her at the front desk, took her "to meet her interviewer." This "receptionist" led her to the basement of the office building and beat her black and blue. He did *not* rape her. The man received one year and a month imprisonment for his brutality. The woman was in psychotherapy for several years and received plastic surgery. Only $4,000 of her expenses were covered through a compensation program for victims. On being told this story, my friend's mother commented, "Well, she shouldn't have gone to the basement."

As one looks more deeply into the study of sexual violence against women, it becomes clear, given the gender and sexual roles of men and women, that violence itself is the issue. Sexual violence is only an extreme point on the continuum of men's abuse of women. As I suggested earlier, men may rape because of their learned connection between aggressive and sexual feelings. This connection is considered part of the development of "normal" masculinity and is supported by pressures from peer groups and by media portrayal of violence against women. Moreover, all forms of male violence may continue to increase if men continue to respond violently to their perception that women today are violating or extending gender-role boundaries. Of course, women are reporting rape to a greater extent than previously; this tendency may threaten male aggressors enough that such aggression will be reduced in the long run.

Many developments give us cause for hope. For example, as noted earlier, research is showing that rape is not something that occurs only between strangers. Also, new helping networks are being developed to support the victims of rape, who are in no position to report the occurrence immediately following the attack without support from friends, family, and those in authority to proceed on the case. Finally, the absence of resistance is now being viewed as indicating a life-threatening situation rather than as indicating consent, and changes in the law are beginning to reflect this perspective.

All sectors of the public are beginning to see that rape is an act of aggression rather than of sexuality, and a constant interchange is developing between (1) the redefining of rape on a personal level and (2) the methods of political and social remedy that women are seeking. This trend can be seen from the emphasis on self-defense, legal reform, and a women-run helping network. Activism against rape has taken many forms—some quite ingenious and promising; for example, women marching through the streets to "claim the night" and men organizing groups called "men against rape." Although these forms of activism are more acceptable to some than to others, they all help to alter the stereotype of women as passive victims of rape and of men as being permitted by our society to engage in unchecked aggression.

12 Gender, Gender-Role Identification, and Response to Erotica

WILLIAM A. FISHER

Concern regarding the effect of exposure to erotic material (pornography) is not unique to conservative segments of the population. Researchers, too, have been trying to understand how erotica influences behavior. In addition, they have been puzzled over the fact that surveys have consistently shown men as more aroused by sexy pictures and stories than women are. The complexities of understanding the arousal process became even greater when experimenters began to find that men and women did *not* differ in their responses to erotica in laboratory settings.

William Fisher makes a very helpful contribution to our understanding in this area with his analysis of the reasons for gender differences in response to survey questions about erotica, and gender similarities in response to erotica in the laboratory. He deals with the complicated research methodology issues in a thorough and unusually clear fashion. Fisher examines the potential interaction of gender-role socialization, the intended audience of most erotic material (men), and typical responses of men and women to erotic material. His chapter is useful for the concerned citizen who wants to understand the complexities of the issues to a greater extent. His chapter is also likely to pique the interest of researchers by highlighting areas where we still have little understanding and by suggesting further experiments. All in all, the notions that men are turned on by stark, raw depictions of sex and that women are turned on by more flowery romantic themes just are not supported by research. Men and women appear to be quite similar in what they find erotically arousing. One major remaining question is "Why do men deliberately put more energy, money, and time into seeking erotic stimulation than do women?" Fisher suggests that this gender difference may be due to the interaction of societal beliefs and gender-role socialization, and he proposes some ways of testing that hypothesis.

In 1902, Iwan Bloch remarked, "There is no sexual aberration, no perverse act, however frightful, that is not photographically represented today" (Bloch, 1902/1974, p. 204). As the quotation from Bloch suggests, pornography is *not* a new phenomenon. In fact, human beings have been producing and consuming erotic imagery since the very beginning of history. Sexually explicit cave paintings and erotic carvings in bone were crafted during the early Stone Age, some 20,000 years ago (Eitner, 1975). The Bible's Song of Solomon is filled with sexual metaphors ("Thy two breasts are like two fawns . . . how much more pleasant are thy caresses than wine"). Sexual imagery is found in the very best of English literature, from Shakespeare's *Othello* ("Your daughter and the Moor are now making the beast with two backs") to Defoe's *Moll Flanders* ("Who was . . . Twelve Year a Whore, five times a Wife—whereof once to her own brother").

Today, verbal and visual erotica exist that would have been considered unthinkably explicit a decade or two ago. Mass circulation magazines such as *Penthouse* and *Playgirl* display erotic photographs that have a level of anatomical detail that was once available only in medical books. These magazines also have columns in which readers may share their most recent sexual adventures. Not to be outdone, contemporary motion pictures also present a variety of sexual material, be it mate swapping *(Bob and Carol and Ted and Alice)*, themes of sex and violence (*Looking for Mr. Goodbar* and *Dressed to Kill*), or straightforward soft-core porn *(Emmanuelle).*

Not surprisingly, the public has become quite concerned about what is perceived as a revolutionary increase in sexual explicitness that has saturated our society. Psychologists began to study this much discussed social issue. Research on pornography began slowly at first, with a few studies in the 1950s (for example, Clark, 1952; Kinsey et al., 1953) and a few in the early 1960s (for example, Byrne, 1961; Levitt & Brady, 1965). Social concern and scientific interest were brought together formally, however, only when President Johnson appointed the U.S. Commission on Obscenity and Pornography in 1968. This commission's work resulted in nine volumes of social science research concerning pornography, and the research interest thus sparked has continued until today. A substantial scientific literature now exists with respect to pornography—who produces it, who buys it, and how it affects behavior.

A very important question that has been studied in recent research involves how men and women may differ in their reactions to pornography, and it is with just this issue that the present chapter is concerned. First, evidence of gender differences in response to erotic material is described. In this connection, the relation of gender-role identification—masculine, feminine, or androgynous—and responses to erotica are considered, although little research has been done on this topic. Then, future research is suggested concerning how men and women—or sex-typed and androgynous people—may differ in their responses to erotic material. Now, without further delay, let us turn to the difficult problem of defining *pornography.*

WHAT IS PORNOGRAPHY?

Before we can examine gender differences in response to pornography, we must first define exactly what is meant by this term. Unfortunately, although there are many opinions on this issue, little or no consensus exists. Legal sources in particular have repeatedly—and unsuccessfully—tried to define "obscenity" and "pornography." According to the U.S. Supreme Court, for example, such material must "(a) appeal to a prurient interest in sex" (that is, "excite lustful thoughts"), *and* (b) be patently offensive because it confronts contemporary community standards relating to the description or representation of sexual matters, *and* (c) be utterly without redeeming social value" (Wilson, 1973, p. 10). In practice, however, it has been exceedingly difficult to say when material does or does not "excite lustful thoughts" or to determine at what point sexual matter is "utterly without redeeming social value." What is more, social scientists have demonstrated empirically that no uniform "contemporary community standard" exists to be offended (Wallace, 1973; Wilson, 1973). In view of such difficulties, it is not surprising that Supreme Court Justice Potter Stewart remarked that although he would not define hard-core pornography "I know it when I see it" (cited in Wilson, 1973, p. 10).

For social scientists, it is not enough to know pornography when we see it; we must be more precise. Although it is difficult to come up with a global definition of pornography where so many others have failed, it is possible to be specific about the kinds of material that are studied under the general heading of "pornography." Pornography can be characterized in at least two meaningful ways:

1. *Explicitness.* Sexual material may be relatively inexplicit (an indistinct, airbrushed nude; an indirect suggestion of lovemaking), or it may be relatively explicit (a close-up color photograph of the genitals; an exact description of penile-vaginal intercourse).
2. *Content.* Any kind of sexual content may be explicitly or inexplicitly portrayed. Sexual material may depict an affectionate embrace or a brutal rape; it may contain common sexual acts such as missionary position intercourse, or less common ones such as intercourse with a Chihuahua, or any other sort of sexual content.

Sexual material may be communicated in virtually any medium from cave paintings to closed-circuit television, from grainy black-and-white photographs to color movies, from sculptures at an art museum to "X-rated" pastries made in the shape of human genitals. As will be shown, researchers have attempted to see if degree of explicitness, kind of content, and the medium through which pornography is presented have different effects on women and men.

Although there are probably many other ways to characterize pornography, specific descriptions of the explicitness, content, and media of sexual material will provide at least a start toward objective discussion. Finally—also in the interest of objectivity—the term *erotica* rather than *pornography* will be used to refer to sexual material (of whatever explicitness, content, and media). *Erotica* is preferred because *pornography* has acquired a negative connotation in everyday use. Now that the issue of definition has been discussed, let us turn to a survey of research on gender differences in response to erotica.

GENDER DIFFERENCES IN RESPONSE TO EROTICA: A DIFFERENCE IN SEX DRIVE?

Across the past 100 years scientific and popular opinion have held that men are, to put it simply, more sexual than women. And men's and women's reactions to erotica have by and large been studied from this lopsided perspective.

> Man has beyond doubt the stronger sexual appetite of the two. From the period of pubescence he is instinctively drawn towards woman. His love is sensual, and his choice is strongly prejudiced in favor of physical attractiveness. . . . Woman, however, if physically and mentally normal, and properly educated, has but little sensual desire. [Krafft-Ebing, 1903/1939, p. 14]

> Professor Higgins was right—men wish that women's sexuality was like theirs, which it isn't. Male sexual response is far brisker and more automatic: it is triggered easily by things, like putting a quarter in a vending machine. [Comfort, 1972, p. 71]

> A man is willing to expend a little time and a few sperm in any mating opportunity and often courts indiscriminately. A female must be more selective, for a mismating can cost her much wasted nurture and lost reproductive potential. [Daly & Wilson, 1978, p. 79]

Assuming that males are hypersexual and females (especially if properly educated!) are asexual, it follows that men should enjoy erotica and be aroused by it while females should show no interest or enjoyment in such material. Interestingly enough, this reasoning has repeatedly been confirmed—at least in terms of survey data that have been collected during the past 25-odd years.

The Survey Findings

In 1953, Kinsey, Pomeroy, Martin, and Gebhard published *Sexual Behavior in the Human Female,* the second volume in the now famous "Kinsey Reports." This large-scale survey of the sexual practices of U.S. women (together with Kinsey's data on men) provided seemingly incontrovertible evidence that men are more aroused by most forms of erotica than women are. Specifically, of more than 6,000 people who were asked, men (77 percent) were far more likely than women (32 percent) to report that they had been aroused by photos, drawings, or movies that portrayed sexual activity. Men were also more likely than women to say that they had been aroused by erotic stories, by pictures of same- or other-gender nudes, or by erotic burlesque or nightclub shows. Men were more likely than women were to prefer to have the lights on during sex, and men's public restrooms—compared to women's—were found to have more sexual graffiti. Thus, with few exceptions, the Kinsey survey shows a uniform pattern of male arousal and female disinterest in erotica.

What has happened in the years that have passed since Kinsey's research? First, there has been a much-publicized revolution in sexual attitudes and behavior during the last 20 years or so. Men (and to an even greater extent women) have recently become much more sexually permissive, and males and females seem to be approaching a single pattern of sexual behavior (Curran, 1977; Fisher & Byrne, 1981). Has the sexual revolution brought men and women closer together in their responses to erotica than they were in Kinsey's day? Apparently not, according to contemporary survey data. For example, Wilson and Abelson (1973) questioned a representative U.S. sample of nearly 2,500 men and women about their experience with and attitudes toward erotic material. Men were uniformly more likely than women to indicate that they had ever seen five different types of erotica, including visual and verbal representations of genitals, oral-genital contacts between a man and a woman, heterosexual intercourse, homosexual activity, and sadomasochistic activity. Men were also more likely than women to report seeing each of these types of erotica during the past two years. Respondents were asked as well whether or not each type of erotica should be available to people of various ages, and in each instance women held more restrictive opinions than did men.

In another survey that is relevant to men's and women's responses to erotica, Nawy (1973) studied consumers of erotic material in San Francisco, California—a city that is widely regarded as one of the most sexually liberated in the United States. If contemporary women are developing an interest in erotica, evidence for such a trend ought to be most visible in an avant-garde locale such as San Francisco. In his research, Nawy observed consumers of erotica at 47 bookstores and newsstands, six arcades where coin-operated movies were available, and 28 "adult" movie theaters. The bookstores showed pictures and magazines that depicted heterosexual sex play (usually falling short of penile-vaginal penetration). The arcade viewing machines featured films of a nude female or of simulated heterosexual activity. The adult movie theaters commonly showed full-color sound films "featuring a young heterosexual couple in bed exchanging oral-genital stimulation and reaching climax in the "missionary position" (Nawy, 1973, p. 149).

What of the clientele of the San Francisco erotic marketplace? They were overwhelmingly male. At the adult bookstores 96.5 percent of the patrons were men, and at the adult movie theaters 96.7 percent of those in attendance were men—despite the fact that heterosexual couples got a discount on their admission price. The clientele of the arcades was exclusively male, but the meaning of the observation is not clear because women were prohibited from entering the viewing machine area!

In addition to these findings concerning exposure to erotic material, survey data shed light on men's and women's arousal responses to erotica. In a study done by Berger, Gagnon, and Simon (1971), a representative sample of U.S. college students were asked if they had ever been aroused by erotica. About 46 percent of the men but only 14 percent of the women reported that they had been aroused by such material. And a representative sample of the U.S. population, surveyed by Abelson, Cohen, Heaton, and Suder (1971), showed the same results—men are still much more likely than women to report that they have been aroused by erotica. Evidence from a variety of large-scale surveys conducted across the past two decades has thus converged to indicate that men are more often aroused by erotica than women are, men purchase far more erotica than women do, and they hold more favorable attitudes regarding erotica. In view of such consistent survey findings, few people have seriously questioned the notion that very basic and broad differences exist in men's and women's responsiveness to erotica.

The Experimental Findings

Experiments provide an alternative to survey procedures for studying gender differences in response to erotica. Survey research, in general, relies on people's reports of their past experience with erotica. For example, men and women might be asked if they have ever been aroused by erotica. Such a survey question would presumably leave up to the respondent exactly what kind of erotica was meant, what degree of arousal was involved, how far back in one's memory to search for such an experience, and so on. In experiments, in contrast, men and women are actually *shown* identical erotic stimuli (such as literary passages, slides, and/or movies), and their reactions to this material are carefully assessed and compared. For example, male and female undergraduates might be shown a film of a young couple petting and having oral sex on a beautiful, sun-drenched beach. These students would then fill out scales to measure their degree of sexual arousal, as well as any other measures of interest to the researcher. Or the men and women involved might agree to let researchers assess their levels of physiological sexual arousal with electronic monitoring equipment. Experiments thus give us a better idea of exactly what kind of erotica people are responding to and just how they are actually responding.

Although experimentation offers these advantages, only quite recently—in terms of the history of sex research—have such methods been used to compare men's and women's responses to erotica. As Byrne (1977) points out, sex research has progressed rather slowly from the study of relatively nontaboo topics to the study of more taboo subjects. Thus it was acceptable to publish clinical studies of "abnormal" sexual practices (Krafft-Ebing, 1903/1939), to discuss the sexual behavior of nonwhite native peoples (Bloch, 1902/1974), and to do research on the mating habits of primates (Ford & Beach, 1951) long before it was permissible to compare experimentally white men's and women's responses to erotica in industrialized nations.

When researchers finally did get around to using experimental methods to study gender differences in response to erotica (for example, see Schmidt & Sigusch, 1970), they must have been shocked by what they found. Contrary to virtually all the survey evidence, men and women showed strikingly similar reactions when they were exposed to erotic stimuli in experiments. These results parallel Radlove's discussion of male and female sexual response in Chapter 4. In glaring contrast with our stereotypes, men and women exhibit much the same reactions to effective sexual stimulation.

Men and women can be similarly aroused by erotic photographs, literature, and fantasy A study conducted by Byrne and Lamberth (1971) provides a good example of the experimental comparison of men's and women's responses to different kinds of erotica. The participants in this research were 42 married couples, students at Purdue University. Some of these men and women were shown a series of 19 erotic slides that portrayed heterosexual, homosexual, and autosexual acts. Others read 19 literary passages that described in words the acts that were depicted on each of the slides. A third group of couples were given brief descriptions of the acts portrayed in each of the slides (for example, "heterosexual intercourse, face to face, female on bottom"), and they were asked to *imagine* what the activity would be like. After 20 seconds of viewing, reading, or imaging each stimulus, the men and women rated their feelings of sexual arousal.

The results of this study proved to be quite enlightening (see Figure 12-1). It can be seen that for each type of erotic stimulus, men and women

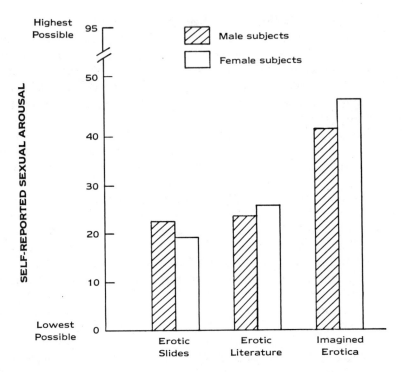

FIGURE 12-1

Men and Women's Self-Reported Sexual Arousal in Response to Three Types of Erotic Stimuli

SOURCE: Adapted from Byrne, D., & Lamberth, J. The effect of erotic stimuli on sexual arousal, evaluative responses, and subsequent behavior. In *Technical report of the Commission on Obscenity and Pornography* (Vol. 8). Washington, D.C.: U.S. Government Printing Office, 1971.

reported feeling virtually identical levels of sexual arousal. Although survey data show that in daily life, men report being more often aroused by erotica than women do, these findings suggest that both genders *can be* equally aroused by various kinds of erotica. It is also interesting to note that men and women both reported about *twice* as much arousal in response to imagined erotica as in response to pictures or literature that described similar sexual acts. Apparently, we do not need to press on with our search for the ideal aphrodisiac—we are carrying around a powerful one already, in our own imaginations (Byrne, 1978).

Similar findings for male-female equivalence in arousal responses to erotica have been reported by other researchers (for example, Fisher & Byrne, 1978a; Griffitt, 1973; Griffitt, May, & Veitch, 1974; Heiman, 1975, 1977; Schmidt, 1975; Schmidt, Sigusch, & Schafer, 1973). Investigators have found that when men and women are exposed to a variety of erotic materials they will—on the average—respond with similar levels of arousal. Nonetheless, it is important to keep in mind that men and women *do* differ in arousal repsonses to specific kinds of erotic content. For example, in the Byrne and Lamberth (1971) study, both men and women agreed that face-to-face intercourse and cunnilingus were highly arousing. However, men (versus women) were more aroused by female masturbation, while women (versus men) were more aroused by erotica that depicted male masturbation. In this case, it seems easy to explain the gender difference in arousal: for heterosexual people, erotic content featuring the other gender (for men, female masturbation; for women, male masturbation) is the most arousing. In other cases, however, it is not clear why—within their generally similar arousal responses to erotica—men and women should differ in response to specific erotic stimuli. More research is needed to specify exactly the sort of erotic content, explicitness, and media that men and women may find differentially arousing. Then research may focus on why, psychologically speaking, such differences occur. For the present, it is important to note that, averaged across a diversity of erotic stimuli, men and women report equivalent levels of sexual arousal, although in specific instances gender differences do seem to exist.

Men and women can be similarly aroused by erotic movies   We have just reviewed experimental evidence suggesting that, in general, men and women can become similarly aroused by erotic slides, stories, and fantasies. Does this similarity of arousal responses extend to other types of erotic media? For example, do the genders differ in their reactions to "hard-core" erotic movies that display petting, coitus, ejaculation, and other such acts? Because movies provide a most lifelike portrayal of erotic content, researchers have devoted considerable attention to gender differences in response to this type of erotic media. We will briefly consider the results of some of this research.

Hatfield, Sprecher, and Traupmann (1978) have conducted one of the largest studies of gender differences in response to erotic movies. These investigators studied the responses of 556 college men and women to six different erotic films. The movies included *Auto-American Dreams* and *Shirley* (which portrayed male and female masturbation), *Rich and Judy* and *A Ripple in Time* (which showed adolescent and older couples engaging in heterosexual activity), and *Vir Amat* and *Holding* (which depicted male and female homosexuality). Hatfield and her colleagues found that men's and women's arousal responses, averaged across this range of erotic movies, were virtually identical.

In another series of experiments, Fisher and Byrne (1978b) examined the responses of single undergraduates and married students to different erotic movies. In their first experiment, the investigators asked gender-segregated groups of undergraduates to view a silent color film. This erotic movie depicted a couple undressing, petting, and engaging in fellatio and cunnilingus, with both partners reaching orgasm (Schmidt & Sigusch, 1970). After viewing this movie, male and female students reported equivalent (and moderately high) levels of sexual arousal. In a second experiment, married student couples participated, and these couples viewed either a silent color film that depicted nudity and hand-to-genital petting (without orgasm), or a film that showed foreplay, oral sex, and intercourse in various positions (with orgasm) (Schmidt & Sigusch, 1970). After viewing these movies, the married men and women indicated privately how aroused they had been by the erotic stimuli. Once again, men and women reported equivalent levels of sexual arousal in response to the erotic films.

In contrast to survey data that show that women do not go out of their way to view erotic movies, experimental findings show that—when presented with erotic films—men and women respond with quite similar levels of arousal. As was the case for erotic slides, stories, and fantasies, however, there are exceptions to the findings for gender similarity in arousal responses to movies. For example, in the Hatfield, Sprecher, and Traupmann (1978) study, it was found that men were more aroused by the female masturbation film, while women were more aroused by the male masturbation film. Also, Schmidt (1975) found that females were less aroused by a film of group rape than men were (see also Malamuth, Heim, & Feshbach, 1980). In each of these cases, it is fairly obvious why gender differences in arousal responses to specific stimuli may occur, within a general pattern of male-female similarity in such responses. In other instances where there are gender differences in arousal responses to specific erotic films (for example, see Mosher, 1973; Schmidt & Sigusch, 1970), however, the reasons for these differences are not entirely clear. Once again, more research is needed to specify just what elements in erotic films may be differentially arousing to men and women—and why. For now, it is important to note that, on the average, men and women report strikingly similar levels of sexual arousal in response to erotic films. Such findings are quite inconsistent with what one would expect based on survey research in this area.

Men and women can be similarly physiologically aroused by erotica We have seen that by and large, men and women report similar levels of arousal in response to erotica. Thus far, however, the data consist mostly of subjective self-reports in which men and women tell us—introspectively—how sexually aroused they feel. Such reports indicate, in essence, how aroused men and women are in their heads. Researchers have also been interested, however, in men's and women's *genital* or *physiological* arousal responses to erotica. Does male-female similarity in response to erotica extend from subjective to physiological indices of arousal?

One of the first large-scale studies of men's and women's physiological responses to different kinds of erotica was reported by Schmidt & Sigusch (1973). These researchers conducted three separate studies in which nearly 600 West German undergraduates were exposed to erotic stories, slides, and movies. The erotica depicted a range of sexual activity including nudity, manual-genital and oral-genital acts, and coitus in various positions. After viewing the erotica, participants in the research were asked to report on their physiological responses. Males indicated whether they had had erections, preejaculatory emissions, or ejaculations; females reported whether they had had vaginal lubrication, breast or genital sensations, or orgasms. Results indicated a high degree of similarity of men's and women's physiological responsiveness to the erotica: between 80 and 91 percent of the men, and 70 to 83 percent of the women, reported some physiological response to the erotic stimuli.

These findings for similarity of men's and women's physiological responsiveness to erotica are not isolated. For example, Mosher (1973) actually found that a higher proportion of women (85 percent) than men (80 percent) reported genital sensations in response to erotic films. In addition Hatfield, Sprecher, and Traupmann (1978) and Fisher and Byrne (1978b) have also found that men and women report similar levels of physiological sexual arousal in response to a wide range of erotic films.

Our conclusion that men and women may be similarly physiologically responsive to erotica is not based solely on men's and women's self-reports of what is happening to their bodies. Julia Heiman (1975, 1977) has used physiological recording devices to assess *directly* men's and women's arousal responses to erotica. In this research, each male student was fitted with a mercury-filled strain gauge to measure the blood volume of his penis, while each female inserted a tamponlike device (a plethysmograph) into her vagina, also to measure blood volume. (According to Masters and Johnson's (1966) research, blood flow changes in the genitals are important physiological indicators of sexual arousal). After attaching themselves privately to the recording devices, the students listened to a series of erotic tapes. According to Heiman, "The great majority of both sexes responded physiologically and subjectively to the erotic . . . tapes. . . . Women, in fact, rated the erotic tapes as more arousing than men did" (Heiman, 1975, p. 92). Thus, evidence has converged from a number of sources to suggest that women are at least as physiologically responsive to erotica as men are. Given the physiological similarities between men and women, these findings make sense. As Radlove pointed out in Chapter 4, both men and women exhibit the same general sexual response cycle. Both genders react to effective stimulation with the identical four phases: excitement, plateau, orgasm, and resolution.

Assumptions about the other gender's response to erotica   One other bit of evidence is pertinent to our discussion of male and female arousal responses to erotica. William Griffitt (1973) has conducted research in which undergraduate men and women first rated their arousal responses to a series of erotic slides. Then they rated how aroused they *thought* members of the other gender would be in response to the slides. Results showed that men and women reported similar levels of arousal in response to the erotica. However, females ascribed more arousal to men than male undergraduates ascribed to women. In other words, despite the fact that they were actually similarly aroused, men felt that women would not be excited by erotica while women felt that men would be very excited by such material! Griffitt has demonstrated in the laboratory that, although men and women do not seem to differ in arousal responses to erotica, both seem to think that gender differences in responsiveness do in fact exist.

Men and women show similar increases in sexual activity after exposure to erotica   One of the most interesting (and controversial) findings of the Commission on Obscenity and Pornography was that erotica has few pronounced effects on the sexual behavior of people who view such material. At the most, it was found that exposure to explicit erotica leads to a short-term (for example, one-day) increase in the sort of sexual behavior that a person usually engages in anyway (see Mann et al., 1974). And, as it happens, research indicates that the effects of erotica on subsequent sexual behavior are quite similar for men and women.

Schmidt and Sigusch's (1973) investigations help to provide an overview of the effects of erotica on the sexual behavior of men and women. As described earlier, Schmidt and Sigusch exposed some 600 West German college students to a variety of heterosexual erotica—films, slides, and stories. A day after exposure to the erotic stimuli, participants were asked to report what sexual behaviors they had engaged in during the 24 hours *before,* and the 24 hours *after* viewing the erotica. Results indicated that most of the men's and women's sexual behavior remained unchanged, but there were some significant increases. Women reported more masturbation, petting, and coital activity after viewing the erotica. They also reported having more orgasms after exposure as well as increases in sexual fantasy, talking about sex, and desire to have sex. For their part, men reported increased masturbation, petting, and total number of orgasms after viewing erotica, and they also had more sex fantasies, they talked about sex more, and had more desire for sex after exposure to erotica. Schmidt & Sigusch noted that "In most cases, the results for men and women show similar changes. Where there were significant differences, the women show a greater change with reference to sexual activation" (Schmidt & Sigusch, 1973, p. 135). It should be noted that other researchers (for example, Byrne & Lamberth, 1971; Hatfield, Sprecher, & Traupmann, 1978) have also failed to find differential effects of exposure to erotica on the sexual behavior of men and women.

In related work on the effects of erotica, Fisher and Byrne (1978a) have found that certain people are especially likely to increase their sexual activity after exposure to erotic stimuli. In particular, it was noted that people who evaluated an erotic film most *negatively* reported an increase in their sexual behavior for the two days after exposure. People who evaluated the erotic film more positively did not change their sexual behavior after exposure. Of concern to the present discussion is the fact that *both* males and females who evaluated the erotica negatively increased in sexual activity after exposure to the film. In contrast, the sexual behavior of those men and women who liked the erotica remained unchanged. Thus, even within the subgroup of people who are most responsive, males and females do not differ in their sexual behavior responses to erotica.

Males respond to erotica with more positive emotions and evaluations than females do . . . maybe According to the Commission on Obscenity and Pornography (1970), "even a brief presentation of sexual stimuli elicits strong and divergent affective (emotional) responses in addition to sexual arousal" (pp. 203–204). Research examining emotional responses to erotica has suggested that, in fact, men may respond to erotica with relatively positive emotions while women may react with more negative feelings. At long last, do we have a genuine, robust gender difference in response to erotica? As we shall see, the answer to this question seems to be an unqualified "maybe."

Several researchers have indeed found evidence that men respond to erotica with more positive emotions than do women. Schmidt and Sigusch (1973), for example, studied student men's and women's emotional states before and after they viewed erotic slides, films, and stories. Increases in negative feelings occurred primarily among student women, who reported feeling more irritated and depressed after viewing erotica. In addition, Griffitt (1973) found that after exposure to erotic slides, women (compared to men) said that they were more disgusted, angry, and nauseous. Mosher (1973) has also found some increase in negative feelings among women who have viewed erotic films, and Griffitt and Kaiser (1978) found that women felt less positive than did men after exposure to erotic slides.

Although some investigators have found gender differences in emotional responses to erotica, others have not. Hatfield and her colleagues (1978), for example, studied the emotional responses of 556 student men and women to a variety of erotic films. Men and women in this research showed no difference in a combined negative-emotions scale that assessed volunteers' feelings of disgust, nausea, anger, and depression. In addition, Byrne and Lamberth (1971) found that married men and women did not differ in their emotional responses to a series of erotic slides. And Fisher and Byrne (1978b) found that male and female students—married or single—showed similar emotional responses to three different erotic films. These investigators did find, however, that single women (versus men) rated the films as more pornographic and had more desire to restrict access to such material. Such negative evaluations of erotica by women are confirmed in some research (Griffitt, 1973) but not in other studies (Byrne & Lamberth, 1971).

Where does this conflicting evidence lead us? There do not seem to be any specific kinds of erotica that elicit gender differences in emotional responses. Much of the research that does show gender differences seems to come before or during the early 1970s. The findings for male-female similarity in emotional response are of more recent vintage. Thus, we could speculate that, with increases in societal permissiveness in recent years, women are now able to feel better about viewing erotica. In any event, gender differences in emotional and evaluative responses to erotic stimuli do not seem to be a terribly strong or consistent phenomenon. Overall, the available research suggests considerable uniformity in men's and women's responses to erotica. Schmidt (1975, p. 355) has concluded that

> In sum, the pattern and intensity of reactions to explicit sexual stimuli are in general the same for men and women. When significant differences between the sexes are found, they represent merely minor shifts in the total pattern. These variations should not divert attention from the fact that women can react to the same extent and in the same direction as men.

RESOLVING THE SURVEY-EXPERIMENT DISCREPANCY IN FINDINGS FOR GENDER DIFFERENCES IN RESPONSE TO EROTICA

Voluminous survey data show that compared to men, women do not often report arousal to erotica, nor do they commonly consume such material. In contrast, experimental research shows clearly that men and women can be equally aroused by erotica. What can be concluded from this conflicting evidence?

It may help to remember that surveys and experiments are designed to answer different questions; therefore, it is not surprising that they give different answers. Surveys tell what men and women *presently do* or have done with respect to erotica. And it is evident that men consume and enjoy erotica, while women do not. Experiments, on the other hand, tell what men and women *can do*, under specific conditions, in terms of their responses to erotica. And, it is quite clear now that men and women can respond to many kinds of erotica with equivalent levels of subjective and physiological sexual arousal and modest increases in sexual activity. Confusion only occurs in making unwarranted jumps from one level of analysis to another. Thus, for example, it is inaccurate to generalize from survey data (which show that women *have not been* aroused by erotica) to the assumption that women *cannot* be aroused by erotica.

On the basis of the evidence that has been reviewed, we may conclude that women can be aroused by erotica, but that they do not purchase and enjoy erotica very often. Why not? There are probably many reasons, but there are three "best guesses" concerning why women do not often exercise their ability to become aroused by erotica.

Sexual Socialization

It seems possible that the acquisition and use of erotica is an "acquired taste," just like the enjoyment of caviar or 12-year-old Scotch (Berger, Gagnon, & Simon, 1971). Social arrangements are such that boys and men have greater opportunity to learn to use erotica, while girls and women are either ignored for or discouraged from being sexual in this particular way (Simon & Gagnon, 1969). This explanation is consistent with social learning and social cognitive theories as described by Parsons in Chapter 1. Differential patterns of rewards and punishments encourage boys and girls to accept the gender-typed behaviors that characterize adult men and women. Children and adolescents, too, may actively monitor their own behavior to ensure that they are behaving appropriately or conforming to expected gender-role norms.

Among their peers, boys may gain social prestige for possessing erotic books and magazines. Once they have acquired these materials, boys may also have more opportunity than girls to learn how to use erotica as a stimulus for masturbation. Girls and women, in contrast, may not be rewarded for contact with erotica during their sexual socialization. Although girls may be quite interested in looking at erotic materials with friends, they are probably less likely than boys to conceptualize their behavior as desirable or consistent with their expected gender role. Furthermore, as Parsons points out, girls are less likely to masturbate than are their male peers (Chapter 1), this factor also suggesting that they will be less likely to learn how to masturbate aided by erotic materials. Following these arguments, then, a clear case can be made for the theory that male-female differences in the acquisition and use of erotica are at least in part a function of socialization differences during childhood.

The Nature of Erotica

A second reason why women may use erotica less than men (despite their equal potential for arousal) may derive from the fact that little good-quality erotica is available for women. Although *Playboy* and *Penthouse* have been refining their styles for years, the main explicit erotic magazine for women—*Playgirl*—first appeared only in 1973. And, it may be that *Playgirl* has not yet hit on the right erotic formula for women. For example, readers indicate dissatisfaction with the fact that all of the penises in *Playgirl* are flaccid, not erect. As one female friend of mine remarked, pointing to a photo of a shriveled penis, "What good is *that?*" In addition, systematic research (Stauffer & Frost, 1976) has shown that women are less aroused by *Playgirl* than men are by *Playboy.* In view of the evidence that has been reviewed, we take this to mean that *Playgirl* is inferior to *Playboy*—not that women are less aroused by erotica than men are. Finally, it is worth noting that a certain amount of erotica pairs sexual content with violence against women (Malamuth & Spinner, 1980). Obviously, such material may tend to repel rather than to arouse many women.

Social Desirability

A third explanation for the fact that women have little contact with erotica has to do with social desirability (or undesirability) considerations. In our culture, it is still quite risky for a woman to be assertively sexual, as would be the case for a female who purchases erotica. Women may have come a long way, but it is still more socially undesirable for women to possess and enjoy erotica than it is for men to do so. Thus, part of women's indifference to erotica may simply be a function of fear of social disapproval. The extent to which such fear may exist is well illustrated by the reaction of a woman college student who had just read *Playgirl* magazine for an experiment:

> I do not care to read women's magazines which play on nude males for attracting its readership. Although the fiction appears to be interesting as well as the film reviews, I would feel uncomfortable reading it because the manufacturer would believe I read it for the nude males. [Stauffer & Frost, 1976, p. 29]

It is worth noting that the same fear of social disapproval that may prevent women from acquiring erotica may also prevent them from admitting on a survey that they have purchased erotica or have been aroused by it—even if they have. As Radlove points out in Chapter 4, North American culture has not traditionally given women the same permission to be fully sexual that it has given men. Because girls and women learn to repress sexual interests to prove that they are "good girls," it makes sense that they will be more likely to have a positive response to erotica when an authority figure gives them the go-ahead. In an experiment, in contrast with a survey, the subjects' responsibility for seeing erotica belongs at least in part to the researcher who presented the erotic material. The fact that an authority figure was responsible for their exposure to erotica may facilitate "admission" of arousal by women in experiments.

On the basis of these three factors (sexual socialization, the nature of erotica, and social desirability), it may be possible to begin to resolve the discrepancy between survey and experimental findings for gender differences in response to erotica. Surveys tell us that men consume and enjoy erotica, while women do not. As noted earlier, I think that women do not use erotica because they have not been socialized to enjoy this practice, because little high-quality erotica is available to women, and because it is socially undesirable for women to use erotica. In experiments, in contrast, we learn what men and women *can do* under specific conditions, in terms of their reactions to erotica. And when we provide reasonable-quality erotica to men and women, under conditions that may minimize fear of social disapproval, they respond with equivalent levels of subjective and physiological sexual arousal and modest increases in sexual activity. Confusion occurs only when we make inappropriate inferences from survey data (which show that women *have not* been aroused by erotica) to the assumption that women *cannot* be aroused by erotica.

One final point is worth noting. Speculations about why women do not use erotica more often are not necessarily recommendations that it would be desirable for women to increase their exposure to erotica (or for that matter, for men to decrease their exposure). Rather, the attempt is to understand why—despite a similar potential for arousal—men and women do differ in their everyday contact with erotica. And, the research suggests that prior socialization, the poor quality of erotica for women, and social desirability considerations may help account for this phenomenon.

GENDER DIFFERENCES REVISITED: RESPONSE TO AFFECTIONAL AND NONAFFECTIONAL EROTICA

On the basis of experimental findings, it seems safe to conclude that men and women have the potential to be equally responsive to erotica. There have been, however, attempts to qualify this conclusion. Some researchers have wondered whether—within their generally similar response patterns— women may be more aroused by romantic, affectional erotica, while men are more aroused by purely sexual, unromantic erotica. As already noted by Hatfield in Chapter 5, such speculation seems to be embedded in the cultural stereotype that women are more concerned with love. In any event, this question was first raised by Kinsey and his colleagues (1953). Recently, a number of studies have investigated this topic. The question is whether or not such research may qualify conclusions with respect to gender similarity in response to erotica.

At first, investigations of gender-specific responses to affectional and nonaffectional erotica presented a mixed bag of findings. For example, Sigusch, Schmidt, Reinfeld, and Wiedemann-Sutor (1970) found that in response to erotic slides "the scenes with high affection . . . were judged by the women as more stimulating" (p. 15). In contrast, Schmidt, Sigusch, and Schafer (1973) found *no* gender differences in response to erotic stories that differed in affectional versus nonaffectional emphasis. And, a study by Jakobovits (1965) showed that women were *more* aroused by "hard-core obscenity" stories than men were.

One difficulty with each of the preceding studies is that the nature of the "affectional" and "nonaffectional" erotic stimuli is not very clear. In the 1970 study by Sigusch and his colleagues, for example, slides depicting the following scenes were considered to be "romantic:" "kissing couple, with naked shoulders, couple in bathing suits kissing and embracing, couple in bed naked above waist (women's breasts not seen) showing affection" (p. 14). Whatever else these slides may portray, they do not seem to convey "romance" very powerfully. In a similar vein, the erotic stories used by Schmidt, Sigusch, and Schafer (1973) differ not only in affectional versus non-affectional theme, but also in the coarseness of the language that is used. Because the stimuli seem to differ from one another in many ways other than the intended affectional-nonaffectional distinction. it is hard to tell exactly what any gender differences in responses might mean.

Problems with the stimuli employed may have contributed to the inconsistent nature of the findings on gender differences in response to affectional and nonaffectional erotica. What is needed is research that presents men and women with identical erotic stimuli that differ *only* in affectional or nonaffectional emphasis. A series of experiments by Fisher and Byrne (1978b) has employed just such a methodology. In their first study, these investigators showed male and female undergraduates a 10-minute silent color film. This erotic movie portrayed nudity, petting, and oral-genital sex to the point of orgasm for both partners. In order to create the "affectional" or "nonaffectional" distinction, this same movie was prefaced with one of two sets of "background information." The undergraduates who viewed the film in the "affectional" condition received a handout that said,

> The scene to be presented takes place in a small apartment in Copenhagen. A young working man and his wife, recently married and very much in love, are just returning from a dance. They are eager to express their love for one another.

Those who viewed the film in the "nonaffectional" condition received the following information:

> The scene to be presented takes place in a small apartment in Copenhagen. A young working man has been approached by a prostitute at a dance and has agreed to purchase her services for the evening. They are just returning from the dance. He is eager to obtain what he has bought, and she is quite willing to fulfill her part of the bargain. [Fisher & Byrne, 1978b, p. 119]

After viewing the movie, the students indicated how aroused they had been by the erotica. Results showed that males and females responded to the affectional and nonaffectional erotica with similar levels of sexual arousal. In a second experiment, the investigators showed a group of married couples two different erotic movies. Each film was prefaced by either the "affectional" or "nonaffectional" instructions (just quoted), or by a "casual sex" instruction, as follows:

> The scene to be presented takes place in a small apartment in Copenhagen. A young working man has met a girl at a dance, and they were sexually attracted to one another almost immediately. They are just returning from the dance and are eager to enjoy the sexual exploration which each is anticipating. [Fisher & Byrne, 1978b, p. 122]

Once again, participants in the study viewed the erotica prefaced by one of the three instructional sets and indicated how aroused they were by the stimulus. Once again, the married men and women showed equivalent sexual arousal responses to the various erotic stimuli. Both genders were equally and moderately aroused by the "affectional" and "nonaffectional" erotica but, interestingly enough, married men and women were most aroused by the "casual sex" theme that portrayed a chance sexual encounter.

One more study, conducted by Julia Heiman (1975, 1977), is pertinent to this discussion. Heiman monitored the physiological sexual arousal of college men and women with the penile strain gauge and vaginal plethysmograph devices that were mentioned earlier. Some of these volunteers listened to erotic tape recordings that described sexual action, others listened to erotic-romantic tapes that combined sex and affection, and still others listened to romantic tapes that had affectional but not sexual content. Results showed that most of the men and women responded with physiological sexual arousal to the erotic and erotic-romantic tapes, but not to the purely romantic tapes. Said Heiman, "Our assumption that women would react only to the romantic tapes, or at least that they would prefer eroticism that was tempered with romance to straight-out sex, was simply wrong" (Heiman, 1975, pp. 92–93). Thus, across a series of experiments that exposed volunteers to clearly distinguished stimuli, men and women show equivalent arousal responses to affectional and nonaffectional erotica. Speculation that men are turned on by "lust" while women need "love" theme erotica seems not to be well founded.

These experimental findings are consistent with some studies cited in Chapter 5. As Hatfield points out, the commonsense view that women are more romantic than men may be overly simplistic. Men and women alike seem to want both love and sex in their intimate relationships. It stands to reason, then, that men and women may not desire different types of erotica.

GENDER-ROLE IDENTIFICATION AND
RESPONSE TO EROTICA

In the early 1970s, "gender differences" research was in its heyday. Psychologists studied male-female variations in conformity (for example, Sistrunk & McDavid, 1971), achievement-related behavior (for example, Deaux & Emswiller, 1974), fear of success (for example, Horner, 1972), and other issues of the day. Before long, however, investigators began to realize that discriminations finer than "male" and "female" were needed. After all, a male can be psychologically masculine, or he can be androgynous, or he can even be relatively feminine, in a psychological sense. By the same token, a woman may be feminine, androgynous, or masculine in her psychological makeup.

Research on gender and reactions to erotica is at the same stage now as traditional "gender differences' research was in the early 1970s. That is, almost all of the work being done treats male-female differences in responses to erotica. Little attention has been paid to the possible relationship of *gender-role identification* and reactions to erotica. Like their colleagues in the 1970s, some researchers see the value of introducing distinctions based on gender-role identification into research on gender differences in response to erotica.

Logically, it seems possible that gender-role identification is linked with response to erotica. The highest degree of similarity in reactions to erotica ought to be observed for androgynous men and women. Because such people share psychological characteristics of both genders, their reactions to erotica ought to be similar. Where male-female differences in response to erotica are observed, such differences should occur mostly among gender-typed people (that is, highly masculine males compared to highly feminine females). As noted earlier, not much research has been done on the subject of gender-role identification and response to erotica, but there is one excellent study (Kenrick et al., 1980) that should set the pace for continued work in this area.

In this study, Douglas Kenrick and his colleagues conducted field research to examine the effects of gender-role identification on approach or avoidance of erotica. Male and female students in an introductory psychology course participated in this research. They were contacted by telephone and told that the psychology department was recruiting participants for research. The undergraduates were told that they could opt for a "neutral" study, involving spatial perception, or they could choose to participate in an experiment that involved viewing an erotic film. The student's choices were recorded, and that ended—for the time being—their experimental participation. One month later, however, the same students were asked to fill out the Bem Sex Role Inventory (Bem, 1974), which classified subjects as either gender typed (that is, masculine men or feminine women) or androgynous. Thus, data were available on students' gender, their gender-role identification, and their willingness to see an erotic film.

The results of Kenrick's research are enlightening. With respect to *gender*, more men (71 percent) than women (53 percent) were willing to volunteer to see an erotic film. In terms of gender-role identification, masculine males were more likely (91 percent) than anyone else to choose to see erotica, while feminine females were least likely (31 percent) to volunteer to see the erotica. Most interestingly, androgynous men (60 percent) and women (67 percent) were moderately—and statistically equally—likely to volunteer to see the erotica. Thus, the effects of gender per se are dramatically qualified by gender-role identification. These findings are presented graphically in Figure 12-2.

Kenrick's experiment demonstrates the utility of examining the links between gender-role identification—as well as gender per se—and responses to erotica. Moreover, Kenrick's findings confirm the general proposition that androgynous men and women may be most alike and gender-typed men and women may be most different in their responses to erotica. (It should be noted, however, that the few studies in this general area do not uniformly support this assumption; see Allgeier & Fogel, 1978; Storms, 1980). In the future, it would seem most useful to examine the links between gender-role identification and the other sorts of reactions to erotica that we have discussed. Do androgynous (versus gender-typed) people, become equally aroused by erotica? Do they show similar emotional responses to erotica? These are but a few of the questions that remain to be answered in continued research on gender, gender role identification, and response to erotica.

SUGGESTIONS FOR FUTURE RESEARCH

Recently, Donn Byrne (1977) has proposed a model for the study of sexual behavior: the sexual behavior sequence. At present, this formulation does not

Part Two Contemporary Perspective

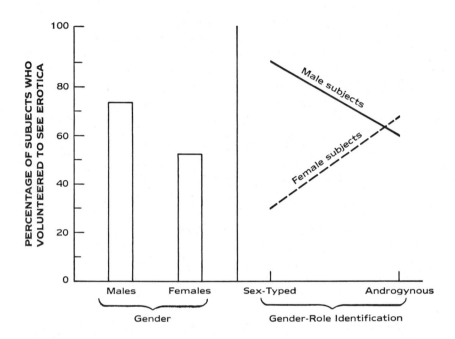

FIGURE 12-2

*Percentage of Subjects Who Volunteered to See an Erotic Movie as a Function of Subjects'
Gender and Gender-Role Identification*

SOURCE: Adapted from data in Kenrick, D.T., et al. Sex differences, androgyny, and approach
responses to erotica; A new variation on an old volunteer problem. *Journal of Personality and
Social Psychology,* 1980, *38,* 517–524. Copyright © 1980 by the American Psychological Association. Adapted by permission of the author.

comprise a thoroughly tested theory, but it does provide useful guidelines for
future research on sexual behavior, including work on reactions to erotica.
According to the sexual behavior sequence, we all learn at least four kinds of
responses to erotica—emotional, informational, fantasy, and arousal. It may
prove useful to examine links between gender, gender-role identification, and
each of these responses to erotica.

Emotional Responses to Erotica

The sexual behavior sequence assumes that erotic stimuli may elicit positive
or negative emotional responses in those who are exposed to it. Have you ever
felt a rush of sexual arousal—or a wave of nausea and disgust—when
looking at a new kind of erotica for the first time? It is thought that such
emotional reactions are learned by way of the association of reward and
punishment with erotic cues during our socialization. If one has been consis-

tently punished in conjunction with erotica, he or she should come to respond to such stimuli with negative emotions. Conversely, a person who has associated mostly positive experiences with erotica should respond to such material with mostly positive feelings.

What is known about the emotional responses to erotica of persons who differ in gender or gender-role identification? We know that women have a tendency to respond to erotica with more negative emotions than men do (Griffitt, 1973; Griffitt & Kaiser, 1978), although evidence on this issue is not consistent (Byrne & Lamberth, 1971; Hatfield, Sprecher, & Traupmann, 1978). Other than that, our knowledge is fairly limited. What is the nature of gender differences in response to erotica of differing explicitness, content, and media? Do gender-typed and androgynous people have—as might be expected—different emotional responses to erotica? How might emotional responses to erotica that are specific to men and women (or gender-typed and androgynous people) affect an individual's other responses to erotica? Such questions may become the topics for future research on gender, gender-role identification, and emotional responses to erotica.

Informational Responses to Erotica

The sexual behavior sequence proposes that, in addition to eliciting emotional responses, erotic material also activates informational responses—learned beliefs and expectancies. Such beliefs (for example, "The picture in this magazine looks interesting") and expectancies ("I bet if I tried it, though, I'd break my back") may be accurate or inaccurate, but it is thought that as long as a person believes they are true, beliefs and expectancies guide their behavior (Byrne, 1977).

Gender and gender-role identification probably have important influences on beliefs and expectancies about erotica. For example, men and women may be similarly aroused by erotica, but men actually use erotica much more than women do. It may be that men have learned positive beliefs about erotica ("Looking at *Hustler* is a real macho thing to do") and related positive expectancies ("Every kid on the block will be begging me to have a look at it") that encourage them to use erotica. In contrast, women—who seem to be just as arousable by erotica as men are—may have learned negative beliefs about erotica ("Sex magazines are unladylike") and may have negative expectancies in this regard ("If I looked at such a magazine, what would people think?") that encourage them to avoid erotica. Differences in beliefs and expectancies may also underlie gender-typed and androgynous people's tendencies to approach or avoid erotic material (see Kenrick et al., 1980). Thus, research is clearly needed to explore the links between gender, gender-role identification, and informational responses to erotica.

Fantasy Responses to Erotica

The sexual behavior sequence proposes that erotic stimuli can elicit sexual fantasies. This is, in fact, the case, and erotica-induced sexual fantasy can be equally arousing to men and women (Byrne & Lamberth, 1971). Beyond that, our knowledge is quite limited. Does the content of erotica-induced sexual fantasy differ for men and women? Do androgynous men and women have more similar fantasy responses to erotica than do gender-typed men and women? Perhaps future research can provide answers to these questions on gender, gender-role identification, and fantasy responses to erotica.

Arousal Responses to Erotica

The sexual behavior sequence assumes that people learn to become aroused by erotica as the result of associating physiological sexual arousal (such as masturbation) with new cues (such as erotic pictures or stories). Research is needed to specify exactly how this process takes place in the socialization of boys and girls. Do the genders differ in the frequency with which they become physiologically sexually aroused at early ages? Are boys and girls encouraged to associate this arousal with different cues? Such research might help explain similarities and differences in men's and women's arousal responses to erotica.

With respect to gender-role identification and arousal responses to erotica, research has only just begun. Have gender-typed and androgynous people learned to be differentially aroused by erotica? Extrapolating from the work of Kenrick and his colleagues (1980), we might expect that androgynous men and women would be the most similar in their arousal responses to erotica, while gender-typed people would be most different in this respect. And, if this is true, the sexual behavior sequence would suggest that androgynous men and women have similar developmental histories of association of sexual arousal with erotic cues. In contrast, gender-typed men and women should have learned to associate sexual arousal with quite different cues.

This speculation, based on the sexual behavior sequence, suggests that future research is needed to examine links between gender, gender-role identification, and responses to erotica—emotional, informational, fantasy, and arousal. On the basis of such information, we may begin to understand better men and women's (or gender-typed and androgynous people's) reactions to erotica.

AFTERWORD

Future Influences on the Interaction of Gender and Human Sexual Expression

A space traveler visiting Earth from another planet a hundred years ago might describe the visit as follows:

No matter where I went to study these odd intelligent beings, one distinction seemed paramount among them. From birth through old age, their behavior and expectations were predetermined according to a minor physical difference in their sex organs or genitals. In most of the lands I visited, those who had protruding genitals dominated over those whose genitals folded inward.

The beings with protruding genitals had power and freedom to do much as they chose. In return for their special privileges, these individuals were expected to provide shelter, food, and protection from hostile neighbors for a selected one or group of those beings who had inward-folding genitals.

The beings with inward-folding genitals led more subordinate, restricted lives. For the most part, their duties consisted of caring for offspring, preparing food, making the shelter more liveable, and gently but dutifully serving the needs for emotional and physical comfort that were expressed by those with protruding genitals.

Mating behavior, too, followed a restricted pattern. The same physical distinction that determined the individual's place in society also influenced feelings about sex and sexual behavior itself. Generally, the individual with protruding genitals was also the more sexually interested party. Traditionally, these beings spent more time looking at sexual artifacts, initiating sexual relations, and chasing after a number of possible sexual partners than did the individuals with inward-folding genitals, who were expected to remain sexually disinterested or passive.

285

Mating rules were so extreme that on some occasions it was considered permissible for an individual with protruding genitals to use force or violence to have sex. Similarly, some individuals with inward-folding genitals learned their roles too well. Even with a sensitive partner, sex for them became a burden, not a pleasure. Passivity and helplessness were not always adaptive.

Punishment was severe for those who tried to break the rules. Those in the subordinate class who wanted to be powerful outside of their shelters, who desired "too much" sex or "too many" sexual partners, or who cared little for nurturing the young were ostracized. Superior-status individuals who had disdain for their greater power and wished to share responsibilities in sexual and family decisions with those who had dissimilar genitals were also punished. Regardless of the beings' original place in society, negative sanctions were imposed against those beings who preferred to have sex with someone with the same kind of genitals. Often, ritual name-calling was used to enforce the traditional social order. For many of these creatures, the worst insult they could give one another was "You are no different from one who has the opposite kind of genitals."

This fantasy about the experiences of a space traveler from the past has a number of implications. First and foremost is our assumption that gender roles have predetermined the course of peoples' lives in most cultures and during most of our history. Until a short time ago, a space traveler would have been able to make fairly accurate predictions on the basis of gender alone about how people spent their days and how they experienced sexuality. With few exceptions, whether the extraterrestial visitor landed in North America or Africa, Toronto or Istanbul, knowledge of the individual's gender would have indicated much that there was to know about someone's likely economic, social, and sexual behaviors. Such predictive accuracy from knowledge of a person's gender would still be available today for the space traveler who landed in many nonindustrialized regions of the world.

In the industrialized portions of the world, however, monumental changes have been occurring. The rigidity of gender-defined roles based on reproductive capacities has begun to yield to pressure from overpopulation, economic necessity, and such social influences as the women's movement, the development of contraceptive technology, and the increasing tolerance for homosexual lifestyles. These factors have fundamentally altered the meaning of sexuality and reproduction.

Conception is no longer a biological inevitability for sexually active people. It is possible to choose when, and whether, to reproduce. Separated from reproduction, sexuality takes on new meanings. It is more possible to have casual, more pleasure-oriented sexual relationships. It is less imperative to find the right man or woman with whom to settle down for life.

Even existing long-term relationships have lost some of their stability. Increasing numbers of people are divorcing or choosing relationships outside of legal marriage.

Freed from the burdens of constant pregnancy and childbirth and beset by inflation, most women now work outside the home. Their new economic positions, although underpaid in contrast with men's, nevertheless afford them the opportunity to reject or delay marriage and to have greater bargaining power within their relationships.

Economic ideology also enters the picture. In our consumer-oriented economy, sex sells. Marketing campaigns suggest a variety of products and ideas for increasing our desirability to others and even for enhancing our own desires for sex. Sexual adequacy and self-esteem are packaged and sold along with magazines, toothpaste, and deodorant.

The purpose of this book has been to review evidence regarding how our lives are changing in association with altered beliefs and norms regarding gender roles and sexual expression, both of which are in a dynamic relationship with each other. Before summarizing and commenting on the contents of this book, we will mention three reasons for caution.

One source of caution is the need to be open-minded when interpreting scientific research. It is all too easy to jump to a dogmatic conclusion on the basis of a few studies. Research in the social sciences usually tells us what *is* but not what will always be or what is ideal for everyone.

The studies discussed in this book do not suggest unalterable conditions. Clearly, different ways of conceptualizing the issues, different populations for study, different research methodologies, and unknown additional variables might have led to somewhat different findings. For instance, most of the contributors to this book would conclude that gender roles are changing and that these changes seem to have positive implications for sexual relationships. Nevertheless, we would not go so far as to insist that liberated gender roles are inherently good whereas the traditional masculine and feminine roles are inherently bad. Just as it is inappropriate to argue that the extremes of masculinity and femininity are natural and normal, it is also incorrect to assume that only androgynous and feminist people can enjoy healthy and pleasurable sex lives.

A second source of caution stems from the fact that our research is embedded in a particular historical era and culture. What we find may be true now but we cannot infer that these results were true for our ancestors or will generalize to future generations. Similarly, our conceptualization of gender role and of sexual behavior is so specific to Western industrialized societies that it would be inappropriate to apply findings among Westerners to those who live in completely different cultures, such as nomads or peasants in the Third World.

Third, we should be cautious because the phenomena we study are themselves changing but our tools for understanding gender roles and sexuality are static. Our efforts at collecting data are like snapshots but the processes we study are always changing—a motion picture of lifestyles. Contemporary North Americans are exposed to a diversity of lifestyles. Families adhering to traditional norms regarding gender roles may live in the same neighborhood as do families following a more egalitarian pattern, singles living in groups of three or four who share responsibilities, gay couples, cohabitating heterosexual couples, and single-parent families. Thus, we have increased freedom to make choices about how we will live, and with whom. But, as Fromm (1941) pointed out in *Escape from Freedom*, the opportunity to make far-reaching choices can be accompanied by considerable anxiety.

Given the static nature of our research technology, we may not be able to separate the effects of particular lifestyles from the effects of taking one particular path when we know that other paths are available. In particular, those of us who were socialized to take traditional roles may experience occasional anxiety, self-doubt, and guilt when we choose newly available egalitarian roles. In measuring various aspects of life satisfaction of people operating with less rigid roles, then, it isn't clear to what extent we are simultaneously measuring anxieties over transition per se as we attempt to determine what costs and benefits are associated with egalitarian lifestyles. Similarly, investigations of traditional people cannot tease out how much their negative experiences reflect misgivings about having had to choose one out of several lifestyles. Anxiety about having made the wrong decision rather than strict adherence to traditional roles could be responsible for family and sexual problems.

FUTURE INDICATORS OF CHANGES IN GENDER-ROLE NORMS

Alternative strategies for examining some of the neglected questions are noted throughout this book. Joseph Pleck (1979) whose work on family work and paid work was described in Chapter 7, has made five specific suggestions for future research strategies. He made these suggestions in the context of increasing our understanding of gender roles and the relative contribution of men and women to paid versus family work. We are broadening his suggestions in terms of their relevance to all the issues covered in this book. We examine the impact of contemporary transitions both as researchers and as individuals struggling to make decisions in our own lives.

First, Pleck says, people need to monitor changes in *responsibilities taken by men and women*. Broadly interpreting his suggestion, researchers should monitor shifts in the responsibilities taken by males and females vis-à-vis gender roles from childhood and adolescence through the retirement years. Second, *patterns of various atypical groups* need to be observed, because some of these groups may have developed innovative methods for dealing with changing roles that may be useful for men and women in general. Third, the part played by various *institutions* in encouraging or discouraging gender-role differentiation should be examined. Fourth, we need to know the *consequences of increased participation* by men in areas traditionally defined as "women's" work and responsibility and by women in areas defined as the domain of men. Fifth, we need to monitor the effects of *educational programs* and *employment practices* designed to increase the ability of people, regardless of their gender, to develop their potential.

Some of these approaches have been used to try to gather information relevant to certain topics covered in this book. We now use Pleck's five suggestions to integrate the contents of this book and to suggest areas where research efforts might fruitfully be directed.

Shifts in Assignment of Responsibility

The term *responsibility* has multiple meanings. One of its meanings carries the notion of skill—the ability to respond: "response ability." A second connotation of the term conveys the notion of duty: someone is responsible for performing certain tasks as a function of his or her role. A third meaning associates the term with guilt or blame. Responsibility has been intimately tied to gender-role expectations in each of these meanings.

Responsibility as skill The topics for which this meaning of responsibility are most directly relevant are those covered by Radlove on sexual response (Chapter 4) and by Fisher, on response to erotica (Chapter 12). In both domains, men have traditionally been seen as having more responsibility. That term applies whether it is used in its traditional sense, meaning duty or obligation, or in the sense of the ability to respond: *response-ability*. They have been taught, and have exhibited, greater responsibility to their own sexual feelings, and to sexual stimulation presented in magazines, books, movies, and on television.

Radlove's research with androgynous and gender-typed women demonstrated that orgasmic responsibility is greater among women who are less identified with traditional roles. From that standpoint, androgynous identification appears to be associated with a strong benefit (if one values the enjoyment of sexual interaction, and we do) for women.

The relationship of androgynous identification and sexual arousal for women, shown empirically, also makes theoretical sense. That is, by taking a more active role during sexual interaction, women may be able to influence the kinds of stimulation they receive so as to increase pleasure and arousal. It is not clear, however, that it would be reasonable to expect a difference in the ability of men to respond to their sexual feelings as a function of being traditional or androgynous in their gender-role identification. After all, active, initiatory behavior is associated with both the traditional male role and with androgynous identification.

On the other hand, Zilbergeld's (1978) analysis of the traditional male role in sexual interaction as described by both Radlove and by Hatfield suggests that traditional men may be overtrained to take responsibility for what happens during sexual interaction. The resultant extreme goal orientation and performance demands, according to his analysis, may actually impede the sense of leisure and intimacy so important for satisfying relationships. Furthermore, the stress on performance may make sexual difficulties, when they arise, particularly stressful for men. Zilbergeld's thought-provoking analysis is clearly in need of empirical research to see if there is an association among gender-role identification in men, the pleasure they derive from sexual interaction, and the degree of stress they experience when occasional — and normal — sexual nonresponsiveness occurs.

The other area of response ability, discussed by Fisher in Chapter 12, involves response to erotic stimuli. He noted that clear differences between men and women in their interest in, and response to, erotica were evident from Kinsey's time to the 1970s. However, with the use of a different research method, these differences seemed to be reduced. That is, although surveys indicated that women are less apt to seek exposure to erotica and less apt to report arousal to it than are men, when men and women were exposed to erotic material in lab settings the gender differences were diminished or eliminated. Whether their sexual arousal is measured by genital recording devices or by self-report, men and women do not generally differ in their arousal from erotic stories and movies presented in experiments in the lab.

Although men and women seem to be equally responsible when exposed to erotic material, we do not know whether such responsiveness is related to gender-role identification per se. Fisher notes that research is needed on the relationship of gender-role identity to response to erotica. It would be useful to conduct such research using both the survey methods, which consistently yielded gender differences, and the experimental lab methods, which have found men and women to be fairly equivalent in their response to erotica.

Responsibility as obligation   Of the three connotations of responsibility mentioned earlier, the meaning of responsibility as obligation is the most intertwined with gender-role expectations. Across the life span, it is difficult to find many tasks that have not been linked either to men and masculinity or to women and femininity. From the first beginnings of sexual contact (courtship or dating) through to retirement, men are expected to take the responsibility for initiating and economically supporting most interactions. Of all the possible benefits to men potentially available as a consequence of the women's movement, one of the most important is the reduced expectation that men must bear responsibility for reaching out, for initiating sexual interaction, for providing economic support of an entire family, and even for fighting any external threats to the family. This last responsibility, a time-honored division of labor, was violated in a 1981 movie, *Raiders of the Lost Ark*. While the hero did battle with the villains in the bar-fight scene, the heroine failed to remain on the sidelines, hands clasped to bosom, screaming, in the way women have always been portrayed. Instead, she joined him in thrashing the bad guys (and she even excelled in her drinking capacity).

But we digress. Gender-role differentiation in the expected duties of men and women was discussed in most of the chapters of this book. A trend toward increasing role flexibility with maturity is evident. For example, in Chapter 3 McCormick and Jesser's description of courtship suggests that older adolescents and young adults adhere to less stereotyped beliefs about seduction and rejection than do the young adolescents described by Zellman and Goodchilds in Chapter 2. Young people continue to stereotype the man as responsible for seduction and the woman as dutifully setting limits on the success of his seduction attempts. Nevertheless, McCormick and Jesser noted that women were just as likely to initiate a flirtation in a bar as were men, and both genders described remarkably similar strategies when asked how they would seduce or turn off a date.

The division of labor by gender has been extremely apparent in the expectations of the roles of men and women in the family, as noted by E. Allgeier in Chapter 7. Specifically, men have been assigned responsibility for the economic support of their wives and children; women have been expected to maintain the house and clothing and to prepare meals for their husbands and children.

Even when women have joined men in sharing responsibility for the economic support of the family, they have still maintained their traditional duties within the home. Most previous studies of the contributions of men and women to paid versus family work indicated that the employment status of wives had little bearing on the extent of responsibility for family work taken by men. After all, food preparation, house cleaning, and the like are considered "women's work." However, just a few years ago, research by Robinson (1977) and Pleck (1979) showed that men whose wives are sharing responsibility for paid work have begun to take on more of the responsibility for family work than was characteristic of men whose wives were not employed outside the house.

We hope that researchers will continue to monitor the relative responsibilities taken by men and women for paid and family work to see whether the tendency toward increased sharing of responsibilities will develop further. In addition, the gender-role identification of husbands and wives should be examined to see whether there is greater role sharing of family work among couples holding androgynous identities than among more traditional couples. In a related area, androgynous fathers are likely to interact more with their children than are traditional fathers.

Gender-role differentiation begins to diminish to some extent during the second half of life, as noted by A. R. Allgeier in Chapter 6. Old age, too, has other advantages. As noted by Hatfield, men catch up to women in companionate love for the first time (Chapter 5). With advancing age, men finally express as much affection toward their wives as heretofore their wives had given them. Promising as these findings are for people who hope to live to a ripe old age, we must recognize that far too little is known about gender-role norms and sexuality among the elderly. Because larger and larger proportions of the population consist of people beyond their reproductive years, we hope that more research will be devoted to this age group.

Responsibility as fault Earlier, we discussed the traditional assignment of responsibility to women for setting limits on sexual interaction. When they "fail" at that task, even when they do not want to have sex, there is a tendency to blame women for their failure in preventing sexual assault or rape. This situation is discussed by Zellman and Goodchilds in Chapter 2, on adolescence, and later, by Cherry in her review of research on sexual violence (Chapter 11). The tendency to blame the woman is more pronounced among people holding traditional attitudes regarding gender roles. Nonetheless, women are blamed to varying degrees by all groups for sexual assaults made on them. As a result, Zellman and Goodchilds argue, most sexual interaction during adolescence involves a sort of sexual combat.

Clearly, young men are expected to demonstrate their masculinity by being sexually aggressive. In contrast, young women are expected to demonstrate their purity by remaining relatively chaste. To the extent that young men and women accept these two different lessons, friction between them is to be expected. Equally clearly, when unwanted sex, pregnancy, or venereal disease does occur, the costs are much greater for women than for men. We are not as pessimistic as Zellman and Goodchilds are, however, in their characterization of adolescent sexual relationships as sexual combat. Many adolescents are able to engage in consensual, mutually satisfying relationships. We do agree with Zellman and Goodchilds that more egalitarian training and more equitable assignment of responsibility are an important part of eliminating assignment of responsibility (fault) to women for unwanted sexual events. The relationship of gender-role identification to the assignment of and acceptance of blame constitutes an important area in need of research.

The assignment of responsibility to men to assume the role of sexual aggressor is also problematic. Until men are taught to separate masculinity from dominance over women, rape and sexual abuse will be pervasive problems. Gutek and Nakamura's description of sexual harassment in the workplace is related to this confusion of male power with sexual aggression (see Chapter 8). Here too, men are disproportionately likely to be the sexual aggressors, with women workers the likely victims. To what extent do unwanted sexual advances punish women for taking on forbidden masculine jobs or reinforce their submissiveness in traditionally feminine jobs? The symbolic meaning of sexual harassment is an area worthy of additional study.

Patterns in Atypical Groups

The second suggested strategy for research involves studying atypical groups to see how they adapt to changing roles. Peplau and Gordon (Chapter 10) provide an excellent example of the application of that strategy to gay couples. They report that some gay couples, particularly early in the gay awareness movement and early in an individual relationship, may adopt dominant-submissive relationships similar to those characterizing traditional heterosexual male-female bonds. However, contemporary gay couples appear to develop patterns relatively free of gender role fairly quickly. Modeling their relationships on a best friend or roommate model rather than on the traditional heterosexual mode, they assign tasks and responsibilities on the basis of individual preferences and skills rather than on the basis of gender. Research on the long-term outcomes of such patterns among gay couples is in its infancy, but observation of these couples may provide useful models for heterosexual couples who wish to develop egalitarian patterns in their own relationships.

Another important source of information about changing roles is suggested by A. R. Allgeier (Chapter 6). He speculates that aging couples, freed from the equation of sexuality with reproduction, may be able to provide models for more sensual and leisurely sexual relationships. Again, there are very few studies on sexual expression among this age group, and research is needed to check the accuracy of this speculation.

The Impact of Institutions on Gender-Role Norms

A third area needing attention involves the part played by various institutions and groups in encouraging or discouraging gender-role differentiation. As we go to press, forces at the highest levels of the U.S. government are clearly attempting to encourage such differentiation. That is, the Reagan administration is supporting a bill known as the Family Protection Act. (Readers may obtain copies of this or any other act by phoning or writing their Congressional Representative and asking for it by name.) If Congress passed this bill, no government funds could be used to support programs or research that might "undermine women's traditional roles." Whether this bill reflects popular opinion, or whether it will shape future opinion, is not known at the moment. The monitoring of ongoing national opinion surveys regarding appropriate roles for women has suggested that there has been increasing public support for egalitarian patterns. If this act is passed, its impact on public attitudes as well as on research and programs needs to be examined.

Ironically, another group in our society has supported similarly repressive positions regarding research on gender. Some scientists, concerned about the discriminatory use of research findings, have either denied the existence of any gender differences beyond those imposed by sexist socialization patterns, or have argued that research that seeks or finds gender differences should not be supported. They assert that such research findings may be used by policymakers to justify continued discriminatory practices against women.

Although women have been the victims of political, social, and economic sexism, and although research finding gender differences has sometimes been twisted to support such discrimination, we don't think that the suppression of free inquiry supported by either of these groups is warranted. People still understand very little about the ways in which gender and gender roles contribute to their lives. Continued research on the topic is badly needed. Regardless of what is found in the future, there is a crucial concept to remember in evaluating the usefulness of that research for the formation of social policies. That concept is known as *overlapping distributions.*

Basically, the term "overlapping distributions" refers to the fact that few differences between men and women appear to be absolute. Most differences are relative. For instance, although the average man is stronger than the average women, knowledge of a person's gender does not allow prediction of the level of that person's strength. The next case in point is even more relevant to the issues considered in this book: Knowledge about the average couple's sexual encounter masks important individual differences. Although the average man is more likely to take the sexual initiative than the average woman, some women are sexually assertive all of the time, and most initiate sex at least periodically.

The concept of overlapping distributions helps explain why social policies based on gender alone are inappropriate. Employment, educational, and therapeutic policies based on gender alone would be both discriminatory and unrealistic.

Besides governmental and scientific groups, there are many institutions whose policies may affect gender-role differentiation. Hospital policies, for instance, may either reflect the attitude that birth is an exclusively feminine process, or they may acknowledge appropriate participation of men in helping during the process of childbirth. Measures of the influence of differences in such policies might include the length and difficulty of labor for women whose labor is or is not attended by their mates, the extent of bonding between father and child, the likelihood of postpartum depression, and the degree of intimacy between new parents.

School policies, also, may encourage or inhibit gender-role differentiation. When the contributors to this text attended elementary and secondary school, no one questioned the rationale for separate physical education classes for girls and boys. As an obvious consequence, most of us were socialized to believe that the physical differences between the genders were so great that "delicate" girls would be at risk if they were forced to play with "rough" boys.

Thanks to recent changes in federal law, today's young people participate in coed physical education with the possible exceptions of contact sports and those activities in which it is reasonable to group students according to ability. Within the context of these coed gym classes, children and adolescents are beginning to question some of the time-honored gender differences that previous generations had accepted as a matter of course. Elementary school boys may be bounced around by the taller girls, who can play games even rougher than the boys do. When this happens, it will be difficult for both boys and girls to believe that boys are always stronger and more competent than girls. In the high schools, the challenge to traditional gender-role beliefs is even greater. Boys may have to swallow masculine pride if they lose out to girls when trying out for a team. (On the other hand, as one female member of a varsity high school team confided, male teammates may try to resurrect the female stereotype by discounting a girl's athletic abilities and attributing her success to being so pretty that she distracts the team's opponents.)

This is a time of transition for young people. In the absence of forced gender segregation in the schools, we may be raising the first generation that will be able to discriminate between real gender differences and differences that are the residuals of stereotyping.

Changes in employment practices, like those that have taken place in the educational system, may also alter gender-role differentiation and its concomitant relationship with sexual expression. Occupations may become less segregated according to gender, thanks in part to affirmative action programs. And such desegregation may contribute to less stereotyped relationships between men and women.

For example, male nurses, secretaries, and nursery school teachers do not fit social stereotypes. In much the same way, female truck drivers, military officers, and computer scientists also fly in the face of traditional gender-role expectations. The very existence of such people may do much to help society accept the fact that individual differences can and do wash out gender differences. As the acceptance of this reality increases, people will probably find it increasingly difficult to continue to perceive and experience sexuality along strictly gender-role traditional lines.

Consequences of Increased Participation in Multiple Roles

Researchers need to measure the effects or consequences of men's participation in areas traditionally assigned to women and of women's activities in spheres formally seen as the domain of men. A broad range of measures is possible here. For example, what are the consequences for children of being raised primarily by their mothers versus being raised jointly by both parents from infancy on? Such egalitarian patterns are relatively recent and still very difficult for many parents to achieve unless they happen to be in one of the few employment areas that permit flexible time schedules. Preliminary research indicates that children with working mothers are less stereotyped in their attitudes about gender roles. However, long-term comparisons need to be made between children with and without working mothers as well as between children who are exposed equally to care by both parents and those who are cared for exclusively by their mothers.

Similarly, such long-term comparisons are needed to assess the effects of role sharing on the quality of the marital relationship. Does such sharing increase the sense of intimacy and understanding between mates, or is an emphasis on differences important for continued attraction and intimacy? Hatfield's review of research on gender differences in the meaning attached to love and sex suggests that some of these differences may be more apparent than real. Nonetheless, the relationship between the belief that men and women differ in their desires concerning love and sex and in gender-role identifications needs to be examined. For example, the belief that women want more love and affection than do men may be more accurate among couples who follow traditional patterns in their division of labor. That is, if a woman remains alone (or with small children) in a house all day, she may strongly desire the stimulation and pleasure of contact with an adult and may look forward to her husband's return from work, anticipating discussion and affection. Is such a desire a characteristic of *women*, or is it a characteristic of people who have been relatively isolated all day?

Similarly, if a man is employed outside the home and is in contact with a variety of people all day, he may return from work feeling rather overstimulated. Home for him, then, is a haven where stimulation is reduced, and he may wish to avoid any intense interaction for a number of hours. Is this set of feelings characteristic of *men*, or is it a characteristic of people who interact with others all day long in their employment setting?

At this point, we don't have the answers to such questions, but changing employment patterns should begin to permit researchers to make some comparisons that would suggest the role of gender versus the role of lifestyle in differing perceptions of men and women.

Educational and Employment Practices

Finally, what is the influence of educational and occupational programs and policies on the development of individual potential? It has been suggested that women do not take education and employment as seriously as do men. There is no masculine parallel to the old saying that women go to college to get their "Mrs." degree. This stereotype is probably partially due to the fact that, traditionally, women are given the titles Miss or Mrs. so that their marital status may be immediately known. In any event, to the extent that people believe that women, compared to men, are less likely to make use of their educational training, admission to and financial support for that training has been less forthcoming for women. Because of such assumptions, one of us had difficulty getting into graduate school despite having test scores and grades higher than any of the other people (men) admitted to the graduate school that year. Such beliefs can function as self-fulfilling prophecies: why invest in education and career training if you aren't going to be taken seriously? Similarly, women may be bypassed for advancement in their employment settings because of the assumption that they will desert their jobs if they become pregnant, or if their husbands wish to transfer to another city.

However, increasing numbers of schools and employers are offering women equal opportunity. Research on the influence of these shifts is badly needed. In particular, what is the effect of such career development on family relationships? In addition, as Gutek and Nakamura note, greater inclusion of women in the workplace has been associated with changes in the work environment (see Chapter 8).

Other, more positive effects may include added pleasure in working with attractive people of the other gender. The consequence of greater contact between men and women in the workplace may be wide ranging, but very little research has been conducted on such effects. For instance, what happens to productivity and job satisfaction in employment settings populated mainly by men (or mainly by women) compared to employment settings populated by relatively equal numbers of men and women? Are extramarital affairs (mutually desired rather than coerced) more likely? Or are people in these settings more likely to learn that attractive individuals of the other gender can be very valuable (beyond their potential as sexual partners) as friends and trusted colleagues? Gutek and Nakamura and a few other researchers have been investigating some of the negative and positive aspects of having both genders in the workplace, but a great deal of work needs to be done with this newly emerging phenomenon.

A BEGINNING, NOT AN ENDING

It is an exciting time to be alive. Gender roles are changing and it seems likely that these changes will have a lasting impact on sexual expression.

There seems to be increasing social permission for people to assume androgynous lifestyles. With such permission, adults may become freer to experiment with new forms of intimate relationships. Indeed, homosexuals and single heterosexual adults have already begun such experimentation, as described in Chapters 9 and 10.

Individual needs, not gender-role norms, may pattern the sexual experiences of future generations. Nevertheless, such experimentation will probably be limited to those whose self-concepts are very secure. Less certain of their core gender identification, children and adolescents may be more likely than their elders to relate to one another along rigid gender-role lines. Continuing rigidity may be especially problematic during early adolescence, when girls stress the need to be well liked whereas boys are more likely to value success in all that they do (Rosenberg & Simmons, 1975). This assumption is consistent with the research described in Chapters 1 and 2.

In adulthood, too, it is likely that experiential variables such as differential exposure to sexual ideas and materials and variations in treatment within important social institutions (for example, the family, schools, peer groups, and the workplace) will moderate the extent to which gender roles and sexuality are expressed by each individual.

What is known today is tentative and subject to revision. A scientific understanding of the relationship between gender-role norms and sexuality is just emerging. We have enjoyed reviewing research and ideas on these topics, and we hope that much of what we have had to say will stimulate further observation and research. We also hope that future generations will have greater freedom for flexibility regarding the expression of their own personal characteristics and feelings. At times, this may mean that women and men will behave in ways very stereotypic of traditional gender-role norms. We hope, however, that a woman's nurturant, cooperative, or yielding behavior will be an expression of her *own* desires rather than the result of her fear of punishment if she doesn't or if she engages in more aggressive, independent, and sexually assertive behavior. Similarly, we hope that expressions of protectiveness and strength on the part of men will be freely chosen and that they will also be free to be tender and passive occasionally, as a function of how they accept such feelings in themselves. Such expressions of nurturance, protectiveness, and sexual feelings mean more to the actor and the recipient when they are freely chosen by the individual, regardless of gender, than when they are expected because of one's gender.

G L O S S A R Y

Key Concepts: Gender and Gender Role

Gender   A person's biological and anatomical sex. Chromosomes, genitals, and secondary sex characteristics contribute to the classification of a person as either male or female.

Gender differences   Ways in which males and females differ in behavior, appearance, or personality. Differences may be related to biological and/or cultural determinants.

Gender role and gender-role norms   Cultural prescriptions for masculinity and femininity. Socially approved ways of expressing that one is a boy/man or girl/woman.

Gender-role stereotypes   A simplified or standardized image of males and females. Gender-role stereotypes often fail to discriminate between true or observable gender differences and illusory differences based on unfounded assumptions.

Gender-role development or gender-role acquisition   Children and adolescents learn to adopt or reject culturally approved gender roles as a result of direct interactions, rewards, and punishments with peers and adults. Exposure to formal education and to the mass media also contributes to the development of gender roles.

Gender-role identification   Self-description of psychological gender. Extent to which an individual perceives self as masculine, feminine, or androgynous. *Masculine* people describe themselves as having personality traits stereotypic of boys or men in the society. *Feminine* people describe themselves as having personality traits stereotypic of girls or women. *Gender-typed* masculine and feminine people have psychological traits consistent with traits ascribed to their anatomical gender. *Gender-reversed* masculine and feminine people have psychological traits traditionally associated with the opposite anatomical gender. *Androgynous* people see themselves as possessing masculine and feminine psychological traits to an equal—and high—degree.

Gender-role attitudes   The extent to which an individual is *egalitarian* or *profeminist* (advocates women's liberation) versus *traditional* (believes that woman's place is in the home and that men should be primarily responsible for the decision making and economic support for the family) in their views about gender roles.

REFERENCES

Abel, G., Blanchard, E. B., Becker, J. V., & Djenderedjian, A. Differentiating sexual aggressiveness with penile measures. *Criminal Justice and Behavior*, 1978, *5*, 315–332.

Abelson, H., Cohen, R., Heaton, E., & Suder, C. National survey of public attitudes toward and experience with erotic materials. In *Technical report of the Commission on Obscenity and Pornography* (Vol. 6). Washington, D.C.: U.S. Government Printing Office, 1971.

Aberg, M., Small, P., & Watson, J. A. Males, fathers, and husbands: Changing roles and reciprocal legal rights. *Family Coordinator*, 1977, *26*, 327–332.

Abramson, P. R. *The sexual system: A theory of human sexual behavior.* New York: Academic Press, 1980.

Adams, M. *Single blessedness: Observations on the single status in married society.* New York: Basic Books, 1976.

Addiego, F., Belzer, E. G., Comolli, J., Moger, W., Perry, J. D., & Whipple, B. Female ejaculation: A case study. *Journal of Sex Research*, 1981, *17*, 13–21.

Alan Guttmacher Institute. *Teenage pregnancy: The problem that hasn't gone away.* New York: Alan Guttmacher Institute, 1981.

Alberti, R., & Emmons, M. *Your perfect right.* San Luis Obispo, Calif.: Impact Publications, 1978.

Albin, R. S. Psychological studies of rape. *Signs: Journal of Women in Culture and Society*, 1977, *3*, 423–435.

Allgeier, E. R. Beyond sowing and growing: The relationship of sex-typing to socialization, family plans, and future orientation. *Journal of Applied Social Psychology*, 1975, *5*, 217–226.

Allgeier, E. R. *Sexual and contraceptive socialization and attitudes among sex-typed and androgynous persons.* Paper presented at the World Population Society Meeting, Washington D.C., November 1975.

Allgeier, E. R., The influence of androgynous identification on heterosexual relations. *Sex Roles*, 1981, *7*, 321–330.

Allgeier, E. R., & Fogel, A. F. Coital position and sex roles: Responses to cross-sex behavior in bed. *Journal of Consulting and Clinical Psychology*, 1978, *46*, 588–589. (a)

304

References

Allgeier, E. R., & Fogel, A. F. Coital position and sex roles: Responses to cross-sex behavior in bed. Expanded version of an article that appeared in *Journal of Consulting and Clinical Psychology*, 1978. Unpublished manuscript, 1978. (Available from Dr. Elizabeth R. Allgeier, Department of Psychology, Bowling Green State University, Bowling Green, Ohio 43403). (b)

Allon, N., & Fishel, D. Singles bars as examples of urban courting patterns. In P. Stein (Ed.), *Single life: Unmarried adults in social context*. New York: St. Martin's Press, 1981.

Altman, I. Reciprocity of interpersonal exchange. *Journal for the Theory of Social Behavior*, 1973, *3*, 249–261.

Altman, I. & Taylor, D. A. *Social penetration: The development of interpersonal relationships*, New York: Holt, Rinehart & Winston, 1973.

Amir, M. *Patterns in forcible rape*. Chicago: University of Chicago Press, 1971.

Antonovsky, H. F., Shoham, I., Kavenaki, S., Lancet, M., & Modan, B. Gender differences in patterns of adolescent sexual behavior. *Journal of Youth and Adolescence*, 1980, *9*, 127–141.

Arafat, I., & Yorburg, B. On living together without marriage. *Journal of Sex Research*, 1973, *9*, 97–106.

Army begins to confront sexual harassment problem. *Los Angeles Times*, December 26, 1979, Pt. VII, pp. 4–5.

Ashworth, C. D., & Feldman-Summers, S. Perceptions of the effectiveness of the criminal justice system: The female victim's perspective. *Criminal Justice and Behavior*, 1978, *5*, 227–240.

Baker, M. J., *The effects of inequity on heterosexual behavior: A test for compensation in inequitable relationships*. Unpublished manuscript, Department of Sociology, University of Wisconsin, 1974.

Baldwin, W. H. Adolescent childbearing in the United States—1976. In *Adolescent pregnancy*. Hearing before the Subcommittee on Select Education, House of Representatives, Ninety-fifth Congress, Second Session, on H.R. 12146, July 24, 1978 (Stock No. 052-070-05549-9). Washington, D.C.: U.S. Government Printing Office, 1978. (a)

Baldwin, W. H. An overview of trends in adolescent pregnancy and childbearing. In *Fertility and contraception in America: Adolescent and pre-adolescent pregnancy*. Hearing before the Select Committee on Population, House of Representatives, Ninety-fifth Congress, Second Session, February 28, March 1, 2, 1978 [(No. 3) Vol. 2, Not for Sale]. Washington, D.C.: U.S. Government Printing Office, 1978. (b)

Baldwin, W., & Cain, V. S. The children of teenage parents. *Family Planning Perspectives*, 1980, *12*, 34–43.

Bandura, A., & Walters, R. H. *Social learning and personality development*. New York: Holt, Rinehart & Winston, 1963.

Barbach, L. G. *For yourself: The fulfillment of female sexuality*. New York: Doubleday, 1975.

Bard, M. The rape victim: Challenge to the helping systems. *Victimology*, 1976, *1*, 263–271.

Bardwick, J. *In transition*. New York: Holt, Rinehart & Winston, 1979.

Bardwick, J., & Douvan, E. Ambivalence: The socialization of women. In J. Bardwick (Ed.), *Readings on the psychology of women*. New York: Harper & Row, 1971.

Barry, H., & Paxson, L. M. Infancy and early childhood: Cross-cultural codes. *Ethnology*, 1971, *10*, 466–508.

Baruch, G. K., & Barnett, R. C. *Fathers' involvement in the care of their preschool children.* (Research Report, NIMH Grant MH-25215). Unpublished manuscript, 1978. (Available from Dr. Grace Baruch, Center for Research on Women, Wellesley College, Wellesley, MA 02181).

Bass, B., Krusall, J., & Alexander, R. A. Male managers' attitudes toward working women. *American Behavioral Scientist,* 1971, *15,* 220–236.

Bauman, K. E., & Wilson, R. R. Premarital sexual attitudes of unmarried university students. *Archives of Sexual Behavior,* 1976, *5,* 29–37.

Bazin, N. T., & Freeman, A. The androgynous vision. *Women's Studies,* 1974, *2,* 185–215.

Beck, A. Sexuality and depression. *Medical Aspects of Human Sexuality,* 1968, *2,* 44–51.

Bell, A. P., & Weinberg, M. S. *Homosexualities: A study of diversity among men and women.* New York: Simon & Schuster, 1978.

Bell, R. R. Changing aspects of marital sexuality. In S. Gordon & R. W. Libby (Eds.), *Sexuality today and tomorrow.* Belmont, Calif.: Wadsworth, 1976.

Bell, R. R. *Marriage and family interaction.* Homewood, Ill.: Dorsey Press, 1979.

Bell, R. *Changing bodies, changing lives: A book for teens on sex and relationships.* New York: Random House, 1980.

Belzer, E. G. Orgasmic expulsions of women: A review and heuristic inquiry. *The Journal of Sex Research,* 1981, *17,* 1–12.

Bem, D. J. Self-perception theory. In L. Berkowitz (Ed.), *Advances in experimental social psychology* (Vol. 6). New York: Academic Press, 1972.

Bem, S. L. *Psychology looks at sex roles: Where have all the androgynous people gone?* Paper presented at UCLA Symposium on Women, University of California, Los Angeles, May 1972.

Bem, S. L. The measurement of psychological androgyny. *Journal of Consulting and Clinical Psychology,* 1974, *42,* 155–162.

Bem, S. L. Sex-role adaptability: One consequence of psychological androgyny. *Journal of Personality and Social Psychology,* 1975, *31,* 634–643.

Bem, S. L. Probing the promise of androgyny. In A. G. Kaplan & J. P. Bean (Eds.), *Beyond sex role stereotypes: Readings toward a psychology of androgyny.* Boston: Little, Brown, 1976.

Benson, D. J., & Thomson, G. *Sexual harassment on a university campus: The confluence of authority relations, sexual interest and gender stratification.* Paper presented at the Annual Meeting of the American Sociological Association, New York, 1980.

Bequaert, L. H. *Single women: Alone and together.* Boston: Beacon Press, 1976.

Berg, D. H. Sexual subcultures and contemporary interaction patterns among adolescents. *Adolescence,* 1975, *10,* 543–548.

Berger, A. S., Gagnon, J. H., & Simon, W. Pornography: High school and college years. In *Technical report of the Commission on Obscenity and Pornography* (Vol. 9). Washington, D.C.: U.S. Government Printing Office, 1971.

Berkove, G. F. Perceptions of husband support by returning women students. *The Family Coordinator,* 1979, *28,* 451–458.

Bernard, J. *The future of marriage.* New York: Bantam Books, 1972.

Bernard, J. Sex-role transcendence and sex-role transcenders. In J. Bernard (Ed.), *Women, wives, mothers.* Chicago: Aldine, 1975.

References

Bernstein, A. *Flight of the stork*. New York: Delacorte Press, 1978.

Bernstein, A., & Cowen, P. Children's concepts of how people get babies. *Child Development*, 1975, *46*, 77–91.

Berzon, B., Morin, S. F., Rochlin, M., & Sang, B. *Panel discussion: Assessment and treatment issues in psychotherapy with lesbians and gay men*. F. Strassburger (Chair), Discussion presented at the meeting of the American Psychological Association, New York, September 1979.

Bird, C. The case against marriage. In L. K. Howe (Ed.), *The future of the family*. New York: Simon & Schuster, 1972.

Blasband, D., & Peplau, L. A. *Open and closed long-term relationships of gay men: A comparative study*. Unpublished manuscript, Department of Psychology, University of California, Los Angeles, 1980.

Blau, F. D. Women in the labor force: An overview. In J. Freeman (Ed.), *Women: A feminist perspective* (2nd ed.). Palo Alto, Calif.: Mayfield, 1979.

Blau, Z. S. *Old age in a changing society*. New York: Watts, 1973.

Bloch, I. *Anthropological studies in the strange sexual practices of all races in all ages, ancient and modern, oriental and occidental, primitive and civilized*. (K. Wallis, trans.). New York: AMS, 1974. (Originally published 1902, translated 1933.)

Block, J. Conceptions of sex-role: Some cross-cultural and longitudinal perspectives. *American Psychologist*, 1973, *28*, 512–526.

Bloom, L., Coburn, K., & Pearlman, J. *The new assertive woman*. New York: Delacorte Press, 1975.

Bohmer, C. Judicial attitudes toward rape victims. *Judicature*, 1974, *57*, 303–307.

Borgida, E. Evidentiary reform of rape laws: A psycholegal approach. In P. D. Lipsett & B. D. Sales (Eds.), *New directions in psycholegal research*. Cincinnati: Van Nostrand Reinhold, 1978.

Boston Women's Health Book Collective. *Our bodies, ourselves* (2nd ed.). New York: Simon & Schuster, 1976.

Botwinick, J. *Aging and behavior*. New York: Springer, 1978.

Bower, D. W. *A description and analysis of a cohabiting sample in America*. Unpublished master's thesis, University of Arizona, 1975. Cited in E. Macklin, Review of research on nonmarital cohabitation in the U.S., in B. I. Murstein (Ed.), *Exploring intimate life styles*. New York: Springer, 1978.

Bower, S. A., & Bower, G. H. *Asserting yourself: A practical guide for positive change*. Reading, Mass.: Addison-Wesley, 1976.

Broderick, C. Sociosexual development in a suburban community. *Journal of Sex Research*, 1966, *2*, 1–24.

Broderick, C. B. *Marriage and the family*. Englewood Cliffs, N.J.: Prentice-Hall, 1979.

Brodyaga, L., Gates, M., Singer, S., Tucker, M., & White, R. *Rape and its victims: A report for citizens, health facilities, and criminal justice agencies*. Washington, D.C.: U.S. Government Printing Office, 1975.

Brooks, N. Rape and the laws of evidence. *Chitty's Law Journal*, 1975, *23*, 1–11.

Brooks-Gunn, J., & Matthews, W. S. *He & she*. Englewood Cliffs, N.J.: Prentice-Hall, 1979.

Broverman, I., Vogel, S., Broverman, D., Clarkson, F., & Rosenkrantz, P. Sex role stereotypes: A current appraisal. *Journal of Social Issues*, 1972, *28*, 59–78.

Brownmiller, S. *Against our will: Men, women, and rape.* New York: Simon & Schuster, 1975.

Bunch, C. Learning from lesbian separatism. In S. Ruth (Ed.), *Issues in feminism: A first course in women's studies.* Boston: Houghton Mifflin, 1980.

Burgess, A. W., & Holmstrom, L. L. Rape trauma syndrome. *American Journal of Psychiatry,* 1974, *131,* 981–986.

Burgess, A. W., & Holmstrom, L. L. Rape: Disclosure to parental family members. *Women and Health,* 1979, *4,* 255–269.

Burt, M. R. Cultural myths and supports for rape. *Journal of Personality and Social Psychology,* 1980, *38,* 217–230.

Butler, R. N., & Lewis, M. I. *Aging and mental health.* St. Louis: Mosby, 1973.

Byrne, D. Some inconsistencies in the effect of motivation arousal on humor preferences. *Journal of Abnormal and Social Psychology,* 1961, *62,* 158–160.

Byrne, D. Social psychology and the study of sexual behavior. *Personality and Social Psychology Bulletin,* 1977, *3,* 3–30.

Byrne, D. The imagery of sex. In J. Money & H. Musaph (Eds.), *Handbook of sexology.* New York: Elsevier, 1978.

Byrne, D., & Byrne, L. *Exploring human sexuality.* New York: Crowell, 1977.

Byrne, D. & Fisher, W. A. (Eds.), *Adolescents, sex, and contraception.* New York: Erlbaum, 1982.

Byrne, D., & Lamberth, J. The effect of erotic stimuli on sex arousal, evaluative responses, and subsequent behavior. In *Technical report of the Commission on Obscenity and Pornography* (Vol. 8). Washington, D.C.: U.S. Government Printing Office, 1971.

Caldwell, M., & Peplau, L. A. *Power in lesbian relationships.* Unpublished manuscript, Department of Psychology, University of California, Los Angeles, 1980.

Calhoun, L. G., Selby, J. W., & Warring, L. J. Social perception of the victim's causal role in rape: An exploratory examination of four factors. *Human Relations,* 1976, *29,* 517–526.

Califia, P. Lesbian sexuality. *Journal of Homosexuality,* 1979, *4,* 255–266.

Campbell, A. K. Policy statement and definition of sexual harassment. *Women in Action,* 1980, *10,* 2.

Canby, V. Sleeper (Review of *Sleeper* by W. Allen). *New York Times,* December 18, 1973, p. 52.

Cann, A., Calhoun, L., & Selby, J. W. Attributing responsibility to the victim of rape: Influence of information regarding past sexual experience. *Human Relations,* 1979, *32,* 56–67.

Cardell, M., Finn, S., & Marecek, J. Sex-role identity, sex-role behavior, and satisfaction in heterosexual, lesbian, and gay male couples. *Psychology of Women Quarterly,* 1981, *5,* 488–494.

Carlson, J. The sexual role. In F. I. Nye (Ed.), *Role structure and analysis of the family.* Beverly Hills, Calif.: Sage, 1976.

Chaikin, A. L., & Derlega, V. J. *Sharing intimacy: What we reveal to others and why.* Englewood Cliffs, N. J.: Prentice-Hall, 1975.

Chappell, D., Geis, G., & Fogarty, F. Forcible rape: Bibliography. *Journal of Criminal Law and Criminology,* 1974, *65,* 295–304.

Chesler, J. Personal communication, March 1979.

Chesler, P. *Women and madness.* New York: Doubleday, 1972.

References

Chilman, C. S. Poverty and family planning in the United States. *Welfare in Review*, 1967, *5*, 3–15.

Chilman, C. S. *Adolescent sexuality in a changing American society: Social and psychological perspectives* (U.S. Department of Health, Education, and Welfare Publication No. NIH 79-1426). Washington, D.C.: U.S. Government Printing Office, 1979.

Chiriboga, D. A., & Cutler, L. Stress responses among divorcing men and women. *Journal of Divorce*, 1977, *1*, 95–106.

Christenson, C. V., & Gagnon, J. H. Sexual behavior in a group of older women. *Journal of Gerontology*, 1965, *20*, 351–356.

Clanton, G., & Smith, L. G. (Eds.). *Jealousy.* Englewood Cliffs, N. J.: Prentice-Hall, 1977.

Clark, L. Group rape in Vancouver and Toronto. *Canada's Mental Health*, 1980, *28*, 9–12.

Clark, L., & Armstrong, S. *A rape bibliography. With special emphasis on rape research in Canada*. Ministry of the Solicitor General of Canada, Communication Division: Ottawa, 1979.

Clark, L., & Lewis, D. *Rape: The price of coercive sexuality*. Toronto: Women's Educational Press, 1977.

Clark, R. A. The projective measurement of experimentally induced levels of sexual motivation. *Journal of Experimental Psychology*, 1952, *44*, 391–399.

Clark, R. D., III, & Hatfield, E. *Gender differences in receptivity to sexual offers*. Unpublished manuscript, 1981. (Available from Dr. Elaine Hatfield, Psychology Department, 2430 Campus Road, Honolulu, HI 96822).

Clarkson, F. E., Vogel, S. R., Broverman, I. K., Broverman, D. M., & Rosenkrantz, P. S. Family size and sex role stereotypes. *Science*, 1970, *167*, 390–392.

Clayton, R. R., & Voss, H. L. Shacking up: Cohabitation in the 1970s. *Journal of Marriage and the Family*, 1977, *39*, 273–283.

Cleveland, M. Sexuality in the middle years. In P. Stein (Ed.), *Single life: Unmarried adults in social context*. New York: St. Martin's Press, 1981.

Coale, A. J. The history of the human population. *Scientific American*, 1974, *231*, 40–51.

Cochran, S. D. *Romantic relationships: For better or for worse*. Paper presented at the annual meeting of the Western Psychological Association, San Francisco, April 1978.

Cohen, J. Male roles in mid-life. *Family Coordinator*, 1979, *28*, 465–471.

Cohen, M. L., Garofalo, R., Boucher, R., & Seghorn, T. The psychology of rapists. *Seminars in Psychiatry*, 1971, *3*, 302–327.

Cole, J. B., & Allen, F. C. I. Contraceptive responsibility among male university students. *Journal of the American College Health Association*, 1979, *28*, 168–172.

Coleman, J. S., Female status and premarital sexual codes. *American Journal of Sociology*, 1966, *72*, 217.

Collins, B. E., & Raven, B. H. Group structure: Attraction, coalition, communication, and power. In G. Lindzey & E. Aronson (Eds.), *The Handbook of social psychology* (2nd ed., Vol. 4). Reading, Mass.: Addison-Wesley, 1968.

Comfort, A. (Ed.). *The joy of sex. A gourmet guide to love making*. New York: Simon & Schuster, 1972.

Commission on Obscenity and Pornography. *The report of the Commission on Obscenity and Pornography*. Washington, D.C.: U.S. Government Printing Office, 1970.

Connell, N., & Wilsen, C. (Eds.). *Rape: The first sourcebook for women*. New York: New American Library, 1974.

Cooper, A. J. Some personality factors in frigidity. *Journal of Psychosomatic Research*, 1969, *13*, 149–155.

Corradino, M. A. *Comparative study of younger and older fathers' sex-role orientations, personal and marital adjustments, parental childrearing attitudes, and fathering behaviors*. Unpublished doctoral dissertation, California School of Professional Psychology, Los Angeles, 1978.

Costrich, N., Feinstein, J., Kidder, L., Marecek, J., & Pascale, L. When stereotypes hurt: Three studies of penalties for sex-role reversals. *Journal of Experimental Social Psychology*, 1975, *11*, 520–530.

Cozby, P. C. Self-disclosure: A literature review. *Psychological Bulletin*, 1973, *79*, 73–91.

Crain, S., & Roth, S. *Interactional and interpretive processes in sexual initiation in married couples*. Paper presented at the meeting of the American Psychological Association, San Francisco, August 1977.

Crandall, E. Personal communication, June 1980.

Critchfield, R. Sex in the third world. In C. Gordon & G. Johnson (Eds.), *Readings in human sexuality: Contemporary perspectives* (2nd ed.). New York: Harper & Row, 1980 .

Curran, J. P. Convergence toward a single sexual standard? In D. Byrne & L. A. Byrne (Eds.), *Exploring human sexuality*. New York: Crowell, 1977.

Cvetkovich, G., & Grote, B. *Current research on adolescence and its program implications*. Paper presented at joint meeting of the Washington State Council on Family Planning and the Washington Alliance Concerned with School-Age Parents, Olympia, Washington, September 1977.

Cvetkovich, G., Grote, B., Lieberman, E. J., & Miller, W. Sex role development and teenage fertility-related behavior. *Adolescence*, 1978, *13*, 231–236.

Daly, M., & Wilson, M. *Sex, evolution, and behavior. Adaptations for reproduction*. North Scituate, Mass.: Duxbury Press, 1978.

Danyiger, K. Mothers' and fathers' roles: Is the mother of young children really liberated? *Nursing Times* (London), 1978, *74*, 1788–1789.

Datan, N., & Lohmann, N. *Transitions of aging*. New York: Academic Press, 1980.

David, D. S., & Brannon, R. (Eds.). *The forty-nine percent majority: The male sex role*. Menlo Park, Calif.: Addison-Wesley, 1976.

Davidson, L., & Kramer-Gordon, L. *The sociology of gender*. Chicago: Rand McNally, 1979.

Davis, J. B., & Skinner, A. E. Reciprocity of self-disclosure in interviews: Modeling of social exchange. *Journal of Personality and Social Psychology*, 1974, *29*, 779–784.

Davis, K. Population policy: Will current programs succeed? *Science*, 1967, *158*, 730–739.

Deaux, K., & Emswiller, T. Explanation of successful performance on sex-linked tasks: What is skill for the male is luck for the female. *Journal of Personality and Social Psychology*, 1974, *20*, 80–85.

Deckard, B. S. *The women's movement*. New York: Harper & Row, 1975.

DeFrain, J. Androgynous parents tell who they are and what they need. *Family Coordinator*, 1979, *28*, 237–243.

Degler, C. *At odds: Women and family in America from the revolution to the present*. New York: Oxford University Press, 1980.

References

DeLamater, J., & MacCorquodale, P. *Premarital sexuality: Attitudes, relationships, behavior.* Madison: University of Wisconsin Press, 1979.

DeLora, J. S., & Warren, C. A. B. *Understanding sexual interaction.* Boston: Houghton Mifflin, 1977.

DeMartino, M. F. Dominance-feeling, security-insecurity, and sexuality in women. In M. F. DeMartino (Ed.), *Sexual behavior and personality characteristics.* New York: Grove Press, 1963.

Deutsch, H. *The psychology of women: A psychoanalytic interpretation* (Vol. 1). New York: Grune & Stratton, 1944.

Deutsch, H. *The psychology of women: A psychoanalytic interpretation* (Vol. 2). New York: Grune & Stratton, 1945.

Diepold, J., Jr., & Young, R. D. Empirical studies of adolescent sexual behavior: A critical review. *Adolescence,* 1979, *14,* 45–64.

Dinnerstein, D. *The mermaid and the minotaur: Sexual arrangements in human malaise.* New York: Harper Colophon Books, 1977.

Dion, K. L., & Dion, K. K. Correlates of romantic love. *Journal of Consulting and Clinical Psychology,* 1973, *41,* 51–56.

Dion, K. L., & Dion, K. K. Personality and behavioral correlates of romantic love. In M. Cook & G. Wilson (Eds.), *Love and attraction: An international conference.* New York: Pergamon, 1979.

Dolan, M. They skip class to avoid sex. *San Francisco Examiner,* July 21, 1977, p. 1.

Do men like women to be sexually assertive? *Medical Aspects of Human Sexuality,* 1977, *11,* 36; 41–44; 50–51.

Donnerstein, E. Pornography and violence against women: Experimental studies. *Annals of the New York Academy of Sciences,* 1980, *347,* 277–288.

Doudna, C., & McBride, F. Where are the men for the women at the top? In P. Stein (Ed.), *Single life: Unmarried adults in social context.* New York: St. Martin's Press, 1981.

Dryfoos, J. G., & Belmont, L. *The intellectual and behavioral status of children born to adolescent mothers* (Final report to National Institute of Child, Health, and Human Development, U.S. Department of Health, Education, and Welfare, November 1979). Bethesda, Md.: Center for Population Research, 1979.

Dukes, R. L., & Mattley, C. L. Predicting rape victim reportage. *Sociology and Social Research,* 1977, *62,* 63–84.

Eagly, A. H., & Anderson, P. Sex role and attitudinal correlates of desired family size. *Journal of Applied Social Psychology,* 1974, *4,* 151–164.

Ehrmann, W. *Premarital dating behavior.* New York: Holt, Rinehart & Winston, 1959.

Eitner, L. The erotic in art. In H. A. Katchadourian & D. T. Lunde, *Fundamentals of human sexuality* (2nd ed.). New York: Holt, Rinehart & Winston, 1975.

Elias, J., & Gebhard, P. Sexuality and sexual learning in childhood. *Phi Delta Kappan,* 1969, *50,* 401–405.

Elkind, D. Egocentrism in adolescence. *Child Development,* 1967, *38,* 1025–1034.

Erikson, E. *Identity, youth and crisis.* New York: Norton, 1968.

Erikson, E. H. *Childhood and society* (Rev. ed.). New York: Norton, 1968.

Etaugh, C. Effects of nonmaternal care on children: Research evidence and popular views. *American Psychologist,* 1980, *35,* 309–319.

Executive sweet. *Time,* October 8, 1979, p. 76.

Eysenck, H. Introverts, extroverts, and sex. *Psychology Today*, 1971, *4*, 48–51; 82.

Eysenck, H. L. Personality and sexual behavior. *Journal of Psychosomatic Research*, 1972, *16*, 141–152.

Falbo, T., Graham, J. S., & Gryskiewicz, S. S. Sex roles and fertility in college women. *Sex Roles*, 1978, *4*, 845–851.

Farley, L. *Sexual shakedown*. New York: McGraw-Hill, 1978.

Farrell, W. *The liberated man*. New York: Random House, 1974.

Federal Bureau of Investigation. *Uniform crime reports*. Washington, D.C.: U.S. Government Printing Office, 1977.

Feild, H. S. Attitudes toward rape: A comparative analysis of police, rapists, crisis counselors, and citizens. *Journal of Personality and Social Psychology*, 1978, *36*, 156–179.

Feldman, S. Impediment or stimulant? Marital status and graduate education. *American Journal of Sociology*, 1973, *78*, 982–995.

Feldman-Summers, S., & Lindner, K. Perceptions of victims and defendants in criminal assault cases. *Criminal Justice and Behavior*, 1976, *3*, 1–14.

Fengler, A. P. Attitudinal orientation of wives toward their husbands' retirement. *International Journal of Aging and Human Development*, 1975, *6*, 149–152.

Firestone, S. The dialectic of sex. New York: Bantam Morrow, 1971.

Fisher, S. *The female orgasm*. New York: Basic Books, 1973.

Fisher, W. A., & Byrne, D. Individual differences in affective, evaluative, and behavioral responses to an erotic film. *Journal of Applied Social Psychology*, 1978, *8*, 355–365. (a)

Fisher, W. A., & Byrne, D. Sex differences in response to erotica? Love versus lust. *Journal of Personality and Social Psychology*, 1978, *36*, 117–125. (b)

Fisher, W. A., & Byrne, D. Social background, attitudes, and sexual attraction. In M. Cook (Ed.), *The bases of human sexual attraction*. New York: Academic Press, 1981.

Fisher, W. A., Byrne, D., Edmunds, M., Miller, T. C., Kelley, K., & White, L. A. Psychological and situation-specific correlates of contraceptive behavior among university women. *Journal of Sex Research*, 1979, *15*, 38–55.

Fiske, M. *Middle age: The prime of life?* New York: Harper & Row, 1979.

Ford, C. S., & Beach, F. A. *Patterns of sexual behavior*. New York: Harper & Row, 1951.

Foucault, M. *The order of things*. New York: Random House, 1973.

Fox, G. L. "Nice Girl": Social control of women through a value construct. *Signs*, 1977, *2*, 805–817.

Fox, G. L. The family's influence on adolescent sexual behavior. *Children Today*, 1979, *8*, 21–25.

Fox, G. L. The mother-adolescent daughter relationship as a sexual socialization structure: A research review. *Family Relations*, 1980, *29*, 21–28.

Franzwa, H. H. Females' role in women's magazine fiction, 1940–1970. In R. Unger & F. Denmark (Eds.), *Woman: Dependent or independent variable?* New York: Psychological Dimensions, 1975.

Freedman, J., Sears, D., & Carlsmith, M. *Social psychology* (3rd ed.). Englewood Cliffs, N. J.: Prentice-Hall, 1978.

French, J. R., Jr., & Raven, B. H. The bases of social power. In D. Cartwright (Ed.), *Studies in social power*. Ann Arbor: University of Michigan Press, 1959.

Freud, S. [Certain neurotic mechanisms in jealousy, paranoia, and homosexuality.] In *Collected papers* (Vol. 2.), (J. Riviere & A. R. J. Stachey, trans.). London: Hogarth Press and Institute of Psychoanalysis, 1922.

References

Freud, S. [*New introductory lectures in psychoanalysis*] (J. Strachey, Ed. and trans.). New York: Norton, 1965. (Originally published 1933.)

Freud, S. [The transformations of puberty.] In A. A. Brill (Ed. and trans.), *The basic writings of Sigmund Freud.* New York: Random House, 1938.

Frieze, I. H. *Causes and consequences of marital rape.* Paper presented at the annual meeting of the American Psychological Association, Montreal, September 1980.

Frieze, I. H., Parsons, J. E., Johnson, P. B., Ruble, D. N., & Zellman, G. L. *Women and sex roles.* New York: Norton, 1978.

Frodi, A., Macaulay, J., & Thome, P. R. Are women always less aggressive than men? A review of the experimental literature. *Pscyhological Bulletin*, 1977, *84*, 634–660.

Fromm, E. *Escape from freedom.* New York: Holt, Rinehart and Winston, 1963.

Fry, W. F. Psychodynamics of sexual humor: Seduction. *Medical Aspects of Human Sexuality*, 1977, *11*, 64; 69–71.

Fulero, S. M., & Delara, C. Rape victims and attributed responsibility: A defensive attribution approach. *Victimology*, 1976, *1*, 551–563.

Fuller, M. *Sexual harassment: How to recognize and deal with it.* Annapolis, Md.: What Would Happen If . . . Publisher, 1979.

Gadpaille, W. *The cycles of sex.* (L. Freeman, Ed.). New York: Scribner's, 1975.

Gagnon, J. Sexuality and sexual learning in the child. *Psychiatry*, 1965, *28*, 212–228.

Gagnon, J. H. *Human sexualities.* Glenview, Ill.: Scott, Foresman, 1977.

Gagnon, J. H., & Roberts, E. J. *Content and process in parental verbal communication about sexuality to preadolescent children* (Project on Human Sexual Development). Unpublished manuscript, Harvard University, 1980.

Gagnon, J. H., & Simon, W. *Sexual conduct: The social sources of human sexuality.* Chicago: Aldine, 1973.

Garblik, P. B. *Acceptance or rejection of sex-role stereotypes as a factor in adolescent female sexual behavior and use of contraception.* Unpublished doctoral dissertation, Education Department, University of Cincinnati, 1978.

Gebhard, P. H. Postmarital coitus among widows and divorcees. In P. Bohannan (Ed.), *Divorce and after.* New York: Doubleday, 1968.

Gebhard, P., Gagnon, J., Pomeroy, W., & Christenson, C. V. *Sex offenders: An analysis of types.* New York: Harper & Row, 1965.

Gelles, R. J. Power, sex, and violence: The case of marital rape. *Family Coordinator*, 1977, *26*, 339–347.

Gibson, I. *The English vice: Beating sex and shame in Victorian England and after.* London: Duckworth, 1978.

Gilder, G. *Sexual suicide.* New York: Quadrangle, 1973.

Gilder, G. *Naked nomads: Unmarried men in America.* New York: Quadrangle, 1974.

Gillespie, D. L. Who has the power? The marital struggle. *Journal of Marriage and the Family*, 1971, *33*, 445–458.

Ginsberg, G. L., Frosch, W. A., & Shapiro, T. The new impotence. *Archives of General Psychiatry*, 1972, *26*, 218–220.

Glenn, N. D., & Weaver, C. N. Attitudes toward premarital, extramarital, and homosexual relations in the U.S. in the 1970s. *Journal of Sex Research*, 1979, *15*, 108–118.

Glick, P. A demographer looks at American families. *Journal of Marriage and the Family*, 1975, *37*, 15–26.

Glick, P. Updating the life cycle. *Journal of Marriage and the Family*, 1977, *31*, 5–13.

Glick, P. C., & Norton, A. J. Marrying, divorcing, and living together in the U.S. today. *Population Bulletin*, 1979, *32*, 1–41.

Glick, P., & Spanier, G. Married and unmarried cohabitation in the United States. *Journal of Marriage and the Family*, 1980, *42*, 19–30.

Gold, D., & Andres, D. Comparisons of adolescent children with employed and nonemployed mothers. *Merrill-Palmer Quarterly*, 1978, *24*, 243–254.

Goldberg, P. A., Gottesdiener, M., & Abramson, P. R. Another put-down of women? Perceived attractiveness as a function of support for the feminist movement. *Journal of Personality and Social Psychology*, 1975, *32*, 113–115.

Goodchilds, J. Personal communication, July 20, 1980.

Gordon, M. The ideal husband as depicted in the nineteenth-century marriage manual. In E. H. Pleck & J. H. Pleck (Eds.), *The American man*. Englewood Cliffs, N.J.: Prentice-Hall, 1980.

Gough, H. *California psychological inventory: Manual*. Palo Alto, Calif.: Consulting Psychologists Press, 1964.

Gough, H. G. Some factors related to men's stated willingness to use a male contraceptive pill. *Journal of Sex Research*, 1979, *15*, 27–37.

Gove, W. R. The relationship between sex roles, marital status, and mental illness. *Social Forces*, 1972, *51*, 34–44.

Green, C., & Green, G. *S-M: The last taboo*. New York: Grove Press, 1973.

Green, R. Patterns of sexual identity in childhood. Relationship to subsequent sexual partner preference. In J. Marmor (Ed.), *Homosexual behavior*. New York: Basic Books, 1980.

Green, S. K., & Sandos, P. *Perceptions of male and female initiators of relationships*. Paper presented at the meeting of the American Psychological Association, Montreal, September 1980.

Greenberg, J. B. Single-parenting and intimacy: A comparison of mothers and fathers. *Alternative Lifestyles*, 1979, *2*, 308–330.

Greer, G. *The female eunuch*. New York: McGraw-Hill, 1971.

Griffitt, W. Response to erotica and the projection of response to erotica in the opposite sex. *Journal of Experimental Research in Personality*, 1973, *6*, 330–338.

Griffitt, W., & Hatfield, E. Gender identities and gender roles: Psychosocial determinants, in *Psychology of sexual behavior*. Glenview, Ill.: Scott, Foresman, in press.

Griffitt, W., & Kaiser, D. L. Affect, sex guilt, gender, and the rewarding-punishing effects of erotic stimuli. *Journal of Personality and Social Psychology*, 1978, *36*, 850–858.

Griffitt, W., May, J., & Veitch, R. Sexual stimulation and interpersonal behavior: Heterosexual evaluative responses, visual behavior, and physical proximity. *Journal of Personality and Social Psychology*, 1974, *30*, 367–377.

Gross, A. E. The male role and heterosexual behavior. *Journal of Social Issues*, 1978, *34*, 87–107.

Groth, A. N. *Men who rape: The psychology of the offender*. New York: Plenum Press, 1979.

Groth, A. N., Burgess, A. W., & Holmstrom, L. L. Rape: Power, anger and sexuality. *American Journal of Psychiatry*, 1977, *134*, 1239–1243.

Guittar, E. C., & Lewis, R. A. *Self-concepts among some unmarried cohabitants*. Unpublished

References

manuscript, Pennsylvania State University, 1974. Cited in E. Macklin, Review of research on nonmarital cohabitation in the U.S., in B. I. Murstein (Ed.), *Exploring intimate lifestyles*. New York: Springer, 1978.

Gundlach, R. H., & Reiss, B. F. Self and sexual identity in the female: A study of female homosexuals. In B. F. Reiss (Ed.), *New directions in mental health* (Vol. 1). New York: Grune & Stratton, 1968.

Gutek, B. A. Experiences in sexual harassment: Results from a representative survey. In S. Tangri (Chair), *Sexual harassment at work: Evidence, remedies, and implications*. Symposium presented at the annual American Psychological Association Convention, Los Angeles, August 1981. (Available on ERIC microfiche, no. ED 210 568).

Gutek, B. A. *Sexuality at work: An empirical analysis*. Book in preparation. (Available from B. Gutek, Ph.D., Department of Psychology, Claremont Graduate School, Claremont, CA 91711).

Gutek, B. A., & Morasch, B. Sex-ratios, sex-role spillover, and sexual harassment at work. *Journal of Social Issues*, under review.

Gutek, B. A., Nakamura, C. Y., Gahart, M., Handschumacher (Jensen), I., & Russell, D. Sexuality and the workplace. *Basic and Applied Social Psychology*, 1980, *1* (3), 255–265.

Hacker, H. M. Gender roles from a cross-cultural perspective. In L. Duberman (Ed.), *Gender and sex in society*. New York: Praeger, 1975.

Hagen, R. *The bio-sexual factor*. New York: Doubleday, 1979.

Hansson, R. O., Chernovetz, M. E., & Jones, W. H. Maternal employment and androgyny. *Psychology of Women Quarterly*, 1977, 2, 76–78.

Harmetz, A. Actresses just fade away at 40. *Buffalo Courier Express*, January 27, 1980, p. C-1.

Harry, J. On the validity of typologies of gay males. *Journal of Homosexuality*, 1976, 2, 143–152.

Harry, J. Marriage among gay males: The separation of intimacy and sex. In S. G. McNall (Ed.), *The sociological perspectives: Introductory readings* (4th ed.). Boston: Little, Brown, 1977.

Harry, J. The "marital" liaisons of gay men. *Family Coordinator*, 1979, *28*, 616–621.

Harry, J., & DeVall, W. *The social organization of gay males*. New York: Praeger, 1978.

Harry, J., & Lovely, R. Gay marriages and communities of sexual orientation. *Alternative Life Styles*, 1979, 2, 177–200.

Hass, A. *Teenage sexuality*. New York: Macmillan, 1979.

Hatcher, P. A., et al. *Contraceptive technology, 1980–81* (10th ed.). New York: Irvington, 1980.

Hatfield, E., Sprecher, S., & Traupmann, J. Men's and women's reactions to sexually explicit films: A serendipitous finding. *Archives of Sexual Behavior*, 1978, 7, 542–583.

Hatfield, E., & Traupmann, J. Intimate relationships: A perspective from equity theory. In S. Duck & R. Gilmour (Eds.), *Personal relationships*. London: Academic Press, 1980.

Hatfield, E., Traupmann, J., Sprecher, S., Greenberger, D., & Wexler, P. *Male/female differences in concern with intimacy, variety, and power in the sexual relationship*. Unpublished manuscript, 1981. (Available from Dr. E. Hatfield, 2430 Campus Rd., Honolulu, HI 96822).

Hatfield, E., Utne, M. K., & Traupmann, J. Equity theory and intimate relationships. In R. Burgess & T. L. Huston (Eds.), *Social exchange in developing relationships*. New York: Academic Press, 1979.

Hatfield, E., & Walster, G. W. *A new look at love*. Reading, Mass.: Addison-Wesley, 1981.

Hatfield, E., Walster, G. W., & Traupmann, J. Equity and premarital sex. In M. Cook & G.

Wilson (Eds.), *Love and attraction: An international conference*. New York: Pergamon Press, 1979. (Reprinted from *Journal of Personality and Social Psychology*, 1978, *37*, 82–92.)

Hatkoff, T. S., & Lasswell, T. E. Male-female similarities and differences in conceptualizing love. In M. Cook & G. Wilson (Eds.), *Love and attraction: An international conference*. New York: Pergamon Press, 1979.

Hayman, A. Legal challenges to discrimination against men. In D. Davis & R. Brannon (Eds.), *The forty-nine percent majority: The male sex role*. Reading, Mass.: Addison-Wesley, 1976.

Hefner, R., Rebecca, M., & Oleshans, O. Development of sex-role transcendence. *Human Development*, 1975, *18*, 143–158.

Heiman, J. P. The physiology of erotica: Women's sexual arousal. *Psychology Today*, 1975, *8*, 90–94.

Heiman, J. P. A psychophysiological exploration of sexual arousal patterns in females and males. *Psychophysiology*, 1977, *14*, 266–274.

Heiss, J. (Ed.), *Family roles and interaction*. Chicago: Rand McNally, 1968.

Herold, E. S., & Goodwin, M. S. Self-esteem and sexual permissiveness. *Journal of Clinical Psychology*, 1979, *35*, 908–912.

Hersh, B. G. A partnership of equals: Feminist marriages in 19th-century America. In E. H. Pleck & J. H. Pleck (Eds.), *The American man*. Englewood Cliffs, N. J.: Prentice-Hall, 1980.

Higginbotham, E. Is marriage a priority? Class differences in marital options of educated black women. In P. Stein (Ed.), *Single Life: Unmarried adults in social context*. New York: St. Martin's Press, 1981.

Hill, C. T., Rubin, Z., & Peplau, L. A. Breakups before marriage: The end of 103 affairs. *Journal of Social Issues*, 1976, *32*, 147–168.

Hill C. T., Rubin, Z., Peplau, L. A., & Willard, S. G. The volunteer couple: Sex differences, couple commitment and participation in research on interpersonal relationships. *Social Psychology Quarterly*, 1979, *42*, 415–420.

Hiltz, S. R. *Creating community services for widows*. Port Washington, N.Y.: Kennikat Press, 1977.

Hindelang, M. J., & Davis, B. L. Forcible rape in the United States: A statistical profile. In D. Chappell, R. Geis, and G. Geis (Eds.), *Forcible rape: The crime, the victim, and the offender*. New York: Columbia University Press, 1977.

Hite, S. *The Hite report*. New York: Macmillan, 1976.

Hite, S. *The Hite report on male sexuality*. New York: Knopf, 1981.

Hobart, C. W. The incidence of romanticism during courtship. *Social Forces*, 1958, *36*, 362–367.

Hoffman, L. W. Effects of the employment of mothers on parental power relations and the division of household tasks. *Marriage and Family Living*, 1960, *22*, 27–35.

Hooper, J. O. My wife, the student. *Family Coordinator*, 1979, *28*, 459–464.

Hopkins, J. R. Sexual behavior in adolescence. *Journal of Social Issues*, 1977, *33*, 67–85.

Horner, M. S. Toward an understanding of achievement related conflicts in women. *Journal of Social Issues*, 1972, *28*, 157–176.

Horney, K. Flight from womanhood, *International Journal of Psychoanalysis*, 1926, *7*, 324–339.

Hornick, J. P., Doran, L., & Crawford, S. H. Premarital contraceptive usage among male and female adolescents. *Family Coordinator*, 1979, *28*, 181–190.

Houseknecht, S. K. Voluntary childlessness: A social psychological model. *Alternative Lifestyles*, 1978, *1*, 379–402.

316

References

Huesmann, L. R., & Levinger, G. Incremental exchange theory: A formal model for progression in dyadic social interaction. In L. Berkowitz & E. Walster (Eds.), *Advances in Experimental Social Psychology* (Vol. 9). New York: Academic Press, 1976.

Hunt, M. *Sexual behavior in the 1970s.* Chicago: Playboy Press, 1974.

Hunt, M. & Hunt, B. Patterns and potentials for the single parent relationships. In S. Burden, P. Huston, E. Kripke, R. Simpson, & W. F. Stultz (Eds.), *Single Parent Family Proceedings of the Changing Family Conference V.* Iowa City, Iowa: University of Iowa, 1976.

Huston, A. Sex-typing. In T. H. Mussen (Ed.), *Carmichael's manual of child psychology.* New York: Wiley, in press.

Hyde, J. S. *Understanding human sexuality.* New York: McGraw-Hill, 1979.

Hyde, J., & Phillis, D. E. Androgyny across the life span. *Developmental Psychology*, 1979, *15*, 334–336.

Ickes, W., & Barnes, R. D. Boys and girls together—and alienated: Stereotyped sex roles in mixed-sex dyads. *Journal of Personality and Social Psychology*, 1978, *36*, 669–683.

Irons, E. S. *The causes of unwanted pregnancy: A psychological study from a feminist perspective.* Unpublished doctoral dissertation, Educational Psychology Department, University of Massachusetts, 1977.

Jakobovits, L. A. Evaluational reactions to erotic literature. *Psychological Reports*, 1965, *16*, 985–994.

Janoff-Bulman, R. Characterological versus behavioral self-blame: Inquiries into depression and rape. *Journal of Personality and Social Psychology*, 1979, *10*, 1798–1809.

Jay, K., & Young, A. *The gay report.* New York: Summit, 1977.

Jesser, C. J. Women in society: Some academic perspectives and the issues therein. *International Journal of Sociology of the Family*, 1972, *2*, 246–259.

Jesser, C. J. Male responses to direct verbal sexual initiatives of females. *Journal of Sex Research*, 1978, *14*, 118–128.

Johnson, A. G. On the prevalence of rape in the United States. *Signs: Journal of Women in Culture and Society*, 1980, *6*, 136–146.

Johnson, L. B., & Staples, R. E. Family planning and the young minority male: A pilot project. *Family Coordinator*, 1979, *28*, 535–543.

Johnson, M. Androgyny and the material principle. *School Review*, 1977, *86*, 50–69.

Johnson, R. W., Doiron, D., Brooks, G. P., & Dickinson, J. Perceived attractiveness as a function of support for the feminist movement: Not necessarily a put-down of women. *Canadian Journal of Behavioral Science*, 1978, *10*, 214–221.

Johnson, R. W., Holborn, S. W., & Turcotte, S. Perceived attractiveness as a function of active vs. passive support for the feminist movement. *Personality and Social Psychology Bulletin*, 1979, *5*, 227–230.

Jones, W. H. Chernovetz, M. E., & Hansson, R. O. The enigma of androgyny: Differential implications for males and females? *Journal of Consulting and Clinical Psychology*, 1978, *46*, 298–313.

Jourard, S. M. *The transparent self.* Princeton, N.J.: D. Van Nostrand, 1964.

Jourard, S. *Self-disclosure: An experimental analysis of the transparent self.* New York: Wiley, 1971.

Jourard, S., & Friedman, R. Experimenter-subject distance in self-disclosure. *Journal of Personality and Social Psychology*, 1970, *15*, 278–282.

Kaats, G. R., & Davis, K. E. The dynamics of sexual behavior of college students. *Journal of Marriage and the Family*, 1970, *32*, 390–399.

Kahana, B., & Kahana, E. How different generations view each other. *Geriatric Focus*, 1970, *9*, 1–13.

Kaltreider, N. B., & Margolis, A. G. Childless by choice: A clinical study. *American Journal of Psychiatry*, 1977, *134*, 179–182.

Kamiat, A. H. Male masochism and culture. *Psychoanalytic Review*, 1936, *23*, 84–91.

Kanin, E. An examination of sexual aggression as a response to sexual frustration. *Journal of Marriage and the Family*, 1967, *29*, 428–433.

Kanin, E. Selected dyadic aspects of male sex aggression. *Journal of Sex Research*, 1969, *5*, 12–28.

Kanin, E. J., Davidson, K. D., & Scheck, S. R. A research note on male/female differentials in the experience of heterosexual love. *The Journal of Sex Research*, 1970, *6*, 64–72.

Kanin, E., & Parcell, S. R. Sexual aggression: A second look at the offended female. *Archives of Sexual Behavior*, 1977, *6*, 67–76.

Kanter, M. K. Psychological implications of never-married females who live alone (Doctoral dissertation, California School of Professional Psychology, 1977). *Dissertation Abstracts International*, 1978, *38*, (9-B), 4464.

Kanter, R. M. *Men and women of the corporation*. New York: Basic Books, 1977.

Kantor, D., & Lehr, W. *Inside the family*. San Francisco: Jossey-Bass, 1975.

Kaplan, A. G. Clarifying the concept of androgyny: Implications for therapy. *Psychology of Women Quarterly*, 1979, *3*, 223–230.

Kaplan, A., & Bean, J. P. From sex stereotypes to androgyny: Considerations of societal and individual change. In A. Kaplan & J. P. Bean (Eds.), *Beyond sex-role stereotypes: Readings toward a psychology of androgyny*. Boston: Little, Brown, 1976.

Kaplan, A., & Sedney, M. A. *Psychology and sex roles: An androgynous perspective*. Boston: Little, Brown, 1980.

Kaplan, H. S. *The new sex therapy*. New York: Brunner/Mazel, 1974.

Kaplan, L. J. *Oneness and separateness: From infant to individual*. New York: Simon & Schuster, 1978.

Kasinsky, R. G. The rise and institutionalization of the anti-rape movement in Canada. In M. A. B. Gammon (Ed.), *Violence in Canada*. Toronto: Methuen, 1978.

Kasun, J. Turning children into sex experts. *Public Interest*, 1979, *55*, 3–14.

Katchadourian, H. A., & Lunde, D. *Fundamentals of human sexuality* (2nd ed.). New York: Holt, Rinehart & Winston, 1980.

Kaufman, A., Divasto, P., Jackson, R., Voorhees, D., & Christy, J. Male rape victims: Noninstitutionalized assault. *American Journal of Psychiatry*, 1980, *137*, 221–223.

Kearney, H. R. Feminist challenges to the social structure and sex roles. *Psychology of Women Quarterly*, 1979, *4*, 16–31.

Kegel, A. H. The physiologic treatment of poor tone and function of the genital muscles and of urinary stress incontinence. *Western Journal of Surgery, Obstetrics and Gynecology*, 1949, *57*, 527–535.

Kegel, A. H. Sexual functions of the pubococcygeus muscle. *Western Journal of Surgery, Obstetrics and Gynecology*, 1952, *60*, 521–524.

Kelly, K. L. Lifestyles of never-married adults. *Dissertation Abstracts International*, 1978, *38* (10-B), 5026.

Kenrick, D. T., Stringfield, D. O., Wagenhals, W. L., Dahl, R. N., & Ransdell, H. J. Sex differences, androgyny, and approach responses to erotica: A new variation on an old volunteer problem. *Journal of Personality and Social Psychology*, 1980, *38*, 517–524.

References

Kerckhoff, A. C. Norm value clusters and the strain toward consistency among older married couples. In I. H. Simpson & J. C. McKinney (Eds.), *Social aspects of aging*. Durham, N.C.: Duke University Press, 1972.

Kimmel, D.C. *Adulthood and aging: An interdisciplinary developmental view* (2nd ed.). New York: Wiley, 1980.

King, H. E., Rotter, M. J., Calhoun, L. G., & Selby, J. W. Perceptions of the rape incident: Physicians and volunteer counselors. *Journal of Community Psychology*, 1978, 6, 74–77.

Kinsey, A. C., Pomeroy, W. B., & Martin, C. E. *Sexual behavior in the human male*. Philadelphia: Saunders, 1948.

Kinsey, A. C., Pomeroy, W. B., Martin, C. E., & Gebhard, P. H. *Sexual behavior in the human female*. Philadelphia: Saunders, 1953.

Kirkpatrick, C., & Kanin, E. Male sex aggression on a university campus. *American Sociological Review*, 1957, 22, 52–58.

Klemmack, D. L., & Roff, L. L. Heterosexual alternatives to marriagew; Appropriateness for older persons. *Alternative Lifestyles*, 1980, 3, 137–148.

Knox, D. H., & Sporakowski, M. J. Attitudes of college students toward love. *Journal of Marriage and the Family*, 1968, 30, 638–642.

Koch, P. B. A comparison of the sex education of primary-aged children in the United States and Sweden, as expressed through their art. In J. M. Samson (Ed.), *Childhood and sexuality: Proceedings of the international symposium held at the Université du Quebec à Montréal, September 7–9, 1979*. Montreal: Editions Estudies Vivantes, 1980.

Kohlberg, L. A cognitive developmental analysis of children's sex-role concepts and attitudes. In E. E. Maccoby (Ed.), *The development of sex differences*. Stanford, Calif.: Stanford University Press, 1966.

Komarovsky, M. *Dilemmas of masculinity: A study of college youth*. New York: Norton, 1976.

Krafft-Ebing, R. von. [*Psychopathia sexualis: A medico-forensic study*.] New York: Pioneer, 1939. (Trans. of 12th edition, originally published, 1903.)

Krause, H. Child welfare, parental responsibility and the state. *Family Law Quarterly*, 1972, 6, 372–404.

Krieger, M. E. *The effects upon the family when a woman returns to school, as reported by wives and husbands*. Unpublished doctoral dissertation, Department of Education, Guidance, and Counseling, University of Pittsburgh, 1977.

Kroop, M. When women initiate sexual relations. *Medical Aspects of a Human Sexuality*, 1978, 12, 16; 23; 28–29.

Krulewitz, J. E., Nash, J., & Payne, E. *Sex differences in attributions about rape, rapists, and rape victims*. Paper presented at the annual meeting of the American Psychological Association, San Francisco, September 1977.

Krulewitz, J. E., & Payne, E. J. Attribution about rape: Effects of rapist force, observer sex and sex-role attitudes. *Journal of Applied Social Psychology*, 1978, 8, 291–305.

Kutchinsky, B. The effect of easy availability of pornography on the incidence of sex crimes: The Danish experience. *Journal of Social Issues*, 1973, 29, 163–181.

Landy, E. E. Sex differences in some aspects of smoking behavior. *Psychological Reports*, 1967, 20, 575–580.

Laner, M. R. Permanent partner priorities: Gay and straight. *Journal of Homosexuality*, 1977, 3, 21–39.

Langhorn, M. C., & Secord, P. Variations in marital needs with age, sex, marital status, and regional locations. *Journal of Social Psychology*, 1955, 41, 19–37.

LaPlante, M., McCormick, N., & Brannigan, G. Living the sexual script: College students' views of influence in sexual encounters. *Journal of Sex Research*, 1980, *16*, 338–355.

Larkin, R. *Suburban youth in cultural conflict.* New York: Oxford University Press, 1979.

Law Enforcement Assistance Administration. *Crime in five American cities, Advance Report.* Washington, D.C.: U.S. Government Printing Office, 1974.

Lee, J. A. The styles of loving. *Psychology Today,* 1974, *8*, 43–51.

Lee, J. A. *The colors of love.* New York: Bantam Books, 1977.

Lehman Schlozman, K. Women and unemployment: Assessing the biggest myths. In J. Freeman (Ed.), *Women: A feminist perspective* (2nd ed.). Palo Alto, Calif.: Mayfield, 1979.

Leibowitz, L. *Females, males, families: A biosocial approach.* Belmont, Calif.: Wadsworth, 1978.

Lein, L. Male participation in home life: Impact of social supports and breadwinner responsibility on the allocation of tasks. *Family Coordinator*, 1979, *28*, 489–495.

Levin, H. Womanizing work. *Professional Psychology*, 1980, *11*, 360–368.

Levine, M. I. Sex education in the public elementary and school curriculum. In D. L. Taylor (Ed.), *Human sexual development.* Philadelphia: Davis, 1970.

Levinger, G. A social psychological perspective on marital dissolution. In G. Levinger & O. C. Moles (Eds.), *Divorce and separation: Context, causes, and consequences.* New York: Basic Books, 1979.

Levinson, D. J. *Seasons of a man's life.* New York: Knopf, 1978.

Leviton, D. The significance of sexual activity as a determinant to suicide among the aged. *Omega*, 1973, *4*, 163–174.

Levitt, E. E., & Brady, J. P. Sexual preferences in young adult males and some correlates. *Journal of Clinical Psychology*, 1965, *21*, 347–354.

Lewis, R. A., Lozac, E. B., Milardo, R. M., & Grosnick, W. A. *Commitment in lesbian and gay male living-together relationships.* Paper presented at the annual meeting of the American Sociological Association, New York, August 1980.

Libby, R. W. Creative singlehood as a sexual lifestyle: Beyond marriage as a rite of passage. In R. Libby & R. Whitehurst (Eds.), *Marriage and alternatives: Exploring intimate relationships.* Glenview, Ill.: Scott, Foresman, 1977.

Libby, R. W., & Nass, G. D. Parental views on teenage sexual behavior. *Journal of Sex Research*, 1971, *7*, 226–236.

Lindemann, C. *Birth control and unmarried young women.* New York: Springer, 1975.

Lindsey, K. Sexual harassment on the job and how to stop it. *Ms Magazine*, November 1977, pp. 47–51; 74–78.

Lipman, A. Role conceptions and morale of couples in retirement. *Journal of Gerontology*, 1961, *16*, 267–271.

Livson, F. Patterns of personality development in middle-aged women. *International Journal of Aging and Human Development*, 1976, *7*, 107–115.

Livson, F. *Personality development of men and women in the middle years.* Paper presented at the meeting of the American Association for the Advancement of Science, Washington, D.C., February 1978.

Long-Laws, J. *The second X: Sex role and social role.* New York: Elsevier, North Holland, 1979.

Lopata, H. Z. *Widowhood in an American city.* Cambridge, Mass.: General Learning Press, 1973.

Lowenthal, M., Fiske, M., Berkman, R. L., & Associates. *Aging and mental disorder in San Francisco: A social psychiatric study.* San Francisco: Jossey-Bass, 1967.

Lowenthal, M., Fiske, M., Thurnher, M., Chiriboga, D., & Associates. *Four stages of life: A comparative study of women and men facing transition.* San Francisco: Jossey-Bass, 1975.

Maccoby, E. E., & Jacklin, C. N. *The psychology of sex differences.* Stanford, Calif.: Stanford University Press, 1974.

Maccoby, M. *The gamesman.* New York: Bantam Books, 1978.

MacDonald, C. *Development of sexuality.* Unpublished mimeographed table, University of Michigan, Ann Arbor, November 1979.

MacKinnon, C. A. *Sexual harassment of working women.* New Haven, Conn.: Yale University Press, 1979.

Macklin, E. D. Review of research on nonmarital cohabitation in the U.S. In B. I. Murstein (Ed.), *Exploring intimate life styles.* New York: Springer, 1978.

Macklin, E. D. Nontraditional family forms: A decade of research. *Journal of Marriage and the Family,* 1980, *42,* 905–922.

Maddox, G., & Douglas, E. Aging and individual differences. *Journal of Gerontology,* 1974, *29,* 555–563.

Mainardi, P. The politics of housework. In R. Morgan (Ed.), *Sisterhood is powerful.* New York: Vintage, 1971.

Malamuth, N. M. Rape fantasies as a function of exposure to violent sexual stimuli. *Archives of Sexual Behavior,* 1981, *10,* 33–47.

Malamuth, N. M., & Check, J. V. P. Sexual arousal to rape and consenting depictions. The importance of the woman's arousal. *Journal of Abnormal Psychology,* 1980, *89,* 763–766.

Malamuth, N. M., & Check, J. V. P. The effects of mass media exposure on acceptance of violence against women. A field experiment. *Journal of Research in Personality,* 1981, *15,* 436–446. (a)

Malamuth, N. M., & Check, J. V. P. Penile tumescence and perceptual responses to rape as a function of victim's perceived reactions. *Journal of Applied Social Psychology,* 1981, *10,* 528–547. (b)

Malamuth, N. M., Haber, S. & Feshbach, S. Testing hypotheses regarding rape: Exposure to sexual violence, sex differences, and the "normality" of rapists. *Journal of Research in Personality,* 1980, *14,* 121–137.

Malamuth, N. M., Heim, M., & Feshbach, S. Sexual responsiveness of college students to rape depictions: Inhibitory and disinhibitory effects. *Journal of Personality and Social Psychology,* 1980, *38,* 399–408.

Malamuth, N. M., & Spinner, B. A longitudinal content analysis of sexual violence in the best-selling erotic magazines. *Journal of Sex Research,* 1980, *16,* 226–237.

Mancini, J. A., & Orthner, D. K. Recreational sexuality preferences among middle-class husbands and wives. *Journal of Sex Research,* 1978, *14,* 96–106.

Mann, J., Berkowitz, L., Sidman, J., Starr, S., & West, S. Satiation of the transient stimulating effect of erotic films. *Journal of Personality and Social Psychology,* 1974, *30,* 729–735.

Marcus, R. Snaring the office wolf. *National Law Journal,* 1980, *2,* 1; 12; 13.

Marecek, J. *Economic, social and psychological consequences of adolescent childbearing: An analysis of data from the Philadelphia Collaborative Perinatal Project* (Final Report to National Institute of Child Health and Human Development, NICHD, September 1979). Bethesda, Md.: Center for Population Research, 1979.

Marlatt, G. A. Exposure to a model and task ambiguity as determinants of verbal behavior in an interview. *Journal of Consulting and Clinical Psychology,* 1971, *36,* 268–276.

Marmor, J. (Ed.). *Homosexual behavior.* New York: Basic Books, 1980.

Marsh, J. C., Caplan, N., Geist, A., Gregg, G., Harrington, J., & Sharphorn, D. *Law reform in the prevention and treatment of rape* (Final report). Ann Arbor, Mich.: Institute of Social Research, 1980.

Martin, D. *Battered wives.* San Francisco: Glide Publications, 1976.

Martinson, F. Eroticism in infancy and childhood. *Journal of Sex Research,* 1976, *12,* 251–262.

Maslow, A. H. *Motivation and personality.* New York: Harper, 1954.

Maslow, A. H. Self-esteem (dominance feeling) and sexuality in women. In M. F. DeMartino (Ed.), *Sexual behavior and personality characteristics.* New York: Grove Press, 1963.

Masters, W. H., & Johnson, V. E. *Human sexual response.* Boston: Little, Brown, 1966.

Masters, W. H., & Johnson, V. E. *Human sexual inadequacy.* Boston: Little, Brown, 1970.

Masters, W., & Johnson, V. *Homosexuality in perspective.* Boston: Little, Brown, 1979.

Mazor, M. Emotional reactions to infertility. *Medical Aspects of Human Sexuality,* 1980, *14,* 32–41.

McCormick, N. *Impact of sex and sex role on subjects' perceptions of social power in hypothetical sexual interactions.* Paper presented at the meeting of the Western Psychological Association, Los Angeles, April 1976.

McCormick, N. B. Gender role and expected social power behavior in sexual decision-making (Doctoral dissertation, University of California at Los Angeles, 1976). *Dissertation Abstracts International,* 1977, *37,* 422-B. (University Microfilms No. 77-1646, 151)

McCormick, N. B. Come-ons and put-offs: Unmarried students' strategies for having and avoiding sexual intercourse. *Psychology of Women Quarterly,* 1979, *4,* 194–211.

McCormick, N. Author's files. Unpublished data, 1976. (Information available from N. McCormick, Ph.D., Department of Psychology, State University of New York College at Plattsburgh, Plattsburgh, NY 12901).

McKee, J., & Sherriffs, A. The differential evaluation of males and females. *Journal of Personality,* 1957, *25,* 356–371.

McLaughlin, S. Expected family size and perceived states of deprivation among high school senior women. *Demography,* 1974, *11,* 57–73.

McTeer, M. Rape and the Canadian legal process. In M. A. B. Gammon (Ed.), *Violence in Canada.* Toronto: Methuen, 1978.

Mead, M. *Sex and temperament in three primitive societies.* New York: Dell, 1969.

Mead, M. A proposal: We need taboos on sex at work. *Redbook,* 1978, *150,* 31.

Mead, M., & Newton, N. Cultural patterning of perinatal behavior. In S. A. Richardson & A. Guttmacher (Eds.), *Childbearing: The social and psychological aspects.* New York: Williams and Wilkins, 1967.

Meissner, M., Humphreys, E., Meis, C., & Scheu, J. No exit for wives: Sexual division of labor and the cumulation of household demands. *Canadian Review of Sociology and Anthropology,* 1975, *12,* 424–439.

Mendola, M. *The Mendola report: A new look at gay couples.* New York: Crown, 1980.

Mercer, G. W., & Kohn, P. M. Gender difference in the interpretation of conservatism, sex urges, and sexual behavior among college students. *Journal of Sex Research,* 1979, *15,* 129–142.

Merit System Protection Board. *Sexual harassment in the federal workplace: Is it a problem?* Washington, D.C.: U.S. Government Printing Office, 1981.

Miller, H. *Insomnia.* New York: Doubleday, 1974.

References

Millett, K. The shame is over. *Ms Magazine,* January 1975, pp. 26–29.

Mischel, W. Sex-typing and socialization. In P. H. Mussen (Ed.), *Carmichael's Manual of Child Psychology* (Vol. 2, 3rd ed.). New York: Wiley, 1970.

Money, J. *Love and lovesickness.* Baltimore: Johns Hopkins University Press, 1980.

Money, J. & Ehrhardt, A. H. *Man & woman, boy & girl.* Baltimore: Johns Hopkins University Press, 1972.

Moore, E. C. Fertility regulation: Friend or foe of the female? In J. Money and H. Musaph (Eds.), *Handbook of sexology* (Vol. 3). New York: Elsevier, 1977.

Moore, J., & Kendall, D. Children's concepts of reproduction. *Journal of Sex Research,* 1971, 7, 42–61.

Moore, K. A., Hofforth, S. L., Wertheimer, R., Caldwell, S. B., & Waite, L. J. *Teenage childbearing: Consequences for women, families, and government welfare expenditures.* Paper presented at the meeting of the American Psychological Association, New York, September 1979.

Morgan, S. Sexuality after hysterectomy and castration. *Women and Health: Issues in Women's Health Care,* 1978, 13, 5–9.

Morin, S. F. Heterosexual bias in psychological research on lesbianism and male homosexuality. *American Psychologist,* 1977, 32, 629–637.

Mosher, D. L. Sex differences, sex experience, sex guilt, and explicitly sexual films. *Journal of Social Issues,* 1973, 29, 95–112.

Murstein, B. I. Mate selection in the 1970s. *Journal of Marriage and the Family,* 1980, 42, 777–792.

Mussen, P. H. Some antecedents and consequents of masculine sex-typing in adolescent boys. *Psychological Monographs,* 1961, 75 (2, Whole No. 506).

Mussen, P. H. Long-term consequences of masculinity of interests in adolescence. *Journal of Consulting Psychology,* 1962, 26, 435–440.

Napier, A. Y. *The rejection-intrusion pattern: A central family dynamic.* Unpublished manuscript, School of Family Resources, University of Wisconsin, Madison, 1977.

National Center for Health Statistics. *Monthly Vital Statistics Report,* 1979, 27 (Supplement, Whole No. 11).

National Commission on the Causes and Prevention of Violence. *Crimes of violence* (Vol. 2). Washington, D.C.: U.S. Government Printing Office, 1969.

Nawy, H. In the pursuit of happiness? Consumers of erotica in San Francisco. *Journal of Social Issues,* 1973, 29, 147–161.

Neugarten, B. L., & Gutman, D. L. Age-sex roles and personality in middle age: A thematic apperception study. *Psychological Monographs,* 1968, 72 (17, Whole No. 470).

Newcomb, M. D., & Bentler, P. M. Cohabitation before marriage. *Alternative Lifestyles,* 1980, 3, 65–85.

Newman, G., & Nichols, C. R. Sexual activity and attitudes in older persons. *Journal of the American Medical Association,* 1960, 173, 33–35.

Newton, N. Childbirth and culture. *Psychology Today,* 1970, 4, 75.

Nieva, V. F., & Gutek, B. A. Women's work: What women want, expect and get. In B. Gutek (Ed.), *New directions for education, careers and work: Enhancing women's career development.* San Francisco: Jossey-Bass, 1979.

Nieva, V. F., & Gutek, B. A. *Women and work: A psychological perspective.* New York: Praeger, 1981.

Notman, M. Women and mid-life: A different perspective. *Psychiatric Opinion*, 1978, *15*, 15.

Orthner, D. K., Brown, T., & Ferguson, D. Single-parent fatherhood: An emerging life style. *Family Coordinator*, 1976, *25*, 429–437.

Parsons, J. Cognitive developmental theories of sex-role socialization. In I. H. Frieze, J. E. Parsons, P. Johnson, D. N. Ruble, & G. Zellman, *Women and sex roles*. New York: Norton, 1978.

Parsons, T. The social structure of the family. In R. N. Anshen (Ed.), *The family: Its function and destiny*. New York: Harper, 1959.

Parsons, T., & Bales, R. F. *Family, socialization, and interaction process*. New York: The Free Press, 1955.

Peplau, L. A. *Power in dating couples*. Unpublished manuscript, University of California, Department of Psychology, Los Angeles, 1977.

Peplau, L. A. Power in dating relationships. In J. Freeman (Ed.), *Women: A feminist perspective* (2nd ed.). Palo Alto, Calif.: Mayfield, 1979.

Peplau, L. A., & Amaro, H. Lesbian relationships. In W. Paul & J. D. Weinrich (Eds.), *Homosexuality as a social issue*. Beverly Hills, Calif.: Sage, in press.

Peplau, L. A., & Cochran, S. D. *Sex differences in values concerning love relationships*. Paper presented at the annual meeting of the American Psychological Association, Montreal, September 1980.

Peplau, L. A., & Cochran, S. D. Value orientations in the intimate relationships of gay men. *Journal of Homosexuality*, 1981, *6*, 1–19.

Peplau, L. A., Cochran, S., Rook, K., & Padesky, C. Loving women: Attachment and autonomy in lesbian relationships. *Journal of Social Issues*, 1978, *34*, 7–27.

Peplau, L. A., & Hammen, C. L. (Eds.). Sexual behavior: Social psychological issues. *Journal of Social Issues*, 1977, *33*, 2.

Peplau, L., Rubin, Z., & Hill, C. The sexual balance of power. *Psychology Today*, 1976, *10*, 142–147; 151.

Peplau, L. A., Rubin, Z., & Hill, C. T. Sexual intimacy in dating couples. *Journal of Social Issues*, 1977, *33*, 86–109.

Perper, T., & Fox, V. S. *Special focus: Flirtation behavior in public settings*. Paper presented at the meeting of the Eastern Region of the Society for the Scientific Study of Sex, Philadelphia, April 1980. (a)

Perper, T., & Fox, V. S. *Flirtation and pickup patterns in bars*. Paper presented at the meeting of the Eastern Conference on Reproductive Behavior, New York, June 1980. (b)

Perry, J. D., & Whipple, B. Pelvic muscle strength of female ejaculators: Evidence in support of a new theory of orgasm. *Journal of Sex Research*, 1981, *17*, 22–39.

Pfeiffer, E., Verwoerdt, A., & Wang, H. Sexual behavior in aged men and women. *Archives of General Psychiatry*, 1968, *19*, 756–758.

Phelps, L. Female sexual alienation. In J. Freeman (Ed.), *Women: A feminist perspective* (2nd ed.). Palo Alto, Calif.: Mayfield, 1979.

Piaget, J. [*The moral judgment of the child*] (M. Gabain, trans.). New York: Free Press, 1948. (Originally published, 1932.)

Pietropinto, A., & Simenauer, J. *Husbands and wives*. New York: Berkeley, 1979.

Pleck, J. H. *Men's new roles in the family: Housework and child care*. Paper presented at the Ford Foundation/Merrill-Palmer Institute Conference on the Family and Sex Roles, Detroit, November 1975.

References

Pleck, J. H. Men's family work: Three perspectives and some new data. *Family Coordinator*, 1979, *28*, 481–488.

Pleck, J. H., & Brannon, R. (Eds.). Male roles and the male experience. *Journal of Social Issues*, 1978, *34* (Whole No. 1).

Pleck, J. H., & Sawyer, J. (Eds.). *Men and masculinity.* Englewood Cliffs, N. J.: Prentice-Hall, 1974.

Plummer, K. Men in love: Observations on male homosexual couples. In M. Corbin (Ed.), *The couple.* New York: Penguin, 1978.

Pocs, O., & Godow, A. Can students view parents as sexual beings? *Family Coordinator,* 1976, *26*, 31–36.

Polatnick, M. Why men don't rear children: A power analysis. *Berkeley Journal of Sociology*, 1973–1974, *18*, 45–86.

Pomeroy, W. B. Some aspects of prostitution. *Journal of Sex Research*, 1965, *1*, 177–187.

Pope, K., Levenson, H., & Schover, L. R. Sexual intimacy in psychology training: Results and implications of a national survey. *American Psychologist*, 1979, *34*, 682–689.

Pope, K., Schover, L. R., & Levenson, H. Sexual behavior between clinical supervisors and trainees: Implications for professional standards. *Professional Psychology*, 1980, *11*, 157–162.

Proulx, C. Sex as athletics in a singles complex. In C. Gordon & G. Johnson (Eds.), *Readings in human sexuality: Contemporary perspectives,* 1976–1977. New York: Harper & Row, 1976.

Quinn, R. Coping with Cupid: The formation, impact and management of romantic relationships in organizations. *Administrative Science Quarterly*, 1977, *22*, 30–45.

Quinn, R., & Staines, G. *The 1977 quality of employment survey.* Ann Arbor, Mich.: Institute for Social Research, 1978.

Raboch, J., & Bartak, V. A. A contribution to the study of the anesthetic-frigid syndrome in women. *Ceskoslovenska Psychiatrie*, 1968, *64*, 230–235.

Radlove, S. Androgyny and sexual functioning in women. (Doctoral dissertation, Miami University, Oxford, Ohio, 1977). *Dissertation Abstracts International*, 1977, *37*, 6410. (University Microfilms No. 77-12, 983)

Radlove, S. *Couples' sexual communication questionnaire.* Survey prepared for couples' sexual communication workshop, Cincinnati, Ohio, November 1979. (For inquiries regarding reprints, write S. Radlove, Ph.D., 7759 Montgomery Road, Cincinnati, OH 45236).

Rainwater, L. *Family design.* Chicago: Aldine, 1965.

Rainwater, L. Marital sexuality in four cultures of poverty. In D. S. Marshall & R. C. Suggs (Eds.), *Human sexual behavior: Variations in the ethnographic spectrum.* New York: Basic Books, 1971.

Rainwater, L., & Weinstein, K. K. *And the poor get children.* Chicago: Quadrangle, 1960.

Ramey, J. *Intimate friendships.* Englewood Cliffs, N. J.: Prentice-Hall, 1976.

Ramsey, J., Latham, J. D., & Lindquist, C. U. *Long term same-sex relationships: Correlates of adjustment.* Paper presented at the annual meeting of the American Psychological Association, Toronto, August 1978.

Raphael, S. M., & Robinson, M. K. The older lesbian: Love relationships and friendship patterns. *Alternative Lifestyles*, 1980, *3*, 207–230.

Raven, B. H. Social influence and power. In I. D. Steiner & M. Fishbein (Eds.), *Current studies in social psychology.* New York: Holt, Rinehart & Winston, 1965.

Raven, B. H. *The comparative analysis of power and power preference.* Paper presented at the meeting of the Albany Symposium on Power and Influence, Albany, New York, October 11–13, 1971.

Reevy, W. R. Child sexuality. In A. Ellis & A. Abarbanel (Eds.), *The encyclopedia of sexual behavior.* New York: Hawthorn, 1967.

Reiss, I. L. *The social context of premarital sexual permissiveness.* New York: Holt, Rinehart & Winston, 1967.

Reiss, I. *Family Systems in America* (3rd ed.). New York: Holt, Rinehart & Winston, 1980.

Resnick, J. L., Resnick, M. B., Packer, A. B., & Wilson, J. Fathering classes: A psycho-educational model. *Counseling Psychologist,* 1978, *7,* 56–60.

Riegel, K. F. Adult life crises: Toward a dialectical theory of development. In N. Datan & L. H. Ginsberg (Eds.), *Life-span developmental psychology: Normative life crises.* New York: Academic Press, 1975.

Riegel, K. T. The dialectics of human development. *American Psychologist,* 1976, *31,* 679–700.

Riger, S., & Gordon, M. T. The structure of rape prevention beliefs. *Personality and Social Psychology Bulletin,* 1979, *5,* 186–190.

Riley, M. R. Aging, social change, and the power of ideas. *Daedalus,* 1978, *107,* 39–52.

Robbins, M. B., & Jensen, G. D. Multiple orgasm in males. *Journal of Sex Research,* 1978, *14,* 21–26.

Robertiello, R. C. Masochism and the female sexual role. *Journal of Sex Research,* 1970, *6,* 56–58.

Robinson, J. *How Americans use their time: A social-psychological analysis.* New York: Praeger, 1977.

Robinson, W. J. *Woman: Her sex and love life* (17th ed.). New York: Eugenics Publishing, 1929.

Rockwell, L. Sex and the single parent. In S. Burden, P. Houston, E. Kripke, R. Simpson, & W. F. Stultz (Eds.), *Single Parent Family Proceedings of the Changing Family Conference V.* Iowa City, Iowa: University of Iowa, 1976.

Rogel, M. J., Peterson, A. C., Richards, M., Shelton, M., & Zeuhlke, M. *Contraceptive behavior in adolescence: A decision-making perspective.* Paper presented at the meeting of the American Psychological Association, New York, September 1979. (Available from Dr. M. J. Rogel at Michael Reese Hospital, 2959 S. Cottage Grove, Chicago, IL 60616).

Rosenberg, F. F., & Simmons, R. G. Sex differences in the self-concept of adolescence. *Sex Roles,* 1975, *1,* 147–159.

Rosenkrantz, P., Vogel, S., Bee, H., Broverman, I., & Broverman, D. Sex role stereotypes and self-concepts in college students. *Journal of Consulting and Clinical Psychology,* 1968, *32,* 287–295.

Rosenthal, K. M., & Keshet, H. F. The not-quite step-mother. *Psychology Today,* 1978, *12,* 82–86; 100–101.

Rossner, J. *Looking for Mr. Goodbar.* New York: Simon & Schuster, 1975.

Rotbart, D. Father quit his job for the family's sake, now hirers shun him. *Wall Street Journal,* 1981, *61,* 1; 12.

Rothenberg, P. B. Communication about sex and birth control between mothers and their adolescent children. *Population and Environment,* 1980, *3,* 35–50.

Rubin, L. B. *Worlds of pain: Life in the working class family.* New York: Basic Books, 1976.

Rubin, Z. Measurement of romantic love. *Journal of Personality and Social Psychology,* 1970, *16,* 265–273.

References

Rubin, Z. *Liking and loving: An invitation to social psychology.* New York: Holt, Rinehart & Winston, 1973.

Rubin, Z. Disclosing oneself to a stranger: Reciprocity and its limits. *Journal of Experimental Social Psychology,* 1975, *11,* 233–260.

Rubin, Z., Hill, C. T., Peplau, L. A., & Dunkel-Schetter, C. Self-disclosure in dating couples: Sex roles and the ethic of openness. *Journal of Marriage and the Family,* 1980, *42,* 305–317.

Rules and Regulations. *Federal Register,* 1980, *45,* S1604.11.

Russell, D. E. H. *The politics of rape: The victim's perspective.* New York: Stein & Day, 1975.

Russell, G. The father role and its relation to masculinity, femininity, and androgyny. *Child Development,* 1978, *49,* 1174–1181.

Russo, N. F., & Brackbill, Y. Population and growth. In J. Fawcett (Ed.), *Psychological perspectives on population.* New York: Basic Books, 1973.

Rychlak, J. *A philosophy of science for personality theory.* Boston: Houghton Mifflin, 1968.

Rychlak, J. *Dialectic: Humanistic rationale for behavior and development.* New York: Karger, 1976.

Safilios-Rothschild, C. *Love, sex, and sex roles.* Englewood Cliffs, N. J.: Prentice-Hall, Spectrum Books, 1977.

Sager, C. *Marriage contracts and couple therapy.* New York: Brunner/Mazel, 1976.

Saghir, M. T., & Robins, E. *Male and female homosexuality.* Baltimore: Williams & Wilkins, 1973.

Salzman, L. Sexual aggressivity vs. passivity. *Medical Aspects of Human Sexuality,* 1976, *10,* 16–17; 23; 28–29.

Sanders, J. S., & Robinson, W. L. Talking and not talking about sex: Male and female vocabularies. *Journal of Communication,* 1979, *29,* 22–30.

Sanford, L. T. *The silent children.* New York: Doubleday, 1980.

Scales, P. Males and morals: Teenage contraceptive behavior amid the double standard. *Family Coordinator,* 1977, *26,* 211–220.

Scales, P. How we guarantee the ineffectiveness of sex education. *Sex Information and Education Council of the United States,* 1978, *5,* 1–16.

Scanzoni, J. H. *Opportunity and the family.* New York: Free Press, 1970.

Scanzoni, J. H. *Sex roles, life styles, and childbearing.* New York: Free Press, 1975.

Scanzoni, J. H. Gender roles and the process of fertility control. *Journal of Marriage and the Family,* 1976, *38,* 667–691.

Scanzoni, J. H., & Fox, G. L. Sex roles, family, and society: The 70s and beyond. *Journal of Marriage and the Family,* 1980, *42,* 743–756.

Scanzoni, L., & Scanzoni, J. H. *Men, women, and change.* New York: McGraw-Hill, 1976.

Schäfer, S. Sexual and social problems of lesbians. *Journal of Sex Research,* 1976, *12,* 50–69.

Schäfer, S. Sociosexual behavior in male and female homosexuals: A study in sex differences. *Archives of Sexual Behavior,* 1977, *6,* 355–364.

Schaffer, K. F. *Sex role issues in mental health.* Reading, Mass.: Addison-Wesley, 1980.

Schaffer, K. F. *Sex roles and human behavior.* Cambridge, Mass.: Winthrop, 1981.

Schafrick, F. The emerging constitutional protection of the putative father's parental rights. *Family Law Quarterly,* 1973, *7,* 75–111.

Schlozman, K. L. Women and unemployment: Assessing the biggest myths. In J. Freeman (Ed.), *Women: A feminist perspective* (2nd ed.). Palo Alto, Calif.: Mayfield, 1979.

Schmidt, G. Male-female differences in sexual arousal and behavior during and after exposure to sexually explicit stimuli. *Archives of Sexual Behavior,* 1975, *4,* 353–365.

Schmidt, G., & Sigusch, V. Sex differences in responses to psychosexual stimulation by films and slides. *Journal of Sex Research,* 1970, *6,* 268–283.

Schmidt, G., & Sigusch, V. Women's sexual arousal. In J. Zubin & J. Money (Eds.), *Contemporary sexual behavior: Critical issues in the 1970s.* Baltimore: Johns Hopkins University Press, 1973.

Schmidt, G., Sigusch, V., & Schafer, S. Responses to reading erotic stories. Male-female differences. *Archives of Sexual Behavior,* 1973, 181–199.

Schofield, M. *The sexual behavior of young people.* Boston: Little, Brown, 1965.

Schriesheim, C. Personal communication, January 10, 1980.

Schumacher, S., & Lloyd, C. Physiological and psychological factors in impotence. *Journal of Sex Research,* 1981, *17,* 40–53.

Schwartz, G., & Merten, D. The language of adolescence: An anthropological approach to youth culture. *American Journal of Sociology,* 1967, *72,* 453–468.

Schwartz, M. A. *Career strategies of the never married.* Paper presented at the annual meeting of the American Sociological Association, New York, August 1976.

Scroggs, J. R. Penalties for rape as a function of victim provocativeness, damage, and resistance. *Journal of Applied Social Psychology,* 1976, *6,* 360–368.

Sedney, M. A. *Sex roles and coping: Comparison of feminine, masculine, and androgynous women's responses to stressful life events.* Paper presented at the meeting of the Association for Women in Psychology, St. Louis, February 1977.

Selby, J. W., Calhoun, L. G., & Brock, T. A. Sex differences in the social perception of rape victims. *Personality and Social Psychology Bulletin,* 1977, *3,* 412–415.

Seyfried, B. A., & Hendrick, C. When do opposites attract? When they are opposite in sex and sex-role attitudes. *Journal of Personality and Social Psychology,* 1973, *25,* 15–20.

Shapiro, H. I. *The birth control book.* New York: St. Martin's Press, 1977.

Sherman, J. A. *On the psychology of women.* Springfield, Ill.: Thomas, 1971.

Shostrom, E. *Man the manipulator.* Nashville, Tenn.: Abingdon Press, 1967.

Sigusch, V., Schmidt, G., Reinfeld, A., & Wiedemann-Sutor, I. Psychosexual stimulation: Sex differences. *Journal of Sex Research,* 1970, *6,* 10–24.

Silverman, D. C. Sharing the crisis of rape. Counseling the mates and families of victims. *American Journal of Orthopsychiatry,* 1978, *48,* 166–173.

Silverstein, C. *Man to man: Gay couples in America.* New York: Morrow, 1981.

Simon, W., & Gagnon, J. Psychosexual development. *Trans-action,* 1969, *6* (5), 9–17.

Simpson, R. *From the closet to the courts: The lesbian transition.* New York: Penguin Books, 1976.

Sinnot, J. D. Sex role inconstancy, biology and successful aging: A dialectical model. *Gerontologist,* 1977, *17,* 459–463.

Sistrunk, F., & McDavid, J. W. Sex variable in conforming behavior. *Journal of Personality and Social Psychology,* 1971, *17,* 200–207.

Skinner, B. F. *Science and human behavior.* New York: Macmillan, 1953.

Smith, J. A. A survey of adolescents' interests: Concerns and information. *Adolescence,* 1980, *15,* 475–482.

Smith, R. E., Keating, J. P., Hester, R. K., & Mitchell, H. E. Role and justice considerations in the attribution of responsibility to a rape victim. *Journal of Research in Personality*, 1976, *10*, 346–357.

Sommers, R. *Personal space: The behavioral basis of design.* Englewood Cliffs, N. J.: Prentice-Hall, 1969.

Sorensen, R. C. *Adolescent sexuality in contemporary America.* New York: World, 1973.

Spada, J. *The Spada report: The newest survey of gay male sexuality.* New York: New American Library, 1979.

Spanier, G. B. Sources of sex information and premarital sexual behavior. *Journal of Sex Research*, 1977, *13*, 73–88.

Spence, J. T., Helmreich, R., & Stapp, J. Ratings of self and peers on sex-role attributes and their relation to self-esteem and conceptions of masculinity and femininity. *Journal of Personality and Social Psychology*, 1975, *32*, 29–39.

Spock, B. J. *Baby and child care.* New York: Simon & Schuster, 1946.

Spock, B. J. *Baby and child care* (3rd ed.). New York: Pocket Books, 1976.

Stafford, R., Bachman, E., & diBona, P. The division of labor among cohabiting and married couples. *Journal of Marriage and the Family*, 1977, *39*, 43–57.

Staines, G., Gutek, B. A., Pleck, J., Shepard, L., O'Connor, P., & Allen, H. *A study of occupational sex typing.* Final Report to U.S. Department of Labor, Grant No. 91-26-76-51. Washington D.C., U.S. Department of Labor, 1979.

Staples, R. *The world of black singles: Changing patterns of male/female relations.* Westport, Conn.: Greenwood Press, 1981.

Starr, J. R., & Carns, D. E. Singles in the city. *Society*, 1972, *9*, 43–48.

Stauffer, J., & Frost, R. Male and female interest in sexually-oriented magazines. *Journal of Communication*, 1976, *26*, 25–30.

Stein, P. *Changing attitudes of college students.* Unpublished manuscript, Rutgers University, 1973.

Stein, P. *Single.* Englewood Cliffs, N. J.: Prentice-Hall, 1976.

Stein, P. The lifestyles and life changes and the never married. *Marriage and Family Review*, 1978, *1*, 1–11.

Stein, P. Personal communication, March 1981. (a)

Stein, P. (Ed.). *Single life: Unmarried adults in social context.* New York: St. Martin's Press, 1981. (b)

Stein, P., Richman, J., & Hannon, N. *The family: Functions, conflicts and symbols.* Reading, Mass.: Addison-Wesley, 1977.

Stephens, N., & Day, H. D. Sex-role identity, parental identification and self-concept of adolescent daughters from mother-absent, father-absent, and intact families. *Journal of Psychology*, 1979, *103*, 193–202.

Stephens, W. N. *The family in cross-cultural perspective.* New York: Holt, Rinehart & Winston, 1963.

Stokes, W. Sexual function in the aging male. *Geriatrics*, 1951, *6*, 304–308.

Stroller, R. J. *Sexual excitement.* New York: Pantheon Books, 1978.

Storms, M. Theories of sexual orientation. *Journal of Personality and Social Psychology*, 1980, *38*, 783–792.

Storms, M. D. A theory of erotic orientation development. *Psychological Review*, 1981, *88*, 340–353.

Stribling, F. T. Annual report of the court of directors of the Western Lunatic Asylum to the legislature of Virginia, with the report of the physician, for 1841. In D. Rogers, *The adult years*. Englewood Cliffs, N. J.: Prentice-Hall, 1979. (Originally published, 1842.)

Strong, E. K. *Vocational interests of men and women*. Stanford, Calif.: Stanford University Press, 1943.

Strong, L., & Nass, G. *Correlates of willingness among college students to participate in prolonged cohabitation*. Unpublished manuscript, University of Connecticut, 1975. Cited in E. Macklin, Review of research on nonmarital cohabitation in the U.S., in B. Murstein (Ed.), *Exploring intimate life styles*. New York: Springer, 1978.

Swan, R. W. Sex education in the home: The U.S. experience. *Journal of Sex Education and Therapy*, 1980, *6*, 3–10.

Swanson, J. Knowledge, knowledge, who's got the knowledge. *Journal of Sex Education and Therapy*, 1979, *1*, 41–46.

Symons, D. *The evolution of human sexuality*. New York: Oxford University Press, 1979.

Tanner, D. M. *The lesbian couple*. Lexington, Mass.: Heath, 1978.

Tavris, C. 40,000 men tell about their sexual behavior, their fantasies, the ideal woman, and their wives. *Redbook Magazine*, February 1978, pp. 111–113.

Tavris, C., & Offir, C. *The longest war: Sex differences in perspective*. New York: Harcourt Brace Jovanovich, 1977.

Tavris, C., & Sadd, S. *The Redbook report on female sexuality*. New York: Delacorte, 1977.

Tennov, D. *Love and limerence*. New York: Stein & Day, 1979.

Terman, L. M. Correlates of orgasm adequacy in a group of 556 wives. *Journal of Psychology*, 1951, *32*, 115–172.

Terman, L., & Miles, C. C. *Sex and personality*. New York: McGraw-Hill, 1936.

Thomas, L. *The medusa and the snail*. New York: Bantam Books, 1979.

Thornburg, H. Educating the preadolescent about sex. *Family Coordinator*, 1974, *23*, 35–39.

Thornton, A., & Camburn, D. Fertility, sex role attitudes, and labor force participation. *Psychology of Women Quarterly*, 1979, *4*, 61–80.

Tietze, C. Teenage pregnancies: Looking ahead to 1984. *Family Planning Perspectives*, 1978, *10*, 205–207.

The Tom Snyder Show. *An interview with William H. Masters and Virginia E. Johnson*. Televised on N.B.C. Television, July 7, 1975. (For inquiries regarding program transcripts, write N.B.C. Television, Programming Department, 30 Rockfeller Plaza, New York, NY 10112).

Traupmann, J., & Hatfield, E. Love: Its effects on mental and physical health. In J. March, S. Kiesler, R. Fogel, E. Hatfield, & E. Shanas (Eds.), *Aging: Stability and change in the family*. New York: Academic Press, 1981.

Traupmann, J. & Hatfield, E. How important is fairness over the lifespan? *International Journal of Aging and Human Development*, in press.

Traupmann, J., Hatfield, E., & Sprecher, S. *The importance of "fairness" for the material satisfaction of older women*. Unpublished manuscript, 1982. (Available from Dr. Elaine Hatfield, Department of Psychology, University of Hawaii, 2430 Campus Rd., Honolulu, HI 96822).

Traupmann, J., Hatfield, E., & Wexler, P. Equity and sexual satisfaction in dating couples. *British Journal of Social Psychology*, in press.

Tripp, C. Can homosexuals change with therapy? *Sexual Behavior*, 1971, *1*, 42–49.

References

Troll, L. E., Miller, S. I., & Atchleg, R. C. *Families in later life*. Belmont, Calif.: Wadsworth, 1979.

Troll, L. E., & Smith, J. Attachment through the life span: Some questions about dyadic bonds among adults. *Human Development*, 1976, *19*, 135–182.

Unger, R. K. *Female and male: Psychological perspectives*. New York: Harper & Row, 1979.

Uslander, A., Weiss, C., Telman, J., & Wenick, E. *Their universe*. New York: Dell, 1973.

U.S. Bureau of the Census. Marital status and living arrangements: March 1977 *(Current Population Reports*, Series P-20, No. 323). Washington, D.C.: U.S. Government Printing Office, 1978.

U.S. Bureau of the Census. Marital status and living arrangements: March 1978 *(Current Population Reports*, Series P-20, No. 338). Washington, D.C.: U.S. Government Printing Office, 1979.

U.S. Bureau of the Census. Marital status and living arrangements: March 1979 *(Current Population Reports*, Series P-20, No. 349). Washington, D.C.: U.S. Government Printing Office, 1980.

Utne, M. K., Hatfield, E., Traupmann, J. & Greenberger, D. Equity, marital satisfaction and stability. *Basic and Applied Social Psychology*, in press.

Veevers, J. Voluntary childlessness: A review of issues and evidence. *Marriage and Family Review*, 1979, *2*, 1–26.

Véitch, R., & Griffitt, W. The perception of erotic arousal in men and women by same- and opposite-sex peers. *Sex Roles*, 1980, *6*, 723–733.

Verwoerdt, A. *Clinical geropsychiatry*. Baltimore: Williams & Wilkins, 1976.

Verwoerdt, A., Pfeiffer, E., & Wang, H. S. Sexual behavior in senescence-patterns of sexual activity and interest. *Geriatrics*, 1969, *24*, 137–144.

Vidmar, N. Social psychology and the legal system. In A. Kahn & E. Donnerstein (Eds.), *Social psychology*. New York: Smith, 1981.

Wabrek, J. & Burchell, R. C. Male sexual dysfunction associated with coronary heart disease. *Archives of Sexual Behavior*, 1980, *9*, 69–75.

Walker, K., & Woods, M. *Time use: A measure of household production of family goods and services*. Washington, D.C.: American Home Economics Association, 1976.

Wallace, D. H. Obscenity and contemporary community standards: A survey. *Journal of Social Issues*, 1973, *29*, 53–68.

Walster, E., Walster, G. W., & Berscheid, E. *Equity: Theory and research*. Boston: Allyn & Bacon, 1978.

Walster, E., Walster, G. W. & Traupmann, J. Equity and premarital sex. *Journal of Personality and Social Psychology*, 1978, *36*, 82–92.

Warren, C. A. B. *Identity and community in the gay world*. New York: Wiley, 1974.

Watson, J. B. *Behaviorism*. New York: Norton, 1925.

Weber, M. [*The theory of social and economic organization*] (A. M. Henderson and T. Parsons, Eds. and trans.). New York: Free Press, 1964.

Weinberg, G. *Society and the healthy homosexual*. New York: Doubleday, 1973.

Weinstein, S. A., & Como, J. The relationship between knowledge and anxiety about postcoronary sexual activity among wives of post-coronary males. *Journal of Sex Research*, 1980, *16*, 316–324.

Weis, K., & Borges, S. Victimology and rape: The case of the legitimate victim. *Issues in Criminology*, 1973, *8*, 71–115.

Weiss, H. D. Mechanism of erection. *Medical Aspects of Human Sexuality*, 1973, *7*, 28–40.

Weiss, R. *Marital separation*. New York: Basic Books, 1975.

Westoff, C., & Bumpass, L. The revolution in birth control practices of U.S. Roman Catholics. *Science*, 1973, *179*, 41–44.

Who should initiate sexual relations, husband or wife? *Medical Aspects of Human Sexuality*, 1973, *3*, 4–7.

Who should take the sexual lead—the man or the woman? *Medical Aspects of Human Sexuality*, 1976, *10*, 30–35; 39; 43.

Wicks, J.W., & Workman, R. L. Sex role attitudes and the anticipated timing of the initial stages of family formation among Catholic university students. *Journal of Marriage and the Family*, 1978, *40*, 505–516.

Williams, J. *Psychology of women*. New York: Norton, 1977.

Wilson, E. O. *Sociobiology*. Cambridge, Mass.: Belknap Press, 1975.

Wilson, W. C. Pornography: The emergence of a social issue and the beginning of psychological study. *Journal of Social Issues*, 1973, *29*, 7–17.

Wilson, W. C., & Abelson, H. I. Experience with and attitudes toward explicit sexual materials. *Journal of Social Issues*, 1973, *29*, 19–39.

Winokur, G., Guze, S. B., & Pfeiffer, E. Developmental and sexual factors in women: A comparison between control, neurotic, and psychotic groups. *American Journal of Psychiatry*, 1959, *115*, 1097–1100.

Wolf, D. G. *The lesbian community*. Berkeley: University of California Press, 1979.

Wolfe, L. *Playing around: Women and extramarital sex*. New York: Morrow, 1975.

Women officers cite widespread sex harassment. *Los Angeles Times*, February 12, 1980, pt. II, p. 4

Worthy, M. A., Gary, L., & Kahn, G. M. Self-disclosure as an exchange process. *Journal of Personality and Social Psychology*, 1969, *13*, 63–69.

Wynne, L. C. Pseudo-mutuality in the family relations of schizophrenics. *Psychiatry*, 1958, *21*, 205–220.

Yates, A. *Sex without shame*. New York: Morrow, 1978.

Yates, A. *The effect of commonly accepted parenting practices on erotic development*. Unpublished manuscript, University of Arizona Health Sciences Center, Tucson, 1980.

Yllo, A. Nonmarital cohabitation. *Alternative Lifestyles*, 1978, *1*, 37–54.

Zabin, L. S., Kantner, J. F., & Zelnik, M. The risk of adolescent pregnancy in the first months of intercourse. *Family Planning Perspectives*, 1979, *11*, 215–222.

Zellman, G. L. *The response of the schools to teenage pregnancy and parenthood*. Santa Monica, Calif.: Rand Corporation, 1981.

Zelnik, M. Sex education and knowledge of pregnancy risk among U.S. teenage women. *Family Planning Perspectives*, 1979, *11*, 355–357.

Zelnik, M., & Kantner, J. F. Sexual and contraceptive experience of young unmarried women in the United States, 1976 and 1971. *Family Planning Perspectives*, 1977, *9*, 55–71.

Zelnik, M. & Kantner, J. F. First pregnancies to women aged 15–19, 1976 and 1971. *Family Planning Perspectives*, 1978, *10*, 11–20.

Zelnik, M., & Kantner, J. F. Reasons for nonuse of contraceptives by sexually active women aged 15–19. *Family Planning Perspectives*, 1979, *11*, 289–296.

References

Zelnik, M. & Kantner, J. F. Sexual activity, contraceptive use and pregnancy among metropolitan-area teenagers: 1971–1979. *Family Planning Perspectives*, 1980, *12*, 230–237.

Zelnik, M., Kim, Y. J., & Kantner, J. F. Probabilities of intercourse and conception among U.S. teenage women, 1971 and 1976. *Family Planning Perspectives*, 1979, *11*, 177–183.

Zilbergeld, B. *Male sexuality: A guide to sexual fulfillment*. Boston: Little, Brown, 1978.

Zillman, D. *Hostility and aggression*. Hillsdale, N. J.: Lawrence Erlbaum Associates, 1979.

Zumwalt, R. Plain and fancy: A content analysis of children's jokes dealing with adult sexuality. *Western Folklore*, 1976, *35*, 258–267.